THE WRITING ROOM

Keys to
the Craft
of Fiction
and Poetry

EVE SHELNUTT

LONGSTREET PRESS

Atlanta, Georgia

For my students

Published by
LONGSTREET PRESS, INC.
2150 Newmarket Parkway
Suite 102
Marietta, Georgia 30067

Printed in the United States of America

1st printing, 1989

Library of Congress Catalog Number 88-083935

ISBN 0-929264-12-6

This book was printed by R.R. Donnelley and Sons, in Harrisonburg, Virginia. The text type was set in Times Roman by Typo-Repro Service, Inc., Atlanta, Georgia. Design and cover illustration by Paulette Lambert.

Contents

Preface

PREFACE

Learning to write fiction and poetry is a process of seemingly limitless dimensions. Eudora Welty writes of having learned how her story "No Place for You, My Love" should be shaped while taking a car trip. Katherine Anne Porter writes in her essay "The Sources of *Noon Wine*" of having reached into memories of her earliest consciousness for images which informed the novella. V. S. Naipaul's novel *The Enigma of Arrival* is intricate for its delineation of a writer's development and the theme of both the writer's and the world's fluidity. Welty, Porter, and Naipaul make it clear that a writer does not once and for all learn to write but, rather, can hope only to understand more deeply how to think about writing.

Creative writing is under study wherever writers live, work, and publish. All writers, no matter where or how they study, must still make their own way, and I doubt that way is ever straight.

Each of us writes having had a particular background, origins in one time and place which cannot be ignored since they are the origins of perception. Yet the writer seeks not to be circumscribed or victimized by that background. Instead, the writer tries to make a separation through form, both from it and from life's mundane disorder in order to assess. The writer seeks, in fact, to use the accidents of birth and subsequent motion in order to gain some mastery of circumstance. Writing is both a process and a product of conceptions and labors performed on the self shaped by society.

Each conception, each labor that produces a work of the imagination (a piece of writing) is different. While we may have found a way to make our latest story, novel, poem, or drama, we nevertheless begin anew with the next not knowing how. In part this is so because, if we are attentive, our writing changes us, its first reader, a special reader for whom the writing is a revelation to be estimated and mined by additional writing.

And as we work at writing, the world changes. We absorb large and small shifts which may affect our work in progress, and in doing so we sometimes begin to feel that the writing profession is a juggling act or a battle always fought on new terrain. We come to feel that our freedoms as writers are small and that what we "mean" in a piece of writing is open for debate with both ourselves and our readers.

But it is possible, I think, to learn, if not how to write, how to embrace the fluidity of the writer's profession, possible, that is, to learn ways of thinking about writing fiction and poetry that make this shifting ground our asset. *Not knowing* how to write the first or next story, novel, or poem can become a process, a stance, a tactic for allowing a writer to feel fiction and poetry as extensions, a formalizing of questions.

In what follows, you will not find absolute definitions of types of point of view or rigid statements about form. Simply, I and a number of other writers I know will share our ways of thinking about writing fiction and poetry, both generally and specifically, since our own stories and poems are included along with essays on the process of writing them. All of us are at different "stages" as writers, but precisely what these stages are can only be suggested. Perhaps a writer's greatest freedom is to develop unpredictably, and the writers included here are evidence of that freedom.

Many of these writers have been students in my classes. They have helped me to create a dialogue about writing. Their work is a measure of the excitement they feel about writing and testifies to the rewards writing can bring. Others are professional writers whose writing I have learned from and whose generosity to fellow writers is worthy of admiration and emulation. Emily Ellison and Herbert Scott in particular contributed significantly with their respective chapters on the novel and poetry. Both demonstrate their long immersion in writing as well as their dedication to helping other writers, not only here but in the numerous classes and workshops they conduct as a natural extension of their lives as writers. What all the contributors to *The Writing Room* share in common is a dedication to writing as a profession that makes us less hidden from each other and ourselves.

Structurally, *The Writing Room* is a weave of both theory and practice. Stories, poems, and essays about the writing of the stories and poems serve not as writing models but as examples of writers at work. The stories and poems in *The Writing Room* were chosen not as models since the idea of models would be antithetical to the overall idea of the writer as shaper of unique materials. I chose the selections on the basis of the writers' *consciousness of form* as that which guides the imagination toward unique expression. It seemed appropriate, then, to include selections by writers at various stages of their development in relationship to form. Above all, I wanted all of the materials to demonstrate the intriguing complexity of writers' situations that has perhaps been best captured by Joyce Carol Oates in the following sentence from *The Profane Art*: "That the writer labors to discover the secret of his work is perhaps the writer's most baffling predicament, about which he cannot easily speak; for he cannot write the fiction without becoming, beforehand, the person who *must* write that fiction: and he cannot be that person without first subordinating himself to the process, the labor, of creating that fiction."

The chapters on such broad topics as "The Problems of Material" and "Point of View" open with an essay which suggests ways of thinking about material, point of view, reading, etc., then move to specific exercises. Theoretical material about the art and craft of writing is always debatable since practitioners have perspectives about writing which have grown from their own struggles with language and form. Writers develop in both agreement and disagreement with other writers. None of us is without our prejudices, nor have we tried to disguise them. After all, we write from *some* perspective even as we keep alert to writing by other writers which could change our thinking. What is offered here, then, is work by creative writers in the process of development and change.

WRITING FICTION

Introduction

Having taught fiction writing for fourteen years at the university level, I know that it is possible to "teach" almost any beginning writer how to write a traditional short story. The traditional story form consists of components, such as characterization, scenes, conflict, resolution, that may be analyzed and practiced. Indeed, in creative writing courses in fiction, students are asked by teachers primarily to write stories because, in part, the size and structure of the story is so "teachable." A novelist seeks to understand and reel in the whale while the story writer nets the fish. Or so it seems.

I have always taught writing the story form, however, while also writing stories myself, and the interplay between my teaching and my struggles with that form cautioned me early about giving any easy lessons in story writing. None will be presented here not only because are there none, but also because presenting the story form as anything but fascinatingly complex seems wrong to me in every way. Any student of fiction writing seeks, I always presume, what I seek as a writer—to shape language and to be shaped by the confluence of language and form in such a way as to recognize the story one writes as one's own, even as *who* one is changes as the result of writing. The undertaking is large, it is difficult, and there are no easy lessons. In writing about the novel form, Emily Ellison circles the novelist's large task, just as those of us writing about the story form seek here to encircle the *questions* writers have about that form.

I have sought to organize what I consider to be many of the fiction writer's questions in a text which will offer something beyond easy lessons. And the section on writing the story ends in an inevitable whimper: *Is* there nothing to do but *begin* now?

Over half of my teaching in creative writing courses consists of "curing" beginning writers of the conception that undertaking expression in creative forms is easy. What follows is not easy. It is, simply, an array of questions presented in such a way as to support the complexity of the writer's task. The section is also, I hope, an invitation to other writers to revel in the demands of writing good fiction. The contributors are passionate about the work of writing because we are experiencing its rewards. We hope for your company.

THE PROBLEMS OF
MATERIAL

*That the writer labors to discover the secret of his work is perhaps the
writer's most baffling predicament, about which he cannot easily
speak, for he cannot write the fiction without becoming, beforehand,
the person who must write that fiction: and he cannot be that person
without first subordinating himself to the process, the labor, of creating
that fiction.*

—Joyce Carol Oates,
The Profane Art

It is intimidating to buy a new ream of paper and realize that in time it will be
covered with words. How? *What* words? Each writer facing blank paper is sorely
aware that the act of writing is an act of will. How difficult it is for a writer to
begin and to continue depends, I think, on how *prepared* to write he or she is.

Preparation for writing means, in part, making time for writing. A regular
writing time is a luxury for many writers, especially beginning writers, and anyone who has made time for writing on a regular basis has, I imagine, done so at
great cost. The desire, the *will*, to write creatively can become a vocation that is
not readily provided time and space in society. We often say we "chisel out" time
for writing, implying that other demands are the rock against which we pit our will
to write.

Time is always at a premium for a writer—society's demands and priorities will
not vanish. Moreover, the amount of time available to each writer is not only
different but different for each writer week to week. Early in my career, as I
wasted time wishing for perfect writing conditions, I finally realized that what was
crucial to my writing was my frame of mind about writing and specifically about
material. Because the amount of time that I have to devote to writing is limited, as
it is for any writer, I began to understand that when I sat down to write I needed to
be prepared to write, prepared to waste as little writing time as possible.

The preparation for writing often happens away from the typewriter and in many
ways can become a studied activity that can help solve the problems of material, of
what to write. While every writer surely makes preparations for writing in different ways, what has helped me and a number of students I've taught is consciously
practiced daydreaming.

But this idea and pedagogy issues from an esthetic: for me, the most powerful
writing occurs when a writer seeks to uncover, to ask questions about, his or her
own way of seeing; when the writer pursues in form the radical events which
bestowed a special viewpoint; pursues those which formed the writer's personality.

What else? I think, until I am reminded by some of my students and many other writers that their preference is for fiction and poetry which carry ideas about issues current in society. And while my esthetic does not exclude creative work that in some way comments on the world we live in, since all writing probably does this at least obliquely, my prejudice is against writing that is merely commentary, no matter how cleverly disguised in form. I seek, then, writing that has issued from the urgency of the radical self.

But what is meant by "the radical self"? The exercises to facilitate finding fictional material (page 15) will help in answering the question. But it is not easy to discover an answer. Most of us share a number of experiences in common: our first day of school, falling in love for the first time, watching television, eating a fast meal at McDonald's, etc. But we bring to all of our experiences very particular perspectives about life. And we formed those perspectives partly through common rituals and also partly through experiences that were singularly ours: the startling events, the painful events, the private celebrations, the unspoken humiliations, the secret loves and hates, etc. These are the times when our personalities are shaken, when we feel something different and especially significant has occurred. The problem for the writer is that many of these significant events lie buried in us. Yet they are the very events that will constitute our best fictions. Not that fiction transcribes our "radical" moments but, rather, that it seeks forms and plots and characters that will allow our unique (and "radical") selves to surface. In preparing to write, it is important to seek what formed the uniqueness of our personalities so that in our fictions we "invent" characters who stand out against society's seemingly common rituals. We feel, as writers, both common and uncommon. If a story is to have tension or conflict, we must remember what can toss a character from his or her ordinary existence within society's flow. We must, when writing, recreate a "radical" experience. In order to do that, we must recognize in ourselves what constitutes the radical experience. We must burrow down in our memories and draw them forth for examination. We must, in other words, remember particular instances when our personalities were being shaped by events and our reactions to them.

Daydreaming as a habit that provides material is merely the strengthening of memory and the odd combining of memories with other memories and with supposition. It is different from merely recalling the radical events of one's life, which would result in purely autobiographical writing. Daydreaming is, rather, an imaginative rearranging of memories and the lifting of memory from the patterns of reconciliation we make in order to put specific memories aside. Writers, in fact, reenter memory to upset whatever peace their minds have made with the past, to make *each time* something new of experience. To use memory as material, a distancing from it is required. To myself, oddly perhaps, I call this separation "indifference to material."

For my students I draw on the board two rectangles set slightly apart, each with a single "door" facing the other, with a passageway between them. Inside one "room" is nothing but the writer and paper, the pen or typewriter (the writer's study). Inside the other is a jumble of memories, suppositions, images, dreams, daydreams—a room seemingly as packed as possible yet endlessly expandable. The writer, I suggest, walks from the empty room, across the passageway, and extracts one item from the jumbled room, returning then to the study, which now contains the writer, the typewriter, and *something*. Of course our memories like the company they keep and want to bring along whole histories of events and situations—it is not easy to isolate an image from its attendant images packed like sardines in a can. But if the writer is disciplined, he thinks about the one image he has brought back—an image, say, of a pair of wooden shoes made and decorated in Holland. That, I suggest, is enough to begin with.

Many years ago I wrote a story to go with my Dutchman's shoes, and the image appeared in two poems as well. I had not thought of the shoes in years when suddenly, as I was sweeping a kitchen floor, they arose from memory. I was not prepared to write then because other tasks needed to be done, and the shoes as an image were (seemed) inconsequential, merely one of dozens of images which floated through my mind as I swept.

But one afternoon as I sat down to write, I said to myself: Why not the wooden shoes this time? I meant only as a beginning, because I've been convinced by experience that whatever we call "inspiration" comes *during* writing. Because of this belief, it matters little to me how I begin: Why not the shoes this time? I made this my proposition: in this story, the shoes will appear. For me, what I term a "proposition" is a mode of self-forgetting, a way to deflect the power of the blank paper to intimidate, a retrieving of an artifact in memory for the sake of investigating it apart from others—a distancing.

And I was immediately amused—how unlikely an image around which to build a story! I noted my amusement because I take seriously the notion that my material resides "over there," through the passageway and behind a door. I had, then, suddenly extracted humor to accompany the shoes, and to recognize that element, I accentuated it. I typed "Feet" on the page as a title: how improbable! I was delighted, since now I had a genuine "proposition," to write a story for which the title "Feet" would be appropriate. As I mused, I remembered an expression I'd heard in the South as a child, someone saying in disbelief or exasperation, "My *foot!*" And now that I had the remembered expression, I would use that too: one of my characters would say it and, furthermore, the expression would be the only time a form of the title would appear—this restriction because while I wanted an anchor for the memories I would pull out one by one, I also wanted freedom in which to explore what nonliteral connotations the word *feet* might have for me.

Opening again the door to the jumbled room, I brought out the place where I had first seen wooden shoes from Holland. But as I remembered, it was dark there, seemingly cold all year, and damp. Mentally I put the memory back because I needed a setting of sunlight to accompany the story's humor, however it might surface. From memory I extracted a place I recalled as having been perpetually sunny though I'm sure it wasn't: Pelzer, South Carolina, where I'd lived for a year. No, I amended, not Pelzer, but *West* Pelzer. Pelzer itself contained the mill village where as children we'd not been allowed to go, and so the memories arose as mystery—how the houses in Pelzer were painted in pastel colors, each with a tiny white porch across the front. When was it I lived there? I asked. But I'd moved so many times as a child, I found it too troublesome to sit figuring out the year— during the Korean conflict or after it? Asking the question, I "had," then, the Korean conflict, and it seemed appropriate, as contrast, to the houses' pastel colors. So it *was* during the war, I decided. Now I had a title, "Feet," an obligation to humor, the village of West Pelzer, Pelzer's pastel houses, and a time.

In my hours of daydreaming, I have considered names, saying numerous names over and over to myself, names which will not obtrude on the southern locales I use in most of my fiction. Now, as I sat looking at my title, I brought them out: Irene, James, Robert, Anna, Anna-Marie, Josie, Claire, Lucy, Romona, Ben, Rosette, Charlie, Patrick-Marion, Fleta . . . I could, I knew, spend an *afternoon* reciting names. I could even get up from the typewriter to flip through story collections—does a name leap out begging to be used? It's a way, one of hundreds, to waste time. But on this writing day, I had my amusement at my title to quell the wasteful habit— "Feet" waited.

So—writing as an act of will—I wrote a sentence, picking at random two names: *During the months of the Korean War, Louise, a mother of thirty-nine, and Josie, her eleven-year-old daughter, lived in West Pelzer, South Carolina.*

Already, what was happening was, to borrow a phrase from the poet Elizabeth Bishop, a "driving to the interior." I noticed that I had written *war,* not *conflict,* because, I realized, I had lived as a child in fear for eighteen months for the life of a cousin who had served in Korea during the "conflict," which in my child's dreams and daydreams was horrifyingly a *war,* as it remains for me. No word we write is without its reverberations in memory.

I reread the sentence, disliking the rhythm of *West* Pelzer and *South* Carolina. I retyped the title on clean paper and rewrote the sentence, omitting the word *West,* keeping the word *war.* This retyping is a manner in which I think, typing in order to absorb what it is I have written. And how much I had committed myself to! If we are genuinely our own first readers, it seems important to absorb the words we use, their suggestiveness. What *had* I written? I considered

Josie. Louise. Ages eleven and thirty-nine respectively. Yet it seemed too much to consider—they had dropped onto the page too quickly. I had, however, daydreamed for minutes about the villages of Pelzer and West Pelzer.

I wrote next: *Across from the railroad tracks, mill children waited on their porches at dusk for their parents to come home. Lined up, their heads made steps. Until the mill closed long after the war was over, this scene was recurring. Nothing appeared to change.*

As I wrote, I realized that I could have gone on describing the mill village for many pages, trying to capture the mysteries it had contained for me as a child. But Josie and Louise *waited*.

Yes, I said to myself, I will make an effort to remember you both are in this story: it was not *my* story I was writing because experience has taught me, too, that our own "stories," representations in language of our radical selves, are best apprehended through others' stories, when our insistence on autobiography is muted. This greater apprehension applies to us as writers, as well as to our readers.

I added, then: . . . *but because the two service station owners built almost identical asbestos-siding homes during that time, Louise and Josie would come to think the pale shades of green and pink belonged to wartime.*

Having now a whole paragraph, I reread it and saw that I had chosen a point of view. The narrator was distant enough to stand back observing Louise and Josie as a unit and also close enough to enter their feelings. The narrator, I saw, moved effortlessly between description seemingly apart from Louise and Josie and description colored by their perceptions: *Lined up, their heads made steps*—surely a subjective manner of measurement although whose subjective assessment makes the metaphor is not stated. I saw, too, that the narrator had a long view of Josie and Louise: "would come [later] to think . . ."

I had, I decided, begun a story which would cover a long period of time in Josie's and Louise's lives. And since this was so, I could, as the writer, allow the narrator to give the reader an overall sense of their lives before I, the writer, would have to decide what Josie and Louise would do. And, I reasoned, if I had the narrator describe the texture of their days in the place they are living, perhaps when it came time for both to act, I would know what they, being themselves, would do.

Implicit in the description of the process I used for this story are several aspects of the process I employ often. I have separated myself as writer from narrator, which I do in thought regardless of how similar the narrator's voice is to my own. This separation seems important for keeping sight of the narrator as simply another *device* of fiction, a carrier of decisions I make as writer. Also implicit is great deliberation over every word, accompanied by a willingness to *wait*—to relinquish a need to know what actions characters will perform, bringing plot to the surface. If the language is deliberate, if each word's nuances are felt by me as I write, I feel assured that my characters will do what previous language has prepared for them to do. I do not *think* in an ordered way. Rather I put words on the page slowly, with deliberation, and read them as *instructions* about orderly assembly of story. In this way, I do not have stories to *tell*, only stories to *discover*. The telling—the manner of using language—is the method of discovery.

I have described, then, a method of beginning. I did go on to describe Louise's bed, a daybed in the living room. Mornings, I discovered, she looked out the windows to a vacant field where a host of daisies bloomed. As I imagined her looking out at the field, I realized she slept alone, and I knew, suddenly, that her husband, Josie's father, was dead, although I did not then know why he had died. His death, however, caused much else in the story to be imagined, and slowly the story unfolded, Josie's and Louise's stories, though it became primarily the girl's story. None of the plot was autobiographical, but all of the details were memories of sights I had seen. What Josie and Louise felt, I had at some time felt, each detail and feeling drawn one by one from the room filled with memory, memories loosened in the jumbled room from their "families" for use in "Feet."

In this method of discovering material, it seems important to refrain from thinking of plot or a story's meaning early in the writing process. *If* writing is genuinely to be a discovery for the writer, and the piece of writing genuinely a creation, then it seems that part of what allows for discovery is the writer's ability to lose himself in words, to sense *their* implications to the writer.

I mentioned that I "knew" Louise's husband had died when I wrote *daybed*. In my mind it was a single bed with bolsters, in the living room. I imagined that Louise would sleep there because the double bed in one of the bedrooms held too many memories of the husband, and then I stored for use later in the story Louise's longing and even something of the husband's character—what is left of him in Louise's and Josie's memories. So much, in fact, had been determined by the word *daybed,* which comes in the fourth paragraph of the story: the sexual aspect of Louise's memories, her loneliness, her vulnerability.

As I wrote, it seemed natural to have a man enter her life for a time. As it turned out, he is the landlord of the rented house, and his own sexual power is represented by the fact that, in the house, there is one room he doesn't rent but keeps locked. He comes one day to do something in the room, and it is then I was able to "use" the painted, wooden shoes, which Josie and Louise see while peeking into the room. The landlord had rented out the house after his wife's death—his belongings, the shoes among them, are artifacts of the marriage. The landlord begins to come frequently to sort through them, and at first he is silent, as though he carries a burden too heavy to speak of. He has, however, also managed despite his grief to incite Louise's sexuality, which she at least knows is a sign of her own repair. Surely the landlord knows this too; and so she taunts him: *"So what did she* [his wife] *die of?'' because now his silence was like a quarrel between them.*

"Of suffering,'' he said.

"My foot!'' cried Louise. And he slammed the door as he left.

The expression recalled from my childhood became Louise's mating call; she and the landlord begin to send Josie away in the afternoons and take her bed.

As it developed, the story is about the tenacity of memory, a meaning that emerged *as* the story was written. Through this method of discovering material first—the story *through* material and then a story's meaning—I have taken seriously the notion that we know what we have to say after we've said it. Here, then, are Josie and Louise in their story "Feet," written early in my career as a writer.

• FEET •

During the months of the Korean War, Louise, a mother of thirty-nine, and Josie, her eleven-year-old daughter, lived in Pelzer, South Carolina. Across from the railroad tracks, mill children waited on their porches at dusk for their parents to come home. Lined up, their heads made steps. Until the mill closed long after the war was over, this scene was recurring. Nothing appeared to change, but because the two service station owners built almost identical asbestos-siding homes during that time, Louise and Josie would come to think the pale shades of green and pink belonged to wartime.

The mother and the child did not keep track of the number of men the newspaper reported were falling in the war. There was no way to tell how many of those who had wanted to die had died, or how many of those who had not wanted to die had died, or how many who had shot off their own toes in their backyards with shotguns were sick to death of not wanting to die.

Still, there was consolation in the field of daisies across from the house. Years later, when Louise and Josie would happen to go as tourists to the cemetery in Arlington, Virginia, they would feel betrayed by white crosses looking so much like a field of daisies.

But now, the mother, who slept on a daybed in the living room, woke each morning to spend five minutes looking out the windows to the field where the slightest wind moved a thousand heads. And Josie, from her window, was looking too—the single eyes of yellow, blinking. In winter, they were apparitions, in memory, all white.

Where was the father, the husband?
He was dead.

In the space Louise's husband once occupied were piles of ladies' magazines, of underwear, boxes, and an empty space on the daybed where the second pillow used to be. The odor of woman was like a third person. They knew he would hate the house arrested in this mess, and their knowledge of his hatred was another odor.

Often over meals Louise said to Josie of their cousin four times removed, "If Harry gets back without getting himself blown to smithereens, we'll clean this place up and throw him a wham-bam party, whatcha say?"

Josie nodded. And Harry did get home much later and they did clean up and throw him a party, but he lost too much sense to notice and sat in an armchair, waving.

Saturdays, to make time meet, Louise gave violin lessons to a girl Louise said was hopeless. Louise made Josie take lessons with the girl. "You play decent," Louise told Josie. "Keep my interest up." Between Josie and the girl, they made Louise concentrate, all songs in three-quarter time.

Sundays they went to church and liked each other in the pews better than they liked each other in the house because in church they sang, one soprano, one alto, and there was no question who would sing which part since nature had sealed in each a particular range. Afterwards they ate chicken, and it was fortunate that Louise liked the breast and Josie liked the inner part of the wing.

On Sundays, too, Charlie, Harry's father, came visiting, even though he did not often present himself but parked his car below the rise in the road or behind the cluster of trees, and when he could hear Louise and Josie cooking in the kitchen or pulling the shades for their naps, he wrote messages in the dirt of their drive with a stick. One Sunday he would write: I WAS HERE. Then next he would follow with WHERE WERE YOU? Or, he would ask, DON'T YOU LADIES EVER STAY HOME? And follow that with GOD IS LOVE.

Josie waited to see HARRY DIED, even though Charlie was a dairy farmer and would never think to write a message like that.

Other days of the week, Louise taught music in the Anderson County Public Schools, schools clustered on the map in the kitchen like shoes under a bed. When Louise first began to teach, she got lost on the country roads and came home crying, her autoharp vibrating on the kitchen table where she dropped it. Now she knew where to go. Every child in the county could play a song on the autoharp. They sang along, "Whispering hope, o how welcome thy voice," and when they had the whole song straight, Louise set the autoharp down on the table so gently not a string moved, and said she was bored to tears.

Would he ever come back?
No.

Louise grew a layer of fat almost translucent as a batiste baptismal dress on a girl who has waited too long to be saved—under the minister's hands and under the minister's robe: water, a prophecy: the body is so tender it falls in time from the bone.

Josie refused to get saved. She took walks in the woods and practiced being a ballerina who does not even need toeshoes.

Harry wrote that almost everyone was dead. "P. S.," he added, "not me," and Charlie drove all the way up their drive to say "Thank God" in Louise's hearing range. Charlie learned, in time, to celebrate by playing checkers in the silence Harry afterwards required, and went ahead and invested in automatic milking machines, contributing to the post-war boom.

Louise rented. While her husband would not come back, there was in life always the outside chance. Women who bought their own homes did not understand men.

Relatives at the Easter reunion said she would be a renter all her life and they said she would have to stop pretending to be so young if Josie was going to look like that: legs toned and eyes toned down.

Because it was a custom, Louise and Josie took to the reunion a cake they had baked for the oldest living relation, who said she would *not* die, yellow cake crumbs sticking to her lips like pollen, her insides, they said, absolutely in shreds.

"Who does she think she *is?* " Louise asked, and they forgave her because of him.

When he was alive, what did he do?
A little of this and that; in bed, the other.

It was what he had been best at that had left Louise house-poor. This one sat at the front of a field. Far back were the railroad tracks, trains keeping so closely to a schedule Louise felt it as an affront. *He* had taught her to be ready at any time, and, then, in those days, if two small boys had put their ears to her chest, between the breasts on the flat bone, they would have heard a humming; they would have jumped back as if they might get run over. Now two boys who were almost men came over on Saturdays to cut the grass, and they wouldn't have thought, looking at her, of whistling. No one knew that flat bone had once almost split like a tie.

And then, at the height of summer, when Louise's teeth itched, the landlord showed up. It was his house, his doors and windows and clustered trees. And, in a way, it was his music trying to float from the house and not making it at all because Louise, in a fit, had said Josie and the girl would, if it killed *her,* learn to play Mendelssohn's Violin Concerto, and the girl's father, who waited in the car in the drive, sent in $2.50 instead of the usual three, not hearing in Louise's lessons a tremolo of hope.

New fat on Louise's upper arms quivered; she rubbed too much rosin on the bow and still, in the heat, it dried out. Josie got slapped on her bare legs so many times so softly that Louise's hand on her legs was a counter-rhythm.

Into all that, the landlord came, and he wasn't anything like the husband, the father.

Was he, in his day, what they called a "natural"?
Louise had put the pillow at the foot of the bed and hooked her toes on the
headboard. That helped.

The landlord knocked one Saturday during a music lesson. The external view would have made neighbors think of a Jehovah's Witness without a partner—the suit, the arranged hair, the valise.

Josie and the girl who did everything a second too late rested their violins on the metal music stand. They heard mumbling and their own white blouses rubbing on their shoulders, then Louise crying out, "You are kidding."

He wasn't. He walked past the space heater and through the space where French doors once hung and past Josie and the girl, Louise running behind him, one hand at her neck as if she were closing a robe. She rolled her eyes at Josie, who was not looking, transfixed instead by his suit, which seemed apart from his motion—containing his fat and possibly a million tiny broken veins such as the ones the afternoon sun caught in his eyes—a suit of herringbone and leg creases and grey pearl buttons to go with his eyes set too close together like "o's" in the word "look."

Then they were into the hall and Josie heard Louise push aside the chenille bedspread which hung over the entrance to the connecting hall. Beyond the curtain was the closed room. Josie imagined the peacock, whose tail feathers splayed the bedspread, had folded like an accordian.

"See what I mean!" Louise said.

In the hall leading to the one room they did not rent, Louise had stored her husband's goods—everything he had owned even though none of it was worth saving and so she had saved it all. It took up the hallway, stacked and piled, uneven shapes in the half-light from the dining room.

How did he die and what was Louise's reaction?

Consequent to a poker game, as the newspaper put it, and Louise, on seeing him and the color of his blood pouring from a hole a gun had made, tightened her muscles until they held and exploded. Her body had rocked, bones against themselves, hence her current layer of fat, against such a time in any future.

"It can't be helped," the landlord said. "I need to see to things," and he moved aside and went past Josie in the doorway and sat in a chair, filing his nails and waiting.

"Well for Christ's sake help me," Louise said, and Josie, followed by the girl, put down her violin and began carrying boxes and suits and hunting gear out of the hallway and into the dining room. As they piled his things around the piano, the landlord watched and hardly moved, sweating in the heat of his still weight. Louise cursed, she said, "My back is killing me." When she looked at her watch, she said, "Oh my God," and scooted the girl out to her father. "Tell him we did theory," she called, "and nevermind the money."

When everything he had owned was out in the bright light of the dining room, Louise pushed back her hair and said to the landlord, "Whatever it is, I hope it's worth it."

He got up from the chair and disappeared behind the door and didn't come out until it was almost dark. Louise and Josie were eating when he came back through. All the time he had been in the room, he had not made a sound, and now, Louise and Josie, tired from listening to nothing, had almost forgotten their own voices. The food tasted like nothing. Then, at the front door, he turned to say to Louise, looking at her without moving his head or his eyes, "My wife died in that room," and then their mouths tasted spit.

After he drove away, Louise sat beating on the table with a spoon. Josie, by herself, moved the belongings back to the hallway and pulled the bedspread straight again, the bird pastel in the muted light.

He came all summer and into fall, except that some Saturdays he did not come, and the Saturdays he stayed away had no pattern to them. He did not say he was coming again or anything about when he would stop coming. Louise thought each time was the last, and she put her husband's belongings back and pulled the curtain. Each time she moved them out again, she said to the landlord, "I can't do this much longer."

The girl who took violin lessons decided to stop taking the lessons, and Josie, having no job to do now that the girl was gone, put up her own violin and the sheet music by Mendelssohn.

Louise and Josie had little to say to each other about the landlord, about his wife. What they thought about, they thought about alone in bed.

Harry came home and Charlie stayed with him on Sundays and did not write any messages. But what Charlie did was expected, and even Harry, like an aftermath of himself, was not a surprise.

It was the little things Josie noticed. The landlord's grey suit seemed each week to contain more cloth. And Louise covered her arms because she was losing her fat. They were growing thin together.

One Indian summer day, the landlord took off his suit coat and, once it was off, helped Louise move her husband's things to the dining room around the table. One night when Louise was hungry before she and Josie had a chance to move the things back to the hallway, they ate with his belongings there, and it seemed he had come to dinner.

The landlord always brought the valise, and both Louise and Josie noticed that, after a time, it began to looked stuffed when he left. The first evening it seemed to Louise that he had something in the valise, she called to him from the couch, "So what did she die of?" because now his silence was like a quarrel between them.

"Of suffering," he said.

"My foot!" cried Louise. And he slammed the door as he left.

"I don't like him," said Josie.

"Like! Like!" Louise's voice had thinned with her body; it was one string.

Then, when even the landlord could see she was tired, the landlord consented one day to try to walk over and around the husband's things and get in without her moving them. And that evening, he stayed for dinner. Louise said such things as, "I get tired of all that driving around," and "There's just so much you can do with kids, and then that's it." And he said, "I can imagine," and "Not bad," of the food, and "I could help you move all that stuff out to the garage."

What sizes had the husband worn?

Coat: 42; shoes: 11 ¹/₂; socks: stretchable; shirt: 16¹/₂; tee-shirt: large; his favorite food was steak; he liked to sing but wasn't good at it; he loved Louise and Josie; he never did discover why, exactly, he'd been born; and when it ended, he had one minute in which to be surprised, and he used that minute instead to notice the shape of Louise's hips, bones pointing inward, as she ran up to him.

That night they moved everything to the garage, and when they had it all arranged, Louise noticed that it had begun to rain, and she took one of her husband's coats off a hanger and gave it to the landlord to wear, and he wore it home.

With the hallway empty, Josie kept the light on, and, for the first time, she looked through the keyhole of the locked door. In the morning light, what she saw was bright, even with the shade drawn. Nothing left in the room at all but a pair of shoes, blue and decorated, with carved toes curved upward and heels low, wooden, aligned on the wood floor, pointed toward a corner.

"Look!" she called, and when Louise came, they both tried to look at once, and then they looked at each other.

After a time, Louise took Josie's room and Josie slept on the daybed. And when the landlord came on Saturdays, Louise gave Josie money for the movies, and when Josie came home, she found them talking in the living room, and Josie went to look in her old room, at the pillow down at the foot of the bed. The room smelled to her like all the weight they had lost.

When he went, he took the shoes, and he never came back.

Louise, some days, would wrap her arms around herself and, while passing by a wall, run herself into it. She said one day, "Let's go see what Florida is like."

They moved and they took all of the husband's belongings and stored them in the new house Louise rented. She taught in a city school and didn't have to drive far. Josie began to get the shape of a woman, and Louise grew fatter. Only sometimes then did she run her body against a wall when passing by. And Josie and Louise both had beds of their own, covered with spreads in the pale shades of green and pink.

Charlie died, but only after Harry died. "Of what?" Louise wrote to Charlie. But he didn't answer, and Louise dreamed once that Harry had died while dancing, his feet of painted wood.

And Josie, who had never seen her father's body undressed in life or in death, asked:

Would he ever come back?

Of course he would.

AFTERWORD TO "FEET"

What is most difficult to express about the writing process is the constant interaction between the use of memory and the technical demands of the particular story. This is especially the case when the story has not been preplanned because no logic anterior to it exists. The interplay between memory and formal demands feels, then, similar to playing a fish on a line, a fish *this* size, with unique movements in response to being snagged.

In the story "Feet," the most crucial decision was that of narrative voice and the narrator's point of view in regards to the emerging material. In the story, the narrator's voice is ironical, deeply enough for me to have decided to accentuate the irony by the device of narrator's questions. To myself, as I formed the questions, I imagined they might be ones Josie would ask, not literally so much as in emotion and emotions' moods; and I imagined they would be asked by her much later, years later, when she extracted a tally from herself. The answers, too, are ironical because they issue from what I imagined as Josie's future deeply ironical resignation to the power of others to transform our feelings. I thought of the resignation not as unhappy but rather as a coat she might put on to ward against cold.

Some readers have mentioned finding the device intrusive, as perhaps it is for a reader who likes his fiction to be purely mimetic, to allow the reader wholly to believe the story is not artifact but "real life."

It is not a relationship I want with a reader because it is one which I have decided supports a sentimentality to which I would like to express opposition in form. I have chosen, instead, to remind the reader, subtly, if possible (for I do not like writer's self-conscious experiments that speak mainly to themselves) that fiction is a tension—between writer, reader, and the infinite number of ways the world construes itself.

For that reason, I am working against a reader's *habits* in relation to the tradition of storytelling. If a reader is inattentive by virtue of the comforts of habit, that reader will slide into a self-induced identification with story, as if he has heard all stories before and can attend only on the level of story's novelty. In "Feet" I deliberately use a storytelling tone, which is then undercut by the question-and-answer sections. The device is a deliberate instrusion that allows questions and answers to be posed in images and juxtaposed images in such a way as, I think, to require a reader's nonhabitual response—what I hope is a deeper, more thought-provoking response. Dutifully, for instance, the answer to the question "What sizes had the husband worn?" issues from the answerer in, initially, normal, habitual ways—the answer seeks to keep concomitance with the question. But the answerer quickly tires of this because the question is irrelevant. It has no relation to the effect another person makes, and it is to the effect that she turns: the husband's puzzlement about his life, his sensuality, his values.

This ploy, as it were, is an attempt to have the reader appropriate the story to himself only after I the writer have sought to break into the reader's habits in relation to storytelling. I do not want the reader to *identify* with loss as much as I want the reader to ask how others posit their effects in us, and why the effects are so powerful. After the reader finishes the story, having read it more than once, I would hope that he or she is less sure about what he knows or imagined he knew about memory. I would like his state to be one of questioning.

But perhaps it is not clear why more overt intrusions into the reader's habits would not better serve my purposes. Certainly any reader picking up a story by, for example, Susan Sontag, Leonard Michaels, or William Burroughs would be alerted to a writer's wish to upset the reader's habits with the traditional story. In my mind an apt analogy between the tactics of a radical experimenter with the story form and my own experiments *within* tradition is between guerrilla warfare and face-to-face combat. Mine are covert sallies onto the battlefield, issuing from a different politics in regards to my imagined reader. The reader I imagine is bound to his habits but can nonetheless accept as a Sunday sport a skirmish on a declared field, in daylight, with both sides facing off squarely. Such a battle is intellectual insofar as it is a game of wits. I seek instead to surprise the reader and, above all, if he engages at all, to engage the reader's feelings and sensations first. I finally believe in the power of narrative, of *story,* which is always more than the sum of its parts.

If storytelling is not mere re-telling, it is more open-ended than any experiment because it preserves mystery. In "Feet" all of the devices are moving the narrative toward the final question and answer, which I hope aggressively flips Death on his head, to be, of course, in another story, turned upright again for another struggle.

EXERCISES TO HELP FIND MATERIAL

The following exercises are designed both to expand memory and to broaden the concept of material for writing. Writers already deeply involved in their relationship to material will find the exercises artificial, and they are. Anyone using the exercises, however, will discover those which stimulate memory and imagination.

1. Reread the stories you have written. Make a list of: a) the stories' characters; b) the stories' settings; c) dominant colors recurring in the stories; d) recurring themes; e) recurring images. In imagination or on paper begin to draw a map of the places you have written about. While it may seem awkward, this exercise will be more helpful if you actually draw the map, capturing, however awkwardly, the way you envision the settings in your work. Add figures to represent the characters, as well as sketches of objects or images that recur. This map will represent the places, people, and images you have "visited" imaginatively to date in your fiction. Drawing the map is a way to bring fully into consciousness the work you have accomplished over time in individual stories.

2. After completing the map and thinking about it for several days, imagine the distance between one setting and another. Imaginatively "drive" between settings while asking, "What exists *between* each place—what people and objects?" List on paper what your imagination yields in response. During another daydreaming session, look at the map or reimagine it, asking whether it is possible to rearrange the components of the map, moving settings, for example, further apart. Would certain characters not have met or come upon particular objects crucial to their stories? Ask how such a change would affect a specific story. Imagine that, with the changes in settings, characters who had not "met" previously are now able to meet. Finally, write on the map or paper the time frame you have used in each story—June-August, 1972, for instance. Do this for stories which do not have specific dates mentioned in the prose. No doubt as you imagined the story you imagined a time. After listing the stories' time frames, imagine how changing the time frame would have changed the stories. Imagine a particular character in a story and ask, "If it is ten years later, where would this character be and what would he or she be doing?" The purpose of this exercise as a whole is to assist a writer in separating his or her personal history or memory as it may be used, however much or little, in a story so that the writer can "play" with the material and become "indifferent" to it in order to stimulate imagination.

3. On a day when you will not write but have time to spend preparing to write, write as quickly as possible on separate sheets of paper the opening words of a dozen stories. Vary the opening sentence or sentences as much as possible. Write enough sentences so that the material seems arbitrary. None of the

sentences *will* be arbitrary, and this is the point of the exercise: to help the writer understand that he or she has some relationship to all the words he or she writes. As Eudora Welty has written, ". . . a writer and his fiction were never strangers."

4. Using an anthology of stories with which you are *un*familiar, copy the first sentences of a dozen or so stories. Refrain from reading the stories. One at a time over a period of days, read the sentences and ask, "If this were a beginning of one of my stories, what would I write next?" The purpose of this exercise is to help a writer understand how much information is given to a reader in every sentence. For this reason, it is helpful to list the components of fiction appearing in the opening lines: point of view, characters, setting, time, mood, action, etc.

5. Using stories written by a writer in a culture different from your own, study a dozen "foreign" stories. Mentally or on paper separate the aspects of the story which seem to be cultural from those which appear to comprise "pure story." Ask how the same pure story could be transferred into your own cultural setting. The purpose of this exercise is to help the writer understand how deeply one's culture affects one's fictions.

6. Using Wallace Stevens's *Collected Poems,* list the colors Stevens uses in his poetry. Visualizing one color at a time, decide what object, place, and time you associate most strongly with the color. This exercise will stimulate a writer's sense of what can "trigger" imagination and memory. It will also remind a writer that none of the words he or she knows is without its reverberations in memory.

7. Consider the foreign language you know best, either the language itself or discrete words from it that you have absorbed into your own language. List the words, including proper names. Imagine using one or two of the words in a story, asking how other prose could make a "place" for the foreign word. Write several sentences in which you practice inserting foreign words into the prose. The purpose of this exercise is to help the writer become more conscious of each word in a sentence. The device used within a story can also affect the style of a story.

8. Consider the art form with which you are most familiar. List the words and images you associate with the art form. The purpose of this exercise is to remind a writer of the range of his or her knowledges and the images they carry. Bringing forth into consciousness such knowledge can affect a story's style by providing a wider range of vocabulary felt by the writer.

9. Make a list of verb tenses you tend to use most frequently in your stories. Reread your work occasionally in a verb tense different from that in which it was written. Notice what changes in the story as the verbs alter. Using stories by other writers, repeat the exercise. A writer using this exercise will discover how radically verb tense affects story as a whole. He or she will also become

more conscious of making a choice when beginning a story, thus avoiding habit or fads.

10. Practice remembering images which recur as you do menial tasks by listing them on a pad of paper you carry with you. Occasionally chose one image from the list and write down as quickly as possible all of the associations you have with the image. By using this exercise, a writer will understand more fully the wealth of material he or she possesses for use in fiction writing.

11. Choosing a story in which a character was viewed by the narrator sympathetically, make an imaginative "case" against the character. Ask from whose viewpoint such a case might be made and on what grounds. This exercise can help a writer understand that all writers bring to their imaginative work our vested interests; that is, writers can carry their quarrels with others into their work. To the extent that a writer is aware of this, he or she has greater imaginative freedom to separate himself or herself from the personal background that shaped personality. Such imaginative separation can increase a writer's material. The exercise is one which stimulates supposition.

12. List the "truths" you hold dear. Imagine a story that argues against several of them. This exercise extends Exercise 11, on a similar rationale.

13. List the fairy tales, myths, fables, and stories that affected you most deeply as a child. Imagine the characters are your contemporaries, fully grown, with their own histories. This exercise is designed to help a writer understand how deeply psychology, individuality, and subjectivity have influenced the contemporary story form. A writer using the exercise would "flesh out" the simple tales with psychological intricacies.

14. List recurring nightmares, dreams, and fantasies. This exercise stimulates memory and consciousness, adding material to the writer's storehouse.

15. List occasions when you are always surrounded by others. Imagine the same occasions with fewer people present or only yourself. Imagine the occasions with yourself absent. As in Exercise 3, this exercise will help a writer make an imaginative separation between himself and his personal history.

16. List the rituals engaged in by those around you, now and during childhood. Focus on those peculiar to the group and not on those the larger society also participates in. This exercise helps a writer see more deeply into the interactions of others.

17. Studying writing by your contemporaries, list techniques used by the writers. Using texts written thirty to forty years ago, separate from List I the techniques writers employ now that were not employed thirty to forty years ago. Ask, "Why has this change occurred? This exercise will help a writer become more conscious of society's effect on creative work. It will also help a writer gain more imaginative freedom by allowing the writer to practice supposition. The writer may ask, "What if *I* prefer not to use certain contemporary devices?"

18. Read a contemporary story. Underline the words that suggest the society in which the *writer* worked. Examine surrounding words for indications of the writer's attitude toward the society. This exercise accentuates Exercise 17.

19. List what you do when you begin writing a story. Ask why these habits have accrued and what the result would be if some were changed. This exercise will help a writer become more conscious of his or her methods.

20. Read carefully a story by a writer whose work you admire. Write a deliberate imitation of some aspect of the story—style, approach to characterization, etc. A writer using this exercise can expand his or her concept of story.

CONSTRAINTS ON MATERIAL

I. Revision

No method or process of building a story works smoothly for a writer every time. In the method I've described, it is not unusual to "discover" the story on the fifth, tenth, or even last page. In such an instance, it is not that *a* story is not underway or finished but, rather, that *the* story the writer wants to claim is discovered only slowly, during a process.

It is customary to term these "wrong" pages *drafts* and to term the "more right" pages *revisions*. Both my students and I have discovered, however, that it is more useful *not* to use these terms, or to use them only very close to the end of the process when a story's "errors" have been almost completely eliminated. We have found, first, that it is too easy to write with inattention when we dismiss early writing as merely a draft. We have also found that the excitement experienced at the beginning stages of writing can be lost when we read a failed draft and understand that the whole thing must be rewritten. It is difficult psychologically to finish even a draft and know that what one faces is reentering the emotions of the story. Often, in fact, a writer does not reenter a story's emotions while making revisions but rather approaches the story's flaws as a technician with a how-to manual. Such revisions may be technically correct but render the story wooden.

I suggest to students that they consider that a story has *begun* only when almost all of its form has been discovered, especially the style and rhythm of language. If, that is, preparation for making *the* story must come during the writing process, if discovery of material occurs *while* writing, it helps to consider the ensuing pages of type not a draft but a preparation. Such a shift in thinking may appear to be only a difference of semantics, but thinking of the labor of writing in this way, my students and I have found that we are able to remain emotionally involved in material through many days of work.

It is not that anyone who knows the basic components of the story form cannot write *a* story. The labor is in search of a story that is somehow one's own, a discovery which the writer wants to claim and have represent him to strangers, to his readers. If, as I often do, I find myself rewriting the first three pages of a story over and over, it is because I don't sense in the material shapes that please me. Or if I find only on the last page of a story I've written the aspects of the material most interesting to me, it is not that I haven't written *a* story but that the story I've written is extraneous language on the periphery of another, more interesting story, perhaps similar but also very different—it will become *the* story. And it is *then* that I've begun.

A writer's "economy" is whatever it takes to get a story that is finished and satisfying to the writer. Katherine Anne Porter may have written some of her stories in one sitting, but in fact those stories were years in preparation. My own economy, which many students have used to good effect, is seemingly tedious. If I complete three pages on the first day of writing a new story, I retype those pages on the second day before allowing myself to begin composing the fourth page, and so on. By a story's end, the pages will have been retyped numerous times. It is a method by which I remind myself daily of the components of a particular story-in-progress, which seems essential since my daily life is filled with typical distractions. The retyping is a very concrete reminder, of myself not as a writer who knows form but as one who is using form *in this way, in this story.*

The constraints on this method are physical: if I allow myself to think about writing page nine, for example, only after typing again pages one through eight, I must have energy in reserve for writing page nine after typing eight pages of manuscript. But this method has proven fruitful because it allows me to reenter each day my character's emotional states, which will be quite different from the emotional state of my own daily, mundane life. This method has also helped me to avoid what is termed "writer's block" since, each day I write, excepting the day I begin a story, I don't have to ask myself immediately if I *want* to write or am emotionally or intellectually prepared to write. *As* I type and read what I've written, I become prepared to continue writing. And the writing assumes a unity which I'm convinced it would not otherwise have.

This method would of course not work with a novel as a whole; it could be used within a single chapter, with rereading of previous chapters serving as a substitute for retyping.

II. Fear of the Unknown

No writer is wholly free. In our storehouse of materials are our obsessions, fears, estimations of human nature, prejudices, memories of radical experiences—all that comprises our personalities, including the mechanisms we trigger to keep our personalities unified. As a result, all of our creative work will be, finally, very like ourselves. We will have a range of writing styles but also be identified as having *a* style—the sum of our approach to form and language. A style is inescapable, and it will be molded partly by our idiosyncrasies and partly by our interactions in society.

The world shifts and as writers we respond; our creative work is written and as readers we respond to its having been made. As readers, we respond to other writers who worked or are working in similar fluidity. What we write, it would seem, is a transcription of tension, of the push and pull between who we are and what we are becoming.

It is easier not to delve into the storehouse of material, not to use writing as a method of self-discovery. A willingness to use writing for self-discovery requires a certain degree of self-trust—trust that experience *has* created a bounty of material for use and trust that we can confront hidden truths about ourselves. We must be prepared to be shocked at times and to be tossed at other times into a caldron of memory for which no shape seems possible.

The personalities we live with daily are not the sum of who we are, and both in dreams and in writing more of who we are emerges. Like dreams, the revelations of writing can be unsettling, can conflict with other images of ourselves. But the writing can also be a release, a sanctioning of our sense that we are more than we seem to others and even at times to ourselves. Both happen, not one without the other, and if we startle ourselves by what we discover in our writing, we also become more knowledgeable about ourselves.

The fear of discovering material brings with it another fear, not knowing how a story will develop before beginning the writing process. For many writers who preplan their stories, language does not rattle the doors of memory or test the reverberations created by words. Rather, it smooths the path already made by logic: these characters, in this setting, will do these preordained actions, and the sum will mean this.

While it could be said that Katherine Anne Porter preplanned her stories, a careful reading of "The Sources of *Noon Wine*" reveals that the novella results from Porter's search for its materials in the deepest recesses of memory and consciousness and that the form and style were carefully attuned to the process of Porter's vision.

What often happens when beginning writers write, however, is adherence to a plan for creative work *without* the long process of preparation which Porter describes and which I have termed "daydreaming." Beginning writers often leap into creative work with mere ideas or imitations of others' ideas, a flimsy facade over which language will be shingled.

Ideas, it seems to me, are so barely serviceable to a writer of fiction and poetry as to be almost useless, which is not to say that writers are not thinking at every turn. But it is a particular kind of thinking, in the service of creative work, a habit of mind that is part of what comprises a writer's materials.

For a creative writer, ideas are shaped into images, within individual words, clusters of words, in scenes, in scenes building one upon another, in contrasts between images, in the rhythms of the language that presents images. All of these stimulate the senses or memories of sensation.

We learn language first in the concrete—the object, then the word representing the object, although this is of course a simplification. But we do first learn sensation, which, as we develop, then separates into an understanding of the cause of sensation and only later into the names we give to identify the sensation and its causes. If writers are often accused of being lost in childhood, it is, I think, because writers must remain highly conscious of sensation and images. For the writer, name and cause and effect are never "givens"; rather, the writer seeks to have seen newly, again, *this* way, the writer's way *discovered* in the act of writing.

Ideas, for writers, are pleasing shapes, shapes that seem authentic within a whole, a larger shape, one not settled upon until the last word is written in a piece (and often a shape is adjusted by later writing, each piece of writing an amendment of a former piece). Language and its arrangement on the page carry the shape and, frustratingly, language is a code we use in society. Language carries the weight of society's interactions, the "meanings" of which are explored partially through language never freed of its users' histories and vested interests. This *beast*, language, is what must carry a writer's construed shapes, and to no reader will the beast look the same. Every reader has his or her history with language.

The writer begins his work on hostile ground, everything about language and the forms it has *so far* assumed designed to obscure *his* vision, whatever it may turn out to be, to misconstrue *his* shapes, however they form, because language is so burdened a medium. We are quite accustomed to this idea in the customs of other countries, where an innocent gift of a particular color of flower may, for example, represent mourning to the receiver. We likewise have our customs with language.

If a writer's shapes are wholly predictable, old ladies will stoop to pet the beast. If the writer's shapes are startling, a hue and cry will go up: "Obscure! Elitist! Aggressive! Nonuniversal! Decadent!" If the shapes are new enough to be good conversation at a dinner party but not so new as to disrupt eating, the writer will become popular, be permitted to tie his beast at the post while he eats. He will be invited to the same houses every season, provided he brings the beast everyone has grown so fond of.

The writer probably understands at the outset how difficult it is to want to invent and share new shapes in society. But beginning writers, I've discovered, rarely acknowledge that part of a writer's *materials* is an estimation of language's inherent difficulty *as* material; rarely, that is, do beginning writers acknowledge that thinking *about* language can provide access *to* language.

A story told in present tense, for instance, focuses by virtue of the immediacy of the verbs on action, event: *When Corrine arrives, she looks around outside for her brother.* While the sentence itself would not seem radically altered by its transposition into past tense—*When Corrine arrived, she looked around outside for her brother*—in fact much about the form of the story will have been affected by the choice of past tense because the narrator is different in *character*. If nothing else, the narrator has relinquished the sense of urgency which present-tense verbs provide. In present tense the story*telling* aspect of the story is deemphasized in favor of inviting the reader to *be* present.

But the change can be even more profound. In past tense a narrator often invites a reader to listen in contemplation to a story whose significance has accrued over time, after a narrator's reflection. The story depends in such an instance upon a narrator's accumulation of events, feelings, actions and the narrator's own view of them. For this narrator, what is important to the story may well be material which resides outside characters' abilities to know, to feel, and/or to understand. In that sense, no "story" exists in present time at all. The "story" comes into being only after the ordering mind of the narrator has accumulated specific data and put a face on it.

No doubt a writer's level of expertise at craft influences his or her range of questions about language. *Finnegans Wake* is a novel that only a mature writer could have attempted, born of Joyce's previous work. But writers whose craft is less sophisticated can nevertheless at least begin to ask difficult questions about language and form.

It is far easier, for instance, to learn how to write one kind of story, to polish it, and repeat that story's strategies in numerous other stories, varying only subject matter. In this way, a writer can avoid confronting his or her limitations and the awkward writing that is inevitable in the beginning stages of experimentation. Indeed, a segment of the reading public encourages writers to remain highly limited by identifying a writer with a particular type of story and encouraging that writer to give them as readers more of the same. Joseph Conrad complained of readers' infatuation with his sea tales, which he knew were far easier to understand than a novel of the depth of *Nostromo*. Conrad was shrewd enough to be able to identify readers' responses that would limit him as a writer and was thus able to avoid the enticement of popularity. Other writers have not been so self-protective and self-challenging.

It is understandable that younger writers often repeat forms they have succeeded with and avoid confronting again the awkwardness of trying to broaden their craft. Often they haven't read broadly enough to appreciate the traps of repetition, written enough to tire of their own repetitions, or imagined the dangers to development of repetition. In my classes, if I observe a writer repeating particular devices, choosing, for instance, the same point of view or narrative style in story after story, I suggest that he or she make a list of the approaches to form and language he or she has employed and then deliberately avoid repeating those approaches in the next five or ten stories. Writers seeking to expand their range of styles and devices need to be patient with themselves as they experiment—the work will, inevitably, be less polished, but, with time, the writer will discover shapes and styles which might otherwise have remained hidden.

The language that comes to mind for a given story is released *by form*. We do not keep the sum of our vocabularies instantly on tap but draw what we need for a situation created by form, by the sense of form that we set forth in the first words of a story we write. While these first words may be revised again and again, the revision is *toward* the elimination of some words in favor of others. The sum of these words will constitute the shape of a written work. Form and language are inextricably bound together.

We *are* as writers imprisoned by our habits as language-users, unable to wrest wholly free. But part of the material that can be available to us can emerge from questioning the parameters of our habits with language. Writers do this at every turn, some more consciously than others, for our society and our time in history will affect our use of language whether we know it or not. Certainly in retrospect we understand our fluctuating creativity. We're accustomed, now, for instance, to the rawness of life rendered in numerous contemporary poems, but each writer participating in, for example, what we now term the "confessional school" pioneered, in form, language, and the "politics" of writing. Can anyone imagine Anne Sexton's poetry existing a hundred years ago when what she had to say would have been unsuitable for a woman to say? Receiving license from both the era she lived in and the urgency of self, she assessed, self-consciously, I believe, her freedoms and approved of them. Their transcriptions became her poems— material won not only through pain but also from a particular time in society. Tragic stories of writers struggling within repressive societies are heightened versions of our smaller conflicts with material. A writer oppressed externally by the state can at least name his or her oppressor. The rest of us must wrest our material from the prisons of the self. Extracting a range of freedom requires heightened self-awareness.

III. Our Myths

A writer's material is not something a writer *has*. It is something a writer develops. Yet, for a number of reasons, it is difficult for beginning writers to grasp this concept in any depth. First, our tradition in America is a realistic tradition, Hawthorne, Poe, and Melville's whale notwithstanding. We have liked our tradition of practicality, our pioneering spirit that made confrontation with nature a virtue of survival. That history has influenced our forms just as the fact of apartheid currently influences the writing of both black and white writers in South Africa.

Mimetic fiction, fiction that mirrors what we take as reality, has been a fiction with which readers could "identify." It is a short step, too short, of course, for a beginning writer to imagine that creative work is a transcription of experience, a report of *what happened*. Older writers who have just begun to write seem especially fond of recording the events of their lives as if exactly what happened to them could constitute fiction. But young, beginning writers also accentuate the importance of their biographies as material. It must seem that they can render most truly, in our tradition, that which they have lived. After all, they have heard the admonition "Write what you know."

These are the writers I ask most frequently to imagine what it might mean to be "indifferent" to their materials. But professional writers, too, can be heard fostering an illusion about "raw" material. Once I heard a writer say at a public reading, "This next story is as autobiographical as you can get." Yet the story was shaped in a way no life or portion of a life is shaped. It *was* in the mimetic tradition, *almost*. I would rather we all declare, "None of our work is autobiographical although we have lived, sensitive, in the world." That would mirror more accurately, I believe, the power of form to transform facts, the power of language to set off differing reverberations for different readers.

The beginning writer is caught, then, by our literary and social history as well as by the fictions we espouse about creative work. One of our most binding myths is that of the writer's "madness." Creative people, we say, are different. We *feel* more, and it is hard to be so sensitive, so hard that we border on madness. Moreover, what makes us like this is a hidden wound which it is better not to explore except in writing and, even there, not to understand *too* well because this wound is, after all, the source of our creativity.

We can, in society, enjoy too much the posture of hand-on-forehead—ourselves as special cases, which has, historically, exempted writers from responsible behavior time and again: if the creative work is *good enough,* we can overlook the behavior. This message is heard by young writers: they come to believe that knowing too much about the writing process will abort creativity. In this scenario of the writer at work, he or she is *given* certain material and his lonely job is to use it up, one neurotic memory, presumably, after another until the mythical "well" runs dry and then, kaput, he's done for. Such a view subverts a writer's materials and development.

No writer develops in a vacuum, and, that being the case, a writer's material issues from the intellectual freedoms he imagines for himself. These can come in the form of questions, of experiments in writing, in supposition, in dreams, in daydreams, in study of other writers, in a self-conscious observation of habits in thought and writing, in skepticism about one's time and society. The *problems* of material are part of what *form* a writer's material. What to write *is* the question.

POINT OF VIEW

No doubt we all learned in high-school literature courses useful ways of thinking about point of view: first-person; third-person omniscient; third-person limited omniscient, etc. But when I notice in fiction-writing courses students working from these definitions of viewpoint, they seem less serviceable, too narrow. In contemporary fiction point of view is the aspect of form that has probably developed the most dramatically. The changes in point of view have mirrored writers' changing assumptions about the world.

If we are a long way now from the epic novels of Tolstoy and Dostoevsky and the grandeur in poetry of Wordsworth, we are just as far in the story form from the tale. Against this canvas of negations, it would seem that we have nothing to tell. Yet, of course, our modern fictions *are* revelatory, perhaps excruciatingly so, especially in European and American works, because they, too often, demonstrate either only inwardness or banality. It is as if we have no territory left to contemplate or render, and how much loss we feel as writers and readers may correspond to how well we know *War and Peace* and *The Brothers Karamazov.*

But what exactly the story is as a form, or the novel for that matter, is in debate, carried on in writing most vociferously within point of view, as it naturally would be. While an individual writer may signal his stance to the tensions in literature carried by point of view simply by choosing to write "traditionally" or "experimentally," the writing he produces is emblematic of a changed and changing world.

While we probably do not have the distance from which to assess in any depth either our current writing or what it bespeaks of us, it is nonetheless possible to survey the tip of the iceberg in order to estimate its hidden properties. Many writers relegate this task to the critics alone, foolishly, I think, but any of us can see, for instance, a difference in Faulkner's assumptions about the world in his creation of Yoknapatawpha County and Ray Carver's domestic tundra. Susan Sontag and Nadine Gordimer appear to inhabit different universes, and they were, of course, shaped by differing tides of history.

But if a society shapes a writer, that writer may also respond within some indeterminate range of freedom and demonstrate his response through point of view *choices.* Faulkner may have inherited a particular social order, but he did not rest in it. The extent to which he rebelled is obvious in the scope of his work. The enactments of history on his characters' very souls permeated Faulkner's vision.

It is interesting to note that in Daniel Halpern's international anthology *The Art of the Tale,* a collection of eighty-two contemporary stories, only five are written in present-tense, and those by Americans, except for one. The exception, "This Way for the Gas, Ladies and Gentlemen," is by the Polish writer Tadeuz Borowski

(1922-1951), and what is so urgent as to require the present tense is his characters' experiences in a concentration camp. By contrast, an anthology of contemporary American stories would contain more than half written in present tense. The question is, *do* we have a justifying urgency or has fad followed what began as a justifying urgency? By and large, our present-tense stories have as their subject matter the trivial upsets of daily life, and we should wonder why.

Is point of view as a technique related to verb tense? Surely not, we may think, yet how else are we to consider the broader definition of point of view that affects specific point of view as a technique—except by asking what its parameters are. A narrator, either in first, second, or third person, tells a story, and in a novel each may be used, with a hidden narrator (the author) behaving as overall narrator. It is the narrator who carries the story's language, even the language of dialogue, since the narrator only illustrates what he, she, or "it" has to declaim or ask with selections of conversation written to progress a story. *How* the narrator sees determines what story is told on the level of plot, and the choices of language convey tone, attitude.

In the tension between ourselves as perceivers of the story—*all* of its materials—and our view of the world within which we decide what we think of the story (again, all of its materials), *a* story is received. *That* story, resulting from the push and pull between reader and writer may be quite different for each of us, depending on who *we* are: how we read, how we have read in the past, what our situation is as we read.

The perpetual debate about literature, about how we write *and* read, our awareness of that debate as writers, can be part of our material for writing and, moreover, probably *is* regardless of how conscious of it we are.

Point of view as a technique in fiction is, for me, at the center of my own private and public debates about literature because, if I want to set up a tension between my writing and a reader, point of view is crucial because it determines other aspects of form. The word *tension* suggests that I, the writer, have something to say about what kind of tensions get set up. This imagined wedge of freedom is hard-won; any contemporary writer with his eyes open probably laments this era so circumscribed by the fact of nuclear weapons, cultures in conflict, all of us set adrift on the current of technology.

Technically, some tensions in a story are easy to construe. When we speak of an "unreliable narrator," we know as readers that what we are being told, perhaps blatantly, is not the truth. The reader's job is to listen to the narrator's version of the truth, check it against his own understanding of reality, and find the narrator in error. But even simple irony has become not so simple when the reader's vision of the objective world shifts. The tensions between narrator and reader that the writer imagined setting up can fade, become distorted. This sort of shift is evidenced in numerous critics' rereading of western literature as a carrier of implicit imperialistic attitudes. Knowledge of a post-colonial world reverberates against the writer's assumptions within a colonial period. I daresay Alice Walker's *The Color Purple* will one day be read differently, just as Conrad's novels are now.

If we ask why American writers are currently writing in the present tense so frequently, we would no doubt need to ask the sorts of questions cultural anthropologists ask (and the questions *they* have traditionally asked are changing). In poetry, a similar technique—the poem addressed to the reader: "you"—raises questions as broad-reaching.

Point of view as a technique in fiction is no simple matter.

In its broadest sense, point of view is a writer's attitude toward the world as that attitude is expressed, exposed, in form. It is, finally, a measure of the writer's experience and intelligence and, a traditional critic would say, his moral fiber. Inexperience and lack of thought can atrophy a piece of fiction quickly because a point of view will be chosen within too narrow a range.

It is common, for instance, for a beginning, very young writer to write of his or her first experience of romantic love, and because, no doubt, the experience was felt as radical, the incident of love is written about as if the writer has not experienced other forms of love, has no history against which to judge the erotic dimension of love. The story's point of view is often third-person, supposedly objective narration in which only what happened is related, as if fact could make fiction. Often the story is written in present tense as a mirror of the characters' urgency. The affair goes badly or well and is over. There is, in fact, no story but rather an incident.

It is perhaps a prejudice of mine to make a distinction between incident and story when much contemporary American fiction is writing about incidents, ripples of experience which suggest that we as a people don't know *what* to think, have moreover forgotten that we once imagined we did, and have now simply given up the larger questions while still entertaining ourselves by reciting our daily human vagaries. And to give such writers their due, perhaps this is so, perhaps such non-stories are political statements, for the writers often have their characters declare their own inabilities to think, have them confess a confusion that requires the characters to exhibit only what happened and how befuddling it all was.

Nevertheless, it is my prejudice to separate story from incident, to care not only about what happened but to be drawn into questions about why. It is handling of point of view that can draw me in. It seems that fiction that only mirrors our confusion as a people allows for no tension to be set up between a writer's materials and a reader. Whether or not it is a habit bred of grand illusion, we seek in our daily lives to understand the tide of humanity accompanying us in its sweep. Finding our questions insufficient to the task, we turn to art to have our questions deepened, discarded, or refined. *Should* art be mere solace, still we are thrown back to inquiry: why does it take the multiplicity of forms it takes and might these forms yet mean something?

Recently I read a novel written from the sole point of view of characters who were sub-normal in intelligence—society's cast-offs in alleys, halfway houses and rented rooms. The third-person narrator never veered from the characters' view-points as they beat one another, had sex voluntarily and involuntarily, with both strangers and family members, etc. I took the novel as a political statement, a one-dimensional statement, since I felt there was nothing else I could do as a reader: the author's only assumption of tension-causing device was scene after scene of hapless incident—characters at the mercy of themselves in a society blind to them, although this blindness had to be deduced since the close adherence to the charac-ters' view prohibited any direct presentation of society's blindness. Suppose, I thought, I had been shown on television scene after scene of brutality toward blacks in South Africa and had no knowledge of apartheid? That would mirror the experience of reading the novel, which might, in a world not desensitized by its absorption of terror, generate a revolution against all brutality, but we know very well that we are confined by our history and the narcosis it produces.

By comparison, Russell Banks's novel *Continental Drift,* about an "average" man, is also filled with brutal scenes. Yet his narrator is exceedingly aggressive, at times rhapsodic, saying: This is a story of an average man who does evil and dies for it. It isn't pretty, the narrator continues, and I will tell his story unadorned so that you, reader, will know men like this exist and why I think they exist. This narrator also aggressively manipulates how the story is told, switching from the main character's story in alternate chapters to the story of a woman whose life is made hideous by this character's actions. Banks's novel announces loudly the terms of the debate it wants to set up, names the tensions Banks expects between story and reader. The difference between the two novels is tremendous, and if, as I did, I argued with Banks's narrator, there were intricacies of characters' thought and actions with which to argue and material upon which to contemplate.

Point of view, then, is the manner in which a writer asks a reader to become engaged. It is an invitation issued by a writer fully aware of competing demands on a reader, and it is perhaps here that writers distinguish themselves most readily. The writer imagines a reader whose interest must be piqued in order for the communication between them to occur. Just as a writer's experience will determine his broad viewpoint, so will experience aid him in imagining to whom his writing may speak. It is no simple task.

It can happen, as it did with Heinrich Kleist, that a writer's sensibilities can so conflict with his own era that a reader not yet born must be imagined—from hope, supposition, a reading of the forces at work in a society. It is too large an issue to investigate here but nevertheless important to mention that a writer's imagined reader may be more difficult to construe if the potential for nuclear annihilation has entered his consciousness as a vision, no matter how starkly or dimly viewed. I doubt that we have begun to intuit how the fact of annihilation's threat to the world has affected our art.

But on the level of our daily immersion in writing, for we seem still capable of pursuing writing, experience is required for a writer to imagine a sophisticated reader. And what *sophisticated* means and portends for a writer depends on his experience and, moreover, the *politics* of his experience: what do we want our writing to *do* in the world?

There is no doubt in my mind that a young writer can best aid himself in answering questions about the imagined reader through reading. But that lifelong pursuit will result in the perpetual fluctuation of the reading writer's particular imagination. Specific questions that relate to broad point of view can, as the reading process continues, help a writer not only formulate questions about material but aid in a definition, no matter how fluid, of the writer's imagined reader.

The following questions are merely suggestive of the many a writer may ask about point of view.

Questions About Point of View

1. What, specifically, makes this story worth telling?
2. Apart from simple plot, what aspects of form are included to engage a reader?
3. Is the story anything other than a transcription of ideas or has it become more than that through its devices?
4. How naive or sophisticated are the ideas lurking in the story?
5. If my perspective on the material is set before I begin to write, how do I make it appear as a discovery for a reader so that the reader will sense the tensions that I initially experienced in order to conceive the material?
6. If my perspective about the material emerges *as* the story is written, how do I order the material? Do I want the point of view to contain a sense of seamless unity as if I knew all along what my discovery would be or should the language and form reflect some of the "raggedness" of faltering discovery?
7. If the story's events are important to my characters, what seemingly peripheral events caused me to understand their significance to the extent that I can use it in a story? Should these peripheral events or some suggestion of them be included in order to enrich the texture of the primary events?
8. How much have I thought about what I will write about? Does my thinking cause my fiction to suggest answers to problems, or does it deepen my own and an imagined reader's questions?
9. Can form help me to discover meaning, and do I even think that meaning is a discovery fiction seeks?
10. Is the particular material of a story engaging me, or am I merely imitating either my own previous writing or that of others?
11. If I write as an act of discovery, how do I know that I will have any control over the piece of writing? Can a choice of point of view aid in handling emerging material?

12. To what extent is time a factor in my understanding of an event, and do I want to give a reader a similar sense of time?

13. If I move back and forth between points of view in a piece of writing, how will my broad point of view about the material be conveyed?

14. Do I question what we term "conventions" in fiction—a pre-established, tacit understanding with the reader—or do I use them unthinkingly?

15. How do I distinguish between fads in prose and long-established "conventions"?

16. Is a sense of place important in this particular piece of writing? If so, how broad should the landscape of place and population be? Does the answer to the question affect specific point of view?

17. To what extent does my knowledge of traditional point of view influence my understanding of point of view?

18. What aspects of the traditional story or novel contradict my view of the world? How, in form, do I contend with the contradiction?

19. How limited is my vocabulary, and how does it affect my range of point of views?

20. To what extent does the role I play in society affect the points of view I use in my fiction? Do I think that my role in society should be mirrored in my work?

21. Do the points of view I use routinely make it difficult for me to discover new stories? If so, how might I manipulate habit and still retain technical control of my work?

22. Do I think that a story changes dramatically if the point of view is changed?

23. When I read a writer whose broad point of view is radically different from my own, do I dismiss the writing or search for understanding?

24. How often do I read work that challenges my own prejudices about writing?

25. Can I identify my primary interest among storytelling devices and give at least a partial answer as to why the interest is dominant?

Note: An excellent analysis of point of view can be found in *The Novel: Modern Essays in Criticism,* edited by Robert Murray Davis (Prentice-Hall). The essay is "Point of View in Fiction," by Norman Friedman.

POINT OF VIEW WITHIN
A STORY'S STRUCTURE

While the previous commentary about point of view focuses primarily on its broader definitions as crucial to the making of fiction, point of view is also a specific technique, which can be studied specifically. Point of view in a piece of fiction determines language, structure, and meaning.

At whatever level of consciousness, a reader asks: Who is the narrator, and what are his attitudes?

Here is the opening to a story titled "Prognosis," which I wrote during a time when I wanted to expand my use of plot (it is a heavily plotted story) and sense of distance from material:

> *They have spent five days crying—all their bodies could tolerate. Ray had spent himself before the windows of the motel room, not looking out so much as not turning around. Ann, his daughter (eleven years old and becoming already the beauty her mother had been), had stayed curled on one of the double beds, all the fingers of one hand stuck in her mouth.*

The narrator, first, is not objective—"all their bodies could tolerate" is a subjective assessment since, presumably, some people can tolerate crying for longer or shorter periods of time. The word "spent" is also subjective, suggesting Ray's physical resources as that which he can use at will, to a tolerable extent. ". . . not looking out so much as not turning around" is also subjective since it suggests more than fact—Ray is *refraining* from turning around, and it is that action rather than looking out the window that occupies him. The statement is also an exaggeration—surely he moved during the five days. And, subtly, "all the fingers of one hand stuck in her mouth" is subjective, in tone and rhythm suggestive of a child, the word *stuck* in particular, as if she had jammed her fingers into her mouth in defiance. Of what? That is suggested in the mention of crying, of Ann's mother, of her beauty and the words "had been." But it is only a suggestion *because* the narrator is subjective and for reasons of his or her own prefers to focus primarily on not the cause of grief but the grief itself.

The narrator is distant enough from the scene to see both Ann and Ray as a unit, "They." And the narrator has mentioned the number of beds in the room—two—as if it were a detail that mattered, and it does, partly so that the reader can see the site of grief and also to suggest the modernity of the hotel room. Later it will be learned that Ann and Ray are in Chicago, but this information is subsidiary to what the narrator perceives as more important information.

The narrator, then, is subjective, observant, cognizant of the mother's absence, specific if not about Ray's age, then Ann's, and, by inference not contradicted by other language, at least allowing the reader to imagine Ray as middle-aged, say thirty to forty. Moreover, the narrator begins the story, invites the reader in *at this point,* with Ann and Ray's grief, then undercuts it by suggesting that grief or, at least, the stage of grief during which tears flow can last only so long. But by focusing on grief as opposed to, for instance, the cause of grief, the narrator is suggesting that grief be the focus, and if not the grief of tears, what else of grief?

The grief has been mentioned, then, at the expense of other details. What is omitted weighs on what is present, as it always does in fiction but particularly in the story form. We do not learn why Ann and Ray are in the motel room—not yet. Nor are we told how they look except in the abstract reference to the mother's beauty suggesting itself in Ann at age eleven. Presumably another narrator might find these omitted details crucial.

An omniscient, subjective narrator, then, is outside the story looking on out of interest in the characters' next stage of grief, which is focused on more than who or what has caused the grieving. In fact, the narrator so focuses on the manifestations of Ray and Ann's grief that it will be five more paragraphs before it is clear that the mother/wife has died in a fire and much later before it is clear that Ray holds himself responsible and indeed may *be* responsible.

But the narrator is also making a preparation for another element of the story, its black humor. Given the subject of death and the solemnity with which the writer is aware it is taken generally, the narrator must quickly establish at least something in "voice" or tone or language itself if humor is ever to rise. The humor is not evident here, but a narrator's voice which will allow it to rise, through a narrator's commentary as well as through juxtaposition of sentences and the rhythms of language, must be established. To my ear, the "place" is paved for humor in, first, the aggressiveness of the narrator's opening line: *They have spent five days crying—all their bodies could tolerate.* A narrator not bent on black humor might have put the same information differently: *They were exhausted from crying* or *They had cried for five days and now found themselves unable to cry.* The word *tolerate* carries reverberations of both exhaustion depleted and exasperation, a signal of giving up, which has been incorporated into society in such phrases as "I can't tolerate that behavior one more minute!" or "He is simply intolerable!" The word used in any way except clinically, as in *he died because his body was not able to tolerate the extremes of cold to which it was subjected,* is exaggeration, a hyperbole used most often when exhaustion is *not* the issue but a signal of feeling.

It should be mentioned here that such careful reading may be given a paragraph by a reader but certainly not with a critic's eye for cause and effect. Having the critic's eye is the writer's job, at least in a story that appears to be within the storytelling tradition. The reader is invited to read a *story,* a narrative, and will most likely be reading at a brisk pace.

If a story's whole can be intimated in its opening, as it often can, Ray and Ann's story is about grief itself and its effects on the living, and this will be the narrator's focus to such an extent that the "story" of how the person who has died came to die and why is subsumed by the narrator's greater interest in investigating the effects of grief. It is a story sympathetic to the survivors, and Ann will be the main character, if it is accurate to deduce that Ray will continue to monitor his movements in an awareness of Ann.

In the sense that story derives from point of view, the *language* of a story derives from point of view, and structure does as well, a microcosm of the story exists in its first paragraph.

Here is a much more aggressive narrator:

It is noon when Claire begins screaming, the high-C of arch suffering (history and waste) in a repertory which will never contain cancer of the bone marrow or one lost eye. So: who cares? Except, afterwards, her body will not look quite the same—puffiness under the eyes and on the belly a mound of fat and in the shoulders what looks like fat but is instead a realignment of wings—clipped, a curving inward like a second set of ribs protecting a second stomach, and she slows down, as if chewing thoughtfully. If anyone were watching, he would pause, the repose of any animal sensing a foreign species, its habits embedded in the brain like teeth.

This narrator is making a special sort of invitation to a reader, and the complexity, density, and idiosyncrasy of the narrator's language will not be taken up by those who do not like flamboyant style as a story's component. Besides wielding language idiosyncratically ("high-C of arch suffering"; "curving inward like a second set of ribs"; "what looks like fat but is instead a realignment of wings"), the narrator is making social commentary through images, and that social commentary is being given as much space as Claire's character, her plight. In fact, that commentary is coloring Claire and her situation for the reader. A certain kind of screaming is termed "arch" and immediately relegated to history and waste. Either Claire or mankind in general indulges in "arch suffering" and, implies the narrator, such suffering is wasteful within a world where others suffer from cancer or maiming. In the question "So: who cares?" is the narrator's implication that a sufferer such as Claire ought to be ignored. Then the narrator amends the suggestion by describing the physical manifestations of Claire's suffering which will later become a part of her. Moreover, the narrator suggests, we as people respond at a primitive level ("any animal") to manifestations of prior suffering in others *regardless* of how foreign the Other is to us, because the Other, the "foreign species," has a presence, "habits embedded," and the presence cannot be ignored for they are "like teeth."

Again, if an unfolding story is suggested by its point of view, this story will be about the effects of Claire's suffering on a larger society. Claire's ostensible story will be overtaken, compete with, the narrator's preoccupation with its effects. It will be, in fact, not Claire's story at all. *By* the narrator, the story will be given to Lucy, Claire's sister, because she is developing a watchfulness which the narrator finds adequate.

The technique of point of view is that which we read *through* for any story at all. Except possibly in the tale, though we are too far removed from the tale to experience it as separate from our heightened interiority and thus ensure a misreading—except in the tale, *two* stories exist within a writer's single story. Then the Reader enters the picture.

Story I: The plot—characters in action, the action beginning at a certain point and ending at a certain point, with some result. This is the ostensible story, a story's surface. This is so even of anti-stories which seek through experiments of language and arrangement to free themselves from traditional storytelling. Readers' habits bring narrative progression even to the anti-story.

Story II: The deeper story beneath the surface of plot. This story is the sum of the materials, conveyed through a narrator's point of view, language, scenes, setting, action, dialogue, all chosen to convey point of view in its broad definition.

Story III: The sum of what a particular reader at a particular time and place makes of Stories I and II in the push and pull between the reader and a writer's story.

When writers become interested in the intricacies of point of view, they can begin to modulate the tensions between reader, Story I, and Story II; can begin, that is, defining story without dependency on plot's variety, on its ability to startle or beguile. Although many startling or beguiling stories heavy in plot exist in literature, in general, plot is the *least* interesting aspect of the story or novel forms. We have, as it were, heard it all before.

Since point of view is carried, as is plot, by language, writers whose primary interest is in a story's sub-surface will pay careful attention to language. We call the selection and ordering of a story's language *style,* and it becomes heightened in importance when plot is devalued. As the diagram below indicates, what I call "lines of tension" are established whenever a story's sub-surface is crucial to its meaning.

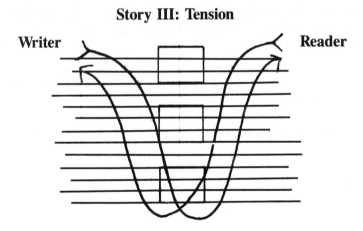

Story I: Plot

Scene

Scene

Scene

Story II: Plot & Narration

Scene

Scene

Scene

Story III: Tension

Writer   Reader

Following a more detailed analysis of the Imagined Reader, I will delve into specific viewpoints and the "lines of tension" each sets up. But at this point to turn again to the reader is important if we are to imagine that our writing is for the sake of communication at some point in time.

THE IMAGINED READER

. . . someone is making this book that we are reading. And, as with all made objects—at least those made by men, not God or nature—it is put together out of bits and pieces, attached to each other by dint of hard work, skill, guile and sheer preservative instinct. But at the same time we are made strongly aware of the maker of this book: of his desires, choices, decisions—ultimately, of the darkness and silence out of which such decisions spring.

*This is done by making the reader himself shoulder the task of the making. For this patchwork, piecemeal object is also a mousetrap, designed to catch the reader. The more he withdraws, tries to establish himself in a safe position above the action, retreats to the safety of his seat in the library, the more enmeshed he becomes in the toils of the book. Once he has started reading this novel [*Tristram Shandy*], there is no escape for him: he is made to give up many of the assumptions he held before he started, and the process is one not just of loss but also of discovery.*

—Gabriel Josipovici,
Writing and the Body

A story is not experienced by the reader as a flat surface. The deeper, more complex a story's sub-surface, the greater will be the reader's intellectual activity and, possibly, emotional and sensual engagement. He can feel as though he has entered new territory, read certain signs for direction, and visited the populace, on some occasions as a privileged guest privy to the inhabitants' thoughts, feelings, and dreams.

If the reader is viewed by the writer as an active participant in the writer's process, a component to be reckoned with, the relevant question is: Who is my imagined reader?

While some contemporary critics are uncomfortable studying literature from the viewpoint of readers' responses and prefer to look at a piece of writing as setting up its own terms apart from readers' history with language and culture, writers nonetheless imagine a reader. At whatever level of consciousness, the action of writing presumes a receiver of the action.

I am speaking of the general reader who reads simply to enrich his life. It is not *for* him, necessarily, that the writer writes; rather, the writer imagines a tension which may be established in a piece of writing and, while establishing it in prose, envisions how the tensions may be perceived, received, taken apart and examined, or, simply, how they are felt.

If we say that a writer is his own first reader, we imply his taking the place of an imagined reader, before the work is ready for reading, for *a* reading. We know, of course, that readers differ. We also know that the writer has difficulties being his own reader because of his subjective investment and immersion during the creative act. This imagined reader is necessarily, then, an elusive character in a process of change as we as writers change. The more we write and then read, the more intricate will the imagined reader's personality become, mirroring our growing sophistication.

If we try, however, to approach the imagined reader tentatively as a component in the writing process, it may be useful to ask first: In this particular story, what would I have a reader *do* with the materials? If a story's whole is more than its parts, it is because, like fabric, it becomes whole cloth as a result of the individual threads' having been woven together. And the reader may try to take the material apart thread by thread. If he succeeds, these are the easy stories, because our finest fictions in both the story and novel forms appear indestructible, so tightly are they woven, so intricately patterned. These are the fictions we stand in awe before and contemplate again and again because they yield enough to fascinate us but not enough to destruct. Tolstoy's *War and Peace* is in this category, as well as Melville's *Moby Dick*. Of modern stories, Katherine Ann Porter's *Noon Wine* appears to withstand repeated readings. And there are many more, in all languages. But what is certain is that many more easily unraveled, flimsy works of fiction exist. The individual writer knows this as fact and is haunted by it. We know that at least some readers have read enough to measure what they read.

It seems to me that the first task of a writer trying to develop his or her imagined reader is to work at curing himself of naiveté through reading. It is a task which can never be completed, but too many beginning writers try to avoid an apprenticeship to literature. A similar tactic by a surgeon would meet with disastrous results, as if there were no need to meet the patient, take his medical history, or keep abreast of technology.

Reading is used by the writer not only as preparation for a career. It can be vital to the ongoing development of a writer's craft and especially of an imagined reader. If I want to imagine a reader who will read my writing, I need to estimate him through my own reading, observing literature that has rewarded him in the past and considering what rewards him currently.

This does not mean, of course, that what is popular must affect what I write. To the contrary, in fact. A writer seeks a reader for his or her particular work in its uniqueness and idiosyncrasy. But part of what a writer does is estimate how his special vision can be *translated* into form, what shapes to draw out of the silence of himself. The form and language of a writer's work are not wholly predetermined, no matter how much he may feel dogged by what has been written before and what is being written now. An imagined reader is a judicious selection of an image from many images of "The Reader."

Writers need to read partly to discover the readers we *don't* want. Calmly and with self-assurance, V. S. Naipaul has stated that he does not write for the masses. When we notice a very young writer's first novel vault him into fame and fortune, enough to give him what we presume in our envy is unlimited freedom for writing, a statement such as Naipaul's seems quite radical. But we can become victimized by rumors of fame and fortune. We can forget to ask of the young writer's work: "But is it any *good?*"

The question is crucial, for the writer can be seduced by images of fame, perhaps now more than ever before since contemporary publishing practices and economics dictate appealing to a mass of readers rather than to readers whose backgrounds in literature make them highly discriminating. To many, being a writer now appears to be a good career *because* a number of young writers have "made it big." It is hard to imagine Poe, for example, enticing others into the writer's career by his image so fraught with anguish. But reviewers now appear to focus as much on the writer as on the writing; we are spoon-fed stories of instant fame with, at best, news that the writer spent a year in a university writing program before his teacher sent the protégé's novel off to an agent and, voilà!— fame.

The writer beginning to develop a relationship with an imagined reader should be wary of the seduction in such stories. It is far too easy for a writer to begin to tailor his or her writing to the fads of the day, especially when it is so difficult for a writer to find shapes and languages for his *own* vision. Yet if he does not, his writing will be ephemeral or like fodder for the herd gathered round the fad. It is, after all, not the *reader's* job to protect a writer's potential; rather, it is the writer's job to imagine a reader he or she wants.

And the imagined reader must arise from a writer's changing estimation of his capabilities; that is, a writer needs to estimate what it is *possible* for him to do as a writer while leaving space for the estimation to grow. For example, as a southerner I grew up reading Eudora Welty's name and seeing her books. As soon as I was sophisticated as a reader, I began reading her work. I was captivated by it, especially by how intricately a sense of place is woven into the fabric of her work. I knew the locales, and I had heard the speech of her characters. When I began to write, I imagined that I, too, would write such stories, and, in some recess of the brain, I imagined having for my own work *her* readers. But as I wrote and read more, as I understood increasingly what had comprised my own personality out of my own background, I began to realize not only our radical differences as writers but the differences in the readers our work appealed to. No matter how much I admire Welty, my relationship to place is different, as have been my experiences with people, if, that is, it is fair to deduce Welty's experiences with people from reading her fiction. Too, I began to understand from reading that *as a writer* and not simply as a reader, my affinity is greater to Porter, to John Hawkes, Gina Berriault, James Purdy, V. S. Naipaul.

When we imagine a reader of our own writing, we are in part assessing our experience in the world and taking into account how it will influence the way we *can* write. For *this* writing we need readers.

But even then we should be cautious that we don't allow our imagined or actual readership to obscure our visions. In creative writing programs, students and faculty worry that their readers—fellow writers and faculty—are too much like themselves. And they know, too, that some writing programs foster experimental writing while others insist young writers ground themselves first in the traditional forms. Some programs expose students only to writing by published contemporary writers as models. Students in writing programs who are interested in protecting their personal visions, *their* writing, assess the biases of any program and compensate for them with broader viewpoints.

It is more difficult, however, to compensate for influences on one's work—especially the work of imagining a reader—when a complex of forces combine to promote a particular kind of writing. A writer whose vision is antithetical to the prevailing mode of writing can feel hapless and depressed. It is easy to assuage depression by asking, "Ought I not revise my vision and write what 'they' want, if I want to publish?" An example of this pressure on a writer is the prevalence of the "minimalist" story, which strips the story down to the basics of plot rendered in "plain" language, which in this case means not the plainness of Katherine Anne Porter's prose in *Noon Wine* or V. S. Naipaul's in *Miguel Street* but, rather, colloquial language which sounds like American speech. Not only is style effaced in the minimalist story; cause and effect are too. As a result, plot is heightened, but only because of other absences since the actions of characters are often trivial, mere incidents of daily life. Meaningful dialogue is undercut as well, because, within trivial events, people appear to talk out of habit since, with cause and effect absent, they have nothing to ponder or to ask. What is left, then, are portraits of incidents in an ambience most frequently rendered through the brand-name products characters use and the television they watch. The stories are about "the way we live now," as a number of reviewers have said, and they have captivated a readership that is itself immersed in cultural changes—the changes in perceptions and realities about the family, sex, money, politics.

The developing writer, however, should be wary and self-protective in the face of this fiction, no matter its readership, even if such wariness means that finding one's readers, as well as imagining a reader whose needs are different, becomes more difficult. It is too easy for the writing in a particular era to appear, in sum, over time, so similar as to be indistinguishable, one story from another, one writer from another. Too, the broad point of view from which such work issues may bear little relationship to one's inherent viewpoint about either writing or the world. And the use of language arising from the broad viewpoint may allow a writer little, in style of language, by which to satisfy the urge to write that was an impetus to writing.

Alongside the "minimalist" fiction has arisen fiction and poetry focusing on what is termed "the working class," meaning blue-collar workers, and "the underclass," meaning groups of people whose education, poverty, mental stability, or intelligence keep them cut off from the mainstream of society. In this fiction, what is new is not such characters, however, since they have appeared in fiction repeatedly over time. What is new is the fiction's point of view since the narrator most often refrains from providing a perspective on the characters' conflicts but rather adopts a viewpoint and language identical with the characters. Because Russell Banks's novel *Continental Drift* contains a narrator who aggressively provides a viewpoint, his novel could be called traditional even though its style often reflects what society considers "blue-collar" ways of thinking and speaking. But his novel is an exception to the general trend in characterizing such people and their lives.

The developing writer who has himself been privy to a wide variety of class structures and strata and thus has material for transformation into fiction by virtue of knowledge and understanding, observing the popularity of this writing about middle-lower, lower, and sub-class characters, would need to ask questions about the imagined reader. These stories are read *not* by the classes they portray, again within a viewpoint mirroring the classes, but by the upper-middle classes, usually. With the narrators of this new fiction relinquishing the function of providing an outside perspective, the reader is given, by and large, what is by virtue of circumstance—the difference between the materials and the class of the reader—a voyeuristic experience. Such fiction does present portraits of characters, of course, but the restrained narrative intervention leaves unclear for what *purpose* the portraits are being presented.

I present these examples of current trends in fiction to suggest that defining an imagined reader is not simple because the reader cannot be imagined apart from his social/cultural position.

The problem of imagining a reader is two-fold, then. As writers we are aware to some degree of the material we have and know that we are to some extent bound to it. As we render it into form, we will interest particular readers by the specific nature of the material itself and by the manner in which it is presented. And we are aware that the reader is a social creature responding to a changing world, making assessments of it, however obscured by prejudice or faddishness. We must maneuver between these claims in order to imagine a reader for our work, and how adroitly we maneuver will in part determine the quality of our work.

A READER'S RESPONSE

What follows are a story and an essay indicating some of the responses one reader had to the story. While both are interesting pieces of writing in and of themselves, they are offered here to suggest the complexity of the reader/writer relationship. The story indicates at least partially the manner in which one writer thinks about form in general and how she applied those overall conceptions within a particular story whose demands were necessarily unique. The essay gives evidence of the reader's overall view of what literature can do and her assessment of one story within that framework. The interplay between story and essay suggests the importance of the tension between writer and reader a story creates and depends upon.

• REPLACEMENT •

by Jane McCafferty

To think after an entire month she was still living in a room she never would have seen had she not felt her longing as dire that night. And yesterday, in the light of a morning moon, she had chopped her hair to look like the girl's, so that next time they ventured into the street, strangers out there might think *mother* and *daughter*. The hair was piled in the corner now, a dark mound on the green wood floor.

The girl was eleven, playing a toy xylophone in the corner, seated on the edge of the cot. She wore a man's sleeveless undershirt like a dress, and on the back of it with a black pen (she called it an ink-pen and would let nobody touch it) she'd drawn a huge sun, and the words KILL ROACHES in the middle of it, in back-slanting letters she said were proof of talent. "I could go into lettering one day," she'd say, out of the blue.

"Katrina," Doreen said.

"Name's Frank."

"Frank, your mother ain't comin' back and neither is Isaiah-Ahmed." (*Beautiful man,* she added in her mind. Even his abandoning her could not bring the rage that might have punctured love, or rather helped the memory of his hands to collapse into something less whole—something that wouldn't, like the hands themselves, sweep over her each time she said his name.)

"We could go lookin' for them again," said the girl. "One more time."

"They ain't in the city no more. I can feel it in my bones."

And the girl pushed the toy instrument off of her lap; the bright metal keys crashed to the floor, a few high notes clinking.

"I'm sick-a-ya feelin' it in your stupid bones," she said.

"Katrina, don't sass."

The girl walked to the high window where the moon could be seen resting on the dark apartment building across from them, scattered rectangular windows brimming with orange light. She had to tiptoe to see out. Doreen applied another coat of lipstick thinking *when,* Lord, *when* will the emptiness go away? She looked

up at the flaking ceiling and watched two roaches circle the light, side by side. So
parallel it was almost for a split second pretty.

"No whales in the sky now," the girl said. "Fish freaks all swam off for a better
place."

"Oh?"

Earlier they had watched the schools of grey clouds swimming across the moon
as if swallowing it. The bright ball of light had burst through the grey flesh to get
back to the sky, leaving behind groping tatters with illuminated edges. "Clouds
think, you know," the girl said once, in the middle of a xylophone song that
Doreen in her mind had been making up words to: He broke my heart with both
his hands, but I can't help to love the man. The man, the man, the man.

The night she had first walked off the street, down the alley and up the fire
escape into the battered room that was turning out to be a home was the night she
had tired of cows. She had gone to visit them for so long after James died, a
weekly ritual, taking the bus out of the city (avoiding the cemetery though it was
what had given her a taste for country air), her own reflection floating in the tinted
bus window above the road. There had been a child that night who kept asking
Why? no matter what the fancy mother said, the mother refusing to acknowledge
the child's attempt to irritate or amuse, responding to each Why? as if it were
sincere and answerable. (Doreen could still hear the woman saying "Because
Daddy thinks troutfishing's the next best thing to dying and going to heaven, that's
why.") And with that the child had lost control; Why! Why! Why! she'd shouted,
and would not stop, until every rider on the bus felt the shame and sadness of the
child breaking down, all rage and tears, and Doreen thinking, I would like to have
that child. I would.

It was always a good thing, stepping off the bus into the utterly foreign smell of
grass and manure, starred breath of earth gathering around her like a cape from a
different world, the bus pulling away and herself in the white dress splashed with
violets which James had bought in another city before the sickness was even
named. She would turn to watch the spewed clouds of exhaust, vanishing.

She had bent down and picked up a white stone that night, and held it tightly,
walking up the road. When the face of James rose in her, it usually took her along
like a chill, but that night his image was strangely powerless, and she felt the
memory as habit, the sadness more like weariness. She owned it then, his death,
controlled it, held to it as one holds to a ball of string, flying a kite, waiting for
wind. She could allow it to rise into space behind clouds, and then there were only
moments when fearing the loss of that loss (the final fear, always) she would wind
the string back in to feel the tugging in her fingers, palm, gut—but gently now,
though still her entire body eventually responded in a moment's dream of
ascension.

She walked as usual toward the farm where her cows were kept, her eyes on
Edgel's house, the white door standing in the stone, long, moonlit, the old fear

filling her—seeing the house as strange, herself being sent to live with odd relatives, a suitcase packed with favorite things—red thermos full of stones, ragdoll, a blue dress that later in a dream Katrina would wear before turning into a bird, and two Almond Joys she'd planned on sharing, already melted.

"So you're Doreen," the older aunt had said, stepping back with critical eyes to appraise, as if to find an essence inside of her that would invite a grown man's touch. And in the house an unhappy smell, and wax fruit on the table. "Tell us about yourself," the younger aunt said. She sat on the red chair while they were on the couch, facing her as if she were an awaited means of transportation that had arrived on time, but damaged. "I'm tidy," she had told them. "And I love to draw."

Not to drown. To be a grown woman walking toward my cows. Already it felt like the last night of visiting. She saw Edgel, the farmer, a thin man walking toward a white shed with rope in his arms. "Edgel!" she cried, but he was too far off. She had dropped the string, kite flying on its own accord now, whipped tail swerving out of sight, the heart on the ground unraveling. The loss now seemed pristine and absolute, and though her stomach ached with the knowledge, it was almost a relief. Was there an animal, small and shivering at the edge of the woods with a human face? And why did no thought startle?

She had moved then beyond all astonishment, save the sudden consciousness of loneliness, how fierce it had grown, how it had made her strange in her own eyes, and worse, someone whom James might hardly recognize. Was part of grief's cruelty to change the bereaved into someone the dead would think strange? For days in the mirror her eyes had looked too luminous. Once she had seen the echo in her brain reflected around her head like a dark halo.

She walked up to the sagging fence and faced the cows that night. Good-bye to twenty-one black Angus. They were soaked in moonlight so brilliant it seemed violent. She stared at them, silenced, and they stared back, their souls in their eyes (or so she had once thought, truly) apprehending the future, yearning to escape into some sleeker form and head down the road at top speed screaming. She had perhaps come to see the cows so regularly because they taught her something of the body's limitations. In a gifted moment she had understood why they were holy and sacred elsewhere. How impossible it was to really look at a cow and *not* imagine something caught inside that flesh. The body *was* a prison, and a cow could teach you that the way a graceful deer never could.

And yet, the body is the body is the self, is what she might have said that last night had she been conscious of her thoughts. She thought of the week before, the white birds scattered around the cows like the cows' ideas; inside the ideas lived the knowledge that she didn't belong *there* either. For all their peace, they were impenetrable, might even be mocking her ritual visits. "Won't come again, good-bye," she had told them finally, then walked to Edgel's front door. (Later she would tell Isaiah-Ahmed of the black flesh of underbelly swaying, how it hurt to see, and how soft the ground felt below her feet when she walked away.)

Edgel had been a contact of sorts; she had gone once with him to a bar in the sticks called "Kings and Queens," barstools with backs like greasy fur-covered thrones, and neither of them had been able to think of much to say, so they'd stirred their drinks and lifted their faces to the TV where an apparently exciting football game was being played; the other people in the bar had their hearts in it. In the end, their mutual lack of love for the sport had bonded them, hadn't it? Hadn't their silence grown comfortably deep in opposition to the crowd's exuberance? She would remember how he told her in the truck, "You're a real nice lady, but we're not from the same world. You'll meet a nice fella someday soon, and I'll meet a nice lady, a bit older named Lucinda or Louise, an *L* name." And she hadn't said, "Why an *L* name?" nor did he explain the significance. So she rode pretending to understand, so desperately wholehearted that it almost felt like real understanding. It became, for a short while, her attitude toward the world.

She knocked that last night on his door, trying to peer through limp curtains into the kitchen. He swung it open and stood with a bottle of half-emptied Scotch in his hand, a tall woman in her sixties standing beside him in shoes most often seen on police. The woman had long hair that she pushed behind her ears.

"I came to say good-bye," Doreen said, and felt the surprising loss of his singleness drop through her like a rock into a pit.

"Enter, honey, and meet Marguerite," he said. The three of them had a glass of Scotch in a low-ceilinged kitchen that smelled like a garage. Pictures of another decade's starlets were taped onto the walls, their old edges curling up as if protecting themselves. "She loves the cows," Edgel explained to Marguerite. "I told her not to go gettin' attached to any one of 'em in particular," he laughed. Marguerite raised a curious eyebrow.

"I'm stayin' in the city from now on," Doreen explained, and Edgel said he could understand why: she was a fish out of water in these parts.

Did he care?

Marguerite poured more Scotch, crossed her long legs, the policeman shoes reflecting dingy light from the ceiling. Doreen saw the two wink at each other, and the single gesture made the echo in her brain so loud that when it came time to say good-bye, she heard her own voice as one wakes in the dark to the siren of an ambulance, thinking *whoever it is, help them, God.*

"I'm starved all a sudden," Doreen told the girl, finishing pretzels, and recalled her mother's "Don't say starved, you don't even know *hungry* much less starved," and her pulling out the worn manila envelope packed full of tragedies, including the bodies of dying black children photographed in magazines, ribs under skin like steps the eyes climbed to get to the faces. "Look at these children!" her mother had said. "You think they don't dream?" And Doreen had merely nodded when her mother went to the State, only to be visited, a woman pumped full of Thorazine on the sixth floor, stupidity replacing terror. "So how the hell is school?" she'd say, laughing in the stale light, winking as if there were secrets being shared.

Doreen had even told Isaiah-Ahmed *that*. And was that precisely when she'd first heard the song of his listening? Even James had not caused so much memory to rise.

"What I mean is, I'm hungry," she told the girl, who was curled on the cot now, having exhausted herself in front of the washstand mirror trying to make a cowlick in her hair.

"And not for another damn donut," she added.

"I could live off air and water," the girl mumbled. "If I had to I could live alone in the park and eat leaves. I don't need a bed, or donuts, or Frosted Flakes, or shoes, even." She was always listing the things she could do without. It was almost a prayer.

"You're a growing girl. You need milk and the like, and certainly shoes. Streets like these would kill your feet."

"I'm a growing boy," said the girl, and yawned. "I'm a wild-cat boy."

"It ain't good to pretend too much," Doreen told her. "You'll forget you're pretending. That's how people get outlandish." Then she added her father's words when she'd been small: "All the lights are on but there's nobody home." But the image of his face came always like punctuation, stopping thought.

"Soon we gotta go to work," Doreen reminded the girl.

"I know."

"You been a big help to me," Doreen said.

"I know."

The room was filling up with grey light. Doreen lit a cigarette. "My mother wanted a gun," said the girl. "In the middle of the night she'd get up on a chair and scream her lungs out if there was a rat. And once she smacked one with her clarinet."

"That's too bad," Doreen said, growing uncomfortable. "Play something pretty on the xylophone. Something to start the day," she told the girl, who didn't move, her green eyes staring into space, then closing.

Doreen got into her work uniform—white pants made of what? Imitation rayon? They itched, and the blouse that would never stop smelling of donuts no matter how long it soaked was a sickening washed-out pink. And she had to wear a small cap, also pink. It was too large for her head, and the peak of it nearly covered her eyes if she wasn't consistent about adjusting it. Sometimes she would tilt her head back just to see. Everyone at the donut shop had to wear this outfit except the girl, whose only job was to clean out the glaze bins and ride on the delivery truck with Doreen, making sure the racked donuts in the back didn't slide off the metal shelves.

Katrina dressed in brown corduroys, held up too high on her waist by a thin black belt pulled to the final notch. She kept the undershirt on, though it was tucked in and hidden by the snow-coat she wore, a green quilted nylon jacket with ribbed cotton cuffs and a detachable hood that zipped up the middle. She detached the hood, then wore it anyway.

Doreen locked the door of the room after making it almost tidy, arranging lipstick tubes on the blue dresser near the metal candlelabrum Isaiah-Ahmed had left behind, Katrina setting the xylophone under her cot near her rocks. Doreen had stripped the beds and hung the sheets on the thin rope she'd stretched across the room near the ceiling. Air that was not fresh, but better than nothing, came into the room each day and took their old dreams out of the sheets (the girl's belief) so they could have fresh dreams each night. It was why the girl refused to sleep with a pillow; dreams could get caught in the feathers.

"I bet we see a clue today," Katrina said, from the back of the donut truck, an old step-van with newly painted sky-blue walls. It was raining. Doreen pretended she hadn't heard the girl, and concentrated on avoiding collisions; the streets in the dark morning were already chaotic, cars and people darting like there were no rules. In the rear-view she saw Katrina stuff a cream donut into her mouth, her black hair still slicked down and side-parted under the green hood. "Taste good?" she said, meaning, really, I love you.

She remembered the first time she'd seen the girl (it was not even months and it seemed years ago) there in Isaiah-Ahmed's room. Couldn't she have said I love you then and meant it just as much as now? Even before Katrina or her mother had spoken a word? And why?

After the cows she had taken the bus back to the city, thinking she would spend some money, cheer herself up a bit. She walked the streets, stopping here and there to look at magazines, cosmetics, candy, and nothing appealed to her. She drank a cup of black coffee at a dim café, a man directly outside her window playing saxophone, his black hands so old they were grey, pink neon bouncing off the brass, while inside she sat burning the roof of her mouth on the steaming coffee, hearing nothing but the music, riding it as if it could carry her up through the dark above the crowd. It wasn't until she left and crossed the street, arms folded, her eyes peering ahead at a corner market, that she noticed the pain in her mouth, tongue rising to test the roof.

The outside of the market was lined with piles of beautifully arranged fruit, lit by streetlight except for the melons, dark in the awning shade. Under one of the highest wooden tables where newly sprayed grapes gleamed, a woman wrapped in a filthy blanket sat rocking, her thumb in her mouth, headlights streaking over her. Doreen looked away to the left and into the eyes of the man who stood beside her, an arm's length away, a maroon apple in his dark hand.

Though their eyes had met for just a moment, the contact seemed prolonged somehow. She looked down at the apple, struck by the hand, the beautiful strength of the fingers. She moved toward the next table, feeling the man was watching her, though when she stole a glance, she found he was not. He was placing the apple into a brown paper bag, and moving toward the pears, his square back to her in a black shirt. *From someplace I've never heard of,* she had thought the instant their eyes had met. What had affected her was their expression, and though she had no words to describe the moment, something in her was already trying to relive it. Again he turned around and looked at her, with no expectation and no defense, the black eyes in the face that for another prolonged moment made the rest of the world a periphery, receding.

She looked away and he walked into the store. She stood near the pears, picked one up, and pretended to examine its bruises with her fingers. The next pear she dangled by its stem, holding it near her face as she watched him through the lit doorway, the way he waited in line, his eyes downcast, squinting a bit. She watched him speak to the clerk, and then knew with certainty (though she could never have explained the source of the knowledge) that he was a man who lived alone (his room seemed to gather around him, the order of it something he worked hard to maintain, a tropical plant on the radiator, dying). He had lived alone for a long time; that was clear. She drank in the precision of his gestures—nothing wasted—as if a great energy were being willed into place, controlled, saved, yes, and incredible silence was trailing him.

Most of all, there was his face.

It was the *effort* in his face that captivated her now, perhaps even more than his eyes had looking into hers. The effort reflecting what seemed an enormous struggle to be *present,* to peer through the brain's echo and thank the clerk sincerely in this world. She saw the profile of his quick smile (he almost winced when he looked at people, as though he saw light). And now he was walking toward the lit door, squinting slightly, thick lips constrained, blinking twice in a sort of nervousness. He passed by her—one more look in the eye which may as well have been an embrace. And following him on the sidewalk she knew thick blue veins branched in his brown arms where he held the bag of fruit. He did not look back to encourage her, and yet she could feel the inevitability of what was happening, desire so deep it dispelled all fear; she imagined he was somehow pulling her along.

They kept an even pace, him nearly a half block ahead of her, people streaming through him, then the same people streaming through her. She imitated the way he held his head perfectly straight, imagining he saw only the night air the way she saw only his back, large and lean in the black shirt.

She walked this way, block after block. When he paused to cross the jammed narrow streets, she too stopped, right in the middle of the sidewalk; anyone watching would've imagined her in the grips of realizing she'd forgotten something, would have expected her to head back in the direction from which she'd come. But he would cross over, and she would walk again, her eyes holding on, bars lined against her heart, keeping it in.

He was stopping now, or slowing down, turning off the street, at last, into an alley; and now her pace quickened. She reached the mouth of the alley; he was not

in sight, but she heard footsteps on iron, and saw the alley led to a moonlit
courtyard, and on the ground against the wall to her left a pair of flowered
underpants lay in the litter near a beer can. She looked down at the miniature faded
roses until the sound of footsteps ceased.

"I see him, I see him, go left! It's Isaiah-Ahmed!" the girl screamed. The rain
was turning to snow, and Doreen took the left too quickly; donuts flew off the
racks. She pulled the truck over to the curb. "Where?"

The girl, looking out the back window, said it was just some guy who looked
like him. *Whoops,* she added.

Doreen looked in the rear-view at the donuts all over the filthy metal floor—the
grime and butts and dust and donuts. "Clean up there, dammit, or my ass is
fired!" she yelled.

"I'm sorry," Katrina said. "I was seein' things."

"Yeah, seein' things. Where's this thing you were seein'?" The girl pointed
ahead to a coatless stranger who smoked a cigar out on the sidewalk. He was half
the size of Isaiah-Ahmed.

"Seein' things," Doreen said.

"I'm *sorry,*" Katrina said. "I *said* I'm sorry." Doreen turned around and
looked at her. The serious white face in the green hood looked defeated, and
suddenly very tired.

Back in the room that night, Doreen read a cookbook she'd bought on sale while
Katrina stood in front of the mirror saying, "If I walked down the street now,
nobody from my other life would know who I was 'cept my mother." She wore a
brown baseball cap bought for a quarter in a thrift store.

"Katrina?" Doreen said.

"Who's that?" said the girl.

"Frank," Doreen said. "You OK tonight?"

"Yes."

"The hat looks good. You look like a real good boy."

The girl sighed and took the cap off. "I bet you Isaiah-Ahmed's married to
another woman," she said. "A real pretty one. And he forgot you was alive, he
don't even think of you, you won't see him again, ever."

Doreen looked down at Katrina's feet, toes curling on the wood. "Oh?" she
said.

"This ain't our home. We ain't home."

"So leave," Doreen said. She closed the cookbook and looked at Katrina. The
girl stared back at her, wide-eyed.

"If you wanna leave, by all means leave."

The girl looked up at the ceiling. "No. But tomorrow I'm goin' out to look
again. Not ridin' in the donut truck."

"Good, fine," Doreen said. "Don't blame you a bit."

There were times when she tried to recount, moment by moment, how she had entered the room. The child's red bike on its side in the courtyard. The grey dog watching from a corner, its eyes almost yellow. The light flicking on and the man above her there in the window, setting the bag of fruit on the sill. He was looking down, but had he seen her?

She saw him start to take off his shirt, just a slice of bare chest, and then she was on the iron steps, ascending. Halfway up she felt the window lit beside her, and turned, and though he looked at her with the same expression he had at the market, now she was terrified. But he had opened the window, the generosity in his face seeming to increase. "Hello," he said. "Are you visiting me? Use the door," he pointed, arms, shoulders, sculpted. And later, seeing his body whole in the dark, a glass of water in his hand like light, she would feel the gratitude (so thorough it transformed), known only by those who have sensed themselves as undeserving in the presence of beauty. And he seemed unaware of the contrast they made, while she saw him more clearly than she would have had she been beautiful.

Was this before or after talking? After she told him about Edgel, losing Edgel, as if the farmer had been her lover. The name of James, the fact of death, she had not uttered until later.

And he had listened, as if with every cell in his body. And she had listened to the sound of listening. What came to her most often was the memory of him above her, looking down, layers and layers, opening. "What can I do for you?" he'd said. "Anything?"

"Just stay here like this," she'd tried to say, but the one word emerging was *this.*

He had brought her back to the beginning of herself; every touch felt like a reshaping.

She would try to stand up, weak-kneed, fingers moving to touch the tiny dots of color love made in the dark, Isaiah handing her the glass of water.

On the second night, late, he had given her a robe to wear; old and flannel with a grey print of coyotes in the mountains. They sat talking and drinking Night Train wine from glasses flecked with old paint; Doreen thought them pretty, a snowstorm.

"My father was a drover," he said, and before she could ask what a drover was, a knock came to the door.

"Ah-Med? Ah-Meddy?" The voice was a bark. "You in there?" And before he could answer, the voice added, "Mother of God, tell what's happening."

"My neighbor across the hall," Isaiah-Ahmed told Doreen, getting up and walking to the door, sheet wrapped around his waist. He opened it to the dim light of the hall, and Doreen saw a hand reach up and settle on his shoulder. "Heart," the voice said. "Give a lady what she needs. Just one."

"I ran out."

"No more?"

"I got only aspirins."

"Well invite us in," the woman said.

Doreen sat further back on the bed, leaning against the wall in the dark, her body braced.

"I have a friend," Isaiah said, and the woman said, "Don't we all."

The next second she and Katrina were in the room, the girl's hair that night resembling the black-penned rays she'd later drawn around the sun on the undershirt. Isaiah-Ahmed bent over and kissed her head, and the woman, seeing Doreen said, "He's the only man my baby lets come near. He's special." Doreen nodded. Isaiah lit the three candles on the dresser. The woman lit a cigarette. Then Isaiah-Ahmed took Katrina's hand and walked her over to the front corner of the room. He put his large hands on either side of her head, tilted it upward, and said something to her very quietly. In the dim moon and silence they were people underwater.

Then they were looking out the window, the girl tiptoed beside him, his back flaring. "It's called a *gibbous* moon when it's like that," Doreen heard him say. "Meaning more than half and not quite whole." The girl said, "Gibbous." And then they turned from the window and faced Doreen, while the woman began pacing as if she were ready to make a speech, one hand on her chin and the other waving the lit cigarette in frantic circles.

Finally Isaiah introduced the girl as Katrina, and the woman pointed to herself and said, "And I'm her mother, Grace Demain," then sat down on the floor, refusing the folding chair Isaiah-Ahmed offered. She brought her legs up to cover her chest; her arms, bangled, wrapped around her shins and she rested her chin on her knees. The girl was back in the far corner with her arms crossed. "So why's it so damn quiet?" she wanted to know.

"Are you from around here?" Doreen said, to be polite. Isaiah came back to sit beside her now. The woman started laughing, though the laughter did not seem genuine; it was more of a cry than anything. "You might not know this," she said, looking at Doreen. "But I'm drunk. I'm so drunk you look like an angel of God. But if I had one of God's blessed pain pills I could pass out good."

"Take four aspirins," Isaiah offered. "It's all I got left."

"Candy shit," the woman barked. And then she introduced herself all over again. "I'm Grace Demain!"—pointing violently at her breastbone. "And that's my little girl Katrina and her father's no good so we won't go home again, right, honey? I'm a house, you're a house, we live inside each other, right, little girl?"

The girl did not answer.

"When she's shy, that means she likes you," her mother said.

Isaiah got up and went to the white washstand on the other side of the room. Doreen could see him reflected in the mirror there. He filled one of the paint-flecked glasses with water and brought it to the woman with some aspirin.

"God bless," she said, and took all the aspirin at once, most of the water dribbling down her face.

Doreen had thought that night: If Grace should ever die, we would take the girl away, comb down her hair, take her to an indoor pool for swimming lessons. Isaiah-Ahmed could teach us the names of the stars in a quiet place. Then a baby sister would come, and I never . . . I would hold . . . I would lean on his arm that way but not too much . . . learning to sing in a different country with camels out the window, real fruit on the sills, Katrina healing.

"For God's sake turn the light on," Grace had finally belted out, and Isaiah said no, it hurt the eyes. Grace smiled, then one side of her mouth collapsed into a frown while the other side remained up, quivering as if yanked by a fishhook. The girl said to Doreen, "She ain't always like this."

"I know," Doreen said. "Don't worry." And how well she knew the child's need to protect the broken parent from eyes that knew no history, and so were cold. An old sense of shame overwhelmed her and she pulled the sash of the robe tighter.

"She can play the clarinet," the girl said to Doreen.

"And someday I'll play for you," the woman said. "Like Benny Goodman," then curled up into a ball on the floor and sighed, her cheek against the wood. She closed her eyes. The three of them were quiet for a moment, staring down at her as if waiting.

"We could all of us live on grass and water if we had to," Katrina said then, and walked over and sat down next to Doreen. "What kind of damn animal is *that?*" she asked, pointing to coyotes, two of them lounging on a flat cliff near Doreen's rib, while Isaiah helped Grace to her feet. "Let's go home," he said, and moved her toward the door and then across the hall. Katrina sighed, then stood up and walked to the doorway.

"You like Isaiah-Ahmed?" she said, turning around to face Doreen.

"Yes."

"Then I like you."

Now Katrina sat cross-legged in the cot, her back against the wall. She had barely spoken all evening, defeated after having spent another day searching the streets. So many hours of insistent peering, so much hope had left her eyes looking too large and hungry. Doreen knew what the girl's day must have been like, strangers in the distance turning into the loved one in fleeting moments of violent expectancy, then the heart sinking again.

"How come ya don't play some music?" Doreen asked, washing the pink uniform in the sink, avoiding her own face in the mirror.

"Why should I?" said the girl, softly.

"You hungry? We could get out of here and get some hamburgers, something good."

"Whatever will be fine," Katrina said.

"Will it?"

A silence fell; Doreen stood wringing out the shirt, and Katrina ran her skinny fingers through her hair. "Do you like your father?" she said. Their eyes met in the mirror.

"I don't exactly know where he is," Doreen said.

"Is he good?" Katrina said.

"I just don't know," Doreen said, and turned around. "It'll be OK," she told the girl, who curled up on the cot.

And Doreen remembered how Katrina looked on Isaiah's shoulders two days after her mother disappeared, four days before he left himself; in the park there had been a moment of clarity that etched itself into her mind, his black eyes turned up to see the girl's face bowed down into his, both of them just about to laugh, red light of sky soaring above the ground, then lowering as if it could care.

Doreen stared out the window at the apartment building across from them; up high in a lit window a red dress was hanging. Had Isaiah-Ahmed been there, it would've been time to eat now.

He had taken bags of fruit each night and sectioned the bright pieces into four portions on blue plastic plates. They had eaten in the room at the end of the hall, a sea-green room narrow as the hallway itself, a door-shaped window looking over the street, the table pushed up against it, a picture of Christ taped up on one of the panes. And he would say the blessing very quietly, his eyes closed, his dark head bowed, the candlelabrum brought from his room on the middle of the table now, flames bending as he prayed:

Sweet Jesus, bless this fruit
And make us whole
Take the pride out of our soul
And move our hands with the impulse
Of your loving. Amen.

Then he would give everyone a speckled vitamin tablet. The fruit, wet and sliced in the candlelight, seemed for a moment untouchable.

"Let's never leave," Katrina said one night, like a second blessing. But Isaiah had put his finger to his lips and said "Shhh," and then for a moment Doreen saw his face held the same expression it wore the night she woke to find him watching her sleep.

And when it had come time for him to say good-bye, he assured her they would see each other again, and if he could he would explain the reason for his leaving. Understand I love you.

She had held to him unable to stop talking. He had not tried to quiet or rush her, had not tried to loosen her hands. And when finally she fell silent he looked down and asked her please to let him go, as if he could not turn and head toward the long mouth of the alley without her finally resigning, body going limp as she wished him what? Good luck? Sweet dreams?

If he could have stood there forever, a man in a courtyard surrounded by buildings where the windows seemed to fall like fire-lit rain that night . . . how much the sight of his body meant to her—would it always be impossible to say?

Watching him walk away was not difficult. What you don't believe cannot hurt. You must go back up the fire escape, into the room, fill a glass with water, and drink.

When the knock sounded urgent in the dawn-light as she woke from a dream in which departure's approach had been somehow sensed, Doreen sat up and said, "Who?"

But she knew who.

And Grace Demain, holding a plaid suitcase and a clarinet in a plastic see-through bag, was a sober woman with new red highlights in her hair asking *Where in the world is Ah-med,* then exploding into a flurry of thanks and apology, while Katrina, crying with joy, slipped into the brand-new coat. It was deep red, with a black velvet collar.

"It's dressy," Katrina said. It came down past her knees and the sleeves were inches too long. "You'll grow into it, Babe," her mother said, and in Doreen's mind it was a man's voice saying, "Pretty little thing, ain't she?"

"Now comb your hair and thank Doreen for everything," her mother said, and Doreen joked that donuts would fly all over hell's creation until she found a good replacement. And then Katrina's things were placed in the plaid suitcase, xylophone on top, and it was all zipped up and they were walking down the fire escape, Katrina holding tightly to the rusty railing, her green eyes peering straight ahead, not looking over at Doreen who was framed in the window watching the descent.

There were no thoughts in her mind as she swept the green floor and arranged the glasses and Katrina's rocks on the dresser. She put the room in order, and gathered her things. The sun was caught in the washstand mirror now, blasting, and the pulse of that sunken light was the last face she saw before closing the door behind her and walking away.

Down in the street, headed back to a room on the other side of the city, she felt like a woman on her way to pay a visit to a dying friend. What was there to say? How had she been? Was she still there at all? There would be photographs curled in drawers, James's clothes still hanging, surfaces silvered with months of dust, awaiting her finger, as if there were a word that might be written there before she cleaned. The sidewalk moved below her like a conveyor belt now, and she was filling up with something heavier than tears, and suddenly it stopped her, whatever it was. She let the crowd pour through her, their legs taking them so quickly in so many different directions. The noise of the city may have been deafening, but Doreen heard nothing and stood now, paralyzed. *The things I didn't tell Katrina.* And Katrina, you grow out of it, you make room, you give yourself away in pieces or whole, and the man who hurts you early on, Love will almost kill him, if you're lucky.

Jane McCafferty's "Replacement"

by Shirley Clay Scott

It must be that the writer, driven as he or she is to reshape ordinary experience in language, lives, even more than most of us, in two worlds—the mundane, two-dimensional, "real" world that Wallace Stevens called "things as they are," and that much more private world of dream and desire that Stevens called "things as they are upon the blue guitar," his synonym for imagination. From both worlds a writer, even a "realistic" writer, receives impetus for story, and from both worlds he or she accrues knowledge, draws inferences, acquires materials. Jane McCafferty's story "Replacement" is noteworthy for its attempt, often successful, to negotiate between those two worlds. In fact, it is probably not an exaggeration to say that the story is about those negotiations.

The "real" world in which the story takes place is a particularly bleak one, contemporary-urban where the things that are include donut shops and pink uniforms that retain the stench of donuts, roaches and rats, cigarette butts and dirt, or contemporary-rural where cows may still graze in rich fields but where human life is played out in sleazy bars with "barstools like greasy fur-covered thrones" and television sets blaring football games to the noisy crowd of drinkers. The descriptions of the real world are not particularly arresting, perhaps by design, perhaps because objective description is not the writer's strength. But when she can bring together appearance and sensation or, better, sensual response, the writing is curious and memorable. For instance the kitchen of the farmer, Edgel, is described as a "low-ceilinged kitchen that smelled like a garage," decorated with "pictures of starlets from an earlier era taped onto the walls, *their old edges curling up as if protecting themselves*" [italics mine]. And later in the story, Doreen is dressed in a robe given her to wear by Isaiah-Ahmed. The garment is simply described as, "old and flannel with a grey print of coyotes in the mountains." But Doreen's contentment to be dressed, after lovemaking, in her lover's robe is later nicely caught by a figure that melds Doreen's body with the robe she wears. Katrina notices how Doreen is dressed and asks, perhaps jealously, "What kind of damn animal is that?" and then points to the coyotes, "two of them lounging on a flat cliff near Doreen's rib."

Description is seldom an end in itself for McCafferty; the concrete realities of the bleak world the story evokes serve to bring into being the straitened lives that exist in it. In this story the writer's interest is in the lives of desperate and crazed women, sometimes dulled by Thorazine, sometimes reduced to the creature's own efforts for appeasement— "Under one of the highest tables where newly sprayed grapes gleamed, a woman wrapped in a filthy blanket sat rocking, her thumb in her mouth,"—sometimes, like Grace Demain, consoled for a time by alcohol or whatever other anodyne comes to hand. Grace Demain, who becomes more than a marginal character in the story, is succinctly but convincingly developed largely through her patterns of speech: "Heart . . . give a lady what she needs. Just one." And McCafferty is compelled by the lives of the children of such women, some of them starved for food, "ribs under skin like steps the eyes climbed to get to the faces," or starved for wonder like the child on the bus trying to ask a "Why?" for which there can be no rational answer, or, like Katrina, starved for love and the self love guarantees but knowing already to refuse that need: "'I could live off air and water,' the girl mumbled. 'If I had to I could live alone in the park and eat leaves. I don't need a bed, or donuts, or Frosted Flakes, or shoes even.'"

The central or point of view character, Doreen, exists in the story both as a woman, not herself crazed and not quite desperate, but comprehending both states, and, through a few brief flashbacks, as one of the children abused by the circumstances of their lives. And so Doreen lives in the "real" world; in fact, ordinarily she refuses to live at too great a distance from its claims, knowing from early in life the dangers of being "outlandish," but it is her fate to acknowledge the force of things as they are and to know at the same time the power and possibility of some other world shaped by need and the imagination out of the most meager materials: "She looked up at the flaking ceiling and watched two roaches circle the light, side by side. So parallel it was almost for a split second pretty."

But only for a split second. For Doreen is presented as a woman chastened by a harsh world and its harshest facts, loss and death. Her capacity to yearn for and to apprehend beauty, whether the beauty of the abstract pattern of the motion of roaches, of clouds that swim across the moon like schools of fish, or of the black body of a man she sees buying fruit in a marketplace, compounds with her capacity to acknowledge horror. The cows she visits for some kind of peculiar assuagement of the pain of James's death are "soaked in moonlight," but she perceives the moonlight as "so brilliant it seemed violent." And she can fancy the cows having escaped "into some sleeker form," but she goes on to guess that they would then head "down the road at top speed screaming."

The horror Doreen apprehends is not simply death and loss, but, as she realizes on the night when James's image loses its power over her and she "controls" his death, "as one holds to a ball of string, flying a kite, waiting for wind," that loss itself might be lost, to be succeeded by an existence so empty as to be intolerable. The passage in which she understands the possibility that James's death might die and anticipates the barren world which she would then inherit is compelling writing, and its impact on the story is amplified by its opening out into a flashback of Doreen as a child, exiled, after her mother succumbs to her own terrors, to the care of suspicious aunts who live in a house with "an unhappy smell and wax fruit on the table."

The present time of the story begins sometime after the death of James, a man realized in the story only by Doreen's love for him and by the intensity of her bereavement. Because Doreen, like Katrina who resists her own need, consciously resists her own capacity for extremity, she refuses to suffer the additional cruelty of death, that it should "change the bereaved into someone the dead would think strange," and she begins to keep company with a farmer, Edgel, who understands better than she the impossibility of the kind of replacement she seeks to effect and who jilts her—though of course that is hardly the word for his defection and *his* replacement of *her* with Marguerite.

Though the loss of Edgel's singleness "drops through Doreen like a rock into a pit," it is really only a parody of loss or a substitute loss. She knows this herself when she realizes she has told Isaiah-Ahmed about "losing Edgel, as if the farmer had been her lover. The name of James, the fact of death, she had not uttered until later." However, it is this substitute experience that opens her to genuine experience again, that makes it possible for her again to feel and own desire.

Her decision, if it is that, to follow Isaiah-Ahmed "of the black flesh of underbelly swaying" brings the world of desire and the world of things as they are into dangerous proximity. The writing registers the tense coexistence of these two opposed categories of reality in a series of structurally similar images that begin when Doreen, during her expeditions to see the cows, steps off the bus and experiences the country air as an element with the power to recall for her the well-being she knew before James's death. This experience does not appear in the story as discursive statement but as an implication of the figure that comes into Doreen's mind as she recognizes the exhalations of the country as "always a good thing, the utterly foreign smell of grass and manure, starred breath of earth, gathering around her like a cape from a different world, the bus pulling away and herself in the white dress splashed with violets which James had bought in another city before the sickness was even named." That is one of the most sustained inventions in the story, carefully cadenced, appropriate to the passage in which it appears and a grounding for a number of other images that answer it in the story.

With the appearance of Isaiah-Ahmed, who seems to Doreen as if he, too, is from a different world, "from someplace I've never heard of," dappled and pied objects, sometimes in and of themselves only part of the debris of the "real" world, single themselves out for Doreen's attention, and often they are irradiated by moonlight or are so light-filled as to be discernible in darkness. The alley down which Doreen follows Isaiah-Ahmed leads to a "moonlit courtyard, and on the ground against the wall to her left a pair of flowered underpants lay in the litter near a beer can." Doreen, intent upon the man she is following, observes the underpants as a small display of "miniature faded rosebuds." Later, after she makes love to Ahmed, who is for her the purest beauty, she tries to stand, "weak-kneed, fingers moving to touch the tiny dots of color love made in the dark." The two of them drink Night Train wine "from glasses flecked with old paint. Doreen thought them pretty, a snowstorm." Each of these images is reminiscent of the starred cape from an unknown world that Doreen is capable of imagining and the violet-splashed dress from an earlier and less painful world that she has in fact known.

Such images are probably only in part the result of craft, for they must come about when the writer is in overdrive, with unusual resources of memory and invention available, the story itself suggesting the forms that will realize it. In this story these dappled or pied objects and Doreen's capacity to perceive them are linked to her sense of a recovered or at least a recoverable self, and they suggest that what one knows as the self is not so much an identity that persists in time as it is discrete experiences of radical desire, fundamentally identical to one another. Even as Doreen understands the longing to escape from the body, she knows that the body, the vehicle of desire, is the self, the product of desire: "And yet, the body is the body is the self, is what she might have said that last night had she been conscious of her thoughts." And when she follows Isaiah-Ahmed, it is because his physicality bespeaks a self that might offer her access to her own being. She knows "desire so deep it dispelled all fear; she imagined he was somehow pulling her along." And indeed, while she is with him, he causes "memory to rise" and he takes her back to "the beginning of herself."

Ahmed, though a more fully realized character than James, is not entirely credible. The writing, particularly of the domestic scenes of Ahmed, Doreen, and Katrina, is not always strong enough to suspend a reader's innate disbelief. But the story works well enough in other ways not to be destroyed by that defect. In relationship to Ahmed, Doreen allows herself the luxury of imagining a world fully answerable to desire—Ahmed and Doreen together, Katrina with them as their child, all of them "in a different country with camels out the window, real fruit on the sills, Katrina healing." And if Katrina can heal, then Doreen, who knows she is only an older version of that damaged child, might heal also. But the world promised by the presence of Ahmed, is finally not available to Doreen, or is available only as desire. Ahmed leaves as suddenly and inexplicably as he appeared, and his departing form offers one more light-filled, dappled image. Doreen's last sight of him is of "a man in a courtyard surrounded by buildings where *the windows seemed to fall like fire-lit rain*" [italics mine]. This last image in the series, though it appears late, actually presides over the story, for as the story opens, in a time after Doreen has been abandoned by Ahmed and Katrina by her mother, the narrator observes that "the moon could be seen resting on the dark apartment building across from them, *scattered rectangular windows brimming with light''* [italics mine]. In this version the image is innocent enough, but the fully disclosed version in the concluding pages, in which the windows "fall" like "fire-lit rain," is an image of barely contained violence, and it seems to be generated by the story's inherent premise, that the self is utterly dependent upon desire in its most unmediated manifestations, and that such desire is powerful enough to violate the very essence it brings into being. This comprehension is the "something heavier than tears" that halts Doreen on her walk back to the room she lived in before she followed Ahmed, and this is the chief thing Doreen would have told Katrina, who has already been tempted back into perilous love by the reappearance of Grace Demain, temporarily "a sober woman with new red highlights in her hair." Doreen phrases what she understands this way: "The man who hurts you early on, Love will almost kill him, if you're lucky."

Jane McCafferty's work is still in progress, but it is already marked by her ability to observe and intuit, to feel and to guess at feeling, and to support her fictions with language that calls upon her own caches of memory and experience, desire and dream.

Specific Points of View
Within Fiction

I. "Attached" Narration

This is a term I use with students to replace the term "omniscient" narrator when that narrator enters the thoughts and feelings of characters. By changing the term normally used in literature courses, I hope to have students experience the viewpoint almost physically as they write, as if when they move from objective narration into the subjectivity of a character they feel "attached" to the character enough to sense his or her sensations, physical movements, moods, voice timbre, etc.

Using this point of view, a writer chooses words to give information to the reader which are *from the perspective* of the character or characters to whom the narration is said to be "attached." The narrator does not step back from the chosen character. He is bound like a Siamese twin—frequently a more articulate twin—and can give the reader information accepted, by convention, as felt or thought, without the words *felt* and *thought* being required, although they may be employed in "limited attachment" when an objective narrator has been established. An example: The character is remembering a time when she saw her father's gracelessness: *Except once, in a grocery store, she saw him break open—the grey suit, the white shirt, the maroon wool tie, Hanes underneath, the wing-tip shoes, the stuffed-in cigarillo, the mouth itself break open, and then no one would have trusted this man—crying and running up and down the aisles, a high, high voice belonging to a cat saying over and over "Oh" because she, his daughter, sat on the floor, holding her foot and watching blood pour from a wound made by a can of green beans falling from a shelf.*

The sentence is long in an attempt to have the reader feel that the character remembers the scene as an assault of memory, in a rush of images, each image recorded because the father's state has startled her and even provided such information about him that she feels pain upon remembering. The sentence begins in truncation—*except*—as if the character has interrupted herself for this memory. The list of what the father wore proceeds objectively until the memory overpowers the character, at which time it becomes subjective: *the stuffed-in cigarillo*. It could also be thought that the phrase *Hanes underneath* is subjective if the writer assumes that the reader will not expect a daughter to list a father's underwear in a list of his apparel. The phrase "no one would have trusted this man" is followed by a dash, as if the character must take a breath before remembering the image of his frenetic behavior. The behavior itself is described in a style meant to mirror her sensations on observing it: "crying *and* running . . . a *high, high* voice *belonging to a cat . . .* over *and over.* After the "Oh" the character rushes on: *because,* and then identifies herself: *she, his daughter,* which places the emphasis on *daughter,* as if she feels the import for his behavior results from the father/daughter relationship and is painful to acknowledge. Then, given the hyperbole of the rhythm of the sentence, the cause of the behavior is saved for the last because the character feels the absurd insignificance of the cause, *a can of green beans,* almost as if the can has by injuring her and releasing the father's response become a metaphor for his vulnerability as father.

The reader receives information in this viewpoint through a filter of feeling and is not distanced from it by the words *she thought* or *she felt.*

This viewpoint has numerous limitations because the narrator is tethered to the character. It is sometimes economical in terms of a story as a whole to give information plainly, not drawing attention to the sensations or thoughts connected to an action: *she sat down.* Usually, then, a writer will combine the subjectivity of attached narration with objective narration. But a balance needs to be struck. A reader will attempt to "see" what he or she is told by narration to see, and an objective narrator places the reader at a greater distance from an object, character, or action than attached narration. Once an "intimacy" with a reader through attached narration is established, care needs to be taken not to have the objective narrator destroy that sense of close knowledge. The unseemly move from one viewpoint to another is termed a *transgression* on the established viewpoint. This occurs most frequently when beginning writers are unaware of the technical skills necessary to convey information vital to the story. It is then dropped in without regard to viewpoint, and such information calls undue attention to itself and to the writer.

On this point, my students and I debate whether or not telephone conversations recorded in dialogue are transgressions when the dominant viewpoint is attachment to only one character. I feel that I have been positioned as a reader with the one character—in his or her room or mind or body or thoughts. The sensation is one of intimacy, as if I as reader were *with* the character. Then the phone rings and the dialogue is written in this manner:

"Hello?"

"Carol! I'm glad you're there."

"What's on your mind, Miriam?"

As a reader, I feel pulled from, say, Carol's viewpoint because I can also imagine Miriam's room, her holding of the telephone, etc. If the story were mine, I would use narration attached to Carol to render not the words of the conversation but her assimilation of them, their effect. My students have insisted that, even within attached narration, telephone conversation rendered in this way has become a convention and is therefore not a transgression on established attached narrative.

Moving back and forth from objective to attached narration, then, must be felt by the writer as a proper flow of information dictated by the story itself. In the following sentence, the writer is seeking to establish both objective and attached narration: *Roselle was tired of the piano, tired on the planks of notes that began each score.* A distance is created by using the character's name and by making a statement *about* her. But a closeness is created by the repetition of the word *tired,* and *planks,* which suggests the formidable nature of piano keys when the player is weary, as if the notes were wooden, large, heavy.

A writer interested in weaving objective narration and attached narration together within single sentences can study the device by using different colored pens to underline objective and attached narration. Students find the exercise helpful not only for learning viewpoint but also for becoming acutely sensitive to the nuances of language. Flannery O'Connor's stories are useful in the exercise since she weaves frequently between objective and attached viewpoints.

If language issues from viewpoint, it is useful to ask to what aspects of characters can words which are subjective be "attached." Each visualization will release to the writer different vocabularies. I've suggested to students that "attachment" can be made to 1) a character's interior voice, which may be quite different from a character's speaking voice; 2) to a character's moods or emotions; 3) to a character's speaking voice; and 4) to a character's physical state. Certain stories for study have proven helpful to students in learning the way a variety of attached narration can elicit a particular vocabulary from a writer. "At the Landing," by Eudora Welty, is interesting to study for attachment to a character's moods or emotions. "The Rocking-Horse Winner," by D. H. Lawrence, is useful to study for attachment to a character's physical *and* emotional state, as is "The Frozen Fields," by Paul Bowles. Grace Paley's third-person stories are interesting to study for their attachment to characters' speaking voices. And Tillie Olsen's "Tell Me a Riddle" is an intricate rendering of characters' interior "voices."

When reading a story specifically for study of attached narration, a writer should notice that the "attachment" is usually limited to one character. Writers make this choice because a story is usually too compact a form to allow for the investigation of more than one character's feelings, actions, and psychology. Tillie Olsen's "Tell Me a Riddle" is an exception, *and* it is a very long story.

I have written several stories myself in which the consciousness of more than one character occurs. It is an interesting challenge because the problem to solve is how to let the reader know who the main character is. My solution has been to double the amount of attached narration for the main character, using attachment to subsidiary characters only when the attachment is to show the consciousness of a minor character that will affect the main character's psychology. And I have used this technique only when another point of view has been used—that of the omniscient, *subjective* narrator, which will be described in the following pages. I have also used the technique only when limiting the characterization in such a way as to make it obvious that the main character is psychologically the most vulnerable character, on the assumption that a reader will feel a particular sympathy for that character and thus be especially attentive to the language depicting him or her.

"Allegro Ma Non Troppo" in *The Formal Voice* and "Questions of Travel" in *The Musician* are examples of such stories. In both, a child, as particularly vulnerable, is the main character.

The Dangers of "Attached Narration": Surveying the Minimalists' Ground

In recent years many, if not most, contemporary American writers have begun to employ a narrator whose language is reflective or imitative of the vocabulary and speech patterns of so-called "average" Americans—the "working class," "yuppies," "suburbanites," "ordinary housewives," the "under-class," the "lower class." The narrators sound like the person next to us in a bus or the person who changes the oil in our cars at service stations. As a result of the prevalence of stories told by these narrators, it has become accepted that this narrative language is *the* language for storytelling. A "movement" has arisen and taken hold.

Since the narrators are presented as being "just like us," which means tentative, unsure of cause and effect, almost overwhelmed by daily life and its swift social changes, buried in life's trivialities, etc., other aspects of story form have also been adjusted to accommodate the equally hapless and ineffectual narrator. Characterization has changed. Characters are now often defined by what they wear and its brand name; by what they watch on television or the lyrics they remember from songs; by the printing on their t-shirts; by the number of lovers they have had; by the economic pressures they face; by how many times they have moved since the divorce; by who keeps the children on weekends; and, now, by how many friends have AIDS. Plots have been reduced to incidents of daily life. Above all, what a story *means* or may mean has been miniaturized into the stories' last-line images, of, often, running in place; spinning; panting; staring vacantly; picking up a telephone that has gone dead; holding a beautiful but empty bowl; holding a chipped water glass; being surrounded with hospital equipment; watching a child turn and look accusingly; etc.

The ending, "resolving" images are particularly telling because they are written in language which has usually appeared nowhere else in the story, language which both the narrator and characters have presented themselves as incapable of using. The effect is of the stories' *writers* becoming suddenly apparent, to extricate characters from stories that could go on forever otherwise because the stories are "slices of life."

These are "minimalist" stories, and what they ask by virtue of what is *not written* is that the reader identify with the characters and incidents and recognize the depiction of their lives. For what purpose is not implied; indeed, the components of the story do not suggest that a purpose might be considered important. The stories appear to be offered as another commodity to be consumed.

The narrations in the stories (and the stories' other components) could be said, then, to be "attached" to a particular view of life which finds humans operating at minimum capacity. But this would need to be deduced by a reader since the stories also relinquish a historical sense of any time when humans were more engaged in their lives. Even recent history, and only in characters old enough to have experienced the periphery of the Vietnam War, is seen as that which might ruin a party, be the pretext for one, ruin a lovemaking session or a family outing—no more than a gnat around the eyes or a scratch on a formica-topped table.

The dangers for a writer of this type of narration and its attendant implications for form appear to be these:

1. The stories issuing from this esthetic will sound so similar as to be almost indistinguishable, increasingly so over time.
2. Because the stories are records of the writers' view of a time in society, they will in time appear dated, old-fashioned.
3. Because the stories have proven so easy to imitate and to have published, a beginning writer could find himself or herself rewarded enough in the short run not to broaden his or her range of capabilities as a writer, which may need to be broad in the long run of a writer's career.
4. Since the "minimalist" story uses flat language in simple declarative sentences, the writer could discover that he or she has relinquished an exploration of the nuances of language in its variety and, as a result, also relinquished language's capacity to uncover complex thought and emotion.
5. With the interpretative function removed from the "minimalist" story, the writer of it may find no avenue in writing by which to explore mystery or the limits of language.
6. The writer of the "minimalist" story may become bored and yet know too little about language and form to contend with boredom through more intricate writing.

II. Omniscient-Subjective Narration: The Disembodied, Intelligent Narrator

This type of omniscient narration is often termed "authorial presence" or "omniscient author" narration. In both teaching and thinking about writing, I do not use these terms because I have found it more helpful to separate the author from the point of view through terminology. By substituting the term "disembodied, intelligent narrator," I emphasize it as a device, a writer's invention. And I also resist the implication that the narration mirrors the *author's* voice, thoughts, psychology. In this way, my students and I are reminded that *all* of a story's devices add up to one, and only one, representation in form of the author and that it is the *sum* of a writer's work that constitutes the "authorial presence." I also sought a term which could suggest sensation since point of view needs to be *felt* as a particular distance from scene or characters. To me "disembodied" suggests floating, hovering, present-in-absence.

When writing a story I never feel that a narrator carries my own voice, no matter how close to my own voice the narrator's may appear to be. This is a discipline for the sake of control over material, both technical and emotional, for a story-in-the-making can elicit from a writer almost overwhelming emotion. And I practice the discipline as a reminder to myself that the language I use daily in speech and sub-vocalizations is *not* the language of my fiction—it is too casual, too disjointed, too irrelevant and often too trivial to seize a reader. I caution students, too, against how their ears have been trained by the media and suggest that they try to offset its effects with broad reading, especially of classical and modern literature and of contemporary writing only in proportion.

A "disembodied, intelligent narrator" is one who does not become a character on the page by appearing physically in the story but who is, rather, a presence to be reckoned with by virtue of the story's language. The language of the narrator is a filter of *subjectivity* through which the information about characters, scene, plot will be given. The subjectivity of the narrator's language will indicate the narrator's *vested interest* in the story's materials. As a result, the tension level of the story will be dual: tension will come from the characters' conflicts and *also* from the reader's looking at the characters *through* the narrator's subjective, idiosyncratic language.

For a reader to reckon with the device, it must be seen as device. That is, a distinction apparent to a reader must be made between *this* narrator and a traditional "authorial presence," which is effaced in vocabulary, tone, and rhythm— the narrative style of Katherine Anne Porter's work, for example. The "disembodied, intelligent" narrator is anything but self-effacing.

This narrator *has* a story to tell, but "he," "she," or "it" is demanding and will not allow the story to unfold without letting the reader know that the unfolding, the very definition of what *makes* the story a story, is the narrator's. For this reason, the narrator's language is idiosyncratic, signaling itself. It offers opinion, metaphor, simile; it uses rhythm, and it reels in the story at its own pace.

Aspects of the form as it is traditionally used may, then, be changed. The flow of the ostensible story may be interrupted by an image which, on the surface, may appear irrelevant, its relevance withheld by the narrator to be reckoned with later. Handling of time may be out of sequence; the time span of the story may be unusually long or short. Dialogue may appear only in bits and pieces or appear particularly articulate or inarticulate. Most pointedly, the story's plot may appear to be not plot at all but, instead, a collection of scenes which on the surface may appear too disparate to constitute plot. Or, conversely, the intrusions of the highly subjective narrator may be buried within a traditional-seeming story, appearing disconcertingly at just the point when the story's flow would appear to be uninterruptible.

The narrator's voice may be ironic, rhapsodic, skeptical, resigned, eager.

Of course the traditional "authorial presence" also permitted all of these tactics.

But it has been interesting to push against the traditions of the "authorial presence." Certainly Faulkner extended the tradition in the Benjy section of *The Sound and the Fury* by rendering in style Benjy's sensations trapped within a subnormal intelligence. Through this narration Faulkner asked the reader to consider the relationship between sensation and knowledge.

Here are examples of various narrators whose idiosyncrasies are apparent. It should be remembered that the narrators are not bodily present in the stories from which the language is taken.

1. The boys in Korea were seeping like mist, whole battalions awash. Then the cases of Spam had to be rerouted.
2. It began in a church, long before she was at all pretty. The day was hot—flies seemed to rest on the ladies' hats of tight, delicate straw. No one cried, as if in such heat the salt would be kneaded in. They moaned. But Lucy's voice was light, a ligature to tie the most delicate wound.
3. Crimson of silk scarves, Rasputin under candles, of tight nylon blouses, or reefs.
4. This is a wedding tour, a cacophony of preparation leading to the dance.
5. Now, if one could see her, she is looking in a mirror, calm, as if that were insouciance itself.

What is not of course demonstrated by the examples is how *story* is derived from this type of narration. The narrator's language, self-conscious, pointing to itself, is, of course, only one device. And the device is usually used in conjunction with both "objective" and "attached" narration. I have also found the device most interesting to use in stories which otherwise appear to be traditional stories. When the technique is used in this manner, a reader enters the story assuming that he is following a simple story of people whose actions will lead them to a place different from where they began. But a reader of any sophistication is also accustomed to "authorial presence" and can accept a narrator whose idiosyncratic language is cautiously announced and subsequently hidden until the ostensible story is underway. Indeed, this is precisely how dual tension is created: the reader believes he is reading one story while the narrator is in fact subtly directing him away from that story.

It appears important, then, either to entertain highly with voice, as Grace Paley's aggressive, subjective narrators do, or to use the device with great restraint within a seemingly traditional story.

The manner in which another writer may consider the "disembodied, intelligent narrator" will depend on the purpose for which he or she needs its flexibility with language. And that depends on what quarrels with the traditional "authorial presence" or the story form as a whole the writer has. Implicit is the idea that a writer investigating the form *knows* the story in its tradition. If the device can be perceived as one which releases language, it can be liberating for any writer who feels pinioned by narrow definitions of story form. It can also release a writer's multiplicity of interior voices, the wide range of those we do not use in society for fear of startling others and ourselves. And flexibility with language can release new material to the writer's imagination.

For moral complexity carried by this type of narration, see Eudora Welty's story "At the Landing" and John Hawkes's novel *Second Skin*.

A Writer's Rationale for Using Disembodied, Intelligent Narration

It may be useful to indicate how at least one writer's interaction in society has resulted in interest in and use of a particular device in fiction. I offer the explanation, necessarily truncated by constraints of space, as an indication to beginning writers that the forms we construe bear an intimate relation to *who* we are. We may begin our writing careers by imitation, but as we become immersed in craft, in the problems of craft, more and more of ourselves is revealed in the craft decisions we make.

In essence, my use of the "disembodied, intelligent narrator" emerged from the following complex of ideas.

At some indeterminate point as a writer, I began to feel that modern psychology had managed to back the creative writer into a corner. From Europe, after Freud and Jung, came a wave of interest in the caverns of the mind expressed newly, in a vocabulary devised or informed by Freud and Jung in their studies of human nature. As pragmatists, Americans began to resolve the appropriately difficult language of Freud and Jung by turning it into therapies for the masses couched in simpler language. We were taught how to speak about our unresolved conflicts, as in such phrases as "This is my father in me talking" or "My id is about to take control of my ego." It became easy for a reader to believe that he knew what motivated characters in fiction, every father/daughter relationship, for instance, having its component of incest.

Simultaneously, with Hitler removed from the scene, we turned to solving domestic repression of women, blacks, homosexuals, etc., just as, for many reasons, the all-American family of Ozzie and Harriet began to disintegrate. Suddenly almost everything that we had taken to be "normal" was now debatable. If we *were* repressed or oppressed, we were going to fight it, if not on the streets then with language.

The fiction writer's dilemma, as I saw it, became acute as a result. If heretofore we had imagined that certain values remained solid in society and that characters could act out their conflicts within these accepted definitions, that time had passed. It appeared to me at least that a writer would now need to define *within a story* all of the terms of characters' conflicts. Further, it would, I thought, be incumbent upon him to discover a language for narration that would resist appropriation by psychology or sociology. That is, the question became, How does a writer invite a reader into the *writer's* vision—psychological, permeated by society, derived of the unconscious—when the reader most likely now thinks he or she has, truly, heard it all before?

Whether or not it results from self-aggrandizement or need, the writer does feel that his or her own vision is worthy of communicating, feels that with a piece of writing something new has been added to the world. The challenge to the writer is to have the reader see *through* a veil of confusion to the "vision," and now the confusion was amplified.

I, too, had absorbed the pluralism of the age, discovering that my very background had prepared me to question a number of old "truths." Yet here was the story form in a seeming solidity of tradition.

As a writer I understood early that my interests lay not in plot unless the plots were tempered by accentuation of other devices, characterization and variety of language in particular, just as, very early, I had read less for plot than for effects of action on characters and for a love of language itself. Both interests had resulted from familial training. As a beginning writer, I became dispirited by the burden of thinking that, with each new story, I needed to conjure some fascinating plot, which I suspected could be believed only if I could manipulate other story devices adroitly. All plots seemed to me to be outlandish, and I quickly began using the method of discovering plot *as* I wrote a story. I fully believed, and still believe, that were I to say to myself the outlines of a plot before my characters enact it, I would find it so ridiculous that I would not write the story. Moreover, I had grave doubts about discovering any story, encapsulating any "vision" apart from language and form that can, if a writer is concentrating, relieve the mind of its banality.

But for deeper reasons I wanted to find readers who, when reading, did not seek that which was shocking, startling, only entertaining, or easily dismissed. I wanted a *non*consumer, one whose history with literature had caused him to know that reading *may* change him, was capable of changing him, sometimes radically. I wanted a reader who had had the experience of particular images from literature having lodged in his mind as intimately as his own personal experience, who possessed images which had become the vocabulary of himself. And this desire of mine, in an age of so much triviality in writing, became a political strategy, so strongly did I rebel against the new "voices" of contemporary communications.

The flexibility of the disembodied, intelligent narrator's language provided a way for me to create stories which asserted both my interest in language and my belief that semblance is wrought over all things.

III. "Objective" Narration

This term has two meanings as they are used in fiction. The term is used to indicate a narrator who does not enter the thoughts and feelings of the characters but limits his reporting to information about actions. This narrator is omniscient. A story's focus will be on action when only an objective narrator is employed. Characters' feelings, thoughts, and motives must be discerned by a reader through interpretation of action and dialogue.

The term is also used to indicate information that remains uncolored by subjective assessment. It applies to a narrator's tone of language as well as to word choice.

Contemporary writers most frequently use this type of narration in combination with others.

IV. First-Person Narration

When a character in a story tells the story in first-person, two (usually) unspoken premises are possible: the "I" is capable of telling the story reliably or the "I" is only partially reliable. In both cases, all information is filtered through the perceptions of the first-person narrator as opposed to the perceptions of a third-person narrator.

In both cases, the choice of narration immediately affects a story's language. That is, the reader will expect language in the story concomitant to the first-person narrator's character, background, social standing, etc. And usually, unless something the character tells us disabuses the reader of the idea, the reader will expect the story to progress linearly, moving from point A to point B to point C, with a focus on story in the traditional sense. Of course a first-person narrator's strategy may be to disclaim linearity; that is, he or she may spend much narrative time explaining why the story cannot progress logically. While this strategy provides narrative flexibility, many writers feel that first-person narration provides a writer with less freedom in how a story is put together than does third-person narration.

Part of the reason for a seeming loss of flexibility is the range of language available to first-person narrators. Writers will often choose only highly articulate characters to tell stories in first-person and often augment their articulateness with retrospection—the story related after the first-person narrator has had time to contemplate, often with part of the story's tension coming from the way events appeared in the past as opposed to how they appear at the time the narrator chooses to tell the story.

But increasingly writers are choosing to have a first-person narrator tell a story in present tense, as if the story is unfolding concurrent with its telling. (This device is increasingly used also in third-person stories, almost as a contemporary convention.) The reader is invited, then, to "experience" the story's unfolding at the same time the main character experiences it. In such cases, a sense of immediacy is created which the plot and theme elements of the story form must satisfy: *what* was so urgent? Or, at least, if a reader is interested in a story's formal properties, it would seem important for the writer to answer, in form, why present tense, whether in first-person or third, was necessary. As it turns out, however, much contemporary writing in first- or third-person present tense does establish a convention—*this* is how stories are told now. And with a reader accepting a convention, pressure for the writer to provide in form a "rationale" for present-tense storytelling disappears—it disappears, that is, for readers who accept the device as a convention.

I still, nevertheless, ask my writing students to know why a story *must* be told in present tense, that is, to question the contemporary convention and not simply to fall into a habit of writing in present tense. Especially in first-person, present tense poses problems of logic. An ahistorical sense exists in present-tense stories. The first-person narrator, then, if he or she wants to give a reader a sense of background, of cause and effect, must resort to the flashback (or, awkwardly, to having characters discuss an event's history in dialogue). The writer must then determine whether the flashback will be in past or present tense. If the background material is in past tense, the flow of the present tense story is broken. If it is written in present tense, the rationale of immediacy, its logic is broken. Often, then, first-person, present-tense stories are either illogical in form or eschew a historical sense, thus focusing on present events only. This focus on present events without background is part of what constitutes the minimalist story: events simply *are*. And a writer choosing to present events in this manner is also choosing, by implication, to present to a reader a point of view about characters and their actions within a contemporary world. That point of view can be summarized something like this: a sense of history has not helped mitigate chaos or "lostness" and therefore it is not valuable.

It would seem important for a writer beginning a story in first-person to imagine the difficulties posed by the choice, which would then, conceivably, allow the writer to imagine ways around the difficulties. First-person present-tense stories are, to my mind, *the* most difficult to write. The difficulties of the present-tense story extend to third-person as well.

An occasion for the story's being told now needs to exist, either on the page or by implication. Often the implication is made by the power of the narrator's emotions: the story *had* to come out. Often, explicitly, the occasion is clear within the plot— *this* just happened and it brought to the fore a previous "story."

First-person also poses difficulties for inexperienced writers because all information given to the reader must have been available to the narrator, by some means. I notice that students often resort to the telephone as a device—someone phones the first-person narrator to convey information vital to the reader.

The largest difficulty, it seems to me, is the difficulty of language in first-person, especially for a beginning writer. If the writer is using material trans-formed from personal experience, a first-person narrator may have a "voice" too close to the writer's and therefore allow the writer to feel too little distance from the character. This will often cause too little transformation of actual facts into fiction, and the writer may end up writing not a story but an autobiography. I often ask students to practice writing first-person narratives of characters quite unlike themselves, to "become," as a method actor might, someone else.

When a writer chooses a particularly articulate first-person narrator, what may result in many of his or her first-person stories is a similarity in tone. When stories are published individually in magazines, this similarity may not be apparent to a reader reading them over a period of time, but it does become apparent within a story collection.

Another problem exists with the highly articulate first-person narrator. The story itself, the plot, is emphasized; that is, implicit is the fact that language and implied intricacy of thought could not keep the character from being at the mercy of events. Education, logic, thought—none of it helped. The story or plot must then contain material which "proves" implicitly to the reader that the first-person narrator was, truly, hapless. This problem lessens in a story told in retrospect since the narrator implies that he or she couldn't "see" the story then but "sees" it now.

Often in contemporary writing, first-person stories are "told" by inarticulate narrators whose backgrounds and educational levels seem, necessarily, to put them at the mercy of events. Focus is on event, on the quixotic nature of life, on "chaos" itself. For the reader, the experience is one akin to voyeurism—the stories, published *for* the literate reader whose education and background prepare him or her to be less at the mercy of events, are tales of lives he or she will never experience. In such a case, the burden of the writer is to give the reader a sense of why the story is important to read, as opposed to a story closer to the reader's own experience, especially in view of the fact that an omniscient, third-person narrator who signals significance through various devices is absent.

THE APPRENTICESHIP

Because writers develop and change with each act of writing and reading, they remain in a perpetual condition of apprenticeship. But I would like to narrow the definition of *appenticeship* to mean the study a beginning writer undertakes in order to learn his or her *craft*. For a story writer, the time of apprenticeship is particularly important—the form of the story is especially demanding because of its compression and unity. Every word in a story needs to support what, at its end, may be thought of as its meaning or effect. It is a form which also requires practice in a particular kind of writer's vision, precisely because of its compression. It is difficult to define specifically what constitutes this special kind of vision. It is a refined selection either of just the right actions for characters *or* language that causes the reader to feel that characters' actions could be no other than what they are. And the reader must feel that what the characters did or failed to do suggests something about life that, at the least, substantiates his or her conception of its complexity.

The story form is *not* what writers do before maturing enough to write a novel, despite this misconception on the part of many people. The form demands utmost discipline, craft, intelligence, vision, and labor. Despite this, it is the form most beginning prose writers first practice, often for no other reason than that its length seems manageable. The logic appears to be that it must be easier to learn as a form than the novel *because* it is shorter. And, too, many young writers are serving their apprenticeships while enrolled in university writing programs wherein the structure of classes makes assigning the story form an easy method of handling the constraints on resources.

But teaching the story form in writing programs are, often, novelists who have written either none or only one or two stories, in which case the intricate demands of the story form may be sensed by the teacher/novelist but may not have been experienced in the depth that the writing of stories could provide. It may well be that some of the changes in the contemporary story are a result of this situation in teaching—a very large number of writers serve their apprenticeships in writing programs, and what their teachers know and do not know may be influencing the contemporary story form. It is a speculation which needs more investigation. What I would like to stress here is that the story form is a difficult form. Its demands are sufficient to require a long apprenticeship.

But how and where? It seems to me that the first consideration a beginning writer might well make is how to be self-protective, which, I have discovered as a teacher, is the *last* consideration beginning writers appear to make. But what constitutes "self-protection" for the beginning writer?

A creative writer begins study and practice having used language all of his or her life, but not having used, for instance, the story form as a mode of expression through language. He or she may have read many stories, but reading is an adjunct

to practice, not its substitute. At the onset, then, a enormous imbalance exists—
knowledge of *one* component of form and absence of practice of the remaining
components of form. Yet point of view dictates *what* language a story requires so
that having a knowledge of language means only that a story writer has language
in a storehouse to be used *if* he or she can discern what language the shape of a
particular story requires.

It is difficult, I've discovered, to have beginning writers recognize the significance of the disparity in their knowledge of language and of form, much less
understand how to be self-protective as learners. It is, for example, perfectly
natural for a person to accentuate his or her strengths and minimize weaknesses.
Beginning writers will quite naturally begin their "assault" on the story form with
language and receive some satisfaction because the beginning writer no doubt was
drawn to investigate creative forms out of a love of language. Some beginning
writers possess such facility for language that I as a teacher have been enormously
impressed by sheer virtuosity of style, in awe of a young writer's ear for language.
But most often the *story* within which the language resides is weak and unconvinc-
ing. The *story* has been *arrested* in terms of its craft *at the level of language,* and
in such an instance, despite my admiration, I feel obliged as a teacher to say that
this is an imbalance that needs to be addressed.

It is difficult for a beginning writer to calm the exaltation of using language for
the sake of using language, and, in fact, the writer would do well to continue
writing freely in paragraphs apart from a story—to write, that is, blocks of prose
as a sort of journal entry or diary. But to address an imbalance of craft, a
beginning writer of the story form needs to assess with a cold eye what it is within
form that he or she does *not* know and with determination set about learning it. In
the story form, language must be *in service of story.* The questions are: What does
"story" mean to me? and How do I go about discovering a story?

What the beginning practitioner in the story form will discover as he tries to
answer these questions is that his exaltation about language has suddenly been
replaced by awkwardness in form. It is a rude awakening, but the discomfort as an
experience may be *the* most valuable lesson a writer can learn. It signals that the
labor of using language *within* form has begun: *this* is what it will mean to attempt
to be a creative writer.

With a writer's apprehension of the difficulty of using language within creative
forms, a complex of understanding at some level has begun. The writer has begun
an apprenticeship to form and has begun to apprehend what it means to be self-
protective. To amplify: a writer's ability to absorb discomfort when confronting the
demands of form allows him also to begin to make his first separation from the
teacher. I do not mean the teacher of a writing class so much as whatever has
positioned the writer to become involved in the demands of form. For some the
"teacher" may be published writers. But, whoever the teacher, once a writer has
confronted the discomfort inherent in the apprenticeship phase of his career, a

separation has occurred which will help the writer in his development. He can now listen and weigh what he hears, asking, Does this "teacher" *challenge* me, challenge me to accept the labor of writing, its discomforts? Until a writer asks this question, he is in one of two vulnerable positions. Either he is looking to a teacher to tell him precisely what is wrong with his writing, or he is refusing to confront what he does not yet know in order to remain comfortable in ignorance or naiveté.

To complicate matters, the beginning writer has not yet begun to define the vision he needs to protect—it is that which his writing will apprehend *as* it is written, and his problem is analogous to an explorer's laying claim to land he has seen only from shipboard yet must send militia to protect without being able to provide a topographical map or a report on the habits of the natives.

Students in writing workshops rarely read the fiction or poetry of their teachers before signing on to be within their sphere of influence, and only some teachers declare their esthetic prejudices. Beginning writers learning from works of fiction rarely read broadly and often supplement their fiction reading with reading of "how-to" articles on story form written by writers whose work they have not read.

Or beginning writers quickly learn how to write one kind of story and repeat versions of it over and over without asking themselves if such a narrow range of craft will truncate their fledgling careers.

If I combine the concepts of apprenticeship and self-protection, it is because I think that a beginning writer (and a mature writer as well) develops most advantageously when his frame of mind is most skeptical and wary, as if he *did* have something to protect regardless of the fact that the "something" has not yet found its full expression in form. He should be wary of what he is told about writing; he should be wary of his own ignorance; of literary trends and fads; of his own comfort in his writing habits. He should be skeptical about the amount of material for writing he has accumulated through experience and about myths that develop about writing and writers' lives.

It is difficult, however, to sustain skepticism as a stance. It is a state of tension. When I have observed students withdrawing from it into despair over their failures to develop as quickly as they imagine they should or into ill-founded self-congratulation over a piece of writing that is simply an imitation of previous writing, I have suggested what they have found to be more productive relief from tension: to accept the idea of apprenticeship.

Apprenticeship focuses on learning craft and allows the idea of high art to rest; creating *art* becomes that which a writer *may* come to achieve but only after a term as an apprentice. The work of learning craft in small increments provides relief from the inherent tension of a writer's position—the "vision" may be apprehended and may be captured but only if the writer is both self-protective and workmanlike.

To be in apprenticeship is to accept certain tasks. I give students a list of fifty short-story collections and suggest that they begin reading them, one after another *as a task,* suggesting that they read consciously for form.

I suggest that students work on memory exercises in some way of their own devising, although I also suggest methods that I have found useful, and that they work on the exercises regularly, as a task.

Often I suggest that beginning writers write a story a week, completing every story no matter how failed, for the experience of grappling with form instead of experiencing only abortive forays into it. I suggest that students practice pushing ahead with their stories while mentally recording every wince at their failures. And I suggest they celebrate small successes, whether a fine image, a section of dialogue, or a scene.

I suggest that students read literary journals, attend readings by both other students and professional writers, and discuss the work presented with fellow writers.

I suggest that students make lists of stories or novels they admire and dislike intensely and that they think skeptically about their prejudices. And I suggest they ask questions of their teachers—why do you have that esthetic, that prejudice?

Serving an apprenticeship is a way of learning responsibility for one's own writing process and development. It is self-consciously accepted service which can help a writer accept the humility of his chosen profession: no matter how much we learn about writing and about ourselves as writers, we will never know enough or produce enough to fulfill a vision well enough *because* the creative act contains inexhaustible dimensions. Every writer is an apprentice. What matters is to know it.

Writing the "Sources" Essay as a Method of Discovery

I developed this teaching method for a course titled "Autobiography and the Creative Impulse,"* designed to be an alternative to the "workshop method" of teaching creative writing. In the workshop method, students write stories or poems, xerox them for classmates to read, and discuss the work as a group with a teacher participating in the discussion. I was curious to observe students' development in a course which took the focus away from student writing and placed it on both the process of transforming experience into fiction and on what, through reading, we could discern were professional writers' transformations of experience into fiction. We read, for instance, Katherine Anne Porter's "The Sources of *Noon*

For teachers who are interested in reading more about the course "Autobiography and the Creative Impulse," see Creative Writing in America: Theory and Pedagogy (NCTE Press, 1989).

Wine," selections from biographies about Porter, *Noon Wine* itself; writing by V. S. Naipaul, his commentary about his own writing, reviews of his work, essays about Trinidad, articles about colonialism, etc. Other writers under study were Eudora Welty and Nadine Gordimer.

Students wrote three stories of their own for the course, each followed by an essay in which they investigated the sources of the stories, to the extent that they were willing to reveal them. In the essays they examined a story's plot and structure, including its images, metaphors, language repetition, names of characters, and so on. I also wrote an essay about one of my own stories. To protect students' privacy, only I read their essays about the sources of their stories; I shared my own. We discussed the experience of having written the essays, discovering how extensive were the questions that arose in regards both to the essays and to their effects upon ourselves as fiction writers.

While our discoveries were too many to relate here, it appeared that all of us had found the essays valuable as a tool in learning more about the craft of writing fiction. Students came to understand deeply that raw experience was useless for fiction unless it was transformed. Most interesting was the fact that we all felt we had uncovered a myth about the creative writer, or relearned its power to obscure what we felt was contrary knowledge, namely that the more a fiction writer knows about himself and his process the more fruitfully productive he can be. We felt, indeed, that we had glimpsed the fathomlessness of the art of using language in form, and it seemed that depth mirrored our own sense of potential within ourselves. The experience seemed empowering, and we felt less victimized by what we perceived to be the myth of the writer's fragile creativity. We felt that we were learning how to be stronger as writers in direct opposition to the notion of creativity's fragility.

Myths do not die easily, for their sources are lost in history. And the idea of delving into one's sources for creative work may be unpleasant for many writers. My prejudice, indeed my experience, is to think that a writer needs as much self-knowledge as he can possibly get. I offer this exercise out of that belief.

How to Write a Story

With the preceding material as preparation, it would seem logical to describe how a story is written. Experience, however, has taught me that doing so would not contribute toward attaining the ultimate goal of a true aspiring writer. Any literate person can write a story, but the aspiring story writer wants to accomplish something much more complicated. He or she seeks to find expression for a unique self through language acted upon by form and through accepting the tension inherent in the push and pull between that which is inarticulate and the ways the complex self can be articulated in the story form. It is possible to write stories and be a stranger to them, to feel *these* are not *my* stories! Indeed, early stories can appear so wrong to a beginning writer that he or she may stop writing altogether because he or she fails to appreciate the level of discomfort writing requires.

Discomfort is an inescapable part of a writer's profession, and the writer about to begin practicing the story form must accept the inevitable rejection of his or her early stories. Liking one's early work too well impedes development; an overwhelming amount of *published* writing is slight, clear evidence of writers' and publishers' easy satisfaction. This has always been true and is true today, for publishers and writing teachers encourage young writers to seek publication early in their careers, an unfortunate symbiosis of an undemanding reading public, the "hungry" writer, and the phenomenon of a large number of creative writing programs in the country.

A writer influences his development *by* what he writes. He will be wise to prepare himself to assess his early efforts, to learn the habits of assessment. In the previous pages I have suggested or implied methods of preparation. These might be summarized in the statement that what a writer does to and with himself is crucial to his development. The desire to write is a planted seed. If it does not remain dormant, the writer needs to encourage its growth with the utmost delicacy, study, care, and thought. *When* a writer has made deep consideration of what it may mean to begin, and only then, it is time to begin.

1. Write a complete—ten- to twelve- to fifteen-page—story. Finish it no matter how difficult and unpleasant the task may be.
2. Wait a week and then read the story. Assess it by bringing to bear all of your intelligence and training in writing and imagination. Continue reading literature and preparing to write.
3. Wait several days and write a new story.
4. Continue in this rhythm until you begin to recognize your work as stories you would want to represent you in the world to *strangers* whose involvement in and discernment about literature you have imagined.
5. Revise or polish those stories.
6. Consider what it may mean to begin a new relationship with a stranger-as-reader and assess the possible impact of rejection by the stranger/reader. Decide how you will contend with rejection.
7. Submit your work.
8. Without waiting for response to a submitted story, continue your work as a writer.

Resources for the Isolated Writer

There are now so many creative writing programs in universities across the country that beginning writers *not* enrolled in such a program may feel left out, indeed, left behind, especially when excessive publicity is given to very young graduates of writing programs whose first books have been published during or soon after their residency in such programs. In fact, most writers who publish have not attended creative writing programs. They are a new cultural phenomenon and how well they serve the cause of writers and literature cannot yet be fully examined.

What writing programs provide most readily for a beginning writer is a readership, of faculty and fellow students. Within the programs, writers find companionship with others whose struggles with language and form are equally dedicated and intense. Writers working in isolation from such programs can provide for themselves, with some effort, an atmosphere as conducive to the study of writing as formal programs provide.

First, seek *a* reader for your work. Even within writing programs, finding the "right" reader is not easy, for that reader needs to be able to *sense* the writer's vision lurking in work not wholly realized. It does little good to find a reader who wants the beginning writer either to write as he does or to provide his favorite type of writing. The reader, then, needs to be one who is willing to do a service—sense what the beginning writer seeks in his work and assess the work within *that* frame of reference, with objectivity born of a knowledge of literature. Since any reader has his or her prejudices, the reader should be aware of what they are and be willing to explain them. But the reader need *not be* a writer himself. The reader who is not a writer may be unable to offer suggestions for revision, but he can perform the invaluable service of telling a writer *what* he has read. The writer listens, assesses the reader's experience with the piece of writing, and is thereby helped to gain distance from it for a deeper assessment himself. When giving a piece of writing to a reader, it is most advantageous for the writer to refrain from talking about the writing before the reader reads it—whatever the writer says will affect the reader's reading. In fact, in classes I ask writers to refrain from talking *after* readers have responded to their work. A writer is so invested in his work that it is difficult to step back from it; the urge is to explain and to justify, not to listen. Verbal restraint can aid in hearing what the reader has said, for whatever use to the writer it may be. A reader provides *information*; questions to the reader can clarify, but statements to the reader tend to cloud.

The isolated writer can usually also arrange to attend public readings, which are listed in newspapers' cultural events sections or are available from university English departments or newspapers. Listening to writers reading their own work can be valuable for a writer working in isolation because he or she can hear the writer talk at least briefly about the conception of what is to be read and then hear how the conception was realized in form.

Writers working in isolation can also attend writers' conferences, usually held in the summer for several days or weeks. At these conferences are professional writers and beginning writers from across the country, gathered to discuss writing. Most conferences are inexpensive. In the spring lists of where such conferences are to be held can be found in *The Writer* magazine and in the *AWP Newsletter,* as well as in *Coda*.

Writers can, of course, form writers' groups, but a word of caution here. Writers forming into groups need to ask themselves what it is they seek from the group. It can be companionship alone, a place where aspirations and frustrations can be shared. If writers meet to read and discuss each other's work, care needs to be taken in choosing members of the group and in deciding what the group will do and how members will behave when discussing others' writing. There are dangers in forming writers' groups. It is possible for a group to become insular, for members to write *for* one another and lose sight of a broader audience. Too, writers sometimes form into groups not to challenge themselves intellectually and esthetically but to solidify narrow views of writing. The beginning writer needs to understand that what he does with himself will affect his development.

Writers working in isolation can also provide a type of companionship and stimulus through reading in general and in particular by reading reviews of newly published books, interviews with writers, and biographies of writers.

What is important is for the isolated writer to estimate the amount of contact he or she needs with other writers *for the sake of his or her writing*. While "talking shop" can be enjoyable, estimating how much isolation is too much is an individual matter which must be sensed. The focus should remain on the *work* and not on the "lifestyle" of "being a writer." Too often talk *about* writing substitutes *for* writing. The writer always needs to be self-protective.

THE COMPONENTS OF
A SHORT STORY

1. **Plot:** the structure of action in a story or novel. The plot answers the reader's question "What happened?" Some contemporary stories appear to be without plot, with disparate incidents juxtaposed against one another. Not all stories, then, have a plot. All traditional stories contain a plot.
2. **Point of view:** the author's basic attitudes and ideas, conveyed through a narrator or narrators.
3. **Setting:** the place in which a story takes place.
4. **Characters:** the people or animals who participate in the action of the plot.
5. **Dialogue:** the spoken words of characters in a story.
6. **Interior dialogue:** the sub-vocal words of characters.
7. **Time:** the span in time of the action.
8. **Theme:** the overall "meaning" of a story, what a story adds up to for a reader.
9. **Style:** the selection and ordering of a story's language.
10. **Form:** the arrangement in a story of the above-listed components.

Additional Words Frequently Used in the Study of Fiction
1. **Irony:** a contrast between the expected and the actual.
2. **Foreshadowing:** preparing a reader for future action or events in a story.
3. **Imagery:** language representation of a sense experience.
4. **Inevitability:** a reader's sense that only what happened in a story *could* have happened.
5. **Cliché:** language which has been so overused as to be ineffective. Also used with fictional situations which have been overused.
6. **Distance:** a measure of a narrator's detachment, tonally, from characters.
7. **Convention:** devices which are accepted through repeated use, such as the device of a narrator's entering the mind of a character to relate the character's thoughts.
8. **Abstract:** the rendering in language of pure ideas.
9. **Concrete:** something with substance that can be weighed, measured, etc.
10. **Pathos:** the sense of pity.
11. **Bathos:** false pathos or sentimentality.
12. **Rhythm:** language with a recurrent beat or stress. More subtle in fiction than in some poetry.
13. **Objective:** in reference to a narrator, *objective* means a nonprejudicial relating of a story's events. In reference to a character, *objective* means that a narrator does not present characters' thoughts or feelings.
14. **Unity:** a sense of wholeness in a story's form.

STORIES FOR STUDY

Writers studying closely the following stories have found that their understanding of form has deepened. I will mention particular devices or techniques in each story which are noteworthy. When studying a writer's use of a particular device, it is easier to isolate the device on a second reading. A third reading can reveal more readily how the device is integrated into the story as a whole. The story titles will be given first, then the author's name, and finally the story collection within which the story was published. Any story can, of course, be studied for its technique. Often students in writing classes will form study groups outside of classes, continuing the close reading methods they have practiced in class with additional stories. Each member of the group brings copies of a story that has puzzled or interested him because of a writer's particular approach to the story form. While these writers read as a daily part of their writing careers, they report that they read more attentively as writers studying device when they separate the activity from casual reading practices.

The Stories:

1. "Mr. Blue," Robert Creeley, *The Gold Diggers*. The prose style in this story is unusual and affects how the surface plot is rendered and even the timing of the information. What happens is revealed slowly through the "filter" of the first-person narrator's perceptions. The prose is stilted, sounding at times almost as if the narrator were stuttering. The plot is almost subsumed by the narrator's attitude toward the event of the story. The prose creates a sense of great interiority in the narrator, which finally places a focus on the inadequacy of language itself to convey not the facts of an event, but its import.

2. "Faith in the Afternoon," Grace Paley, *Enormous Changes at the Last Minute*. Grace Paley's narrator in this story is aggressively assertive, colloquial, "loud." Written in third-person, Faith's history (and her particular story) is conveyed by a narrator who is decidedly subjective. The narrator assumes as much importance in the story as Faith, announcing himself or herself as vital to the story in the aggressive opening address to the reader: "As for you, fellow independent thinkers of the Western Bloc." Paley is known for her style of narration and particularly the stance her narrators take in relationship to an imagined reader. Both are evident in "Faith in the Afternoon."

3. "Time Did," Nadine Gordimer, *A Soldier's Embrace*. "Time Did," atypical of Gordimer's stories of the effects of apartheid on South Africa's black, colored, and white populations, employs the device of narration in first-person with the first-person narrator addressing a "you," who is a former lover. She handles the device especially well, making the information the reader needs mesh seamlessly with the knowledge that the "you" presumably already possesses.

4. "January," Fred Chappell, *Moments of Light*. Amazingly, this very, very short story is, genuinely, a story and not a sketch, in two complete printed pages. Characterization seems full, a sense of place is established, and dialogue is artfully handled.

5. "Pages from Cold Point," Paul Bowles, *Collected Stories*. In this story, the device of an unreliable narrator is handled especially deftly so that the story's tensions are deeply embedded in characterization as well as in plot.

6. "Everything That Rises Must Converge," Flannery O'Connor, *The Complete Stories*. O'Connor's handling of narration is especially smooth in this story, as the narration moves back and forth between "objective" and "attached" to Julian, the main character.

7. "The Displaced Person," Flannery O'Connor, *The Complete Stories*. Political themes are successfully integrated into characterization and plot.

8. "The Dead," James Joyce, *Dubliners*. This story is particularly useful for studying how a story's form is affected by the writer's choice of *when* to begin a story and how to approach event peripherally until the story rises as if spontaneously from description.

9. "Araby," James Joyce, *Dubliners*. Not only does this story have a superior opening sentence, it also demonstrates a story rising from a narrator's recollections "in tranquility," when retrospection, over many years, brings forth story from incident.

10. "Bogart," V. S. Naipaul, *Miguel Street*. Naipaul's first story demonstrates the beauty of economical writing in very plain language to great effect when the writer has an ear for rhythm of sentences. Each sentence reverberates so that the story seems rich and long.

11. "In the Miro District," Peter Taylor, *In the Miro District and Other Stories*. Typical of Taylor's leisurely narrations in which place and social mores are explained by a narrator telling a story in retrospect, "In the Miro District" is valuable for study especially for slow revelation of character.

12. "Motion of the Heart," Josephine Jacobsen, *Adios, Mr. Moxley*. All of Josephine Jacobsen's stories are carefully made to bring forth a character's moment of recognition of a profound change in himself or herself. "Motion of the Heart" is noteworthy for its deft handling of the delicate material of a woman's coming to know of her fiancé's homosexuality. The story can also be studied for methods of preparing for a crucial scene.

13. "Nights in the Gardens of Spain," Gina Berriault, *The Infinite Passion of Expectation*. The difficulties of writing about artists are many. In this story, a classical guitarist is convincingly portrayed by means of juxtaposing him against a younger protégé at the story's beginning and a masterful guitarist at the story's end. Through this technique, the main character is made believable, his art thoroughly integrated into story.

14. "Myra," Gina Berriault, *The Infinite Passion of Expectation*. Myra, the main character, is placed within a narration about class differences and gender

differences. She nevertheless emerges not as a type but individualized. This story is worth study for its handling of characterization within social themes.

15. *Noon Wine,* Katherine Anne Porter, *Collected Stories.* Studied alone, this story is masterful for its clarity of narration—a seemingly effortless style—Porter's handling of time, and moral complexity in story. Read along with Porter's essay "The Sources of *Noon Wine,*" in *Understanding Fiction* (Brooks and Warren, editors), a student of fiction may benefit from noting how a writer's deepest memories are transformed into fictional material.

16. "No Place for You, My Love," Eudora Welty, *Collected Stories.* Description of place is so artfully interwoven into this story that setting becomes almost a character in the story. Story *derives* from setting.

17. "Powerhouse," Eudora Welty, *Collected Stories.* A *tour de force* of narration—sensuous, lyrical, rhythmical, with characterization rising out of the narrator's perceptions rendered almost as a part of the setting. This is an example of a narrator who is not physically a part of the story's action but who is obviously intimate with the story's setting.

18. "The Ugliest Pilgrim," Doris Betts, *Beasts of the Southern Wild and Other Stories.* Worthy of study for its interweaving of humor and pathos.

19. "Strong Horse Tea," Alice Walker, *Black Short Story Anthology,* edited by Alice Walker. In this story, situation and characters are introduced almost immediately, which adds to the reader's sense of the typicality of the character's dilemma, although characterization is strong.

20. "The Swimmer," John Cheever, *The Brigadier and the Golf Widow* (also in *Collected Stories*). "The Swimmer" is ususual for its handling of realism and metaphor. The story is both realistic and surrealistic.

21. "The Seed," Pierre Gaspar, *Beasts and Men.* This long story is especially interesting for the disparity between its lyrical prose and its quiet violence of action.

22. "A Perfect Day for Bananafish," J. D. Salinger, *Nine Stories.* Beneath a portrait of a charming encounter on a beach lurks a deeper story of pathos. The story is worth studying for the smooth handling of the tensions between the surface story and the story beneath the engaging surface.

23. "Going to Meet the Man," James Baldwin, *Going to Meet the Man.* This powerful story can be usefully studied not only for its depiction of the paradox of terrifying forces clashing, but, possibly more interestingly, for the moments of quiet reflection which bespeak psychological destruction.

24. "How I Met My Husband," Alice Munro, *Something I've Been Meaning to Tell You.* Munro's ear for speech is noteworthy. Here she incorporates dialogue in order to advance story without having dialogue seem artificial.

25. "Nothing at All," Robert Walser, *Selected Stories.* Walser's stories are short and read like fables, this one in particular. It is interesting for the narrator's chatty, offhand manner, which establishes quickly a reader's sense of intimacy with the main character, defined primarily by her dilemma.

26. "Winter in July," Doris Lessing, *African Stories*. While interesting for its handling of a difficult subject, "Winter in July" also demonstrates that length of story is an important consideration. Here, Lessing allows the story to unfold slowly while covering a long time period, but at the same time giving a sense of time's having stopped in each scene.

27. "Tell Me a Riddle," Tillie Olsen, *Tell Me a Riddle*. The narrative voice in "Tell Me a Riddle" is unusual. It flows easily between distant, although subjective, narration for the giving of fact, to narration indicating characters' interior monologues, to language representing psychological states. Dialogue is rendered as merely the *least* that is "said." The effect is unusual because the plot is immersed within "voice" even as outside event affects characters' lives considerably.

28. "The Apprentice," Eve Shelnutt, *The Love Child*. This story is unusual for its heavy reliance on imagery and rhythm of language.

29. "Silent Snow, Secret Snow," Conrad Aiken, *Collected Stories*. This story is particularly interesting to study for a narration designed to suggest sensation and the mind's quarrel with sensation. The form of the story itself reflects this push-and-pull of language, with scenes of a boy's interior state alternating with scenes of society's interruption of his interiority.

30. "Cutting Edge," James Purdy, *The Color of Darkness*. In this story, as in other of Purdy's stories, the reader is tossed into incident with little preparation through prose about characters' situations. In "Cutting Edge" particularly, the characters are almost instantly in conflict, which will bring forth the depth of their terrible hate and dependency. The story is especially economical in its suggestion of characters' histories while also suggesting how their histories color their every movement, thought, and conversation.

31. "My Dear Palestrina," Bernard MacLaverty, *A Time to Dance and Other Stories*. Differences in class and the expectations of each, in an Irish setting, are the tensions against which a young boy's innocence is portrayed. The story is interesting to study for MacLaverty's delicate handling of the thin line between bathos and pathos.

32. "Beyond the Pale," William Trevor, *The Stories of William Trevor*. Trevor is a master of irony, particularly evident in "Beyond the Pale." The story can also be useful for an examination of slow revelation of character and conflict.

33. "The Valiant Woman," J. F. Powers, *Lions, Harts, Leaping Does and Other Stories*. This is an adroit example of a writer's portraying a story which the characters are unaware is happening: the story itself is the narrator's in the sense that the selection of materials adds up to much more than incident in a typical day of the characters.

34. "Another Love Story," M. F. K. Fisher, *Sister Age*. This story is interesting particularly for the way in which every scene is artfully chosen to lead toward a character's moment of revelation about herself.

35. "The Maid's Shoes," Bernard Malamud, *Idiots First*. This is an example of a modern tale. The narration is straightforward, objective, and focused on plot. It is interesting to compare the story with another story whose narrator is less effaced and imagine how "The Maid's Shoes" could be changed from a tale into a more contemporary form.

36. "Visions of Budhardin," Stuart Dybek, *Childhood and Other Neighborhoods*. Dybek's special talent is to make modern myths from the characters and settings of Chicago neighborhoods, as he has done in "Visions of Budhardin." The story exhibits both rare exuberance and pathos, an unusual combination.

37. "Maria's Girl," Beverly Farmer, *Milk*. In this first-person story, an incident of childhood incest is reflected upon by the main character in such a way as to focus a reader's attention on the question of a character's reliability as the teller of his own story. Because of the delicate handling of narrative voice, the story is especially interesting to study for the device of unreliable narrator and the depth of tension it can give a story.

38. "A Mother in India," Sara Jeanette Duncan, *The Pool in the Desert*. This is an interesting example of a story which covers a long time period, seemingly necessary for the main character's understanding of herself. Length, in this case, seems necessary.

39. "City of Boys," Beth Nuggent, *The Norton Anthology of Contemporary Fiction*. Rhythmical language as a device is particularly strong in this story and seems to transform the plot.

40. "A Father's Story," Andre Dubus, *The Times Are Never So Bad*. This is a story in the form of a confession, an interesting example of the genre. It is interesting particularly when contrasted with Paul Bowles's "Pages from Cold Point."

A READING LIST:
SHORT FICTION

This list is of collections of stories that my students have found helpful in understanding the variety and complexity of the story form. I ask students to read collections by a single author instead of single stories by a variety of authors represented in anthologies. This affords a reader an opportunity to observe a writer manipulating form and language and places the reader's focus on the writer-at-work and subsidiarily on the individual stories.

I. The collected stories of:

Conrad Aiken
Isaac Babel
H. E. Bates
Jane Bowles
Paul Bowles
Kay Boyle
Anton Chekov
Joseph Conrad
A. E. Coppard
Guy de Maupassant
Fyodor Dostoevsky
William Faulkner
William Goyen
Nathaniel Hawthorne
Ernest Hemingway

Henry James
Franz Kafka
D. H. Lawrence
Katherine Mansfield
Sean O'Casey
Flannery O'Connor
Frank O'Connor
Katherine Anne Porter
Elizabeth Spencer
Jean Stafford
Peter Taylor
Leo Tolstoy
William Trevor
Eudora Welty

II. Selected Stories
Nelson Algren. *Neon Wilderness.*
Djuna Barnes. *Spillway.*
John Barth. *Lost in the Funhouse.*
Donald Barthelme. *City Life.*
Samuel Beckett. *Stories and Texts for Nothing.*
Saul Bellow. *Mosby's Memoirs.*
Gina Berriault. *The Infinite Passion of Expectation.*
John Berry. *Flight of White Crows.*
Doris Betts. *The Gentle Insurrection and Other Stories.*
Heinrich Boll. *18 Stories.*
Jorge Luis Borges. *Labyrinths.*
Harold Brodkey. *First Love and Other Sorrows.*

Truman Capote. *A Tree of Light.*
R. V. Cassill. *The Father and Other Stories.*
Fred Chappell. *Moments of Light.*
Julio Cortazar. *A Change of Light.*
Robert Creeley. *The Gold Diggers.*
Isak Dinesen. *Stories Out of Africa.*
José Donoso. *Charleston and Other Stories.*
Sara Jeanette Duncan. *The Pool in the Desert.*
Stuart Dybek. *Childhood and Other Neighborhoods.*
Stanley Elkin. *Criers and Kibitzers, Kibitzers and Criers.*
Beverly Farmer. *Milk.*
Dorothy Canfield Fisher. *Four-Square.*
Pierre Gascar. *Women and the Sun.*
William Gass. *In the Heart of the Heart of the Country.*
Nadine Gordimer. *Selected Stories.*
James B. Hall. *The Short Hall.*
John Hawkes. *Lunar Landscapes.*
Josephine Jacobsen. *Adios, Mr. Moxley.*
Ruth Prawer Jhabvala. *An Experience of India.*
James Joyce. *Dubliners.*
Janet Kauffman. *Places in the World a Woman Could Walk.*
Heinrich Kleist. *The Marquis of O.*
Jerzy Kosinski. *Steps.*
Tommaso Landolfi. *Gogol's Wife and Other Stories.*
Mary Lavin. *Selected Stories.*
Doris Lessing. *African Stories.*
Jacob Lind. *Soul of Wood and Other Stories.*
Robie Macauley. *The End of Pity and Other Stories.*
Bernard MacLaverty. *A Time to Dance.*
Bernard Malamud. *The Magic Barrel.*
Thomas Mann. *Stories of Three Decades.*
Gabriel Garcia Marquez. *No One Writes to the Colonel.*
Jack Matthews. *Bitter Knowledge.*
Carson McCullers. *The Ballad of the Sad Café and Other Stories.*
James Alan McPherson. *Hue and Cry.*
Yukio Mishima. *Death in Midsummer and Other Stories.*
Wright Morris. *Real Losses, Imaginary Gains.*
Alice Munroe. *The Beggar Maid.*
Vladimir Nabokov. *Nabokov's Dozen.*
V. S. Naipaul. *Miguel Street.*
Grace Paley. *The Little Disturbances of Man.*
J. F. Powers. *Prince of Darkness.*

Reynolds Price. *The Names and Faces of Heroes.*
James Purdy. *The Color of Darkness.*
Tillie Olsen. *Tell Me a Riddle.*
Cynthia Ozick. *The Pagan Rabbi.*
Alan Sillitoe. *The Loneliness of the Long-Distance Runner.*
Bruno Schultz. *Street of Crocodiles.*
Isaac Singer. *Short Friday.*
Christina Stead. *The Puzzle-Headed Girl.*
Theodor Storm. *Rider on a White Horse.*
Barry Targan. *Harry Belsen and the Mendelssohn Violin Concerto.*
B. Traven. *A Night Visitor and Other Stories.*
John Updike. *The Music School.*
Edith Wharton. *Roman Fever and Other Stories.*
William Carlos Williams. *The Farmer's Daughter.*
Stefan Zweig. *The Royal Game.*

Recommended Books
About Fiction Writing

Maurice Blanchot. *The Siren's Song*.

Cleanth Brooks and Robert Penn Warren, editors. *Understanding Fiction*.

Janet Burroway. *Writing Fiction: A Guide to Narrative Craft*.

Robert Murray Davis, editor. *The Novel: Modern Essays in Criticism*.

Gabriel Josopovici. *The Lessons of Modernism*.

_____. *The World and the Book*.

_____. *Writing and the Body*.

V. S. Naipaul. *The Enigma of Arrival*.

_____. *Finding the Center*.

Charles Newman. *The Post-Modern Aura: The Act of Fiction in an Age of Inflation*.

Joyce Carol Oates. *The Profane Art*.

Flannery O'Connor. *Mysteries and Manners*.

Frank O'Connor. *The Lonely Voice*.

The Partisan Review. Fiftieth Anniversary Issue.

William Peden. *The American Short Story: Continuity and Change, 1940-1975*.

The Essays of Katherine Anne Porter.

Philip Rahv. *Essays on Literature and Politics*.

_____. *Literature in America*.

Alain Robbe-Grillet. *For a New Novel*.

Salmagundi. Spring/Summer 1986, Numbers 70-71.

Lionel Trilling. *The Liberal Imagination*.

Eudora Welty. *The Eye of the Story*.

Virginia Woolf. *The Moment and Other Essays*.

• ON THIS ROAD •

by Jessie Vanamee

Late at night Mrs. Bease clucks her tongue, climbs out of bed, and finds her way to the phone. "Operator? Operator, connect me with the police." She speaks finally with Lieutenant Keller, who rubs a hand over his stiff spiky hair and listens to her story again, without listening, without hearing a single syllable. He stares instead across the desk and through the wall, through the houses down the street, home to his own television; because he can hear the World Series in one earphone while he listens to Mrs. Bease through the other; and if he opens his eyes and stares hard, he can almost see it, moment by moment, pitch by pitch.

He knows Mrs. Bease's story; he can rattle through his *yeps* and *nopes* and *I'll send a car right down* without missing a hawk or a spit or a slide to first. But when he hangs up, it's just a second before he remembers to call out. It is just a millisecond—time for an out at third and a *damn* that primes his voice—before he shouts to the dispatcher:

"Mary, send around a car to Henry and Janice's."

Mary doesn't even bother to answer because she knows that Keller is listening to the game, and she already sent a car around as soon as she picked up the phone and heard Mrs. Bease's wet, whiny voice asking for Lieutenant Keller.

She hadn't listened in on the conversation because she had heard it all before. A headset was clamped around her skull like an insect, and she was talking into the wiry leg that hung in front of her white, even teeth. Mary transferred the call; she radioed for someone to get over to Janice and Henry's and not to spend all night there.

Mary never supposed that the voice was whiny because Mrs. Bease really didn't like calling the police. She never thought that Mrs. Bease had to wake up and walk through a dark hall and down cold steps to telephone, to ask them to check up on her dead husband's niece.

It was cold down there with the heat off, "though your voice, Lieutenant, is very calming. I would call them myself, but you know how they've pulled that phone out again." Mrs. Bease never did say to him or to Mary that she crept down those stairs in the dark, one concave wood step at a time, gripping the banister with both of her hands, because she wasn't about to turn on a light and advertise to the whole world that she had gotten up and called the police.

She never said that she had the operator connect her every time because in the dark alcove under the stairs, where the heavy metal phone sat on a tiny table, there was no stray moonlight to shine on the round face of numbers; so even if she knew the number she couldn't dial it in the dark.

But her thick forefinger could run around the rim in that pitch black stillness and find the O, the last hole. That is, after she had waited, and listened, and imagined again that her husband Gus would have snapped on the lights and gone stomping over there himself to settle them down; would have gone with his pants over his longjohns, his boots unlaced, and would have stayed there until it was quiet. He would have come back shaking his head in the gray light of dawn and whispered through a sweet smell of cigarettes that someday Henry was going to get himself shot and that Janice could take on Henry and him too if she would just bother to.

Mrs. Bease stood in the darkness, with one hand on the receiver, one finger in the O, and waited with Gus alive again for a moment behind her eyes. The darkness was replaced by his saggy trousers and his old shirt. Then she heard a crash from next door and she snapped back into the night; she dialed the operator; the operator connected her, and she asked for Lieutenant Keller.

"I think he's shooting up the sofa again," she said, with one ear plugged against the noises.

Now she waits for the squad car and leans her head against a pane of glass. Moonlight shines down on her white robe and her white hair, lighting her up. She stares, never knowing that she glows like a white moth. She just wonders what's happening next door.

And now that the police are on their way she wonders where that blond girl is tonight. The girl, Louise, who stays up so late with Janice and Henry on their porch. Stays, sitting in the bleak light from the bare bulb inside the house. Mrs. Bease has not actually had to call so often since Louise moved in up the road. She has wondered what similarity there was between that blond girl and Gus. What soothing effect? When Louise stopped by to visit once, Mrs. Bease searched her face, looking for Gus.

Louise said she was from Albany, three hours from here. She works in the Pottery. That's why she came. Her clothes are always gray with dust. Mrs. Bease is from Albany too, although she never mentioned it. She barely remembers it. She has never been back since she married Gus. She has really never gone much of anywhere since she moved into this house. She knows everyone on the road, knows all about them, but she stays pretty much alone.

Louise, on the other hand, came alone, and as soon as she moved into the tiny house up the road, Mrs. Bease noticed her slipping in and out of Janice and Henry's house. She carried their children around like they were her own. She had never met anyone here before, but she already knew everyone like Gus had. Mrs. Bease looked for Gus's calm in her face, and she saw his smile that served Janice and Henry like a stiff drink.

The police arrive and glance at Mrs. Bease from the corners of their eyes.

Louise's eyes are closed as the police car drives by, and she is just on the edge of sleep. Those blue lights flashing by her in the dark make the slightest imprint on the inside of her eyelids and she begins to dream.

She dreams she is at the Pottery working on a bowl that is seven feet tall. She is reaching up to smooth the rim when the police drive by and yank her into the car.

"We're going to see Janice and Henry," they say.

"See, there she is like a goddam white bat, just staring." Officer Stoll looks away from Mrs. Bease. He pounds on the door, eager to get inside to the crashing and shouting, away from those white eyes. They left the bubble light on, so Mrs. Bease flashes white and then blue.

Everybody who lives on the road wonders what goes on between Janice and Henry. Most of them watch from a distance. Henry logs with horses. Every June Janice walks around the house sweeping the floor and squatting, until a baby drops out of her. Someone might call Dr. Sal, a midwife, who might stop in, but no one suggests that Janice go to a hospital.

Actually, only some wonder, in those six or seven houses on the road. It is really the women who talk about them sometimes, as they wrap up balsam candles in the Gift Shop, or sit together at coffee breaks in the Pottery kitchen. Or they sit watching their children tumble over each other and wonder. Maybe on the day of Mrs. Bease's latest phone call, or maybe a week afterwards. The days drain into each other on this road.

These mothers have noticed what Mrs. Bease has noticed. Janice and Henry have calmed down since Louise has come to town.

But when Louise told these mothers that she works with each day in the Pottery that she had gone to the river at midnight with Janice, eyebrows shot up in speculation. As far as any of them knew, Janice hadn't been up to that in almost a year. One morning one of their husbands had found Janice's clothes by the river, and he brought them to Henry, inquiring whether Janice was home or if they should drag the river. Janice was standing at the woodstove cooking up bacon.

"Come on in, Steve, thanks." She gave him breakfast. He and Henry ate in silence with the children crawling between their legs under the table.

The women raised their brows and wondered if Louise had gone along for the adventure or as a lifeguard. Louise took her turn watching their children; these mothers felt their babies were safe with her, even if she didn't have any of her own. Louise had rubbed her eyes, and they looked at her roughed-up knuckles.

"You must be tired," one said. "Why don't you go on home?" But she stayed all day making tea cups and then stayed late into the night throwing her own pots. She threw and rethrew and never kept a thing.

Louise opens her eyes because she really can't sleep tonight, and maybe she'll go down to see Janice. She lies there watching the dim blue light sweep through her room. But she doesn't really see it as she stares, so for a while she doesn't even wonder where it's coming from.

Today she watched the children. Louise does not watch them so another mother will take her children away for a morning while she does her shopping or washes her long blond hair in the sink. Louise has no children, no dogs, no fish, so she does those things as she pleases, when she is not working at the Pottery.

Louise makes her own time to slip to the next town for a long afternoon lunch with that mechanic who is married and handsome.

She watches the children for other reasons: so she can borrow someone's station wagon; so Rudy will sit up with her at the Pottery some night when she is firing; so Henry and Janice will set aside a cord of firewood for her this winter and help her stack it outside of her tall, thin house.

Today she watched the children and mused. Emily came running toward her, and she mused that this sweet child looked like both Janice and Henry: that she had Janice's firm bones and broad shining cheeks and Henry's slight, wiry frame and his fierce black eyes. She mused as she watched Emily pick up her little brother JoJo under his arms and carry him over, lunging side to side, one giant step at a time, that these two had seen what she had not seen, but only heard about—what she could not quite imagine.

She held out her arms for little JoJo because he had scraped his palm. His eyes were full of tears. He shied, and Emily took him back saying, "I'll do it." Emily spat on his palm and dabbed the cut clean.

Louise gets up and goes to the window. She goes blank when she tries to imagine Henry hitting Janice because she doesn't know what to see; because she knows that in fact Janice is about six inches taller than Henry. If she thinks for just a moment, if she stretches her imagination the tiniest bit, she can see Janice flicking Henry away like a fly. If she really thinks for a few uninterrupted minutes, she knows that Janice could crack his jaw with a solid hit and that with her knee in the nape of Henry's neck, Janice could snap it like a carrot. So the vision never comes clear to her, and Janice's split lip and blue wrist never seem real; they are unimaginable.

But Henry's cast was real enough. A tree split up and fell on him in the woods, Janice said. He had made a splint and crawled a mile out of the woods to his truck and driven home with a crushed leg. That seemed real enough because Henry, with his black scary eyes, would do anything that he set his mind to.

In the Pottery kitchen one woman said, "Louise, last time Janice went to the river she got washed a half a mile down stream and walked up into my door. Dick just about died. She was buck naked."

Louise nodded as though she could imagine that.

"'Course she wouldn't fit into any of my clothes, so she had to take Dick's. Never did give 'em back."

"She didn't?"

"She musta forgot. But she was shining that night. Couldn't stop talking and singing. Still gives me a turn when I see her in Dick's corduroys."

When Louise talks with the other mothers and tongues are clucked, it seems to her like they can see something she can't. Tonight Louise strains in her disbelief to imagine Henry belting Janice or kicking her calf with those lace-up boots that he oils so often. He's always dipping into a jar of Neat's Foot Oil and working the leather. She can imagine him sitting on the kitchen bench near the woodstove, the flies settling on his shoulders; can see him dropping the cigarette he's rolling or dropping the boot that he's rubbing with his warm fingers. She can imagine those black eyes losing sight with fury.

That's easy because Henry's eyes dart around without seeing anything, until they fall on the boots, or the bowl he is carving, or the tackle he is cleaning, or the chainsaw that he's taking apart; then they rest still and flat.

The faintest waves of blue light pulse in her room. She stands at the window staring down the road. Did the police actually come for Janice and Henry, or is Mrs. Bease dead from a stroke in her kitchen, just like her old husband Gus two years before?

The first time Louise saw Henry's tongue snap out and grab his moustache he was angry at Janice. Instead of saying a word or moving from the sawhorse, he looked at *her*, at Louise, straight in the eyes. She sat still and let her gaze drift to the ground and lit a cigarette to cloud the air.

That was last autumn, when she had only known them for a few months. He sat and smiled at her, and the air had shimmered.

Tonight she remembers when their phone rang after dark. She saw Henry reach behind Emily and crack the cord out from the wall, quietly, and then tap his feet. She has seen Janice pick up a baby and walk out of the house into the night. She would stand up quietly to follow or to drift up the hill to her house.

But sometimes Henry's black eyes focus up at something that Janice says or on Emily or JoJo, on some conversation between Louise and Janice, and those lizard eyes crinkle up into a smile, or maybe a laugh, and Janice smiles too. Sometimes Louise finds Henry sitting next to the stove with the newest baby, Hal, napping on his shoulder and Janice piling through a box of old photographs. Janice gets her a cup of coffee and keeps sorting. When Janice and Henry are like that, Louise sits alongside the two of them and soaks them up.

But tonight, even though she tries, she can't keep from drifting to the other parts of Janice and Henry: to that time that she was spread out on the grass watching their children, when Henry came up behind her, silent as a spider, with an axe in his hand, and paused for a moment, looking down. He looked down, those eyes creeping sideways, and those sunken cheeks filling out with a grin, and that dirty hair standing up, one thick brow jumping; and he kept on walking. Then there was a smile with a flash of good humor and surprising good will. She smiled back up into the sun.

"Hi, Henry."

He paused with his eyes, and he didn't say "Hi," but instead the gentlest singsong phrase, "Mmmmm, good enough to eat," and kept on walking.

Louise watched JoJo, Henry's three-year-old, run and follow him all the way to the edge of the woods. The boy stopped there, lingered, and watched as Henry disappeared without a backward glance into the trees, the handle of his axe bobbing like a tail.

She held her breath and bunched her hair into a blond sun on the top of her head. When JoJo came back to the other children, she picked him up and held him to her. He struggled because he wanted to play. Louise just held on tight, terrified; but she kept thinking about those thin hips swaying away in those dirty brown blue jeans.

And she thinks about opening her eyes in the darkness of this same room—this third floor of her house—when there was no flashing blue light, hearing the door creak open down in the kitchen; reaching silently for her pants, fumbling for her jackknife in the dark. She heard boots lumping up the steep wood steps to the middle floor, then a creak on the cot, and she wondered if her mechanic had gotten drunk again.

The rain had called Mrs. Bease out of her bed that night, not sounds from next door. She stood at her window and saw Henry through the steaming rain. He tumbled down his porch steps and shook his head like a dog. He started to walk. When he glanced towards her house, he didn't see her. There was only a sliver of moon that night, and her robe was dark. That night she was upstairs, safe, at her bedroom window.

She watched him walk all the way up the hill, and after the longest time she saw, or she thought she saw, him slipping behind Louise's house. But that was ridiculous. She couldn't even see Louise's house from there. Still, she stood peering up the road.

There was rainy silence for so long that Louise almost thought that the person had gone to sleep. Finally, she heard the cot creak again and heard the clump of boots up the stairs to her bedroom.

Tonight, as she remembers the dark outline rising from the floor, she turns again toward the stairs. The silhouette grew in front of the streaming window. There was the black design of thin shoulders against the glass.

"Henry," she said.

Henry stood still as a stack of wood. But he was breathing. When he started to walk over to her, creaking the boards, Louise said, "Get out, Henry," in her dullest voice, "get out."

Henry stopped moving, then he turned, and slowly, slowly walked to the stairs. Louise saw his shoulders jump as thunder cracked outside. He glanced back, his eyes opened for a second, and for an instant they looked desperate. He ran down the stairs. Louise never heard him walk away from the house. She sat until dawn, imagining him crouched on the cinder block in front of the kitchen door.

Mrs. Bease pressed her face to the glass when she heard the crack of thunder, and she thought it was a shot. She was afraid for Louise. Finally, when she saw Henry coming down the hill again, she hurried down the stairs. She had two canes, and she called after him.

"You come back here. You've killed her." She came out into the rain—outside for the first time in months. "Come back here, Henry. I'll kill you."

Henry went to her, but Mrs. Bease wouldn't stop shouting.

"Mrs. Bease," he said, "Mrs. Bease." She was crying. Henry picked her up around the waist, light as a sack of twigs, and carried her into her house with her canes dragging on the ground.

"Shh," he said, clumping up the stairs, "I didn't kill anybody." He carried her up to her room. "Now change your goddamn clothes or you'll get pneumonia." He left and walked back out into the rain, down the road this time.

Louise remembers that night each time she sits on the porch with Janice. Each time Janice wonders aloud if she should leave, if the balance is unequal, bad to good; if Henry is bad enough to bother leaving; if Henry balances out worse than equal.

Louise sits and tries to weigh the balance of telling Janice, with her four babies, about Henry's visit. That would surely tip the scales.

She can't speak up. The first day she didn't know how to say it. And in just one day the secret was not about Henry, but between her and Henry. Now Henry always smiles at her, his teeth spanning wider each time.

But still, tonight, she can't envision why the police have come. Many times as she walked down the road on her way to the Pottery, she wanted to tap on Mrs. Bease's door and ask, "You're the one who calls the police. What happens in there? What did Gus see?"

Louise knows about Gus's visits even though she has only lived on the road for a bit more than a year. She can barely breathe tonight for all the stories she has heard.

Everybody is a tangle of rumors. She seems to be the only one who has not always been there. All that is really real to her on this road is washing her hair in the cold tap water, cool wet clay on her hands, and her afternoon mechanic off in the next town. His wife is as unbelievable as Janice's split lip.

Louise can't see Henry's arm dart out to grab Janice and slap her because that little wiry fierce-eyed man wouldn't stand a chance against Janice. Her wide hips sway with assurance when she perches one child on the right and the other on the left and walks around the house.

When Louise is not at the Pottery, gray with clay and thick with dust, she spends her days with Janice. They sit on the porch watching Mrs. Bease bob behind her windows next door.

Sometimes there is a moment on the porch when Louise knows she could ask Janice point blank what the story is. Today, for instance, she could have said,

"Janice, where'd you get that lip? Why don't you break his arm and be done with
it? Why don't you kick him out?''

Instead she had jostled baby Amy in her arms and walked into the kitchen for a
cigarette. But later she did stop by and see Mrs. Bease.

Mrs. Bease ignored the noise until she realized it was someone knocking at her
door. She was surprised to see Louise, but she offered her a cup of coffee and let
her sit down.

"You're the one who calls the police," Louise said. Mrs. Bease sat up straight
and pulled her solid feet back a full inch. Then she stood up and walked to the
window.

She pointed out. Janice was walking up the road to the apple orchard at the top.
JoJo dragged behind her holding on one of her arms while Emily ran in and out of
the drainage ditch. Janice had Amy slung over one boulder hip and Hal strapped
on her stomach. Her horsetail hair fell in a coarse braid down her back, and that
pink and white skin gleamed on her cheekbones.

"Gus's great-grandmother was an Indian. Gus had that broad face too." She
took a photograph from the table and pushed it toward Louise. "See how Janice
just blends in, right? You can tell she's his niece." She held the photo up next to
Louise's face. "You don't have the cheeks. It's in the eyes. Those eyes."

"My brothers are twins," Louise said.

"Do you have a picture?" Mrs. Bease asked. Louise shook her head. "Nothing
wrong with a picture," Mrs. Bease said, putting the photograph back on the table.
"You sure do remind me of him.

"Gus used to call her in for coffee," she said, looking out the window after
Janice. "When Gus was alive, Janice would sit and drink coffee with us. Is she
pregnant?"

"No," Louise said, "I don't think so."

But Mrs. Bease had started to talk. Usually she was silent as a tree, but she kept
on, not about Janice and Henry, not about herself, but about Gus. As she talked she
saw how Louise first smiled, and nodded, and then stopped smiling. At dusk she
backed slowly out of the house. But Mrs. Bease was glad she was gone. She was
glad to be left with Gus alive again; between Janice's cheekbones and Louise's
eyes, he was back.

Louise stands in the middle of the room rubbing her arms as though she is
washing off slick clay with the blue lights. She thinks about Mrs. Bease's question.
Janice says that nursing actually makes women more fertile. Janice and Henry
aren't very keen on plastics or pills.

Louise wonders finally about the midnight swims in the river. Everyone knows
about them. What other mothers on this hill drift away into the wilderness at night?

She drinks coffee with them sometimes, but they're beginning to keep silent
around her. She still has the faintest scars on her knuckles from the time she went

to the river with Janice. Janice had torn through the woods shouting, and Louise ran after, half afraid to follow, half afraid not to. Janice had gone right into the water in her jacket, jeans, and boots.

"Too cold for skinny-dipping," she called and pushed out farther. "Goddamn."

Louise watched for a few minutes before she waded in. Janice was holding onto a boulder and was hard to pry off.

"Damn kill-joy, go home," Janice said, shivering. But she followed Louise to the bank, and they stumbled slowly up out of the water.

There are only one or two, mostly her actually, with her empty nights, who linger on with Janice. Linger until midnight, when Henry is asleep upstairs or out somewhere; linger to drink beers and sometimes gin, but not often because when Janice is sober she's afraid of the river, and gin inspires her to swim.

Or Henry stays up and Louise wanders home, and maybe Janice and Henry fight and wake up Mrs. Bease. Or maybe Janice forgets her rules, and then wakes up the next day spitting dry white words and braiding her stiff, tangled hair with regret; and speaking fearful thoughts about babies to Louise through their coffee.

But that's the Janice that Louise likes. The one who sloughs off those children and goes wild to the river. Sometimes Louise feels as blind as a stone, as though her eyes are lined with clay. Because as she stands by her bed and concentrates with all of her rational might, she doesn't have any notion, no notion at all, why Janice is drawing this life out for herself. Louise can see four babies and maybe a bulge at Janice's waist, maybe not, and Janice's clear white-blue eyes that shake with anger when she thinks that she's done it again, and there's another baby coming. Louise wonders how it can be possible, that things that Janice doesn't want to happen, do happen. To Louise, each movement and each laugh and toss of Janice's big arms appears intentional, each spit seems to be a spit of control—the lid slammed down on a decision.

Everybody has wondered about Janice and Henry. When Mrs. Bease called the police in the middle of the night, all the machinations of justice were thrown into gear. The lieutenant nodded his head yes, Mary sent out a car, and the officers stepped up onto Janice's porch, around the old stump stools, the empty gas cans, around the old sofa with white bulbs of stuffing popping out.

This night they knock on the door, shying from Mrs. Bease's blue and white face. They walk inside with relief, hearing the crashes and Janice's voice hissing. When they get in, Stoll glances up at the grate in the sagging ceiling to see if Emily's little face is pressed there.

And when they walk in the door, Janice and Henry are at a standoff. Henry is in the kitchen with his boot in his hand, turning it over and over, his slight shoulders hunched. Janice, fierce as a big rat, is tapping her heels with an old plastic whiffle-ball bat. The officers come in and say hi, can they be of any help.

Stoll flicks his eyes to the other officer because they have missed it again. Janice and Henry are standing as though they never moved. The big pottery bowl is smashed on the floor, and the splatter of pot roast and gravy looks like an accident.

Last time when they arrived, Henry had had his shotgun in his hand and all the windows in the living room were blasted open: black jagged holes of cold autumn air. He had stood alone with his gun, the waving floorboards creaking under his feet like snow. Janice had been sitting at the kitchen table sipping her coffee and feeding Amy.

So most the people on the road know Janice and Henry's story, but even the ones who see it right up close don't know the story.

These officers know the story so well that they look forward to the visits. Janice has her hip thrust out and a cool beer for each as a way to thank them for their trouble.

The next day Janice goes out with her children, and they walk straight up to Louise's tiny kitchen for a morning chat because, really, the other mothers on this road are a little uncomfortable with Janice and, actually, in person, they keep their distance.

Janice talks again about going to Virginia, where there is a farm house that some relative from that box of old pictures left to decay. She will go with the four children and leave Henry to his shooting and his logging and his horses. Since she is talking to Louise, she expects a serious nod and a pressing for *hows* and *whens* and *can I help.* When Louise is practical, like those mothers, she thinks that Janice should hurry herself out of her present life; should dash that Henry on rocks, drop him in the river, and let him drift away like kindling.

But she finally can't be bothered to say so because last night her room was filled with a blue light that crept into her dreams and forced her awake. Even when she closed her eyes, the light flashed through the lids. She went downstairs, out onto the road, and she saw the police car parked in front of Janice and Henry's house. She walked down the hill, getting more curious with each step. Just as she was going to creep up the porch steps and look inside the window, she glanced over and saw Mrs. Bease, glaring white and blue in her window. Mrs. Bease, motionless and flashing, was watching her. And Louise saw herself. She saw herself creeping to the steps of Janice and Henry's house in the middle of the night, peering silently into the light and the violence; she saw Mrs. Bease, watching her, soaking her up like a year's fascination, and she knew that it wasn't Gus she resembled, but the old woman herself.

So the next day Louise doesn't bother to shy from the invitation to come to Virginia, to leave next week. She doesn't murmur about commitment to the Pottery or the mechanic because she is finally beginning to know this scenario. Instead she nods yes, "Sure, Janice," but stares through Janice to some other thing that she has been wondering about: about that mechanic's wife. She really listens only with one ear as Amy climbs up her shirt to grab her neck.

After a while, Janice heads back down the hill. The air is clear and the leaves are red and falling; the snow will be coming soon. Louise knows that Janice loves the winter, that Janice has purged herself with her talk of escape. Louise watches them walk away, and she sees Janice wave to Mrs. Bease, who shimmers white as a snowflake in her window.

Then the next day before dawn, Janice bundles those children up and climbs into the truck with Henry. They go into the woods. He chainsaws, and she splits wood, always keeping an eye on Amy, who crawls around the woodpile, and Hal, who sleeps in a lined orange crate. Emily and JoJo disappear and return. When they go home, their faces are apple red and tired, and they go to bed as soon as it is dark. So when Louise wanders down the hill that evening for a beer, she finds a dark house and silence, and she hears herself breathe out relief as she turns to go home.

"On This Road": Telling the Story

The process of writing a short story differs for me with each attempt. The approach that I used for "On This Road" was not planned or rigid. I knew in general what I wanted the story to be about, but I backed into it, trying one and then another character to tell it through. Each step I took seemed to circumvent the story. It was a long time before I settled on the final route.

Mrs. Bease was the character I began with. It was a woman like her who sparked the story, an old woman who watched from behind the chained door of her apartment. I saw her and wondered what she was watching and listening to, all locked up like that.

I used that woman's telephone once when I was locked out of my apartment. Her phone was just inside her door in a small foyer. She let me in and stepped aside, holding onto her walker as I called. There was a straight mahogany chair with a horsehair seat and a round phone table. They were fine antiques, incongruous in the small, peeling building. Her telephone was old and very heavy. As I dialed the realtor to get a key, I wondered if she had ever needed a weapon because that phone receiver would be a good one.

It was simple to imagine what would scare her so much that she would lock herself in and simultaneously fascinate her so deeply that she would open her door and expose herself, despite her fear.

I decided to write about what she was hearing. The presence of violence changes everyone, hidden violence even more so: because it is so clumsy and apparent, keeping it hidden requires complicity from everyone who senses it.

The predicament I created for myself with that decision surfaced quickly. I wanted to tell a story about violence, but it was violence that no one had seen. The characters whom I imagined performing it had obviously witnessed it, but they would by nature be too close to describe it without telling their own stories. I didn't want either of their stories. I wanted the story of their violence and their love—and its effect on Mrs. Bease.

She was the one I began writing about. I spent a long time with her. In an effort to distance myself from the real situation from which she had sprung, I took her out of the city. This was to clean the slate, so I could imagine her as I wanted and not be hindered by her real, straight gray hair or the scars and dents on her metal door.

I was concerned with two things. The first was what actually happened next door; the second was the character of Mrs. Bease as a voyeur. I wanted her to be gripped by what went on next door enough to tell the story.

I wrote about her as a longtime neighbor of Janice and Henry. I wanted a sense of permanence and inevitability in their coexistence. They would be part of each other's usual scenery.

The problem was that Mrs. Bease became too familiar with Janice and Henry to describe their story clearly. I imagined her as living next door for so long that she had become accustomed and inured to their lives. She had to push them away in order to live her own life. She would let real fear for them in only at night.

At the same time she was a character who was helpless to get in close enough. I had locked her up, put her behind a window, in a pitch black foyer with a whole yard separating her from Janice and Henry. I gave her a head full of her dead husband and all her losses. As I tried to imagine what she did and thought about all day, I saw her tangled up in her own history, engrossed in what was missing from her own life.

Finally, I supposed that perhaps the strongest effect that Janice and Henry had on Mrs. Bease was to remind her of her loss of Gus and set up chains of events that would lead to a strange longing in her for Lieutenant Keller.

At this point I could have pulled away, erased this Mrs. Bease, and made another old lady, who was nosier and more mobile. But I liked Mrs. Bease. She seemed like the right neighbor; the kind that would survive for a long time next to Janice and Henry.

The jump from Mrs. Bease to Louise was not far although it took me a long time to make it. It was not far because I didn't want them to be too different. The story just needed a character who was not locked away, who could get in closer to Janice and Henry and really feel the shock waves from their fights.

I thought about using the police or a babysitter. Someone who actually saw the blows. But I finally realized that seeing the violence was not important. It was as unimportant as describing the minute physical action of pulling a trigger. The repercussions were at the center of this story.

So, oddly, as soon as I found Louise, a character who could actually see the fights if I wanted her to, I shifted my concern to the billowing silence sent out by hidden violence—to what the silence rustled up in people, specifically in this new character, Louise.

I should add at this point that when I turned to insinuation, Janice and Henry were suddenly easily conjured. Once I decided only to suggest what actually went on between them, I knew I would have to do it with their actions rather than their thoughts. They are the luxurious characters for me, whom I step back from, and allow their actions or scenes to spell out their characters. The pictures of Janice strapping children on her hips and Henry walking into the woods with his axe handle bobbing came easily into my eyes.

To get in close to Janice and Henry, Louise had to be a camouflaged character. She would not be a policeman or a babysitter. She needed to be low-key and versatile. The job I gave her, her age, and her quietness made her unremarkable. She was a character who was able to sidle up to the people on the road almost unnoticed. She had nothing apparent at stake. She was a stranger, so the women would be interested in her only in the beginning, as an oddity. She could move in and out of their houses, the Pottery, and even the mechanic's arms without raising any eyebrows too high.

I presuppose that if you imagine a character clearly, you know some things that they would or would not do. Louise was someone who would let herself all the way in, while Mrs. Bease kept herself back, held away by her own history. Mrs. Bease and the women on the road kept their eyes blinded with the clay that Louise tried to wipe out of her own. Louise was allowed, and allowed herself, to live vicariously. She was fascinated with watching all of Janice and Henry: their violence and their domestic togetherness.

Ironically, such a passive, chameleon of a central character needed to move in a dangerous world, a world that was exciting. Otherwise there would be no story, just a bland woman living day to day. Her life was so calm and interior that she needed to be poked at by the twigs of other people's chaos, to be shocked into considering herself, into being an interesting character.

Here were two elements I could work with: a world of violence that I had no way to describe and a character who needed to be startled awake.

The only way such a passive character could get involved in such a world was vicariously, as a voyeur. Louise did not pull Henry into her bed that night (although it might have been interesting if she had). She did not go visit and interrogate the mechanic's wife, or tell Janice about Henry's visit, precisely because this story needed a voyeur, a hungry exaggeration of the watchful woman on the road, of Mrs. Bease, and even the wide-eyed police. They were the simple watchers who knew what was going on but stayed distant enough to keep their own lives separate and uninvolved.

To get close enough to tell the story, Louise needed to be completely absorbed by the role of voyeur. Keeping her own life intact had to be dependent on her involvement with other people's danger. The relationship that developed there was perfectly complementary. Her companionship and silence could be exchanged for vicarious domesticity, sexuality, and violence.

This is where the story shifted again. Now it was centered on a character being shaken awake by something so fascinating and awful that it had become invisible to everyone around her.

With these parts of the story turning over, I still had to build its practical frame. One thing was clear to me as I kept writing. I knew that at least parts of the story had to be told in the present. I thought that they ought to be the parts that were most difficult to believe, that seemed least real: Mrs. Bease's dark trip to the telephone, the police station scene, Louise's blue-flashing bedroom and her sleepless night, and the policemen's frightened trip up Janice and Henry's porch steps.

These were the bizarre scenes that happened again and again, composing an ordinary routine. They became so mythologized by the characters involved (except Louise) that they were performed almost ritualistically, like a dreamily remembered dance, and then forgotten in the daylight. These scenes would disappear for the characters themselves so quickly that I knew that I had to write about them in the present. That was the closest I could get. I wouldn't describe the violence, but at least I could erase the barrier of time and mythology between it and the reader.

I also wanted to make it clear that the stories were not just rumors, imagined and spread by the women on the road or by Louise. If Louise's reliability was suspect, I didn't want it to be over the fact of violence. That was the given, the splash on her face that made her start opening her eyes.

For me the scenes that seem most real are the ones Louise remembers, the scenes from the past: when Henry snapped the phone cord from the wall, or when Louise and Janice sat together on the porch, or even when Louise told Henry to get out of her bedroom. Those scenes do not need the immediacy of the present tense because they are bearable memories for Louise. They burned clearly and distinctly for her.

The action of the story (from Mrs. Bease's phone call to the arrival of the officers at Janice and Henry's) took place within a twenty-minute time frame for similar reasons. Those blossoms of violence burst and disappear so rapidly that it was hard to remember them; but the memory, however quickly masked and dimmed, spreads thin roots around everything and everybody nearby. The roots lay gently wound around the everyday ordinary life of the people on that road. I wanted to get the facts down as quickly as they actually came, to explain the reluctant watchfulness of the community—and the tug on Louise.

When I began this story, rather than having a clear, linear tale to tell, outlining the plot and characters and then filling them in, the opposite happened. The form evolved only after circling the characters and subject for a long time. The difficult part was finding which part of the story to close in on, which character to tell it through—which character I knew best. The evolving intention of the story determined its shape. I began with the trappings and the folk. They came easily, touched off by that woman in her chained apartment.

• A PLAIN SENSE OF THINGS •
by Paul S. Allison

Elizabeth awoke because there was no cry; the sun streamed across Harry's thighs. She walked slowly to the baby's room. She already sensed, her feet on tiptoe, that Katherine was not breathing, had probably stopped breathing hours ago. And she stared into the bassinet where Katie lay, the knowledge setting in so swiftly and fully that there was only time for a gasping intake of breath before acceptance.

They both had cried when the baby's pale chubby face had been covered at the hospital. But she had cried for the sadness of it. The tragedy of death. Then there was the cool grip of calm which took her through the funeral, through the empathy of friends, through the packing of toys and infant clothes into boxes to be stored in the hot sloping attic.

A few weeks later, when she realized that she had not escaped grief by this calmness but had embraced it, she felt she had done something noble. She had resisted Harry's tears in the beginning, and now she resisted his cheerfulness. She knew his cheerfulness was only partly put on. He really had gotten over it, she thought; this added effort was for her sake. But she would sit in the rocking chair—the one they had found in an antique shop together for the nursery, the one that creaked just enough to comfort—and she would ball her fingers into fists and think, This is not something I will get over. I do not want to get over this. And the chair would creak its comfort. She would imagine herself the subject of a painting. Everything in shadows, or silhouettes, the one-word titles etched on gilded plaques beneath each frame—*Sorrow* or *Mourning* or *Grief.*

Sometimes she would go to the attic and feel the bassinet, smell the blanket, look at the clothes, when she felt as if she could fly—a good day. But these days were rare, monitored, easily kept in check. She wanted most of all to remain in this state, to maintain the balance. I will not yield to extremes, she would think, I will not lose her completely. She envied women of other countries who were permitted to wail and weep for days, wearing black for the rest of their lives, an eternal state of mourning.

They had decided to come to the lake with Dan and Maggie and their girls after all. The plans had been made months ago, "And besides," Harry had told her, "it will be good for you to get away from the house." So they had gone, in separate cars, to the same cabin they had rented the year before: a small A-frame with the tall windows and a red roof. It was tucked into a grove of pines a dozen yards or so from the lake bank. Sara and Amanda, the girls, loved the smell, exclaiming that it smelled like Christmas.

It had rained the first day they arrived at the cabin. Elizabeth spent most of the afternoon cleaning and unpacking their things. From the bedroom she could hear them on the porch complaining about the rain. "Maybe we'll go fishing later," she heard Harry say to the girls. "Fish like the rain."

"Well I don't like the rain," Sara said.

"Well I don't like worms," said Amanda.

Elizabeth sat on her bed, concentrating on the sounds of the voices and the rain, trying to ignore the creaking of the porch swing which creaked too loud and too long: the sound seemed to solidify in her throat; when she swallowed she could feel it wrench in her gut like a hook.

The following day was glorious. As soon as they awoke, the children wanted to go swimming. So after breakfast they all went down to the lake. They ran ahead of her, throwing their armloads of towels, lawn-chairs, and suntan oil on the sand, rushing toward the water. The soles of their white bare feet—even Harry's— reflected the sun in flashes as they ran. Harry looked over his shoulder, inviting her with a thrust of his head, but she waved him on to join the others on the dock.

Sara and Amanda, the children, had already jumped into the water, noses held, squealing. Dan and Maggie watched over them, and from her stance among the discarded towels, Elizabeth watched Harry run between them and dive into the water with the girls. He poked out his head a moment later, flipping his hair so that water sprayed in a wide glittering arc above them, splashing into tiny spittle pools on the surface of the black water. She waited for the deep laughter to come from his mouth that was opened and stretched into a smile. Even from this distance she could see the white of his teeth, the pink of his tongue. And when the laughter did come, she had already stiffened, a preparation, and was unaffected.

"I will stay here," she had told them softly, wondering as the words came out when she had acquired this new way of speaking—like a child, choosing short articulate sentences, carefully forming each word as if she were practicing. Maggie had whistled through her teeth and put a hand through her light hair then. Maggie who had had three miscarriages before her first girl, Sara, was born. Maggie who had tried to comfort her, who kissed her forehead with quivering lips, who stood by, poised to receive the breakdown that would surely come—"Surely at the funeral it will sink in," Elizabeth had heard her say to someone. But the funeral had come and gone. And on the bank then, Maggie had raced away with them, only Harry looking back.

Even now, at the lake, Elizabeth felt Maggie's scrutinizing gaze every so often. Was she still expecting her to fall apart? She watched them all. The sun: so bright that she had to squint to see beyond the shadow of her hand; the lake swirling dark ripples against the boat that was too red, too small, too perfect roped around the splintered wooden pole on the other side of the dock. This could be a painting or a dream, she thought, shutting her eyes against the pleasure and letting the sinking feeling that she welcomed now pull like a coarse string through her body from the inside out. Her legs folded beneath her; she felt the string pushing out between her shoulder blades, forcing her onto her side. Arms and legs sprawled at first, then tucked: curled against her stomach and still-tender breasts.

She hadn't wanted to come here. When Dan and Maggie had asked them if they still wanted to go to the lake with them and the kids, she had wanted to cancel. She considered it a trap. But she had agreed because it would have sapped her strength to come up with reasons to refuse. Anyway, Harry wanted to go, and how could she say no to him about this? He meant well. They all meant well. And she had to admit, now that she was here, that the sun felt wonderful. The air was warm and blew her hair across her eyes. She listened to the splashings on the lake, the squeals, the shouts. It was harder, here, to keep the balance.

She tried to remember Katherine's face. The baby had just begun to develop distinctive features: the nose had lengthened, the space between her nose and lips had broadened, the lips themselves fuller. Lying in the sun, her body tingling with warmth, she brought forth the image for the thousandth time. She wished suddenly that she had seen her die. It would be impossible to forget. Had she cried out, her eyebrows coming together, her angry face pouting? Had her eyes been opened or closed? Had she just stopped breathing as she slept, serene, relieved? "It's a mystery," the doctor had said. "It's as if they just give up." Elizabeth hadn't, until then, thought of life as something so difficult to keep hold of.

I could die here, she said, talking to the man that woke her, who she couldn't see because of the sun in her eyes. Until he spoke she thought this was still a dream, the man would make love to her silently, touching her until she would awake—a frequent dream—and she moved her head to smile. But he said her name, "Elizabeth," softly, and she started, sitting up, sniffing the breeze that was filled with the scent of wet hair and skin.

"Harry?"

He brushed the hair from her face. "Come and swim."

She rubbed her eyes. "Swim?"

"Come and swim," he said again, putting a hand on her arm and stroking.

"You go."

"Come on."

She shook her head, knowing he wouldn't stop now. He thought he was winning by getting her out of the house, to this place of lovely scenes. But this very knowledge secured her, and she let him tug. He pulled on her arm until she stood up. He pulled too hard; the squeeze of his hand left white marks on her wrist. How simple it was for pain to make her come alive.

Dan and Maggie were in the water now, the children in the perfect little red boat, splashing them with the oars.

"Come on, baby."

This was said softly: a gentle command. He would be hurt, but she only walked a little way with him, down to the edge of the water, where tadpoles darted away from her toes which clouded the water with dust.

"You go ahead," she said to him, giving him a push as he watched her from over his shoulder. It would have taken so little to make him happy then, but the only thing she could do was to splash water at him with her foot. He smiled anyway, even laughed to make her feel less guilty. She heard the sounds from the children calling to her, beckoning Harry who had already dived and disappeared only to emerge farther off, leaving no mark, no path for her to follow even if she had wanted to.

All this was for her—a push to get her to live again. The lake, the cabin, the company. They were becoming impatient with her. They wanted her to return to them. She squatted, feeling the seat of her bathing suit moisten from the water. The tadpoles drew near after she had become still. She looked up when Maggie pulled herself from the water onto the dock like some graceful fish. Elizabeth watched her shimmering calves as she approached. The tadpoles scattered again when Maggie knelt beside her, her knees sinking into the soft water's edge, her hair dripping.

"Let's go into town, Liz," she said, "just the two of us."

Elizabeth wiped her mouth with the back of her hand, feeling the cold water against her lips. She didn't want to go. She wanted to go back up on the bank and sleep in the sun. "Why?" she asked.

"Well, we should probably get some groceries. We've gone through just about everything we brought with us—and the kids will be hungry."

Elizabeth looked out to the boat. Harry and Dan were gripping either side of it, rocking it; the girls were screaming in gleeful terror. "Which kids are you talking about?" She said it out of habit, a joke between them about their husbands. She added quickly, "I suppose you're right." She didn't look at Maggie's face, which she was sure held a smile. Maggie lunged at the opening.

"Do you remember when we were here the last time, we rented that crazy touring bicycle-for-two?" Maggie laughed, and touched Elizabeth's shoulder. "God, you were so funny—and that cat! You swerved to miss a cat and ran us right off the road into a ditch, oh, God!"

"I remember," she said firmly; she wanted to avoid more remembrances. She stood up and walked in up to her thighs, then dove into the water. It was cold, freezing. She wasn't prepared for that. Her entire body seemed to contract, then explode from the shock; the air rushed from her mouth. She turned in the water and pushed off the bottom with her toes. She emerged, gasping, rubbing the water-slicked hair from her face, trembling as if she had been struck.

"Are you all right?" Maggie said, walking toward her.

"I didn't think it would be so cold," she said. She rubbed her temples with the heels of her hands.

Maggie laughed. "This is mountain water, remember?"

Elizabeth walked up the bank to the towels and wrapped herself in the one she had been lying on, hot from the sun. Maggie called to the others, telling them that they were going to town. They all stopped splashing for a moment and waved. "Good-bye, good-bye," they called; even the children's voices sounded conspiratorial to her.

Inside, Elizabeth threw her bathing suit over a chair and smoothed her stomach with her hands. Except for the stretch marks and slight bulge, her body, too, had betrayed her. There had been times, when her stomach had swollen, her navel crushed and red, when she felt as if her body was no longer hers, but existed only for "the child," that she would have given it up. Her body had disgusted her then. It repulsed her now. She dressed quickly. She heard Maggie humming loudly in the next room a song that was vaguely familiar. Just then, Maggie began to sing the words to the end of the song:

> But you'd look sweet
> upon the seat
> of a bicycle built for two.

Maggie sang in a loud, self-mocking voice, obviously wishing to include Elizabeth in her joke. She frowned as she pulled on a baggy red t-shirt. It was that song that had prompted them to rent the two-seater bicycle last year. Elizabeth had found it in one of the old songbooks in the piano bench there. She didn't play well, but she had mastered that one, and they had all sung it one night after Maggie's girls were in bed, when they were all a little drunk, Maggie and Dan dancing around the room, she, sitting on Harry's lap, fingers working the keys. Almost a year to the very day. She was angry. She hadn't wanted to think of that.

Maggie came into the room, smiling. "Remember that song?" she asked. Then she laughed and walked over to the window, humming again. "I can't think of the first lines though—how's it start, do you remember, Liz? It's a woman's name— Lucy or Gracie or something."

Elizabeth sat on the bed and put on her shoes. "I don't know," she said. Maggie turned from the window and looked at her. She came and sat next to her on the bed. Elizabeth stiffened and let her foot drop to the floor. She felt Maggie's eyes on her, expecting next an arm around her shoulder or a kiss on the cheek, or perhaps Maggie herself would begin to cry, hoping it would trigger something in her. Elizabeth met her gaze.

"Why won't you let me help you?" Maggie said.

"How on earth can you help me?"

"I know how you're feeling—"

"You don't know how I'm feeling, Maggie." Elizabeth stood up and walked to the dresser. "You think it's the same, you and me, but it's not the same."

"Of course it's not the same," Maggie said. "But I know what it's like to lose a child. After the third one, I didn't want to try again. He was my only boy, you know." She stood up and walked over to Elizabeth. "Things will get better," she said. "I promise."

Elizabeth smiled and glanced at Maggie. "You're right. How much money do you think we'll need?"

Maggie stepped back and looked at her. "I'll get my purse," she said and walked into the other room.

Elizabeth opened Harry's wallet to get some traveler's checks. As she placed it back on the dresser, the flap which covered the photos fell open. On the front panel was Katherine's baby picture. Elizabeth stared at it in confusion. Five days old, black matted hair. She wondered if he had just forgotten to take it out. Surely he knew it was there. She put the wallet down and went to the window. Harry was lying on the dock with Dan and the kids, stretched out in the sun. Did he look at it often, she wondered. Did he cry over her still?

"Ready, Liz?"

Maggie was calling from the front porch. Elizabeth went out to meet her. Sara and Amanda came running when they saw them heading for the car. The skirts of their pink and green bathing suits flapped as they ran.

"Bring us something," Sara said.

"Popsicles," Amanda chimed, "with ice cream in the middle."

Elizabeth sat in the driver's seat and dug for the keys in her purse. She couldn't enjoy the girls. They made her uncomfortable. When she looked at them, she could only picture them as a part of a trio, Katherine the third, in a yellow bathing suit with bright blue flowers splattered all over it—forever missing. Elizabeth actually heard that in her head— "forever missing." She found the keys and started the car.

Maggie told the girls that they would bring something back for them. "Behave yourselves," she said as they backed away. "And don't drown while I'm gone." The girls giggled and ran back to the water. Maggie said that as a joke, but immediately turned to Elizabeth with wide eyes. Elizabeth wouldn't smile to relieve her. Maggie waved feebly to them as they drove away.

They didn't talk until they were on the main road into town. And then only Maggie said anything. She suddenly laughed and said, "Daisy!" Elizabeth just looked at her. "Daisy!" she repeated. "That's how the song starts, remember?"

The general store, like the cabin, though rustic, was full of all the modern conveniences. When they entered, Elizabeth smelled coffee. There were small bins of various brands below the counter, and the aroma filled the small store. It made her feel hungry. The place was crowded, being Saturday afternoon. People moved slowly down the narrow aisles with their baskets, smiling an "excuse me" to one another. One very large woman seemed to have the only child in the store. Elizabeth heard his voice coming from within the maze of aisles.

"I love this place," Maggie said. "It has absolutely everything."

Elizabeth nodded. She felt comfortable here. She almost wished, now, that she had come alone. She was unknown here. This was a welcome change from the expectations and knowledge of the others. She picked up a wooden basket for the groceries and walked across the shiny hardwood floor to the canned goods aisle. A man smiled at her as he reached for some chicken soup, and she was grateful that she could simply smile back. It was a relief to know that these people didn't care anything about her, whether she was happy or unhappy, whether her baby had died or not, whether she was sick or healthy. And as she wandered down the aisles, she relished her own anonymity. She smiled a greeting to everyone she saw, she even offered to reach a box of cereal one woman was having trouble with. Maggie shopped beside her in questioning silence except for an occasional inquiry. "Do you think this is all right? Does Harry like tuna?"

The line at the check-out was long. They set their baskets down on the floor to wait. Maggie flipped through the local newspaper. Elizabeth watched the others in line. The woman with the boy was in line a few yards behind her. She was extremely fat, with a small bosom and large hips and stomach. The boy was about four years old. He was continually busy, handling the groceries in the basket, fingering the candy on the opposite shelf. Every time he did, he received a firm slap from his mother. She couldn't move fast enough to hit his bottom every time, so she just struck anywhere—his shoulder, his hand, his back, his head. Then she would laugh an apology to those around her. She was showing off. She never told the boy to stand still or to stop or to behave, and except for a brief pause to rub the slapped place, the boy went right on fingering everything. It was a game. They both enjoyed the attention they were getting.

Elizabeth watched them until she couldn't stand it anymore. She turned away in disgust but could still hear the slaps, the short yelps from the boy, the laughter of the woman, and she wished that someone would make them stop. It wasn't the abuse itself that made her angry, but the flagrant show for attention. They were begging to be noticed, to be reckoned with. They were a freak-show, their abnormalities taken from behind the curtain and put on display.

The line was moving. Elizabeth lifted her basket to the counter behind Maggie's. The clerk smiled sympathetically at them—his apology for the woman's behavior in his store. She glanced back to the woman. She was staring at her son who had just taken a candy bar off the shelf. He held it at the tip; he was threatening to open it. They stared at each other, mother and child, for a moment. Then, as if on cue, as if this had been rehearsed for hours, they moved at once, the woman bounded to him, but the boy was quick, and ran toward the counter. He bumped against Elizabeth's leg. "Sorry," he said, pausing. The woman grabbed hold of his shirt while he paused. The candy bar dropped to the floor beside Elizabeth's foot. Elizabeth saw the look of triumph on the woman's face, eyes sparkling, as she began to spank him. Elizabeth shuddered, felt herself breathing heavily. She bent down and picked up the candy bar that the boy had dropped. She stepped toward them. "You dropped this," she said to the boy, holding out the candy bar. But he backed away from Elizabeth and drew nearer to his mother, who put a protective arm around his shoulder. This infuriated her. She threw the candy bar at the boy's feet and walked over to the counter and paid for her groceries. Maggie watched her with a slight smile on her face. As they walked out, Elizabeth heard the woman spanking the boy again.

"You drive," she said, throwing Maggie the keys. "I'm too angry."

Maggie laughed and started the car. "It doesn't seem fair, does it? That a woman like that has children."

"I really don't want to talk about this, all right?" and Elizabeth turned on the radio.

At supper, Elizabeth knew that Maggie had told everyone what had happened at the store. She had taken a nap while Harry filleted and fried the fish that the girls had caught while they were gone. Now they ate in silence. She felt them watching her. Even the children seemed to watch her with anticipation, as if they were waiting for her to perform for them or hand them candy or win a million dollars.

Harry leaned toward her. "How's the fish, babe?" he asked.

"It's fine."

"I caught the biggest one," Sara said. "We had to throw two of Amanda's back."

Amanda pursed her lips and stuck a fork into her fillet.

"Daddy said we can fish in the boat tomorrow," Sara said.

"Do you want to come with us, Aunt Liz?" Amanda said.

She didn't look up. She poked a French-fry with her fork. What did they want from her? What was going on? She looked around the table at each of them, and it dawned on her. They thought it was over. They thought she was "cured." They thought that her outburst this afternoon had been the culmination and disintegration of her grief, that in one swift blow, everything would settle back to normal. They were waiting for her to crack a joke, to go to the piano and play "Daisy, Daisy," and in the quiet and stares her mind seemed to stammer. She couldn't focus on anything and forgot what she had been thinking. She put her fork down and closed her eyes. Harry touched her arm.

"Elizabeth, are you all right?" he said.

She looked at him, and remembered the picture. "Harry," she said, "you keep a picture of Katherine in your wallet."

He kept staring.

"I saw it. Right in front. Her hospital picture."

"Yes," he said.

She stood up. She went into the bedroom and got her purse. "Do you know," she said, coming back to the table and opening her purse, "that I don't have one picture of her? There isn't one thing that I have left of her." She dumped the contents of her purse onto the table, spilling drinks and clanking the plates. "Do you know I thought I could control this?" she said. She looked at Harry. "Isn't that a scream?" And she went out of the kitchen, out of the cabin, and walked down to the dock.

She stepped into the red boat and sat facing the lake. The sunset was breathtaking. From habit, she tried to counter her senses by recalling the things that would make her remember the pain—Katherine's picture, her sweet face against the blanket, the coffin, the lacy dress, her white stern expression. But it had little effect. Instead, her body came alive. Sitting there, she felt as if she had been lifted and emptied into the air. Her thoughts flew, hovering through her senses, attaching briefly to only what she could see or touch or hear or smell or taste.

She lay still in the boat, listening to the quiet splash of the water against its sides. It was still there, the pain. She had been afraid of losing it altogether. But it was there, lodged within her: a comfort. She dipped her hand into the scarlet ripples of the lake. The water was unexpectedly warm, and it sent tingles up her neck and down between her shoulder blades. And she thought, I will watch this sunset until all the colors are gone. When the colors are gone, I will go back.

Finding
"A Plain Sense of Things"

I wanted to write a story examining grief. That is the one thing of which I am absolutely sure. The rest is speculation. Yet, even as I say that, I know very well that some elements in the story have a more direct correspondence with reality than others. The most difficult part of writing an essay about the sources of a story is that sometimes you just don't know. At least that is the game I like to play: to pretend that my genius allowed me to create something outside of myself, that I had been inspired. The truth is, I think I know what many of the sources are for this story. The problem is, I don't know whether or not to divulge them.

Also, many of my intentions changed, as the story changed, during its writing, so that now, as I recall the primary sources behind the story, I realize that those very sources are no longer the direct motives behind the final product but simply an antecedent to the secondary sources which were demanded by the very act of writing. This, to me, is significant. If the story dictates the sources that I used, then can I really talk about the "sources" of a story? Or should I talk about the story itself: how it changed, how it demanded change?

Also, there is the problem of defining the source of a story. Does the source of a story define the people, events, and places which influence the characters, plot, and setting in the story, or does it define the motives, emotions, and preoccupations which lie behind the writing of the story itself? And, more important, how much does the writing "process" affect the sources that have been chosen?

In this essay, I wish to explain the changes in my story from the first draft to the final product, why I thought those changes were necessary and how those changes refocused my intentions for the story. In doing so, I hope to examine some of the obvious sources as well as the more subtle ones.

As I said in the beginning, I wanted to write a story about grief. This subject deeply interested me because grief seems to be a no-win situation. To cling to the lost is to give up living; but to grieve for the lost is to lose them altogether. I wanted to write a story that explored the dynamics of the grieving process, the subtleties of the typical "denial, mourning, anger, acceptance" sequence, and even to have a character who fought against that "given" kind of response.

But I am already ahead of myself. "A Plain Sense of Things" began in the midst of another story. I had become bored with a story I was working on, and to prevent myself from wasting the whole afternoon staring at a computer screen, I began to write something new. I had been preoccupied with this idea of grief for some time, and the new story quickly molded itself to accommodate this preoccupation. It began like this:

> *In the beginning it was as if she were dreaming. The sun; so bright that she had to squint to see beyond the shadow of her hand; the pond swirling black ripples against the boat that was too red, too small, too perfect roped around the splintered wooden pole of the dock.*

I knew, from the very start, that the character was grieving a death. At first, I didn't know whose. But as I continued writing the scene, it became clear that it was the loss of a child. For one thing, I had unconsciously chosen to make the character a woman. In the first sentence, "she" had been used over "he." Secondly, the more I wrote, the more I felt the grief to be a private, possessive kind of grief, a grief that manifested itself from within the body, that she would feel to be hers alone.

The story continued from that point in the same vein. But a problem soon developed. I had been writing the story in attachment to Elizabeth, and, by doing so, I wasn't sure if the reader could understand what had happened. I certainly didn't want the story to be a "Can you guess what is ailing the heroine?" kind of story. And I didn't want the story simply to be about a woman losing her child. I wanted the story to focus on grief. I wanted Elizabeth's grief to be the story. So I backed up and began the story with a paragraph that got everything out in the open: "Elizabeth awoke because there was no cry." With the child's death at the beginning of the story, the reader had to focus not on the sentimental material of the baby's death, but on Elizabeth and her grief. In this way, the story is truly hers.

I don't believe that Elizabeth is based on any particular person in my life. Perhaps she is a conglomerate of many individuals. For me, it is difficult even to picture her. It is possible that she is more symbolic than actual, which may be a problem with the story. The two characters in the story that I do know were based on real individuals are Maggie and the woman in the store.

Maggie was loosely based on a relative of mine. From her, I borrowed all the physical attributes—a husband, two little girls, three miscarriages. But Maggie's personality was her own. In Maggie, I found a woman still so torn by the loss of her first three children that she needed the grief of Elizabeth to sustain her. But Elizabeth was not willing or able to share her grief. Maggie, then, appears to be overbearing, nosey, and insensitive to Elizabeth when, in reality, she is simply crying out to grieve the children whom she had never properly grieved. The fact that Maggie's miscarriages are considered "lesser" deaths is most clearly seen when Elizabeth tells her: "You think it's the same, you and me, but it's not the same."

There is a tug-of-war between the women: Elizabeth wants to suspend her grief, "to maintain the balance" so she won't lose her daughter altogether, while Maggie tries to push Elizabeth into grieving so that she can share in it, and, by her doing so, Maggie can experience the release of her own bottled mourning.

The woman in the store is based very closely on a woman I saw in a grocery store in my hometown. She did very nearly the same thing to her child—I can't remember if it was a boy or a girl—but I remember it was the same game they played: slapping and defying for attention. I used this scene at a point when Elizabeth had wanted to escape from the responsibility of friendship and love into the anonymity of strangers. With strangers, she could choose what she wanted to reveal; she could avoid grieving by avoiding those who expected her to grieve. But this woman, this fat, attention-starved woman, and her son showed her the impossibility of such a life. Anonymity was a fantasy. When Elizabeth reached for the candy bar, she unconsciously gave up her last attempt at isolation.

The setting of the story was taken from a memory I have of a fishing camp my family went to in Canada. The lake was dark and ice-cold. There was a long, skinny dock that we fished from, where we caught tadpoles. And there was a red boat that I refused to get in to fish. The cabin in the story is a glorification of the one we stayed in, but the smells and the atmosphere are the same.

I wanted to use a setting in the story which would contribute to Elizabeth's crisis. By getting her away from the house, away from the immediate reminders of her daughter's death, I thought I could really get at the heart of the matter. A vacation, then, with Dan, Maggie, and the kids, which had been planned before Katherine's death, was an ideal way physically to relocate Elizabeth in the story. This very basic change at the beginning of the story began the escalating changes which caused Elizabeth to evaluate the conditions of her loss.

That, of course, is what finally happens. The story is a kind of emotional picaresque. Though she does eventually plunge into what may be called the normal grieving process, she resists it every step of the way. In the beginning, she refuses to live. She protests the death of her daughter by refusing to live without her. She is content merely to exist. This protest so drains her emotionally and physically that she has no strength to refuse her husband when he wants to take her on vacation. There she is forced to live. She must communicate, however minimally, with Maggie and Dan and the kids. Her body feels the warmth of the sun, the coldness of the lake. She is reminded of the past that existed without her daughter and faced with a present that reserves no space for her. Then, feeling pressures of her surroundings, she tries to find solace in the company of strangers but is shown that that, too, is not a viable solution.

When Elizabeth sits at the supper table with everyone assuming that she has been "cured," she realizes how isolated she has become. She exclaims, "There isn't one thing that I have left of her." She has stripped herself of everyone and everything except the pain of her loss which she feels "in her gut like a hook." This realization of isolation and pain takes her out to the water and to the sunset where she is able to use the pain, "a comfort" now, as a path to a new kind of order for her life. There, she finds freedom and beauty in her pain. There, she awaits her return to a plain sense of things.

The title, "A Plain Sense of Things," is taken from a poem by Wallace Stevens called "The Plain Sense of Things." More aptly, it came from a line from that poem: "After the leaves have fallen, we return/To a plain sense of things." At first, I had used that line as an epigraph for the story and had given the story the title "Tadpoles." But while I was revising the story, this original title became inappropriate. In the first draft, the story had ended when Elizabeth noticed only the physical world around her; she had minimalized her loss to the thought that a tadpole might rub against her fingers. This ending was unsatisfying to me. It seemed to work against the entire story by forcing Elizabeth into the very predicament that she had tried so desperately to escape. The irony was unrewarding and unwarranted.

So I took out the tadpoles and made her view the glory of the sunset along with the pain of her loss. By experiencing the extremes of both the physical and emotional worlds, she finds a place to stand. "A Plain Sense of Things," then, becomes a more appropriate title and is reflected in Elizabeth's final thoughts: I will watch this sunset until all the colors are gone. When the colors are gone, I will go back.

• LIGHT ON THE RETINA •

by Mary Anne Tumilty

Ever since her father had left, when Claire's mother looked at her, she saw somebody else.

"Stand over there against the wall so I can see what you look like."

Claire, standing there, fidgeting shyly in the long green skirt and sweater her mother had just bought for her, was almost the same size as her mother now, and under the sweater there was the beginning of form and shape.

"Stand still and let me look at you." Then there was that awful sigh as if Claire had done something wrong. "I don't think there is any of me in you, or at least none that I can see," her mother said at last, disappointed.

Sometimes Claire stayed in the bathroom, looking at herself in the mirror, to see if she could find her mother's part. But the first thing she saw was her eyebrows. They were her father's, thick and dark, exactly like his. She liked her eyebrows. At twelve she was old enough to know the difference between dramatic and plain. The rest of her face belonged to her father, too, her feminine features built on his masculine structure.

Sometimes, Claire thought her eyes were it. Small turned-down ovals that didn't match. At school this year, when the nurse had given her the eye test, she had missed the bottom row.

"OK, honey, let's just do the last line one more time to make sure."

Claire hated it when the nurse called her "honey," like she was a baby or something. I know everything I need to know, Claire had wanted to tell her. I know what's important, and I don't need some strange woman dressed up like it's Halloween to tell me. Then the nurse had smiled at Claire and handed her a slip that said her mother should take her to be examined by their family eye doctor as soon as possible. The word "examined" upset Claire, and she put the slip in the back of her desk at school where no one would find it.

Her mother wore glasses. But only when she drove the car or when she went to the movies. Her mother's eyes were perfectly fine for reading books or for sewing Claire's clothes. They were perfect for details. As far as distance was concerned, her mother told her it wasn't all that difficult; after a while she could recognize shapes, and then she could easily make up the rest to fool people into thinking she saw what they saw. Maybe that was why she had trouble seeing Claire.

Before the Christmas holidays, Claire's teacher, Miss Evans, angry that cigarette butts had been found in the girls' bathroom, ordered the class to clean out their desks.

"Take everything out. I'm going to inspect every single desk in this room."

Claire's desk was always organized. Health, Science, and Math on the left, English, Reading, and Spelling on the right, with the three pencils the school district provided separating them. Bored with this ritual Claire considered beneath her, she began obediently stacking her books, one by one, on the top of her desk, when the white slip fell to the floor right in front of Miss Evans.

"What is this, Claire? You mean to tell me this has been sitting in your desk since October. I'm surprised at you, Claire."

Claire blushed. "I guess I just forgot."

"Well, I'm sending a note home to make sure your mother sees this."

Claire watched Miss Evans march up to her desk with the condemning white slip in her hand. And then that idiot Joshua laughed at her.

"What's the matter, 'fraid I'll call you four eyes, huh?"

Claire glared at him; no boy was going to bother her. "What do I care? I'm better than you at everything." And she turned her back on him letting him know he wasn't worth her time.

"You're just a dumb, ugly girl, that's all," he said.

When Claire handed her mother Miss Evans's note, Claire knew her mother would start up.

"Great, just what I need. How can I afford something like this right before Christmas? Well, your father will just have to pay for this. You can take this note with you when you go to visit on Friday."

Claire looked at the Christmas tree, stunned. "Aren't I staying here with you for Christmas vacation?"

"Your father wants you to spend at least a little time with him. I think he wants you to see the restaurant."

Claire stared at her mother, forgetting that her mother would be able to see the small details.

"Just for overnight, OK?" her mother said then.

In her bedroom, Claire's thoughts spread out thinner and thinner, like the dim pink light of the lamp on the dresser. Her mother was still mad that he, he always gets everything his way, had a restaurant and she had Claire. Claire lay on the floor listening through the furnace register while her mother complained to the washing machine down in the basement.

"It's not fair, nobody cares. What do I get to do? All the things no one else wants to do. I'm sick and tired of it."

Then Claire could hear her mother crying. She closed the register up tight and lay on her bed watching the goldfish her father had bought her swim in its bowl, telling herself never mind, it'll be all right.

Together they packed her things into the good blue suitcase, her mother wanting to make sure about her underwear and pajamas, as if these intimate details could communicate her anger to him. Claire could have told her that she was wasting her time, her father never paid any attention to details, he could care less. At last her mother laid the nurse's white note on top of the new green skirt and sweater and zipped the suitcase closed.

At the Mobil station on the highway, Claire's mother put her on the Greyhound bus.

"I want you to have a good time, OK?" Then she hugged Claire and stood back staring at her as if this would be her last chance to find it, the tiny part that was hers.

Claire waved good-bye. "Don't forget to feed my goldfish," she said, instead of something else.

All the way there on the bus, Claire practiced remembering. When she got home, her mother would ask a thousand questions just like she did when Claire came home from gymnastics practice.

"What did the coach say? Did you stick your back walkover on the beam, What about vault, Did the coach say anything good, Were any of the other mothers there, Who did you talk to, What did your friend Rachel have to say?"

Claire had memorized her answers so that it was like a litany at Church.

"Nothing much, Good, We didn't do vault, Rachel wasn't there."

It would be the same when she came home from her father's. Claire wondered if her mother could see words the way other people saw things.

The name of the restaurant was "Teddy's." Before that it had been a Howard Johnson's with blue walls and an orange roof. But the previous owner had repainted the whole building beige and remodeled the inside so there was no way anyone would mistake it for the old place. Since the name had been Teddy's when her father had bought it, there was no sense in changing it now. On the sign out front, just beneath "Restaurant and Lounge," he had written the message "Under New Management" so people would know.

When the bus left Claire off out in front, it was already dark even though it was only five o' clock. At first she thought it was wonderful. All around the building, the bushes had been strung with tiny white lights so that when the wind blew, the lights danced like a thousand tiny tinkerbells. Inside, standing in the doorway, Claire saw there were Christmas wreaths hung in the windows at each booth and plastic garlands of poinsettia that edged the big mirror behind the bar. By the cash register, someone had set up a small artificial tree that was decorated with the silver rings from the tops of beer cans. From this distance, in the dim light, they looked like shiny, fillagree ornaments. Then Claire heard the tinny Christmas carols and she remembered who she was, a twelve-year-old girl whose father now owned a restaurant. The cheery music suddenly sounded out of place, somehow sad and pathetic because the restaurant was practically empty. Her father stood behind the bar. She waited for him to turn around and see her.

"Hey, there's my girl!" He came right over to her, hugging her as if they were any other normal father and daughter. Then he pinched her cheek hard, embarrassing her.

"I'm too big for that, I'm in the sixth grade now," Claire said, rubbing the spot with the fingers, knowing there was a big, ugly red splotch there. Her father laughed, and his laugh sounded the same to Claire as the fake Santa Claus's at the mall.

They sat in one of the booths and ate the special because he wanted her to try it.

"It's very good, come on, you'll love it."

Claire did love shrimp, but not like this, all buried inside a thick, greasy breading. She liked shrimp the way her mother made them, delicate pink bodies floating in garlic and butter. Her mother had not cooked shrimp since vacation last summer, when it was still the three of them together in the house at the beach, before everything had changed.

To be polite, she ate it all, letting him think he was right about her. In the cheap glass of the salt and pepper shakers, she saw the reflection of herself and her father, perfectly reproduced.

Her father's apartment had only one bedroom so he said he would sleep on the couch. He wanted to watch TV anyway, so it was no problem. Claire liked the idea that she could shut the door of the bedroom as if outside this room the rest of the world no longer existed. Alone at last, she laid her suitcase on the floor next to the bed and took out her pajamas. Then she unfolded the green skirt and sweater and laid it out across the suitcase so that the wrinkles would fall out. She sat on the bed and undressed, watching herself in the mirror, pretending not to notice her last year's school picture displayed on the dresser. The girl in that picture was smiling.

Later, after Claire had brushed her teeth, she lay in her father's double bed staring up at the ceiling not seeing anything, worried that there was some detail she was missing.

They did not go back to the restaurant again. The next day, Claire, dressed in the green skirt and sweater, went with her father to the eye doctor's. It was not a real eye doctor's office like the one her friend Rachel had gone to, but one of those one-hour places at the mall with an optometrist on the premises. Her father said it would be just as good.

Myopia was the word the "doctor" used.

"It's nothing serious, really a very minor problem. You probably won't even have to wear your glasses except to see the blackboard at school."

The receptionist wanted Claire to try on a pair of rose-colored frames.

"This is our most popular style." She handed them to Claire, showing off her long red fingernails.

Claire ignored her choice and pointed to a pair of black wire-rimmed frames while her father watched.

"Let me see, honey." Claire turned in her chair. "You look just like your mother," he said.

Afterwards, they went to the pet shop. Claire saw a miniature castle with tiny towers and tiny windows painted silver, the silver paint shining in the store's bright light. She took it to the counter, and the clerk wrapped it up in tissue paper.

Later that afternoon, with the small, white package on her lap, Claire rode home on the bus, waiting until she was safely back in her own room to separate carefully the thin layers of delicate paper, at last setting the castle where it belonged, in the center of the goldfish bowl.

Christmas passed quickly, almost like any ordinary day, the specialness gone. Claire accepted this as if she had expected it to happen, the same way she had accepted taking the ornaments off the tree when Christmas was over, figuring that was the way it was supposed to be.

Claire was glad when vacation ended and it was time to go back to school. At school, at least, there was the rhythm of the regular routine. She started wearing the glasses at school all the time. Everything was fine until one day at the end of January Miss Evans sent all the girls down to the nurse's office. The nurse handed each girl a tiny white booklet with long pink ribbons decorating the front and the word "Congratulations" written across the top in fancy letters. Claire opened it up and read: "There are a lot of important changes about to happen in your life. How will you handle the new person you are about to become?"

"Does she think we're stupid?" Claire whispered to Rachel.

When the nurse was finished explaining everything, they went to the library where the boys stood in little groups, snickering and laughing. Then that awful boy, Joshua, pointed to Claire in front of them all, calling her "abnormal."

Caught off guard, Claire tried to challenge him. "What are you talking about?"

"Here, look. It says it right here in the dictionary. Myopia is an abnormal condition. So there."

Claire blushed, angry at herself for allowing this boy to see her embarrassment. Then she excused herself and escaped into the girl's bathroom, where the cheap mirror blurred her features into somebody she had never seen before.

At dinner that night, Claire's mother asked why she never wore the green skirt and sweater to school.

"I paid a hundred dollars for that outfit. I wish I had known you were only going to wear it once."

Claire stared down at her mashed potatoes.

"You are wearing your glasses, aren't you?"

"Unhuh." Claire bit her lip.

"Honey, what's the matter?" From across the kitchen table her mother squinted at her.

"Nothing," Claire said, ready to cry. "Why can't everything just be the way it was?" Suddenly pushing her chair back, Claire ran upstairs to the security of her bedroom, leaving her mother sitting at the table, with one forkful of mashed potatoes frozen in midair.

Three weeks later, in the middle of the night, Claire's goldfish died. Claire reached down into the cold water and lifted the limp body out of the silver castle and laid it gently in an old jewelry box lined with cotton. Without telling her mother, she buried it under the bush right outside the front door. In the morning, Claire put on the green skirt and sweater and went down to breakfast wearing her glasses. Surprised, her mother clasped her hands together in front of her and said, "Oh, Claire, you look so grown up."

Years later, as a woman, Claire would look back and squint at that moment way off in the distance, unable to see anything but the small green blur of herself standing there in her mother's kitchen. Like her mother, she was a victim of that abnormal condition of the eye where distant objects are distorted by light and the truth becomes that flawed image of memory that nothing can correct.

Point of View—The Key to "Light on the Retina"

" . . . whatever you invent is true, even though you may not understand what the truth of it is."   —Flaubert

The truth is, this story came unexpectedly. It was the result of a simple assignment presented in class after a discussion on point of view. Realizing our class's most common mistake with the short story form was an inability to stand back from characters and observe them, the professor asked us to try a more structured method of thinking. She passed out what looked like an ordinary writing assignment, repeating that it was only something to consider. It was not mandatory, more a polite suggestion than anything else; something at least to try, when so far, everything else had failed.

The short paragraph at the top of the page read: "Write three or four scenes based on the following information: A man, separated from his wife and child, has bought a B-grade restaurant. The man, who is possibly the main character, invites his ten-year-old daughter to visit him and to see the restaurant."

I remember reading over it quickly with reluctance, thinking this is someone else's idea. I'm no good at artificial exercises.

While the professor directed the class to pay attention to point of view, "Decide whose story it will be, the father's, or maybe the little girl's," my mind answered automatically the girl's, even though, at the time, I had no intention of writing a story. Another student asked, "What do you mean by a 'B-grade' restaurant?" I knew immediately, had in fact already decided what the restaurant looked like, and while the professor explained, I pictured a place I passed every day on my way home from class. I had been inside only once, five or six years ago, but suddenly I was standing in the doorway of Teddy's watching the bartender wipe the spills off the bar with a soiled dishtowel. The professor interrupted my daydream with, "Play around with it. See what you can do, and we'll talk about it next time." I quickly scanned the list of questions to consider, reading only the first few.

"When does the story take place? How does the girl get along with her father? What is her life like without her mother?"

Then I folded the paper in half and stuck it the back of my notebook, deciding to forget about it.

Later that evening at home, while I watched my eleven-year-old daughter brushing her hair, I thought how much she looked like my husband. How there seemed to be nothing about her that physically resembled me. Her nose and mouth, definitely her eyebrows, even the shape of her legs were exactly the same as my husband's. As I sat there watching her pull her hair back into a practical ponytail, I thought, they even think alike. They are both logical and good at math, both highly disciplined and athletic, both successful. At that moment, I realized the one similarity between my daughter and me was her only flaw, her eyes. She had just failed the eye test at school. This was the origin of the sentence: "When Claire's mother looked at her, she saw someone else."

The next morning, I sat down at the kitchen table with only that one idea and began to write. In the confusion of breakfast, Claire began to take shape and form on the page, a real person sitting there at the table between my daughter and me. Once I started, I didn't stop to think technically, as a writer.

This thought process was the major difference between my three previous failed stories and this story. In those other stories I had been involved in a terrible struggle with scene, character development, and tension. I had spent weeks agonizing over every detail in those failed stories, but with this story there was no time to think or worry over words and plot. I was in a hurry to keep up because the presence of the character was real.

I knew things about Claire I had never known about any other character I had ever written about. I knew her mother had found the teen bras she had bought Claire, still in the unopened boxes, stuffed in her bottom dresser drawer under the sweaters, where Claire had hidden them. I knew Claire's self-consciousness when she had to walk up to the front of the room in school to explain a math problem on the blackboard. I knew why she stood there embarrassed, with her shoulders turned in. And I knew Claire would never admit the real reasons for any of these things to anyone, least of all to herself.

My mind focused on Claire and her mother to the extent that I did not exist. It was the same feeling as that of a daydream. I was a million miles away, the "real" place I sat in did not exist. It was a physical change as well as a mental change. What amazes me the most is that this took place in my kitchen with two kids talking, a dog barking, and the phone ringing.

The real question, though, is why this change in thinking happened. Why now, what did I know now that I hadn't known before? Obviously, I had a far greater understanding of the short story form, having spent eight weeks studying technique and structure, painstakingly examining the work of professional writers, sentence by sentence, in order to analyze their methods. Now I knew about point of view, and I recognized that one scene should lead smoothly into the next. I understood the importance of choice in language because I had learned to be a highly critical reader.

Suddenly, I realized with this knowledge of structure, I also had the freedom to imagine. The assignment, which I thought I had discarded, was the reason. Even though I had initially resisted the idea of arbitrary characters and situations, these very limitations had given me "distance," that ability seemingly to forget plot and the technical questions of form that originally had been uppermost in my mind. As if a tremendous weight had been lifted from me, the structure of the assignment supported the technical aspects of my story so that my ideas were suspended effortlessly, the same way the delicate superstructure of a bridge supports its weight over an expanse of nothingness. I didn't worry about what Claire would do next. Even though she was a character in a story, she responded to her circumstances the same way a real person responds to the events around him. No character in a story worries what he will do next; he reacts to a given set of circumstances the same as a real person reacts to the events around him. I had been told this a thousand times; now I understood.

Of course, the specific details of this story came from my own memories. What is interesting, though, is I have never been in exactly the same situation as Claire or her mother. There are, however, direct emotional parallels between us. We have in common a whole set of feelings, the same sensibilities, as if we had grown up together, lived in the same neighborhood, gone to the same school, and had been taught the same morality. We both had to rely on our own strength of character, and we both had to make the same choices.

When I was in the sixth grade, I also had to start wearing glasses. At first, I thought this was wonderful. For some reason, I took this as a sign that I was grown up. When I tried on my friend's glasses to see how I looked, I became a whole new person, totally different from the old me. But when I went home and told my mother, she was upset by the extra expense of an examination, plus a pair of glasses. I still remember sitting at a desk in the doctor's office trying on frames, knowing full well my mother would care only about how much they cost and not about how I looked, the same as Claire's mother. Unexpected expenses became major tragedies.

We were broke because my father was putting himself through college. He had no time to spend with anyone, least of all me, his oldest child who should know better and be a help, instead of a pest who wouldn't let him concentrate and study. I resented the fact that he sat night after night in the kitchen with the door closed.

As far as I was concerned, my father left me. I came to accept that fact, the same as Claire did. It was difficult, and to this day it still bothers me. Probably for the same reason it bothered Claire. It seemed that at the very moment I needed my father the most, he chose something else as being more important.

However, Claire's mother is not my mother. She is an invention, a complicated combination of my real life and my imagination. She is more like the mother I have been to my daughter. I know how the mother in the story feels when she says all she ever gets to do are the things no one else wants to do. This bitterness comes from the time I have spent alone with two small children and that sense of separation and divorce I have felt because my own husband is always at work, never at home. But what really forms the mother's personality and makes her unique is that she is nearsighted, capable of seeing only fine details. It is only a coincidence that I am also nearsighted and wear glasses. I didn't think about that or its significance in the story. The glasses were part of Claire's mother and were important to mention only because Claire herself thought of the similarity. I used what details I needed unconsciously, going back and forth, seemingly without effort, between my memory and paper, into an odd storehouse where the appropriate image lay ready and waiting.

There are also present-time memories in this story associated with my daughter. Only a few months before this, I had bought a matching green skirt and sweater for my daughter. She loved it and asked to wear it all the time. I kept saying no, wait, wear something else. I was afraid if she wore it to school it would get ruined and then she would have nothing special to wear later. After Christmas passed, she never asked to wear it again. Now I was the one asking constantly, "Why don't you ever wear your new green skirt and sweater?" I realized later that when she had worn it, all our relatives had told her she looked exactly like her mother. I found it hung all the way in the back of her closet.

The goldfish was of great significance also. My daughter had had her goldfish for almost two years when she found it lying motionless in its bowl, on the same day she had to quit the gymnastics team because of an injury. "Why did it have to die today?" she wanted to know. Needless to say, she cried and I did too, for the passing of something that could never be again. We still have the goldfish bowl in the vanity under the sink in the bathroom.

To be honest, I didn't realize most of this until now, while writing this essay. And that is why this story succeeded. It was Claire's point of view, not mine.

I can see now there are really two stories here, the actual and the invented, and that both are the product of my own flawed vision. They are both equally imperfect, and neither one is really true. When I went back and reread the assignment the professor had handed out, I saw I had misread it, completely ignoring a whole section dealing with two other characters. I had seen only what I had wanted to see, the same as Claire. Like Claire, I base knowledge on imperfect memories, and the truth becomes nothing more than a uniquely personal mistake. For the writer, then, the trick is to take this ordinary, everyday fault and turn it into a work of art.

• FAITH •

by Beth Watzke

The graveyard still borders DeClancey Street, the high metal bars of its fence set against the long curve of road as it stretches out to the highway. Each bar stands sentinel, protecting the stones of each past life from the mindless rush of traffic moving ceaselessly back and forth, pouring out of town only to return along the very same road, as we all must return, to the very same place.

Beyond this fence which I so often scaled (being unable to squeeze through its bars) the graveyard unfolds in green rolling hills, twisted paved roads, beaten gravel and dirt paths. Trees of oak and elm loom everywhere randomly throughout it; far from following any neat orderly pattern it remains untamed, I am pleased to see, possessing still the wild, primitive quality that teased us, so young then, beckoning us to skirt its borders in packs at night, baying at the moon like unleashed wolves, or during the day, at twilight perhaps, hesitant, startled by the crunch of gravel beneath one's feet, awed by the infinite variety of death. The inevitability of adulthood did seem like a kind of death to us. In defiance, again at night, we would cavort, scheming how to outwit the time pressing in upon us, and the stones, trees, rocks, grass, leaves, the very air around us seemed to whisper urgently: here, among us, you are free. No one of us shall ever tell what we witness, shall ever declaim, lecture, shake a head or point a finger. Here you may do—no you *must*, you must give rein to all those forbidden urges tingling so eagerly up your strong young spines—quickly, they whisper eagerly, and *now,* as if all the dead may then participate through us in life once again. Here, surrounded by death, protected by it, all is permissible—we alone know the evil of desire not acted upon.

In the car, as we whiz past the street leading to Cindy's house (and is *it* still there too I wonder?) my mother starts to cry. My father glances at her and reaches across to take her hand and squeeze it affectionately, saying nothing as he never says anything unnecessarily. I lean across the backseat and wrap my arms around her, rub her shoulders, nuzzling her graying curls. "Oh, Emily,'' she says, patting my hand. I know she is crying from the tension of my visit, her extreme happiness and equally extreme apprehension, and because, along a small gravel path just off the highway, beneath a weeping willow tree, my youngest brother is buried. A simple flat square stone marks his grave. I am sure she cannot come near the cemetery without thinking of him, recalling his last words to her, recalling the loss, though not in the same way, of each of her children. To give life to them, to hold them, raise them, love them—and then to lose them one by one. The letting go which she may never be able finally to accomplish. Perhaps she is thinking of me, her only daughter, trying to fathom my own relentless hanging on, thinking: will my daughter ever wake up? I suspect she is neither fooled, nor satisfied, by the tasteful skirt and blazer, the sensible pumps, the sensible haircut, the god-damned sensible glasses. She senses still the restlessness which weighs upon me heavier and heavier each year. She senses it because she shares it, she bequeathed it to me, it is our link, mother and daughter, this restless yearning beyond the ordinary, foolishness of course, for there is nothing that does not become ordinary, and so she fights to control, to subdue this yearning as she has all her life, much as she fought to subdue me, much as I wrestle too for release, or, if that is imposs-ible, at the very least, to reconcile myself to the impossibility, to make peace with it, to learn to live with it and not against it.

In this house I am not myself, exactly, but only a part of myself, my mother's daughter, the daughter of my father. The overall pattern of our lives together enduring, so seamless on the face of it, supported entirely by her belief, her life, which is his work. My room hovers in time, forever pastel, neat, clean, awaiting my return. I unpack carefully, taking care to hang each dress properly, fold each sweater neatly into its proper drawer.

The safest, in fact the only socially sanctioned, form of release for that which has driven me back here is to eat, which I do recklessly, with great abandon. The evidences of my passion are the cavernous bites I take out of the thick steak she sets before me, the heaps of sour cream oozing out of my potato, and more salad, oh yes, please, more.

"Would you like a glass of wine, dear?"

A glass, *a* glass, one single solitary glass, not a carafe, not a bottle, not a mug, not even a thimble or an eyedropper, but only—a glass.

I smile sweetly at my father. "Yes, please."

Yes please! Yes *please*. Oh Emily, my dear, what is happening to you? Where did you go? I see her now sitting across the table from me, hunched over her plate, scheming, working out the intricacies of the fabrication she will tell them later in order to be free that evening. Her hair hangs in her face, gets mixed up in the salad oil; she refuses meat, thinks wickedly of all the associations the word "meat" brings into her mind, guiltily stuffs another piece of bread in her mouth. It isn't *really* a lie, she tells herself—I really *am* sleeping over at Cindy's, and her parents *will* be there, she thinks vaguely, knowing that it wouldn't matter if they were there or not, that they won't be seen the entire evening.

The week before, in art class, she and Bill had gotten into trouble once again. They always sat together at the back of the classroom, giggling and teasing each other for that too-brief hour each day. That day she had accidentally knocked the paints off her desk, spilling them all over the floor. Bill got a wet paper towel, and as she knelt to wipe up the spill, he reached out and held her hair back so that it would not get in the paint. Emily slowly wiped up the paint, sensing intimacy along the back of her neck, mixing the reds the blues the yellows into a thick swirl on the floor. They both became hypnotized by that swirl slowly evolving, rotating in on itself, spinning colors towards the center, when—"Bill!"

The spell was broken. That was Mr. Fish, the art teacher. They glanced up together then and saw him motion with his hand, frowning, and shake his head disapprovingly. Whatever he had seen bothered him. Bill let go of her hair, and as it fell forward in a wave, she sat back on her knees and looked at him. He grinned.

"He thinks I'm making a pass at you."

Oh how I pondered the meaning of that statement! The concept of a "boy-friend" was alien to me, after all—but Bill was my best friend who was a *guy*. And what *constituted* a pass? If a pass had indeed been made, what was my role, which reaction was the correct one, the most appropriate?

Unable simply to *know,* or even to *act,* I analyzed instead, tried to pin down, to reason out the spontaneous, the unreasonable.

And here I sit, still trying to reason out—what? The same people sitting around the same table in the same house in the same town—the same yet not the same. I help myself to another generous portion of salad.

"Would you like another glass of wine, dear? There's a little bit left."

"Yes, please." I can't help grinning at my mother, who smiles timidly back. "You're awfully quiet tonight. Thinking of anything in particular?"

"Only of myself. In high school. You know." The way I used to be, I think to myself.

My mother beams. "Oh we're so proud of you, dear. You have matured *so much*. You were such a little terror back then."

I stab at the salad and change the subject. "Tomorrow I think I'll go visit Jimmy's grave. I haven't been to see it in so long."

Indeed, I haven't had the nerve to go there since he died. Except that once.

"Well, that might be nice. If you like we could stop by Eicher's and pick up some flowers, or maybe a nice plant—"

"I think that perhaps I ought to go alone." I stop; can think of nothing else to say. I am surprised by the stinging in my eyes. One day both you and I shall go there, mother. We will go there and finally rest.

"Oh—of course, dear," she hushes me. "Of course." Her tight smile fails to mask the shadow of concern flitting over her face. My mother is perpetually waiting for that day which will never come, the day I come home to say Guess what? I'm getting married, and here he is, doctor, lawyer, or Indian chief, most likely. Or the day I place in her arms her first grandchild, so she can be a *real* mother again, or the day I gush about the wonderful fascinating job I have found, which satisfies me in *every* way, emotionally, spiritually, intellectually, aesthetically, indeed, even physically. My life-enhancing "career" at the library. It seems my mother and I must carry the burden of each other's dreams.

The smell of the old books with which I work, emanating from the stacks like waves of heat, has begun to suffocate me. Each book stands upright on the shelf, one squished in next to another, rows upon rows upon rows. Buried lives. Not long ago, on my daily walk to work, I stopped a block away from the library's big double doors and could not move. I was unable to enter the building. Shaking, terrified, I had to sit down on the nearest bench for at least an hour and cry for a while and smoke one cigarette after another, before I was finally able to collect myself, locate within myself whatever courage it took to approach the steps, climb them, and walk through those doors, and face once again those rows upon rows upon rows. It was then that the memory of that night in the graveyard rose up before me like the sight of land to one who is drowning. Struggling to grip the shore with my toes, I called my parents that evening with the news that I was coming home.

Cindy's house is still here, but of course Cindy isn't. A little dog greets me eagerly, a mass of wriggling fur, and yips jumping up to lick and nip at my face as I lean down to return its greeting. When I was a very little girl, the first thing I ever wanted to be was an animal. Not an animal *doctor,* mind you, but the animal itself, I wouldn't settle for anything less. The elderly man who comes to the door graciously gives me permission to walk his grounds, to enter the graveyard by way of his own unofficial entrance.

I had known that Cindy lived near the graveyard, but not that she actually lived more or less *in* it. That night graduation was a week away, and we killed (I believe that term is still in usage) case after case. Just after midnight the boys began to arrive. We had let it be known that this was to be a girls-only party, confident that this would guarantee their presence. The awareness that just up the driveway behind a small scraggly row of hedges loomed the graveyard was the most power-ful intoxicant of all. The room smelled sweetly of smoke, Woolworth's perfume, and leather and cigarettes. The music got louder: the Stones, Zeppelin, Crosby Stills Nash & Young, Sly and the Family Stone, Zeppelin, The Who, Janis, Hendrix, Cream, and always and forever Zeppelin. It must have been very late, perhaps nearing or even after two in the morning when Cindy got the dynamite idea to take what was left of the beer and go into the graveyard to the Black Angel.

"What about cops, man?"

"Are you kidding? It's so dark up there you can see their headlights from a mile away. If we just shut up and get down real low, they'll never see us. I do it all the time. The Angel's in the middle of it anyway, none of the neighbors'll even *hear* us. C'mon!"

Everyone grabbed whatever beer they could and whoever they could. We poured out of the house, up the drive, and leapt the hedges, whooping and hollering until we were out of reach of the streetlights and enveloped in the velvety blackness of the graveyard itself. Then all noise subsided except hushed whispers and giggles and the occasional "Shit!" as someone walked into a stone. For a long time there were cries of "Cindy, where the hell are you?" or "Cindy, we're losing you!" and her answers alone guided us—"Shhh, shut up you guys! Over here, over this way . . . feel the path?"—until our eyes finally got used to the dark, and we could discern the white gravel path.

I walked, or stumbled, to be more precise, at the back of the pack, alone, head down, staring dumbly at the path in front of me. I had felt as deliciously scared at the outset as anyone else, but once I had been swallowed up by that darkness I had remembered quite suddenly that if I simply walked past the Angel and continued to follow the path's curve up and over its small hill, I would come eventually to my brother's grave. One year now since we buried him, and it was this month too, May, I thought. I felt myself pull away inside from the group, different, older, and I knew then that I would indeed have to make that pilgrimage. I had no boyfriend to retire to the bushes with, after all, and I was no longer in the mood to spend the rest of the evening tormenting those who did. When we reached the Angel, I stood off to one side, staring up into her dark quiet face. I finished the beer I was drinking and suddenly angry, threw the can at it, just whistling past her bowed head. Then I turned and, under cover of darkness, I continued up the path alone.

The hedges now are thick and very tall, shielding the house from the graveyard's view. I walk through a trim arch up along the path toward the Angel. The story of the Angel is a legend we all thrived on—there were many versions of the story, but the one I knew went like this: a very old and cruel man married a lovely young girl who eventually died of his mistreatment. In a fit of guilt, he had her buried in the very center of the cemetery, and for her grave he had made the white marble statue of an angel. She is very tall and her wings reach out framing the grave beneath. The old man saw the Angel placed upon the grave, and then he went away. Soon after this he died, alone.

As the day passed and the twilight began to come on, the Angel began to darken. She grew darker and darker, and when the sun rose, she was a deep rich ebony black.

Even now the Angel's smoothness has not given way to the elements. Though she is chipped in places and at the very bottom, at her feet, are scratched the initials "E + B," she still gives off a faded gleam at this particular time of twilight. The moon is out, it can be *seen*.

I continue up the road, careful of the gravel because of the heels of my shoes. As the slope of the hill crests and levels off, the path curves, and I can see the tree that shares my brother's grave. I approach it steadily—no one else is around, only *they* can see. The air is cool, smells of coming rain and wet dirt. The grass thick and soft, smelling of ripe bananas. The mound of the grave gives a little under my feet. I put my glasses in my pocket and take off my blazer, unbutton my shirt and pull it out of my belt, throw off the belt, kick away my shoes, but I want to *feel* the grass, so I reach up and off come the pantyhose too.

Crazy woman! What are you *doing* here? Out in the middle of a graveyard, alone, ripping at her clothes, trying to get back, to be what she once was, to find what she has lost.

But I do feel better, calmer. I sit down on the grave and touch it, read it. I reach out and squeeze the grass and then lie down, resting my face in its coolness, remembering.

"Em?"
"Hey—Em!"
So he *had* come tonight after all. He was following me up the path.
"Hey, Em. Where ya going?"
I slowed down, and he ran to catch up with me. I came about to his shoulder.
"You shouldn't walk around here by yourself, ya know?"
I didn't know what to say—couldn't think, except, "I'm just going to see my brother, that's all."
"Oh." Whatever question he held in his mind must have been answered because he swung into gait alongside me as if it were the most natural occurrence in the world, as if he knew me *that well*. Perhaps he had somehow sensed something in me, though exactly what I don't know. I often wonder what was behind that "oh," what was in his mind that sent him after me—I can't make it out.

When I saw the tree I began to run, and I ran until I came to Jimmy's grave and fell on it. The wind flared up then, just as it is doing now. I pressed my hands flat against the stone and looked up at the moon and the sky filled with stars. I heard him walk up, so I stood up awkwardly, shaken at having shown so much, wiping my face and nose. Bill didn't say anything, only came up and stood behind me very close, lacing his fingers in mine and squeezing my hands, bending down and resting his face, his mouth and beautiful big nose against my shoulder, his long hair brushing my cheek.

Perhaps I should stop here; perhaps the story *should* have ended there. What instinct drove me—what was it that compelled me to reach up and grab his hair and begin, begin to kiss? How did I know to turn, to reach down and fumble, the both of us down and fumbling desperately, because it was not, you see, sweet and romantic and gentle, it was desperate, driven, horribly frustrated until locked together. We simply clung to each other, panting, until he knew to move and then it hurt and I could not help crying out which only excited him more until we were both crying out loudly.

We fell asleep, sweating but warm as long as we held onto each other. Are you all right he whispered and yes I whispered, hiding my face in his hair. He smelled like a drunken high-school boy. I felt my brother, the peacefulness of his presence.

I sit up. It is beginning to get dark—the sun is almost completely gone. The wind is faster, colder, so I find my jacket and put it on and gather up my things, each shoe, the belt. When I find my hose, I stoop to put them on, and then, suddenly, I decide to leave them here. I don't *know* why. I end up tying them to one of the branches of the tree, as high up as I can climb.

Was it all so *very* foolish of me?

Sources of "Faith"

This story came out of a merging of emotion, memory, and imagination. The place where the particulars of these fuse, connect, is the story. It feels like weaving or knitting or playing the bass.

The present emotions I feel shape the story by guiding the choice of material, giving rise to memories and images. It is a selective process, and, again, what guides that process, I feel, is present lived emotion and experience joined with imagination and my knowledge of the short story form.

The key, or way in, to the story was the narrator/point of view; once I discovered it, the various juxtapositions of memories both real and imagined could be linked through the voice of this narrator. Without the informing intelligence of this narrator, the story could not have been told.

For example: Emily herself could not have told you the meaning of what occurred at the graveyard—what she confronted and what she learned—at the time that these events actually occurred. Because she was seventeen at the time, she could not have the distance needed to see the implications of what had happened. And I thought that if I used a third-person narration attached to Emily, there still would not be enough of a true change in Emily as the seventeen-year-old that she was to warrant a story. Yet I did feel that a first-person narration of some kind was needed, that only Emily herself *could* tell the story.

While I mulled over this problem in my mind, the problem itself guided my memory toward certain memories that would eventually reveal to me the narrator I would need. I wanted the story to reveal "something" about death, loss, grief, and regeneration. Yet, if Emily at seventeen told her own story, it would have gone something like this: on graduation night I went to a big party at my friend's house, we all got drunk, went into the graveyard behind the house, where I visited the grave of my brother and, quite unexpectedly, I made love on that very grave. The "moral" of the story would then seem to be: if you are afraid of death, and grieving, and aging, go to a graveyard, have sex and you will be liberated! This is not what I felt the story was or wanted to say.

My imagination then began to play with time. What would happen to Emily, what would she be like in ten or fifteen years' time? What if she grew up to be quite a different person than the one she had been at seventeen? Suppose she grew up to see herself as a person who had been broken in, so to speak; what if all the energy and desire that asserted themselves in that graveyard found no outlet or release, but were smothered, repressed? This led me closer, this question, to my

narrator/point of view by revealing to me the differences between Emily then and
Emily now as she sees herself and feels herself to be. Emily now is looking back at
Emily then. This pushed me towards a narrative voice.

Why? Why is Emily looking back? Clearly circumstances of her present life are
urging her to do so. Why? What is she seeking? That I did not know as I began to
write the story, though I intuited that she was seeking to reconnect and regain the
energy and desire, the rebellious and independent nature and spirit of herself then,
which she felt she was perilously close to losing altogether now. Some inner
conflict was tearing her apart, a conflict which she must go back to resolve and
mend. She herself may not know exactly what she is seeking, but she does know
that she must go back and make some attempt to reconcile herself to herself.

However, in this essay I am working backwards towards the story, as this realization was the last step in forming the story. Because as I ruminated on these
problems, my mind was busy selecting and playing with memories and images.
These images were, I believe, guided by my search for a narrator, as if sub-
consciously my imagination was selecting out memories and creating images based
on them that would point me in the "right" direction.

I started with the graveyard. It was a formative place in my childhood and
adolescent years. I simply let my memory and imagination meditate on it as a
place. The Black Angel. Funerals. There really is a house right next to it where my
friends and I would gather and party and eventually go out into the graveyard,
scaring ourselves silly running around in it. My brother is buried there. This led
me to memories of my family's connections with it, which led me to think of the
differences between my own family and Emily's family. I saw then that her family
could be used (that seems like a cold, cruel word) to reveal even more the inner
split, the conflict within herself which Emily seeks to resolve by showing where
the roots of that conflict lay. In her house during those years, from Emily's point of
view, she may have been fighting a losing battle to hang onto her own personality.

Again, behind all of this was the question—what happened to Emily?—
continued to preoccupy and guide me. I had now the scenes beginning to form
themselves into some kind of order vaguely in my mind: the graveyard, the family
at home. These scenes are connected by the family's, and more specifically
Emily's, personal relationship with that graveyard—the fact of her brother's death
and of his grave located there. It was at this point that I remembered the many
parties I myself experienced there. Quite quickly, I imagined Emily at one of these
parties, I saw her going out into the graveyard with her friends, and suddenly,
aware of her brother's grave, feeling scared, alone, and older; I saw her leave the
party to walk up the path alone to go see his grave. I imagined that she had not
seen the grave alone since the funeral. I imagined these things, I did not analyze
them, or even write them down yet. But I saw again quickly that something was
missing. What happened? What happened at her brother's grave?

I wish I could explain what brings these questions into my mind. They simply
come into it, as if my subconscious is way ahead of me and is trying to point me

in the right direction. My mind is working very quickly at this point, and if I stop to think now why did I think that? I disrupt the process; sometimes I even feel that if I stop to write it down too soon I will stop or at least trip up the process. I do not wish to explain or analyze Emily, I simply want her to help me to tell her story, to get at and get a handle on her story.

Now I would guess that what happened to Emily then in that graveyard on that particular night contains the seeds of Emily's conflict now, or at least reveals a hint, a clue to the nature of that conflict. Perhaps something happened which revealed something to her about herself (again, not then at age seventeen, but only now, at age thirty-five—perhaps it is this memory she has been repressing, this memory which now, because she feels she is losing her grip on herself, losing sense of who she really is, and this is tearing at her, now it rises up into her mind and she knows she must move to confront it and learn from it, and in doing that, she regains whatever it is she feels she has lost.

But I, the writer, still do not know exactly what happened in the graveyard that night.

I can say that I "made up" what happened at the graveyard. But I don't feel those words adequately describe this process, because I did not do it consciously— I did not say to myself, she goes up to the grave and a boy follows her and then, let's see—well what could be more obvious? They have sex. That's the story. It would not be a story if that were all that happened. It is curious to note that the way by which the image itself came into my mind seemed to point me towards a deeper understanding of that image and also of Emily herself.

Here is how this image made itself known to me. I went about my daily and nightly life. In the back of my mind the story is always with me, formed into the question, what happened to Emily that night?

That weekend I went to see some friends of mine who play in a rock band. Maybe it was the fact, it just occurs to me, that I was surrounded by loud rock music and had had a few beers (well, maybe more than a few) so that I was in a state similar to the one Emily herself was in that night. Not only physically, but emotionally. I have been going through my own personal loss, and I was feeling a little bit lonely, though not enough to truly depress me.

I was sitting there, slightly drunk, feeling an odd mixture of elation and contentment and loneliness. I began to focus on one particular young man playing in this band, and I began to think what a fine looking young man he was. And pop! At that moment I got the image of Emily making love with Bill on her brother's grave. Not only the image (as if I were looking down at them from a tree, the very tree Emily climbs herself at the end of the story) but even the *name* Bill also. And it can be no coincidence that the physicality of Bill in the story is modeled on the particular young man I found myself briefly enamored with that Friday night.

All I can offer by way of explanation or theory is that the combination of my subconscious mind's obsession with the core problems of the story; my own common state with the Emily of that night; the power of fantasy which put me in a daydreaming state (a state in which one's mind is wide-open, so to speak, relaxed, a free state of such intense activity one loses sense of one's immediate surroundings)—all these conspired perhaps to give me the central image I needed in order finally to fuse all these threads into a story, linked by the form of the narrative voice, because I saw quite clearly then that a much older Emily would be going back to confront and relive that memory, that experience, in an attempt to regain and reconnect with the self, that part of herself, which she feels she has lost. Emily herself says "The memory of that night in the graveyard rose up before me like the sight of land to one who is drowning." Now *that* image, unlike the one I have just described, I got quite consciously from Homer's *Odyssey*. I mention this by way of comparison. And also, that memory, and that experience, is entirely Emily's own, not mine.

What *did* happen in the graveyard? It is not that the act of sex alone "saved" or "liberated" Emily, then or now; our sexual acts are what we make of them. Emily makes of it an act of regeneration. She herself asks why, why did I do it? Not only why, but how, how did she know what to do? She had no physical experience with boys—so she was acting purely on instinct. In a moment of despair and loss, she reached out to another human being and he answered her. She acted as if "all the dead may then participate through us in life once again."

Why indeed? Why, given the state of our world as it is today, do we continue to reach out to one another? It would be easier, perhaps, to withdraw—Emily tried to do that and it almost tore her apart. Instead she made that journey back (not only physically, but also through memory) in search of the self she felt she had lost that night in the graveyard. In giving herself to that regenerative process, what was she acting upon? What lay behind her instinct to reach out, to make the journey back? It was that question which led me to my choice for the title of the story.

• THE ARABESQUE •

by Barbara H. Hudson

Sometimes Arden's mother would get them up in the middle of the night to clean the house. The first time Arden was four. The room was dark, and her mother stood in the light from the hall.

"It's time to get up," she said and turned on the overhead light, and Arden saw the crack that began above the door and ran across the ceiling. Her sister Kate rose from the other bed. The ceiling was blue, and their beds were white. Her mother wore an old print dress and tennis shoes. "We're going to clean. Before your father gets home." She turned and moved away, her feet soft on the carpet, heavy against the stairs. Soon *The Firebird,* by Stravinsky, filled the house.

"Come on," said Kate, pulling at her arm. "Get out of bed. Get out."

"What is Mommy doing?" Arden asked.

"Hell," said Kate, who was nine. "I don't know."

Arden had never heard her say that word and she was scared.

Later, when the beds were made and the baseboards dusted, they sat at the kitchen table eating cornflakes; their mother was talking. "I'm going to paint the living room today. Kate, when you get home from school, Arden and I will have painted the entire living room. What color shall we paint it?" She turned to Arden. "My little angel, what color shall we paint it?"

Arden was worried. She had no idea how to paint. "I don't know," she whispered.

"Think," her mother said and rose from the table.

Arden heard the car door slam, and she slipped out of her chair.

"Sit down," her mother said. "I'll greet your father."

"This is terrible." Kate twisted a piece of her long blond hair tighter and tighter. "Maybe you should go with me. Maybe I should take you to school."

Their father, who was a doctor and who had been up all night working in the Emergency Room, walked into the kitchen. His fine light hair fell across his forehead, his shoulders sagged, his eyes slipped past theirs and dropped to their shoes. He touched them on their heads. "How are my girls?"

"Fine, Daddy," Arden said.

"Yeh," said Kate. "Just fine. We've been listening to *The Firebird.*"

"Oh?" He raised his head and looked at their mother.

She smiled, her face radiant, one hand pushing her dark hair from her oval face. "Go upstairs and get in bed and I'll bring your breakfast. Whatever you want. Just tell me. Whatever. Waffles, strawberries, whipped cream."

He reached out his arm and drew her to him, and she laughed. "Your mother is crazy," he said and kissed her nose.

They painted the living room that day, while her father slept upstairs. First they stood in the cold gray outside the paint store until the man with the key came. "Colors!" her mother said. "Show me all your colors!" Arden chose white for the walls—Silver Butterflies, or something like that—and a very light pink for the molding. Fairy pink, she called it. And later when they were almost finished and her father was at the top of the stairs, asking if he could come down, her mother shouted, "Wait," and said, "Here, Arden, right here. Paint a fairy." And Arden painted a little pink fairy on the wall where the edge of the desk would cover it.

It was a strange and wonderful day. And a horrible night. When her father left again for the hospital, her mother wouldn't let them go to sleep. Arden was so tired, but her mother kept shaking her or slapping her face. Kate was supposed to be dancing to *Swan Lake*—she wore pink tights and a black leotard and her black ballet shoes.

"Wake up," her mother said. "You're being rude. Kate is dancing for us." And Kate would lift her arms into a big circle one more time. Arden couldn't help it. She had never been so tired.

Finally the phone rang and their mother went away, long enough for them to climb the stairs and crawl into their beds, still clothed. Kate locked the door.

It wasn't the first day her mother had been like that, Arden was sure—people don't go mad overnight—but it was the first day she could remember. A whole day. From beginning to end.

Later she would ask Kate when it started, and Kate would say, "I don't want to talk about her."

One day Arden tried to tell her father. She was six and had walked out of her first-grade class where Mrs. Engelhardt spoke softly and looked at her with steady eyes. Arden was going to clench her teeth and catch the bus and ride home with children who yelled. But there he was, all by himself, waiting in the old Chevrolet, and she didn't even ask why.

"Bright Arden," he said and touched her hair. "How are you?"

"I'm fine, Daddy," she answered.

"Are you always fine?" he asked. "Are you always bright and fine?"

"Yes," she said and rolled down the window to feel the warm air. "Did you save anyone last night?"

"Yes," he said. "We saved a mommy who took too many pills."

"What kind of pills?" she asked and watched the trees go by. They were covered with pale green buds.

"Sleeping pills," he said. "She thought she wanted to sleep a long time, but maybe she really didn't. Maybe she wanted something else." He put on his sunglasses. "To be happy. Happy people don't take too many pills."

Arden didn't say anything for a while. They passed the yard with the willows and the creek bank covered with late daffodils. "I don't think I would have saved her," she finally said, thinking of her own mother.

"What do you mean?" he asked, raising his sunglasses.

"Then I could sleep at night."

"What's the problem, Arden?"

"I have nightmares," she said. It was always one hand. Always going for her face. Sometimes with talons. Sometimes changing at the last into something else: a bird that would light on her shoulder, a butterfly that would brush her nose. On the bad nights she would crawl into Kate's bed, and Kate would let her stay.

"Have you told your mother?" her father asked.

She shuddered. He didn't understand.

He said it again. "Have you told your mother?"

"No." She looked down at her dress. They had picked it out last week, and it was wonderful, finding the dark blue with pink flowers. But now she had to wear it every day, and she didn't like it anymore. Every morning her mother sent her back upstairs to put it on. She wanted to tear it into pieces.

"Maybe I should tell her," he said.

"No," she said. "I think I made it up. I sleep fine at night."

He put out his arm, and she moved across the seat and let him hold her until they got home. Then she kept her distance. It was safer.

Some days their mother didn't even get up, and they would tiptoe down the stairs and into the kitchen. No chaos. Order and peace. Heaven. They would eat their cereal and smile. Once Kate leaned over and kissed Arden's cheek for no reason. Arden started to cry. Then she began to laugh, then they were both laughing, loud and hard, and Kate took the cereal box and dumped the cornflakes on the table, and they began to throw cornflakes in the air, all over everything. They smashed them on the floor. Arden climbed on the table and let them fall through her hands like rain, and Kate pretended she was taking a shower. Then they got out the brooms and swept them around the kitchen and finally out the back door, where Brothers Grimm, the dog, began to eat them.

On those days their mother might still be in bed when they came home from school, the house just as it was when they'd left—curtains drawn, her door still closed, no music, none of her smells. Suddenly Arden would miss her and want to sneak into her room, but Kate would say no, not when Daddy's in there. He would come out later, his hair rumpled, and take a shower. They didn't bother him. He would speak when he wanted to. And later they would eat pot pies together, and he would tell them about his patients. Very sick people, sometimes children, who would probably die unless he were there, and sometimes even that didn't work. He would leave for the hospital, and they would do their homework and go to bed and still their mother wouldn't get up.

When Arden was eleven and Kate was sixteen, they moved into a new house with all new furniture. Arden's bedroom was white with blue trim, no cracks in the ceiling, and Kate's was pale green like an aquarium. Their mother hired a house-keeper who came twice a week, and they thought that maybe she wouldn't get them up anymore. Besides, if Kate locked her door, then Arden couldn't get in when she had a nightmare. In the old house, locking the door had sometimes worked. Arden would hear her mother's hand on the knob, then the pull on the door that wouldn't open. Sometimes she went away and never said anything. Other times she banged until Arden opened the door. "Get your sister up," she'd say. "We have work to do."

One night in the new house Arden woke up because Kate was yelling.

"I'm not going to get up anymore," she shouted. "You can't make me. Some-thing's wrong with you."

"What's wrong with me?" her mother yelled, her voice growing until it swal-lowed all sound.

"Nobody's mother does this," Kate shouted, but her voice quivered.

"How do you know?" her mother yelled. "How do *you* know?" Arden could imagine her reaching for Kate's shoulders, and she began to tremble.

"Don't touch me," Kate yelled. Then Arden heard the slap, and Kate was silent.

Someone moved down the hall and stood in the doorway, but Arden didn't move. She tried to breathe as though she were asleep. One breath in. I can change this into a dream. Hold it. Slowly let it out. I can make this person disappear. Hold it. Slowly let it out. But maybe it was Kate. Maybe she had slapped their mother. Suddenly Arden wanted to open her eyes, to whisper, Kate come here. But no. It wouldn't be this quiet. Slowly let it out.

After a while, her mother turned on the light. She moved into the room and sat down on the edge of Arden's bed and ran one hand over her eyes, again and again. "I'm sorry," she whispered. "I'm sorry." She sat for long time looking down, that hand passing over her eyes. "I'm so sorry." Finally she stood and straightened her dress. Her eyes brightened, and she lifted her long fingers to touch her brow, as though to remember something. "We have work to do. Before your father gets home. I'll put on the music." She moved down the hall. Stopped. Came back. "Maybe you could tell Kate." She was gone again, her feet on the stairs.

Arden could hardly get out of bed, but she crept down the hall and found Kate on the carpet, face down, crying.

She knelt and whispered in her ear, "She says she's sorry."

"I don't care," mumbled Kate.

The music was coming up from downstairs. Arden whispered louder, "I think she really means it."

"Go away," said Kate. "Go away forever."

Arden got up and left the room. She didn't know what to say. Even now it was hard. Pushed out into the cold where it was dark with no moon. No one left. A door slammed shut and a note shoved beneath it. Don't come back. You've taken the other side. Find your friends among the traitors.

She went downstairs and their mother left Kate alone and Arden polished the silver.

Later that morning Kate talked to their father, and after a few days, he put their mother into the hospital for a while. Arden missed her in the afternoons when she came home from school. At night she had the same dreams. In the morning she wasn't sure how she felt. Their father's mother came and cooked runny scrambled eggs and talked to herself as she moved about the house. Arden worried that she might suddenly discover she wasn't talking to anyone. Kate loved her and broke into her murmurings to chatter on and on as she followed her from room to room. Their father kept to himself: he went to the hospital and he went to visit their mother. Never again would he laugh and say that she was crazy.

When their mother left it was fall. When she came home it was winter, and they were all waiting for her—Kate, Grandmother, Arden. They sat on the sofa and watched the late afternoon snow fall, the squirrels at the birdfeeder. Kate was talking to their grandmother, using a name she'd heard. "Mema, I saw this boy again yesterday."

Arden was trying to decide what she would do when her mother walked through the door. Would she stand and say, "I'm so sorry, Mother. What have they done to you?"

"He walked me to my locker, you know, kind of slow, like he wanted to ask me something."

Maybe she would yell from the sofa, "Why have you come back? I don't want you here."

"Finally I just said, 'Do you want to ask me something?' He looked me straight in the eye and said no. I was so embarrassed." Their grandmother coughed.

She could run up the stairs, into her room, lock the door, crawl under the bed. "But later he came back and said, 'Yeh, do you want to go out?'"

Or she could stay on the couch and not move and not say anything.

Their grandmother lifted a wrinkled hand and picked a piece of lint from the sofa. "Ask your mother about it, Kate. Give her a day and then ask her. I think she'd want to know."

Kate took her grandmother's hand and squeezed it. "You tell me. *You* tell me what I should do. Should I go out with him? Should I call him up on the phone and tell him to pick me up across the street? At the Stanways' across the street?"

Their grandmother lifted her other hand and touched Kate's hair. "Ask your mother, dear. You don't need to send him across the street."

"Hell I don't. She doesn't give a damn." Kate stood up, and Arden moved over and put her head on their grandmother's lap. She didn't know her grandmother that well, but when she saw her touch Kate's hair, that was what she wanted to do. Her grandmother began to stroke her head, and Arden began to cry. She couldn't help it. Then Kate began to cry. She sat down and put her head on Arden's back and Arden could see their grandmother's arm come around to touch Kate while she stroked Arden's head, and their grandmother began to hum softly, nothing Arden knew, but it was a wonderful song.

Then the car was in the driveway and they all straightened and sniffed and smoothed their dresses, and it was almost like nothing had happened, nothing with their grandmother that is, too much of the other had happened to forget now.

Two car doors opened and closed. The trunk slammed. Boots crunched through the snow on the stone path. Then onto the porch. The door opened, and Arden's father stepped in with a suitcase. He looked taller than he had that morning, his shoulders more broad. Her mother followed, dressed in new clothes: a long red coat, a brilliant scarf, strands of her dark hair electric in the dry air. She paused for a moment, her eyes uncertain, her hands at the scarf. Then she laughed and threw her arms wide. "I almost went crazy," she said. Arden ran to her—she couldn't help it—and her mother pulled her close and whispered, "Do you still love me, little angel?" And she smelled like she always had.

"Yes," Arden whispered back. She did in that moment. It was a true answer but not complete.

"And Kate, what about you?" She extended an arm. Their father was beaming. Their grandmother rose from the sofa. Kate didn't move.

"Do you want me to lie?" Nobody said anything. "I think you are the most wonderful mother in the entire world. You are such a wonderful mother I think you should teach classes, and I will personally invite all my friends who have never been here—all my friends who ask, 'Why don't we go to your house?' and I say, 'It smells bad. A cat died underneath it.' Do you know how many cats have died underneath our house?"

Arden began to scream. That's all she could remember. Screaming as her father took her outside where the snow was falling. He picked her up and began to swing her slowly around and around, like he'd done when she was five, when she would laugh and ask for more. She was small and thin for eleven, and he swung her until she was quiet. Then he stopped and held her for a while. Finally he said, "It's time to go in now," and they went in together and nothing more was said about it.

Life together was too much for them. Arden could see that now. Too intense. People cannot live like that for long.

When their mother came home from the hospital, she was different. She had fooled Arden that first afternoon, but gradually Arden began to see that her mother's mountains and valleys had been stretched by some hand, maybe her own, into one long thin line. She rose in the morning at 7:00; she went to bed at 10:00.

The housekeeper came three days a week and did all the cleaning. She attended the Medical Auxiliary luncheons and ran a few errands. She and Arden went to Kate's ballet recitals where she sat quietly and clapped with no sound. Sometimes she would say, "Arden, why don't you have a friend over to spend the night?" and she asked nice questions of Kate's boyfriends—what they liked to do instead of what their parents did. She and their father went to the symphony once a month, and Arden watched them leave, her father's arm wrapped around her mother.

Arden was happy; she slept well at night. Sometimes she would sit on Kate's bed and they would talk about those bad days when their mother was mean, the good days now that she was nice, and oh yes tell me and smile big, isn't it easier, especially for our father, who has to work so hard anyway. And for us too, because we're young and have to navigate such a complicated world. And for our grandmother, who won't have to worry so much anymore. Yes and giggle, our heads together, murmuring, muttering, trying to make her sounds of wandering through the house. And for our mother too. It must be easier. Of course we can't ask her, how do you ask someone "Are you happy now that you're not crazy? Do you know what a bitch you were?" But surely she was happy, or she wouldn't be so nice. Yes, Mother, we want so much for you to be happy.

Finally one night after Kate had gone away to college, to a small school in North Carolina where she could study dance, their mother sat down at the kitchen table and lowered her head into her hands. "I have a terrible headache," she whispered. "Please call your father." Arden ran to the phone, her whole body shaking, and she dialed as fast as she could, but when she came back her mother had lost consciousness, her head on the table, her hands limp. The ambulance came, and she was gone.

Later her father called. "Arden," he said, "your mother died on the way to the hospital."

"I see."

"We think she burst an aneurysm."

"Thank you for calling, Dad." She put down the phone, walked into her bedroom, crawled under the bed and went to sleep.

During the service her father leaned over and whispered, "I always knew she would die before me." Then he leaned the other way and said something to Kate, who smiled, a grim sort of smile, their grandmother beside her, but Arden could see only her black hat. She was overwhelmed with relief: they had escaped, all of them. The past would die with their mother, and Arden would live on as somebody else, not trapped on a wall behind the edge of a desk. She could be anyone. Her mother could be anyone. They were all free.

And for a while it worked—that vigorous suppression of history. But eventually she wore out—what with all the energy it took just to live—and her mother came rumbling back. In women who laughed too hard, who were too kind, who had long fingers and dark hair.

Then it was summer, and Kate was home. She was nineteen and Arden was fourteen, and one day Arden was sitting in the bathtub, clothed and dry, trying to remember the song her Grandmother hummed. She looked up, and Kate stood in the doorway, dressed in her leotard and tights.

"It's gone," Arden said. "I can't remember."

Kate walked into the room, bent low and peered into her eyes. "How long have you been in the bathtub?" she asked.

"I don't know." She looked down at her clothes and couldn't remember when she'd put them on.

"Don't let her do this to you," Kate said and grabbed her shoulders.

"What?"

"She's making you crazy. Do you hear me?" Kate shook her. "Do you hear what I'm saying?"

Arden pushed her hands away and stood up. "She's dead."

Kate rolled her eyes. "Can't you see?" She lifted her long fingers and touched Arden's forehead. "You can't get rid of her without destroying your mind."

Arden sat down again in the bathtub and put her head on her knees. "Sometimes I want her back."

"You miss somebody else," Kate said. "Somebody else's mother," and Arden began to cry.

"Maybe you miss me." Kate climbed into the bathtub and sat facing Arden, her knees pulled to her chest. "We had the same mother." Kate took one of her hands. "She was a strange woman."

"Not always," Arden said.

"But we didn't know her long enough," Kate answered.

"I was alone with her when she died."

"She died in the ambulance."

"But I thought I'd killed her, that I'd done it without even realizing, and Dad was calling to ask me why."

Kate pressed her hand.

The words kept coming. "Then he told me and I was so happy. She was dead and I hadn't killed her. I could love her always and things would be better, but they're not. They're worse."

She looked at Kate, who was quiet for a moment, before she released Arden's hand and rose from the bathtub. "This is what you do," she said, and Arden followed her into the living room, where Kate stood in the middle of the Oriental rug, in first position, her shoulders back, her chin lifted, her heels, calves and fingertips meeting. "This is what you do. You take your mother," and she pushed onto her toes and turned, stepping with the leg that would become her base, one arm moving forward, lifting with her upper body, the other leg and the other arm rising slowly behind her. "You take your mother, and you turn her into something else."

It was the most beautiful arabesque Arden had ever seen: one long smooth arc stretching from Kate's fingertips to her pointed toe and the leg on the carpet so straight and sure. "Do you see?" Kate asked.

"Yes," Arden whispered. "I think I do."

On Writing "The Arabesque"

To describe how a story comes into being is an amazing proposal, overwhelming, especially for someone who struggles with language. The struggle goes something like this: What are the words that do justice to what I've perceived? And what, in fact, have I perceived? I find that I live in a world made of threads too tangled to sort neatly, and that is one reason why I write stories.

When I finished "The Arabesque," and I use the word "finished" conditionally, I thought, "Here is a story that has very little to do with my childhood. I could even let my mother read it." Have I? No. She wants to read everything. "Not yet, Mom," I say, "I'll let you read it when it's finished."

I didn't set out to write a story about my mother, who is much more complex than any one character could ever be. I simply set out to write a story.

Last winter I used to ride home from Pitt on Thursday nights with a woman named Ann, a graduate student in psychology. Thursday was her day to work at the Counseling Center at Carnegie-Mellon, and sometimes she told me about the students she'd seen that day, not using their names, of course. Thursday was my night for English Literature 293, Modern Critical Practice, and afterwards I was ready for something mundane like psychotherapy.

One night Ann told me about a young woman whose mother had been abusive, both physically and emotionally. The last thing she said to me as I got out of the car was, "The mother would get them up in the middle of the night to clean the house."

When I sat down at my computer a few days later, knowing I had to begin a story for a workshop, those words surfaced as part of the first line. As I typed them, I had no conscious idea of where I was going. My experience as a child was very different: my mother hired a woman to do the cleaning and was unusually conventional in many ways—but she did like Stravinsky's *The Firebird*, which seemed an appropriate piece of music for early morning housecleaning. I can remember sitting in the den before I was old enough to go to kindergarten, troubled by Stravinsky's chords and terrified by the album cover, a picture of a flaming bird, red against black.

So the story began with a sentence, and immediately I perceived that Arden's room was dark and her mother was standing in the light from the hall. Her mother turns on the light— "It's time to get up"—and Arden sees the crack in the ceiling, an image that seemed perfect for the chaos I knew was coming.

The crack itself belongs to a blue room I slept in from the time I was in a crib until I was ten, when we moved to a new house with no cracks. I don't remember when I first discovered the crack, but looking at it became a nightly ritual. During the day I didn't notice it at all, but lying in bed at night, in the dark, with the light from the hall, I would find it above the door and follow it across the ceiling, down the wall, and into the closet where it disappeared. Somehow following that crack every night reassured me that I would fall asleep, what seemed to me then such a fragile act, with no way of making certain it would happen, though it did—night after night, mysteriously, without my ever knowing exactly how I'd done it. The crack was an image of control for me, of things out of control for Arden: one thread in my story.

And as I think about all the threads, my story seems to be woven out of more than I even know exist, more than I can take into account with any measure of certainty: they start out as one color in memory (the crack in my bedroom), to become another color that forms another memory (the crack in Arden's bedroom), to become still another color as I try to sort their meaning, and so the process continues. As I've said, there is no neat ordering of threads in my way of perceiving.

I've told you about The Firebird and the crack in the blue ceiling, but I don't want to tell you everything I know, limited as it is, because a story is an intensely private matter. And I have discovered that in a story I reveal all kinds of secrets, dressed in other clothes. Some of them I've consciously dressed myself; others slip by to later throw open a coat and say, "Surprise!" Either way I would rather work with clothed secrets than write something that begins, "My mother worked hard to make us believe that our family was normal and healthy and happy, but she couldn't erase the symptoms of our disease." Yet even as I write those words, I realize that they could be a dressing up, the beginning of another story. And if they were, I would feel safe. But were they the beginning of a personal essay, I would not. One some people call fiction, and the other they call truth. Perhaps that ordering is not as neat either.

Returning to my truthful account, let me say that I shared my blue bedroom with my older sister Becky, and though Kate does not equal Becky, I know that she is in the story because I have four sisters, one older and three younger. When the story was being discussed in a workshop, someone said, "Why don't you make Kate and Arden one person?" "Hmm," I answered, with proper workshop etiquette, knowing immediately that I didn't like the idea. It was important to me to explore how two sisters would survive the mother I put into the story. Becky and I never went wild with cornflakes, but maybe I wish we had.

So the mother gets them up. "We're going to clean. Before your father gets home." He has to be gone, I realized, or the mother couldn't get away with what she's doing. Unless he were abusive as well. No, I decided. He's negligent. Overworked and negligent. But where is he? At the hospital. A doctor. But why would he always be there at night? He works in the Emergency Room and will come home while they're eating breakfast. And so my story progressed, each line pressuring the next, as I watched for what happened, always asking, "Is this what it would be? Why or why not?"

As I wove my threads together, pulling in strands from all kinds of places, I asked myself all kinds of questions; and every time I sat down to work on the story, I started at the beginning, asking the questions all over again before I went any further. So the process of revision was very much connected to the process of writing, which is how I write and which is why most of my significant revisions tend to come at the end of a text.

My first ending was very different: Arden's father finds her clothed in the bathtub, and she is older: a young woman living in her own apartment. My husband, who is often my first reader, wasn't satisfied. It seems too removed in time from the rest of the story, he said. Maybe something could happen with Kate. Ah yes, I thought.

The ending with the father might have worked with some major revision, but I think the ending with Kate works much better, and my husband's comment helped me to understand something different about the story. I moved Arden back in time and put her in the bathtub. What would happen if Kate found her? I began to ask, and a thread which had been submerged in the story began to surface—Kate's dancing. Maybe some of you think that my sister Becky was a dancer. Maybe not. I don't think I could have written the ending if Becky had been the dancer. I wouldn't have known what Kate would say. Even then, it surprised me: a secret I'd kept from myself.

Someone in my workshop said the ending made it Kate's story, but in my reading, it is still Arden's. All stories contain other stories, but Arden is the one who finally demands something from Kate in her passive, repressed way.

When I was four years old, I almost drowned in our neighborhood swimming pool because I hadn't learned to swim yet, and in my attempt to walk from one side of the shallow end to the other, I stepped into water over my head, and suddenly I was struggling to breathe. My father was in the deep end and didn't see me, and it was my sister Becky who rescued me, not because she was capable of moving me into shallow water, but because she was someone for me to hold on to until the lifeguard saved us both. I will never forget the image of her seeing me and turning to swim my way.

The analogy is not perfect, but Arden is the one who will remember the arabesque. Perhaps Kate will remember as well, but not in the same way. She already knows how to swim.

· THE BELLS OF ST. CATHERINE'S ·

by Don Minkler

The sky bleeds orange as the sun drifts toward oblivion for the third time this week. The field below waves back and forth, sometimes still, as the sharp October air settles, and moves across the prairies of Arkansas. Men drift home. Women bake hams and pour milk. The village of Joplin stands quiet and lonely with its unused stone jailhouse the only reminder of a time, 150 years ago, when black people were slaves and the farmers proud.

The sign on Route 17, stuck in sand, white, with blue trim and letters, bent at the waist, beaten by dust, greets folks that cross the Missouri border and drive for another half-hour or so:

Welcome to the Town of Joplin, AR.

Po ulati n: 1442
Elevatio : 995 Ft.

That is, unless you stand atop Jackson Rock, in which case your elevation becomes 1020 Ft.

The stairs behind the Gregory house, the ones that ascend to the porch and the back door that extends from the kitchen, have an elevation of 1004 Ft. Below these steps, halfway down Main Street, between Sam's Saloon and Walgreen and across from the police station/fire station, Arthur Gregory sleeps on a cot, snoring, moving his lips every second or two, maybe coughing. His wife, Alice, that is, Alice as in Alice in Wonderland, where her mother got the name, leans on the counter in the front room of the shop, reading a novel by William Faulkner. Her bookmark, a sales receipt from Walgreen, sticks up, ten pages beyond the page she is reading now. This is the point where Alice, forty-two-year-old Alice, with red hair and baggy dress, will stop reading and wake up her husband, Arthur, forty-six-year-old Arthur, with gray hair and crooked teeth, and tell him it is time to close the shop.

Always, it seems, Alice will walk into the shop, where the lawn mowers and tractors and little whiny engines are repaired, and kiss Arthur on the cheek, rubbing his stomach in such a way as to arouse him from sleep. Arthur will rub his eyes, grunting about what time it is, and sit on his cot. If his cigarettes are not in his pocket, he will ask Alice where they are. If they are in his pocket, he will ask her for matches. Arthur will then extend his hand to Alice, she, her hand to him, and she will help him up. It is not that she has the strength to lift him from the cot, the cot that sags near to the floor. It is the touch of her hand and the quick smile that gets Arthur from his cot. His gray hair muffed and matted in the back, Arthur will rub his hand through this and lean forward to kiss his wife on the lips while he grabs the small of her back.

"Good morning," he might say, even though it is evening. Or "I guess it's time to get up." Then he will go about his business of cleaning his tools, turning off the air conditioner, and locking the door. In summer, this process is slow, in winter, quick.

This October, this fall day, none of this happens. Alice reaches the ten-page mark, the spot where the Walgreen receipt sticks from the book. She glances outside, out through the clean picture window that shows the shop to the rest of the world. The rain falls gently, clinging to dust on the road, bringing mustiness to the air. Alice moves her Walgreen receipt twenty pages beyond where it is and continues to read.

Twenty pages later, she reads twenty pages more, and so on, until she has finished the Faulkner novel. As the orange in the sky turns to purple and then brown and as the gray clouds turn black and the rain hits the road and the shop window and the Ford in front, Alice sighs. She forces herself into the back room, letting the swinging door go back and forth and to a halt before walking further into the shop.

"Get up, Arthur. Get up, it's late." Arthur rolls to his side. Alice does not walk forward. "Get up, Arthur. It's after seven." Arthur rubs his eyes and sits up.

"Why is it so late? Have you been baking again?" His voice is not accusing, but childlike.

"Get up, Arthur. We have to go to church." Alice returns to the front room. The door sways behind her. Arthur is puzzled for a moment at her curtness, but the thought passes out of his mind as he begins his chores. A minute later, Alice returns.

"What are you doing? We have to go to church."

"Now?" Arthur grumbles under his breath and shuffles his feet as the rag in his hand cleans a socket wrench. "Why do we have to go now?"

"Just . . . let's go."

"Jesus Christ." Arthur lays the wrench on a battery charger, and the rag wipes his hands. "I'll be there in a minute." Arthur walks up the fourteen steps to the porch that extends off the kitchen.

Inside the house, Arthur sits at the kitchen table with the cereal boxes and butter dish, again rubbing his eyes as he tries to wipe the tiredness from his body. He cannot remember exactly why they are going to church. He knows somebody has died, or someone is being remembered, or maybe it is Easter. Who knows. He rubs his head and walks to the bedroom, the one they sleep in, not the one that has a library in it. Arthur is a man who does what he is told, and he has been told to put on his Sunday clothes, so he will put on his Sunday clothes.

The sky rests, black and speckled, as Arthur and Alice enter the nave of their church. The carpet between the rows of pews retains the footprints they make as they walk down the aisle until they have selected a pew nine or ten rows back. The couple kneels briefly, Arthur coughing and sitting first.

Someone has died, his wife told him. Her Aunt Margret, the one who used to do ironing for neighbors. Arthur doesn't remember her.

The plain glass windows along the edges of the pews allow Arthur to view church members and neighbors walk the sidewalk toward the church door. He watches them cut across the browning Kentucky blue grass and push the bronze bar that releases the white, chipped opening to the building.

Alice hands her husband a bulletin, blue and white with a picture of the church sketched on the front.

The Forsters, the ones with the turkey farm across the county, and the Yeomans nod greetings to Alice and Arthur before they slip into the pew in front of the two.

The funeral bores Arthur. He sleeps through communion, knocking his chin off his chest, waking with a jerk, as the organist begins hymn 304, "Lord Have Mercy on Us." Alice looks with scorn at him as he fumbles for a hymnal and stands up to join the masses. In his mind, Arthur struggles to remember who Aunt Margret was. Could it have been that loud red-haired bag of flesh who sometimes left apple cores on their lawn? No, that's Alice's cousin. Alice grabs Arthur by the arm and leads him from the pew to the back of the church where the Forsters engage them in frivolous conversation. Alice seems anxious to leave, telling the Forsters that they are sorry that they will miss the burial, wasn't Aunt Margret such a wonderful person, and maybe we'll see you in church on Sunday.

"That wasn't so bad, now was it?" Arthur says to Alice as he takes her hand in his and they start out across the Kentucky blue grass toward the Ford. "I still can't remember who Aunt Margret was. She wasn't the one who gave us the brown china for our wedding, was she?"

Alice takes her hand from Arthur's and folds her wispy arms across the chest of her baggy black lace dress. She says nothing as she climbs into the Ford.

Arthur turns his head toward hers as he clicks the ignition key forward. His smile is gone, and he wonders for a moment if Alice is going to start menopause, or maybe she is suddenly disgusted with him. He waits for Alice to turn her head toward his, but she does not. Her eyelids open and shut slowly, reflecting from the windshield a sadness not seen before by Arthur. The Ford slips into drive, creaking and tapping up the hill toward the road.

"I'm pregnant."

Arthur jams the car into reverse, retracing the last forty feet or so of road.

The quick stop jerks back and forth the heads of both passenger and driver.

"Say that again?"

"I'm pregnant."

"Haha!" Arthur raises his hands as far up as they will go in a Ford, slapping the roof. "Haha! You wouldn't kid me now, would you?" He looks at her, then at the road, then again to Alice. "A kid! My oh my, I'm so happy!" A tear drips to his cheek, sliding towards his lip. "Haha!"

Alice appears embarrassed by the whole tirade.

"Arthur, you're stopped in the middle of the road. Don't you want to move?"

The night air brings a chill. Arthur rolls his window closed. He leans to kiss his wife, but her face is not there. She pushes him away, moving toward the door. She brings her knees to her chin, letting the black lace gather around her waist. She cries.

"I'm scared," she whispers.

Arthur drives home, silent.

When they arrive at Gregory's Motor and Engine Repair, Arthur climbs from the auto, closing the silver door gently. With his right arm under her knees and his left arm around her waist, he pulls her person into the outdoors and carries her up the staircase to the porch that extends off the kitchen. Her body is placed on the bedspread, smooth and fresh-smelling, and her teared face on a flowered pillow. Arthur puts her shoes, black flats with delicate bows, under the bed. He caresses her neck and her cheek and begins to get undressed. His mind fills with excitement and dread as he lays the brown suit gracefully at the foot of their queensize bed.

His eyes are wide and his senses alert when he pushes between the worn print sheets an hour later, drunk and frisky. Alice is breathing deep and smooth. Arthur lies awake for three hours.

For the last four months, Alice has been subdued, passive, and often spiteful. The funeral this time is for that lady who throws apple cores on the lawn next to the Ford. The Gregorys walk the grass and the cement to the church with pondering steps. Alice crosses her arms across her chest, keeping two or three feet between herself and Arthur. He has come to accept this response from his wife, as she neither talks at home, keeps house, or participates in business. Her life is eating, she has gained thirty-two pounds, and sipping wine, white wine, the cheap stuff. Arthur nagged her for a week or two, "Why isn't the bed made? Are we going to eat tonight?" But he is not the nagging type, she knew it, so did he. The work that needs to be done, wash, bookkeeping, is done by Arthur. The bed is never fresh and clean, the dishes never go in the cupboard. The butter dish has been empty since news of the pregnancy. Arthur, although he tries to remain spirited, attempts to make conversation, now spends most of his time in his own imagination, where he is now.

He lets Alice open the white chipped door to the church, following behind, playing in his mind a game of catch with Isaac, his soon-to-be son. Alice insists she does not care, boy or girl. Arthur thinks sometimes that Alice wants a miscarriage. Our couple, the Gregorys, slip into the back pew of the church, the short pew with no arm on the right side because a pillar holding the ceiling is there. He kneels, she sits, not even opening a prayer book. With no window to view the outside world from—the frigid white world, lifeless and clean, lonely—Arthur sees the altar, square, wooden, with faded green draperies, and the minister, with exciting smiles and gestures and a monotone voice. The hymns begin, and Arthur stands automatically, reaching to lift Alice. She stands, but sits after the first verse. Arthur hears few sobs during communion and wonders why this lady had many less friends than the last lady. Was she a mean person? The only thing he can remember is the apple cores that he always picked up. She seemed, to him, a pleasant sort.

When the final chord is played, thunderous and evil, the congregation in the rows ahead swoop to greet the Gregorys, or Alice.

"Congratulations! Are we due soon?"

"You look wonderful, Alice. It takes a lot of courage for a woman your age to get pregnant."

Some gray lady, in orthopedic shoes asks, leans towards Alice, and whispers in her ear, "Tell me, honey, was it planned? These things happen, you know?"

Arthur shakes a hand and then another. Alice speaks little, politely nodding, smiling, then grabbing Arthur by the arm and dragging him to the parking lot.

"Why don't we stay a little longer?" Arthur says to Alice as they plod across the snow field before the car. "We haven't spoken to the Forsters in so long. It would be really nice to speak with Bob Forster."

"You know I'm tired, honey. Can we please just get home?"

Her smile, her tone, is light, scratchy, suddenly manipulative and demanding. It is a tone he has heard many times before, a tone that has caused him many times to hold his tongue, changing the topic, walking away. He is hurt this time. She has twisted his heart. A mother who has denied a child's most favorite wish.

The street lights, the few on Main Street, glow. A life is inside each one. Arthur becomes jealous, suddenly, of the lamps, slowing the automobile to stare at each one. They seem so . . . so . . . bright. No stars tonight. No wind. Just the pitter, tap, tap, whirr of the rusting Ford and the rush of rubber on gravel as Alice and Arthur halt at the entrance of Gregory Motor and Engine Repair.

As the couple stumble from the cabin of the Ford and stiffly climb the fourteen steps to the porch that extends from the kitchen, Alice balances herself on the railing, one step at a time, breathing, stepping, near tears. She reaches the landing, the porch, leaning, slanting her body on the wall outside the kitchen. Her hands find her face, her neck leans forward.

"Help, Arthur. My God, I just can't take it anymore. I'm just so tired. I'm tired." She looks for stars with tears in her eyes. "I never wanted this, Arthur. Please help me, Arthur."

Arthur stumbles, shifting his weight and his boots. His hands move up his sides, crossing, then uncrossing. His eyes avert the painful glance of his wife. Finally he takes her hands in his, moving forward, stepping gradually. When their faces become close, hers turns to the side, the ice wind catching her hair, his hands.

"I'm sorry, Arthur, so sorry." The last words straining, squeezing from her soul.

After a minute, seeming like a whole hour to Arthur, he asks, "Why? Why are you so . . . what's wrong?"

She does not speak, choosing instead to turn away, to the door, and go inside to bed. She does not undress. Arthur finds an empty gin bottle in the cupboard. He throws it at the cereal boxes, dominoes now, and sits on the floor. He will sleep here tonight.

It has been six years now, since the birth of Elisha. Six years now since that night when Alice and Arthur slept apart. Alice is happy now, Arthur has decided, being happy now himself because he is relieved. She is free, gregarious again, but somehow vacant. Her life is filled with cleaning, helping with math, making dresses, funny, odd dresses with uneven seams, but dresses nonetheless. She and Arthur talk before bed, whispering as they had done years before, sometimes still giggling. Arthur thought once this to be silly for a couple of their years, fifty and all, but he passed it off. Who knows what everyone else does? These moments keep him vital, in times such as now, when the motor shop must be mortgaged.

His daughter seems to love her mother, running near her in the full grass field behind the store, waving and smiling in those funny dresses, red and yellow, and orange. His daughter seems to love her father, pulling his legs, twirling his hair, folding and unfolding his trouser cuffs. She enjoys most of all the stories he tells, all made up, from the Land of King Isaac, a fairy-tale land the two of them live in every night before bed.

The stars begin to arrive, bringing along the moon and removing the clouds. Crickets. Evening birds. The shriek of children yelling for more fun and faster games. Orange oil rolls across the sky, steady, slowly. Alice, knitting, Arthur, wiping his tools, sip wine as Elisha, in the yard below, a kingdom to the throne that is the porch above, spins, transfixed by the specks above. Her legs are whispers and her face aglow as she runs, runs across the field into yards down the road and further down the road, and Arthur can no longer see her. He turns to Alice and smiles, holding his hand to her as she takes it, softly, returning the smile. Her knitting needles drop from her lap, and there is a screech and another screech and metal violates metal, and metal violates cement and there is another screech and everything is silent.

Flowers cover the end of every pew. Organ pipes groan of death and pain. The minister, graying now, recites prayers from memory, as Alice melts with tears in the arms of her husband, saying "My God, my God." Arthur does not hear the prayers, doesn't hear the organ, only the cries of his wife, throbbing, her handkerchief on the ground. He rubs hair from her eyes, blue, and red, unhappy, as he helps her sit for the homily. The coffin is next to them, in the aisle, in a mahogany cart, draped in white, fresh linen. The dust in the air, stuffy air, causes tears in Arthur's nose and eyes to suffocate him. His wife shakes softly by his side, rising to sing but not singing. When the service ends, the people, hundreds of people, hold the hand of Mrs. Gregory, touching her black lace dress.

"I'm so sorry. I'm so sorry."

"She's in God's hands now, honey. He will take care of her."

Some lady with thin, gray hair, staggering with a cane, leans to Alice, brushing her ear. The lady can't speak and she wobbles away. Alice is steady throughout the process. She says nothing, nodding, accepting the touch of this crowd, doing its best to heal her. Arthur is less able to handle the crowd, choosing to remain behind his wife, holding her shoulders beneath the black dress, staring at the windows as the people retrace their steps over the Kentucky Blue grass, to their cars and to their homes. He imagines Elisha as she would be on Christmas and Easter, bounding toward the white chipped doors, screeching, jumping, her lace white dress with the uneven hem, dirty as she sits on the ground waiting for her parents to catch up. He imagines Elisha as a boy, Isaac, in a blue suit, clomping to the door in new hard shoes.

"Hurry up, Daddy! Hurry up, Mommy! We'll be late!" Isaac leans against the doors and raises his arms. "Am I getting a tricycle this year, Mommy?"

Arthur feels tiredness in his whole body. He squeezes Alice's shoulders. She does not respond, and he squeezes again, letting a tear rest on his lip. Alice rests her head under the chin of her husband, offering a hand along his side to soothe him. She nods ahead, thanking her friends, cousins. Arthur remembers that night so long ago, leaning, crying, against that cracked red brick wall outside the kitchen. He sees Alice toss her head to the left, and he feels his own fear and pain with every pore of his body. He begins to weep. A friend, Mr. Forster perhaps, offers his hand to Arthur.

"I'm so sorry, Arthur. I'm so sorry."

Arthur nods in response. "Thank you." He shakes hands as friends and cousins and neighbors pass by. People he knows, people he has seen, a man in a gray pinstriped suit, a lady with curls and dimples. The crowd recedes, and Alice and Arthur remain in the church with the shoebox of a coffin that contains their daughter. Dark men with gold watches from the funeral home slide the cart with the coffin out the front door, squeak, squeak, swish, and Elisha lies in the back of a hearse. Rain clouds soften the evening, a mist forms around the church as Alice and Arthur descend into the backseat of a long, sad car with shining wheels. The driver does not turn his head as the car pulls out of the lot and up the hill to the road.

Without warning, without Arthur even noticing, rain begins to dribble on the hood of his car. A minute later he turns the wipers on to remove the streaked specks of water from the windshield. Alice sits close to his side, one arm interlocked with his, the other, still gloved, holds a bouquet of white roses. Arthur wants to speak, but nothing he can think of sounds any good. With his right arm, he pulls Alice closer. Her gentle weeping moves with the rain and, soon, the storm explodes. The Ford curves into the engine shop, and Arthur covers his wife with his waterproof coat as they ascend the porch steps. Inside, Arthur fumbles with his tie and with his shoes as Alice sits on the edge of the bed, the fresh, clean bed, folding his things for him.

Alice stands, grabbing her husband around the waist. Her hair, in the dim bedroom light, shining, wispy, is the hair of Elisha.

"You know something, Alice?" Arthur smiles through the shadows of the room, his throat sore and full of tears. "I love you . . . I love you very much."

Alice holds his waist, through his undershirt, even tighter and begins to sway their bodies in a rhythm, back, forth. Over the top of that glistening wisp of hair, Arthur turns his head away from the silver-framed picture of their daughter in a yellow print dress with her two front teeth missing. Her left knee is dusted with sand. Her face is flushed with the joy of slides and swings.

Outside, the rain is no more, leaving behind a silence that accents the rose red glow of the horizon, miles away, outside of Joplin. The grass fields remain still, waiting for nothing but the morning dew. Men read their newspapers, smoking cigarettes, drinking gin. Women dress their children for bed, placing them in Mickey Mouse pajamas and raspberry sheets. If you listen close, with your radio off, and your TV down, you can hear the bells of St. Catherine's. It is seven o' clock in the city of Joplin, AK.

About "The Bells of St. Catherine's"

Point of view is the primary structure around which this story is built. The form, three funerals and a scene in the yard, is very simple. The point of view, disembodied, with an intelligent narrator, is relatively simple. It is these two things, these static objects, that allow us to see the characters in their world.

The decision on point of view was made early in the writing, during the opening scene with Alice and Arthur in the engine repair shop. Only a narrator, detached, or disembodied, from our characters could see the town and the sign and the women pouring milk. Only a distant narrator could have seen Alice and Arthur at the some time. But to create a sadness, or any kind of emotion in this story, we must know someone. We must be inside someone's thoughts and feelings, or the story is only about a town. At first, I planned to tell of Alice's and Arthur's feelings. But this is a complicated task, and the story would lose its simple nature, this simple nature presented in the first paragraph, during our view of the village, a tone which must not be disturbed. The choice of Arthur as our "informer" seemed natural since we see, by her actions in the shop, that Alice is troubled. In order to include Arthur in the story, he must show us his view of the trouble. This also keeps a balance, maintains the even tone, and keeps the story from being a *Better Homes and Gardens* version of "Middle-Aged Pregnancy." A simpler reason is that I am male.

This point of view takes us throughout the story, letting us see the funerals and the sadness of both characters, as well as Arthur as the more giving person. Alice is less aware of Arthur's feelings and her own surroundings. The point of view also lets us see the whole at the end: We draw back from the town with our distant narrator and listen to the bells and watch the sunset.

The form, although simpler, was less apparent to me until later on in the story, during the second funeral. In keeping with the simple tone of the story, it is easier to see subtle change in people if we see them in the same situation at different times in their lives. Of course, form of some sort is always necessary or we see no change at all. This story is more low key, less haphazard, than other stories I have written. I had always tried to write things that were exciting—blood and guts—in every paragraph something new. I tried here to be calm. I tried here to let the characters speak for themselves. Sending the Gregorys to another funeral took care of all these things.

What solidifies the form is the ending. We pulled into town at the beginning, so we must pull out at the end. This ending did not come naturally for me, although it seems natural now. It was not until I looked at the story as a whole, and at the narrator, that I saw the form for what it was. My first endings stopped abruptly at the close of the third funeral. But if you drive onto a bridge, you must drive off. We must leave Arthur and Alice where we found them to live their own lives again. It is at this point that form and narrator are most important because the story takes control of itself. It had to end this way.

If the form and point of view are our creek bed, static and simple, then it is our characters and the little details that will be our water and give the story motion. A lot of the details—the town, the church—come from things I know. I went to Joplin for two days, many years ago, to visit my cousins, the turkey farmers. The Gregorys' church and the minister remind me of my own church and pastor, with the white chipped doors and the Kentucky blue grass.

But the story here is the relationship. The Gregorys love each other. They have been married for a long time, and they have routines. Each has a distinct personality. Arthur is not too educated, slightly absent-minded, a happy-go-lucky kind of guy, a dreamer. Alice is more educated, or at least more interested in things of that sort. She reads Faulkner. She is moody. Deep down, she really cares for Arthur. Both of these characters draw something from my own personality, but appear as opposites in many ways. In the opening scene, we seen an immediate contrast, with Arthur sleeping away the end of the day, while Alice does her "front desk work," reading a book. Right away we have two distinct people, we know they care about each other, which makes us care about them. We also have a conflict, a small one, on the first few pages. These three things are in keeping with the tone and purpose of the story. The conflict is not exaggerated, the people are ordinary. And they immediately have human characteristics both good and bad, which seemed important.

From this opening scene, the rest of the action is a playing out of each character's reactions. Arthur falls asleep at the funeral. The funeral does not mean much to him. Alice is curt and continues to get even curter in the next scenes.

But we know that Alice treats Arthur well on ordinary occasions. The change in her reaction begins the story. I did not decide to have Alice be pregnant until just before she announced it. There were other possibilities: cancer, menopause, or maybe she found another guy. Menopause, I knew nothing about. Cancer is too depressing. Pregnancy should be something happy in people's lives and, again, keeps the story two-sided.

As the story progresses, we see our characters stretched to limits as Arthur does his best to care for his wife as she loses control of herself. Each becomes more human. Arthur retreats into his own fantasy world a little farther. Alice cannot deal with her own situation although she does ask for help once or twice from her husband. My usual method is to go overboard with pain or trouble, but I tried to keep Alice real and a little caring with the scene on the porch steps after the second funeral. She knows what she is doing, but she cannot help her actions. That Arthur sleeps apart from his wife for the only time in their marriage shows two things: both how bad things have gotten, and how much Arthur and Alice really mean to each other.

The baby is born and life is almost back to normal. The daughter wears dresses that Alice tries so hard to make, with crooked seams. We also see later that Arthur really did want a boy although he accepts his daughter very well.

The scene with Elisha is almost too good to be true and is dreamy. She spins. No words are spoken. The sound of children playing is everywhere. Alice is also vacant. Maybe she was happier without the baby at all.

Having Elisha die was the last major decision I made in the story; it fit the form of the story. We must return to where we began. Elisha's birth created a change in our characters, but her death creates a bigger one. Things will never be the same. This, again, maintains a balance of sadness and joy in the story. Alice, in her personality, has an underlying pain, a crookedness, like her dress seams. Elisha's death is inevitable.

This brings us to the final scene, the third funeral, where Arthur finally pays attention. He has more trouble dealing with the people and the church than Alice does, and he hurts very much. The people at the funeral comfort our couple, but, once again, nothing is perfect as the coffin is a shoebox and the driver in the car does not care.

As the narrator pulls away from the town, character and form come together to show the empty pain of Alice and Arthur as we leave them in an embrace with only a picture of Elisha. The town is still the same. The bells still ring. Others lead their lives. Although things are the same on the outside as they were six years ago, Alice and Arthur will always be without something.

As they embrace, they replay, almost, the opening scene, with Alice waking Arthur from his afternoon nap. But they may love each other that much more, as the bells ring for everyone, but especially for them.

• THE HARLEQUIN •

by Daniel Lowe

"So what is it—a woman, a wound, or Wall Street?" Raphael's teeth looked whiter than they should have in the lamplight that reflected off the canopy. He reached across the table and tapped the glass into which Reynolds squeezed the juice of his lemon slice. Reynolds took a swallow and felt the mixture immediately sour in his stomach: he'd eaten almost nothing. He hadn't appreciated the waiter's alliteration, had hardly heard the words.

"None and neither. I'd think by now you'd know my habits." A woman, waiting across the street for the bus, sat on the table where the boy had sold the figures. Tables lined the windows of the stores that had sponsored the children's festival. Though it was past ten, in this section of town there was no threat of theft.

"Enough to know that you're usually in bed by now," said Raphael. "And with four fewer drinks in your belly." Reynolds smiled at this. He took an ice cube from his glass, wrapped it in a napkin, and after loosening his tie ran it along the inside of his collar. *For a waiter, you assume a lot of familiarity.* But this he didn't say.

"Suppose I show you something I bought today," said Reynolds. From his pocket he took the carved soldier's head the boy had been trying to sell. He placed it on the table in front of Raphael.

"A sleeping man standing in a hole," said Raphael.

During the first two evenings of the festival, the boy had stood still and quiet as the figures in front of him, if not for his constant fingerings of his cashbox's slots. Reynolds guessed he was ten years old—his ribs countable, his cheeks nearly meeting inside his mouth—but the line of blue hair above his lip betrayed him. The boy hadn't looked above the waists of the mothers of the other children, for whose paintings, photographs, and late August harvests the festival was held, as they scolded him for his presentation. "This is unacceptable. Where's your mother? This is unacceptable."

"You're really too clever," Reynolds said to Raphael. "The fact is that this head belongs to the unfortunate soldier who stood with his back to his wooden army and was decapitated for his troubles. The boy charged me a dollar for it."

Raphael slapped a moth from the table lamp.

"Sounds like a fair price to me. And what of it?" he said.

Reynolds took the figure off the table and ran his fingers over its eyes, nose, and mouth. "I suppose it didn't strike you that the violent poses of all those soldiers he was selling were the reason why the chairman and all those mothers were up in arms?"

"Prudes," Raphael said. "And besides, lots of kids like violence, Mr. Reynolds. You never played at war when you were a boy?"

Frustrated, Reynolds thrust the figure in front of Raphael's nose. "Does this look like a man who's just had his head removed?" The features of the soldier's face were serene, untroubled. "And all of them had the same expression, victims and victors."

Raphael shrugged his shoulders. "Well, then, may they rest in peace."

The last day of the festival, the boy had begun shouting, and didn't stop even when he grew hoarse, hurting business, the waiters complained. When Reynolds, out of his office early that afternoon, sat down at his table, he listened to the boy's pitch three times through: "These figures, people, I carved them myself. I'll show you the knife, with the splinters still packed in the case. Can't you see, my friends, how the sun shines on the soldiers' bayonets? Looks like real metal, ladies and gentlemen. Buy some. Should I beg? Please buy some. They're going cheap today." But if he meant to, the boy aroused no pity, as he hardly varied the words or their tone when he repeated them, and the waiters applauded when the Chairman walked over, took the boy by the flesh of the arms (his shirt hung over his chair), and shook him until he stopped. He was quiet until Reynolds, swallowing twice from his glass, half-crossed the street; then he began shouting again, even as Reynolds stood at the booth and held the head of the soldier. "That'll be a dollar for the head, five dollars for the body, and ten dollars for the whole set." The boy stared into Reynolds's chest. "You won't sell these, and you should know it by now. Can't you do cows, or sheep, or horses?" "That'll be one dollar, mister." Reynolds noticed the larger figures below the table, half-hidden in a box. "What do you have there?"

"You can be remarkably insensitive," Reynolds thought, as Raphael lifted his hand away from his face. But he said, "Maybe you have time for a little story."

Raphael sighed so heavily that the moth was blown away from the lamp again. "Sorry, Mr. Reynolds, but duty calls." The light obscured the pupils of Raphael's eyes. "As long as you're overindulging?" He pointed to the glass.

Reynolds smiled and raised a finger.

"Perhaps later for that story."

The story that Raphael had heard before: "I don't dream, but I have a flawless memory. Give me a date, and you'll have my history for that date only." That Raphael would be interested Reynolds didn't consider. What had begun to concern him—his justification for drinking—was the boy's invasion of that history.

Reynolds dipped his finger into his glass and stroked his forehead.

"March 25, 1948: my father is in the garage, running his file across my sled blades. He says, 'You're not gonna lose any races with this thing, but if some kid runs in front of you halfway down the hill, you'll cut him in two.'" Then Reynolds's father winked down his nose, not at Reynolds, but at the boy, who was whittling a chunk of firewood in the corner where the shovel and brooms were stored.

"Even though he's wasting that firewood, do you understand?"

Raphael set Reynolds's drink down in front of him, and Reynolds stirred it once with his finger. "Should I walk you home tonight?" Raphael asked before he left again.

"June 14, 1950: my father has bought us cheeseburgers in compensation for his leaving. My brother used the bun to wipe the fog his breath made on the window and, when he saw the new Rambler, said, 'Sleek.'"

Reynolds looked into his father's gray eyes. "One thing you should remember, boy," he said. "And that's that cheeseburgers are more reliable than people." He winked down his nose again. "And as for him—" he pointed to the boy, still whittling on the couch— "hell, I don't know, tell him to join the circus."

Reynolds opened his eyes and sipped from the glass. Drinking had slurred the streetlights into a beam.

"What concerns me," Reynolds said, "is the inconstancy of my memory. That no more belongs to me than the boy."

A woman had stopped beneath the canopy and was looking at him; he thought he recognized her as the mother of one of the festival children.

"Pardon?" she said.

"I'm sorry," said Reynolds. "I've had too much to drink." He left a ten-dollar tip for Raphael and stood up to leave.

At the booth, the boy had taken his dollar and placed it carefully in the cashbox. "The figures in the box are not for sale."

"Your daddy was in the War," Reynolds's mother said, peeling boiled eggs in the sink. "But he never fought. He worked on jeeps. Don't you remember how black his fingernails were when he came home?" Reynolds nodded. At the table, the boy was paring a mound of potatoes, and Reynolds's mother smiled down on him.

"It's something to be good at a thing, isn't it?"

"My mother would like to meet you."

Reynolds squinted into the sunlight he had hoped would ease his headache. He had been sitting no more than five minutes at his table, his fingers supporting his head at the temples. The boy, whom Reynolds hadn't expected to see again, set a crude figure of a man's face in front of him, along with a wooden sculpture of a cow, which, if not for the paleness of the wood, might have been pretty.

"I suppose you want me to buy these, too," Reynolds said, concealing his pleasure under the weight of his head and the steady heat of noon.

"That one," the boy said, pointing to the figure of the face, "is one of those you asked to see yesterday. The other is a cow for you to keep. You won't get milk from it though."

Reynolds wouldn't smile, though the boy didn't seem to expect him to. He was dressed in a yellow shirt too tight at the shoulders and had scrubbed his face, but

Reynolds saw dirt in the streaks of sweat that lined his neck. Raphael arrived at the table, and, knowing when to keep quiet, took two plates from the large brass tray and set them down noiselessly. He had given the boy precisely the same lunch he gave to Reynolds Saturday afternoons. And alongside Reynolds's plate was a note folded once that read, "You're more charming than I thought. The manager says he's been here since 8:00 A.M. R." Reynolds slid the note into his vest pocket.

"What's your name?" he asked.

But the boy had begun to eat and was so absorbed in that that he hadn't heard the question; he was shoveling peas with his bread, lifting the slice of beef with his hands so that its juices dripped from his fingers and down his wrists. Reynolds watched him for some time before he spoke.

"There are proper ways to eat, especially when you're trying to make an impression." But the boy continued, finishing quickly, then rinsing his fingertips in the water glass before drinking from it.

"My name is Thomas," he said. "And I was hungry."

"Tell me, then," Reynolds said, "why your mother starves you."

For a moment, the boy's blue eyes seemed to deepen a shade, and the air cooled between them, the boy tightening his fist, trembling even, as if in the change of temperature he might shatter.

"I do well by her," he said. He looked into Reynolds's face for the first time.

"And she wants to meet me." Reynolds didn't go out with women very often, and the thought of meeting one who couldn't afford to feed her son did not excite him. His interest was in the boy.

"First this man." The boy patted the figure of the head, so simple in form that it was ugly: slits for eyes, holes for a nose, and lips pinched into an expression of idiocy.

"So you had a model for this one," Reynolds said. In the boy's face for the first time was the fear that Reynolds wouldn't go with him.

"Does that mean you won't come?" he asked.

"I wouldn't buy this one, you know."

"I'm not selling it," the boy said.

The fat lady was so large that she absorbed all the other carnival sounds inside the tent where Reynolds and the boy stood: the barker may as well have been mute. She slapped her leg and pulled her dress down between her knees before the boy skipped across the floor and crawled up on her lap. She smiled and stroked the boy's hair, then the line of his mouth, finally kissing him. But when she slapped her other leg and motioned to Reynolds, he shook his head. The boy frowned, and she said, "You're jealous."

Under the canopy that had whitened in the sun, the brightness only now receding as they walked, Raphael rubbed his thumb and forefinger together while he stood at Reynolds's empty table; he wouldn't ask for the money at the evening meal, he'd pretend not to remember at all, Reynolds knew, as Reynolds pulled the extra twenty-dollar bill from his vest pocket, the vest that now lay like a blister on his back. Still, he had forgotten to pay, and that would further dim the pupils of Raphael's eyes. The boy had wrapped his shirt around his neck so that it hung like Reynolds's tie; he carried the figure in his hand.

They walked without speaking, though the boy, watching Reynolds sweat said once, "It's only two miles." Each block they walked led into the poorer sections of town, where the buildings had fewer windows and the heat loosened chunks of brick that lay in the drying grass between the walls. A woman with her chin resting on an upper-story window sill, drying her hair in the sun, watched Reynolds as he passed. From another window, a boy dangling a note on a string to a girl in a room just below snapped it up when Reynolds walked by, and said, "Mister, I can get a hundred bucks for that jacket, sweat and all, in fifteen minutes."

After a while, Reynolds touched the boy's shoulder and said, "You live here, don't you?"

"Not here," the boy said and pointed to the sidewalk. He was obviously poor, but Reynolds wanted the boy to be wonderful. For a moment he feared his normalcy: that this boy, fatherless, was using him as a father this one afternoon.

A man was sitting on a porch swing of a house between two taller buildings. He stroked a dog that was slavering at his feet. A woman was at a clothesline in the front yard clipping on sheets that had no chance of drying in the humidity.

"We're here," the boy said. The woman went inside when she saw Reynolds and the boy come up the walk.

"Tommy," the man said. He wore a baseball cap and had a ball in his hand, and his eyes were the type that would draw his visiting grandchildren out of their mother's arms; but he was still too young for that. A pair of scissors lay on the swing beside him; the dog's hair had been clipped away from its face and chest.

The man's face looked like potato skin, and when he looked at Reynolds, its creases deepened to the blue of Reynolds's suit.

I wear this even on Saturdays so you . . . but Reynolds didn't say the words or even complete the thought. Nothing in the man's body suggested he was the boy's father. The boy had set the figure down on the porch.

"If his mother's been asked to give him up," the man said, "I'm not the one who can adopt him because I can't afford it. But he's a good boy, and I'll attest to that for anyone who *can* take him." He tossed the ball to the boy, who fumbled it once, then rolled it to the dog.

"Somebody needs to teach the boy to play ball, though," the man said. "I tried for two weeks once, and you could have dipped the ball in glue and he still wouldn't have caught it." The boy sat down on the porch and stroked the dog's head. From inside the house, Reynolds heard the rattling of pots and pans. A faucet was turned on once.

"Didn't think they'd ever take him away from his mother though."

"I really don't know what you're talking about," Reynolds said at last.

"You mean you're not from some agency, or something like that?"

"No."

The man watched a neighbor, her face shaded by her hat brim, pass along the street. He waved and spoke her name.

"Then you're marrying her," he said.

"If you mean the boy's mother, I haven't even met her. He brought me here because he said that you were the model for that.

The man's face reddened, and when he stopped stroking the dog, it raised its head and licked his hand. The boy picked up the ball, rolled it back, and continued to behave as if he were deaf.

"The boy carts those things around like they were dolls. Hell, he's got hair on his face. Look, a mustache, for Christ's sake, and he's got these dolls . . ." He shook his head, and for a moment the street was so quiet that Reynolds could listen to the boy breathing.

"Hell, Tommy, you come around once in a while to pet the dog, I don't care, but you start bringing other people, especially dressed like that . . ." He pointed his thumb at Reynolds, then to the screen door. Now the house was quiet. The rhythm of the porch swing chains hadn't altered since they'd come.

"Mister, I wish you were from some agency. His mother, Christ. Once, when he was only four years old, she thinks he gets too dirty from a little game of catch, and to punish *me,* or something, she fills the tub almost to the rim, and of course the boy slips when he takes one step into the tub and slides right under the water face up, too scared to even thrash around. And his mother doesn't even move. I have to haul him out myself . . ." He raised his hand as if to hit the dog.

The boy had turned away, his eyes covered by his hands, when the woman came to the screen door. Her damp dress clung to her legs.

"It's time for your soup," she said.

Raphael plucked the twenty-dollar bill from Reynolds's thumb and forefinger.

"I couldn't tell you why I went along with that boy today," Reynolds said. "I don't belong there."

Raphael laughed and sat opposite Reynolds at the table; the shadow of the canopy darkened his face.

"You better suppose that the ballplayer bedded the kid's mother, especially if he talks you into visiting her."

Reynolds sipped from his wine glass.

"And what happens if I do?"

Raphael laughed again, took Reynolds's glass, and placed it in front of him, then from his pocket took the figure of the cow that Reynolds had left and balanced it ridiculously so its udders were dipped in the wine. He waved his hands over the glass like a gypsy and said, "You won't like her much, but she'll raise an unrequited passion in you to such a level that she'll shatter your heart, and you'll spend all the winter months sitting at my table and mumbling like an idiot."

Raphael slid the glass back across the table to Reynolds, and a passing car lighted his hair and momentarily fixed his blue eyes.

"Why in the world, when you look the way you do, do you call yourself Raphael?" Reynolds could barely distinguish Raphael's wink.

"My mother and father liked the name."

The boy was in such a hurry that he released Reynolds's hand as he took the back fire escape two steps at a time. For a moment Reynolds saw the highrise as the backdrop for the boy's dreams, in front of which his figures danced like marionettes. Reynolds hadn't recognized the streets the boy led him through; the boy had held his hand almost the entire way, though Reynolds hadn't seen him for the week that followed their visit to the ballplayer. Reynolds even thumbed through the phonebook once, forgetting, ridiculously, that the boy's *first* name was Thomas.

At last on the landing, Reynolds could still feel the street noise vibrate through the metal railings. "I don't see how you put up with the stench," he said.

"It doesn't smell here," the boy said.

"You misunderstand me."

But the boy had opened the door, and inside was not the desperate neatness that Reynolds had expected. They had walked into a small kitchen that led to another room; plastic dishes were stacked at the sink, towels slung over the faucet head. On the floor were toys and books too childish for the boy, one opened to a page with a little girl dressed in a sailor suit, her hand shading her eyes as she looked off the edge of a cliff. The print was so large that Reynolds could read it standing:

> *Bobby Shafto's gone to sea,*
> *Silver Buckles at his knee.*
> *He'll come back and marry me,*
> *Bonny Bobby Shafto!*

"She's in here," the boy said and took his hand again.

She sat in a straight-backed chair between two small mattresses, the boy's near the box that Reynolds recognized from the festival and the woman's beneath the one window that showed only another building and a corner of the sky. She was not pretty. She was dressed in a pale orange dress, a slip falling beneath the hem, her hair stringy in the humidity, her face narrow, pale, with eyes too large for her head. Behind her was the toilet and a tub in a closet-sized room that joined another apartment.

"Thomas says you are good but fastidious," she said. "And I *am* sorry."

She spread her arms as if showing the room. There were so many clothes, toys, and books on the floor that Reynolds felt the entire room was balanced on them, and if she dropped the cup she was sipping from, the floor would fall into the room below.

"So will you stay with us for a while?" she asked.

"I don't believe I could stay here ten minutes without retching."

The woman started to laugh, but no sound came from her mouth. She pulled her dress down over her slip and tapped her fingers to her lips.

"For us, neatness is a pretension."

"So, then, what? Do you want a donation?" He now realized the boy was an extension of his mother. She looked away.

"Have I asked for money?"

The boy had flopped down on his mattress and seemed to be counting his fingernails.

"You send the boy out with those figures to earn pennies that no one is about to give him, since no one will buy figures he probably didn't even carve."

She sipped from her teacup, and Reynolds glanced at the print left by her mouth, then walked to the window and saw the moon rising over the corner of the building.

"You don't work, do you?"

"No."

"And the boy does?" He couldn't lend his voice the anger he'd intended.

"You're so much in love with him that you'd believe I chose this apartment just so he could watch the moon rise."

She set her teacup on the floor, and the boy picked up a book near his bed and began thumbing the pages.

"I can hear you, you know," he said, but more as a statement of his presence than over concern for what they might say.

"You should be sleeping, Tommy," she said.

"Mother."

"Say a prayer."

He folded his hands.

"Baby Jesus, meek and mild,/Hear this prayer from a child."

That Reynolds would never recognize the names the boy spoke, that he didn't hear his own, did not disturb him. On the street a bus went by, and the windowpane, loose in the frame, rattled behind him. The boy slept almost the moment his mother kissed him. Reynolds didn't believe the woman, whose name he still didn't know. He did not love the boy but felt his presence now only as loss, a shape cast by his mother's affections and his fatherlessness, the figures of the heads he had carved a parade of men the woman had known, from whom she could no longer differentiate, from which the boy didn't care to select.

"You're thinking," she said, "of the time I almost let him drown, which of course is far from the case."

"No," Reynolds said.

"But you have a pool so well paid for that the water doesn't even ripple when you dive in."

She walked to the kitchen and washed two bowls, cups, and spoons and set them aside on a towel. The boy slept without moving. Reynolds was watching him when she came back.

"He isn't so much a boy that you should ask him to say childish prayers."

"He has the presence of an adult, but he is a child." She knelt beside him and stroked his hair at his temples, smiling a little. For a moment, Reynolds felt the weight of their isolation.

"The man he took me to meet says you don't deserve him."

She stood up, her knees cracking with the movement, and turned out the lamp in the room. The light from the outside window filtered through her dress and slip, and Reynolds could see the silhouette of her body.

"Enjoy the figures he carved for you," she said, "because he won't care for you much longer."

"And what does that mean? I suppose I should never expect to see him again?" Reynolds turned to leave, but she was on him so quickly that she would have knocked him over if he hadn't braced himself on the door. She breathed into his face.

"You want to know about his father?" she said. She took his hands and pressed them between her legs. "He was good with his hands."

The boy couldn't come within a foot of hitting or catching the ball. Even Reynolds's mother refused to cheer, and the woman who did yelled so loudly that her voice echoed off the faces of the children in the field. The man with his dog, sitting next to Reynolds on the bench, tugged once at Reynolds's cap. Then he leaned over and whispered into Reynolds's ear, "Hit the ball and touch the Lord, hit the ball and touch the Lord."

"Tell me the woman's name."

"Caroline."

"And the rest of the nursery rhyme?"

"Bobby Shafto's fat and fair,/Combing down his yellow hair,/He's my love for evermore,/Bonny Bobby Shafto!"

He had not touched her since. They walked along the midway of a large amusement park, Caroline between Reynolds and the boy, the air cooling in the September evening. She had told him that she took the boy once a year to the park, but usually in July. When a roller coaster roared by their heads, she said, "The riders seem almost resigned."

She let Reynolds pay for the boy's rides without comment, and only when he bought him a funnel cake did she say "We can take care of that," but the concessionnaire had already taken the money, and she didn't protest. The boy seemed to climb aboard the rides out of a sense of duty and was more interested in the booths where barkers were waving dolls and stuffed animals, and young men tried to throw rings over soda bottles or shoot basketballs through undersized hoops.

The boy had continued to come to the restaurant, usually to eat, saying only a few polite words to Reynolds, and leaving when he finished. He had not brought any more figures, and Reynolds knew that he was feeding the child. Once he had walked with the boy and his mother in the park, but they had met him there, and they spent most of their time watching a man throw a Frisbee to his dog. This evening, Reynolds had gone to their apartment to pick them up and glanced once inside, where it seemed nothing had been displaced from his earlier visit. A photograph of an old man and woman was on the top of the refrigerator; this he hadn't remembered.

The boy couldn't burst any of the balloons with the darts the barker placed in front of him in sets of three.

"I wouldn't have let him drown," Caroline said to Reynolds quietly. "When he was pulled out of the bathtub he wasn't even choking. He was under the water, see, with his eyes open, not even afraid, and something was pretty in that . . ." Her eyes widened when the balloon popped. The barker raised the boy's fist as would a ring announcer.

"And another big winner, folks, and another big winner." The boy held a toy kangaroo that he turned over several times in the lights.

"Here," he said to Reynolds, folding his fingers around it. "You like animals, don't you?" In her presence, Reynolds at times forgot the boy worked with wood at all. He walked in front of them, crushing kernels of popcorn beneath his shoes.

"Why does he carve the soldiers?" Reynolds asked. The lights of the carousel spangled Caroline's face.

"You haven't seen prices in a dime store lately, have you?" The boy wrapped his arms around his shoulders, as did Caroline; the wind was almost too cool for early autumn.

"He carves what he wants to and tries to sell them to help out. Sometimes, I tell him what to say."

They stopped at a Ferris wheel, and the boy dug into his pocket for the tickets Reynolds had given him.

"Do you ever ride with him?"

"No," she said.

"Well, then, it's time you did." Reynolds laughed and, with one arm, picked up the boy, who was far heavier than he'd expected, and with his free hand tugged at Caroline's wrist. Neither of them smiled or resisted, even when the ticket-taker let him lift them into the seat and lock the bar over their legs. The wheel spun around three full times before they started laughing. And then it seemed they couldn't stop, the boy's head tucked under his mother's arm, their breath, even at a distance, discernable in short bursts. The man at the controls grinned each time Caroline's dress flew up on the descent. Reynolds listened to the sound of their laughter grow and dissipate as the wheel spun around.

"So she washes only enough dishes for the next day, the next meal?" Raphael asked.

"Yes," Reynolds said. "She seems to believe her situation is insistent."

"What do they eat?" Raphael asked.

Reynolds shook his head. Raphael's eyes were half-closed, the restaurant empty.

"Raphael," Reynolds said. "Come here, Raphael."

She was already on the other side of the door, the boy, he assumed, sitting on his mattress.

"Thank you for taking us," she said. "We had a fine time."

"I would like to come in and help him go to sleep."

"He doesn't need you for that," she said, not smiling, and latched the door. But before he started down the fire escape, the boy had opened the door and placed another figure in his hands. In the dim light from the streets, Reynolds couldn't distinguish its features. He ran his fingers over its face.

"It's from smoking." The man across from Reynolds tapped a tooth with his fingernail, then brushed a fleck of dust from his worn black suit. He wore mascara on his eyelashes, and his face looked rouged.

"The yellow teeth." He smiled again. "Yes, you could scrape the color off my cheeks with a fingernail and turn my hair gray with a few good washings. I'm pretentious, I'm pretentious."

Reynolds hardly remembered coming in or sitting down with him at the table. He only now heard the large woman behind the bar, singing songs in a brogue, the few men and women at the bar raising their glasses and joining in at the chorus.

"The boy gave me the figure," Reynolds started to say.

"And it's not much of a likeness, is it? No, you needn't show it to me, I remember it well enough. Forgive him though. He was very young then. Much younger."

He sipped carefully from his glass, his shoulders hunched over, as if he were cold and drinking coffee rather than beer. He glanced at Reynolds from over the rim and with his free hand pointed toward the bar.

"Oh, she'll get to you. Don't worry; I suppose I'm being impolite. But she enjoys her songs, you see, and it brings the older customers in. She won't forget you, wait and see."

Reynolds didn't recognize any of the songs the woman sang, and his host listened for a long time, his eyes closed, his head bobbing slowly from side to side. When he drank, his mouth left lipstick on the glass.

"Soon enough," he said, "I'll get her to sing 'When Irish Eyes Are Smiling.' At least you might know that one and sing along with her."

He lit a cigarette, smiled, and tapped the filter against his teeth. Reynolds had almost expected to find the boy, but could see him nowhere.

"About the woman," Reynolds said at last. "The boy's mother."

"Caroline?" he said. "Oh yes, beautiful. I could tell you a story or two about Caroline. She loved me well enough. Oh yes, we loved each other, more than you would probably like to know."

He laughed then, as if he saw something in Reynolds's eyes, and tapped his cigarette several times in the ashtray.

"But I am not the boy's father. That I can tell you. Though I could have been. If you understand my meaning."

He winked. Reynolds hadn't noticed the singing had stopped until the woman, a green towel draped over her arm, set a glass of beer down in front of him. She lay her damp hand on the back of his neck.

"Anything else, sir?" Her accent was not the least bit Irish. Reynolds shook his head. The mug was warm to the touch.

"So. You're interested in her. Caroline, I mean," the man said.

"Yes," said Reynolds.

"But you know nothing about her really. Nothing. You've seen her—what?"

"Three times." Reynolds drank from the glass; the beer was warm and bitter.

"So you're interested in her, but you have no knowledge of her, no history. And you're a cautious man. That's it, isn't it?"

"Yes," said Reynolds. "That's it."

"So I could tell you something about her," he continued, hardly waiting for Reynolds's response. "Something like, for instance, that she lived on a house on a hill, where her father raised apple trees and her mother milked cows, and on frigid December mornings she'd jump from the loft into stacks of hay, and how once, to make her laugh, her father stuck a stub of corn cob in his ear and pierced his ear drum and, no doctors nearby, went along half-deaf the rest of his life."

Reynolds could no longer look at him. He glanced once at the woman, still singing behind the bar, then looked into his glass.

"But no, that's not it, is it? You want something closer to *me*. Here: It is an October morning. Cold, yes, but the sun warm on her flesh, and you walk amidst old buildings, the ivy yellowing on the walls, your shoulders folded towards each other to protect your intimacy; and the football game, of course, has no players, no people in the stands, just the odor of her rust-colored sweater, which you mistake for a moment as the odor of sunlight, and what matters is that she lies back in rustling clean linen, her hair as smooth as flax, her mouth tasting faintly of whiskey, her neck and breasts of cinnamon, her belly of licorice, her thighs of clove . . . that's it, now, isn't it?"

He had slid his chair around the table, and his mouth was so close to Reynolds's ear that he could have kissed it.

"You are loathsome, Mr. Reynolds," he whispered at last and then spat into his glass.

Behind the bar, the woman's cheeks had flushed red as she sang in soprano, extending the last syllable of each line:

> *Her voice is raw and sweet,*
> *Her voice is raw and sweet.*

Reynolds had hardly noticed the progression of autumn, and he drew his jacket more tightly around his ribs. The tables had been taken in from the sidewalk at the restaurant, and this night it had closed early. Reynolds stood a long time at the window, watching a young woman wiping each table and setting down a new place setting for the morning meal.

"Your father," his host said, sitting on a stack of books near Reynolds's bed, "is old now. Truth is, you pass him on the street, and his pale eyes wouldn't even blink."

Reynolds had recognized the woman from the photograph that hung in Caroline's kitchen; she moved from basket to basket of apples, her eyes closed.

"Now these are yellow delicious, these are red, these Macs,—McIntosh, I don't think you know the name—and these Jonathans, small for this season."

The boy plucked a blade of grass from near his grandmother's feet, pinched it between his thumbs and made it whistle. He had driven the boy out for the visit, his suitcase between them in the car. They had spoken hardly at all after his mother had kissed him and, squeezing Reynolds's hand once, whispered, "Come back and tell me how he does." The boy had pointed out a deer, a cow, and a horse he saw along the road, and Reynolds had said, "You don't have to show me these things just to please me," and then ran his fingers through the boy's hair.

"Ha! There, see? I was right," the woman was saying. "That's a life in a business. I swear, I could do the same thing with my nose." She took a deep breath as if to prove it, then picked the largest apple from one of the baskets and handed it to the boy.

"Caroline says you took her to the fair," she said. "We used to win prizes for these apples every year there, every year, in whatever category we cared to choose."

Most of the trees had lost their color, and the boy kicked through the leaves in the yard. Next door was a house with a rusted red tricycle in the front yard and a tire swing. A toy tractor lay on its side.

"Tommy," the woman said. "You know you can go over and play if you want to. Those people won't mind. It looks like they're inside sleeping anyway."

As Reynolds walked with the woman towards her house, the boy slid himself through the center of the swing, looked up at the sky, and spun in slow circles. The house was warm, heated by a small stove in the kitchen. There were pictures and small porcelain figures on several small tables, many more in a china cabinet.

"Sit down, and I'll make you some coffee." She found a tea kettle and set it on the stove. "It's been a long time since Caroline sent Tommy out here with a man. So maybe you're something special."

"I think it's convenient for her," he said. "Though I don't understand why she didn't come along with us."

She placed a small pitcher of cream and a sugar bowl in the middle of the table; both had yellowed with age, and there were fine cracks in each.

"She doesn't like it much here since her father died. They were pretty close."

The coffee was hot and the cream sweet and rich.

"See, I believe in working," she said. "There was always so much work to be done around here I thought being close was a waste of time. Not much satisfaction on a farm except in work."

Through the window, Reynolds could see a young girl come from the house and climb onto the tricycle. She rode around the yard as the boy stood on top of the tire, holding to the rope. Reynolds could hear their voices but was unable to discern what they said.

"See, I loved him, her father, but just like I should. Not like Caroline." She sighed once. "I keep these things around, the pictures and trinkets and so on, so that when she does come—Caroline, I mean—she'll be happy, comfortable. But it doesn't seem to make that much difference."

The woman stirred more cream into her coffee and watched the boy herself for a while. He sat down with the girl at the base of the tree, and each was eating an apple.

"Caroline treats him like he's strange," she said. "But here he acts normal. Look, he's happy eating." They had exchanged what was left, and the boy was peeling his with his knife, the skin falling to the ground in one long strand.

"That's where we store them." The woman pointed toward a door that must have led to the cellar.

"On good weather days in the winter, people will stop by to pick up a bushel. That's the thing, apples *last*. They get a little sticky towards the spring, but they last."

The boy came in the door, breathless from running, his face red from the cold. "The picture, Grandma. Where is it?"

"I think you showed it to her last time," the woman said.

"But she wants to see it again." The woman pointed to one of the small tables, and the boy took it and ran out the door again.

"Of his father," the woman said, before Reynolds could ask. "I just think it might be embarrassing for that little girl. He shows it every time, and the little girl must say something to her folks."

"He and Caroline never speak of him, at least they haven't to me," Reynolds said.

"I couldn't tell you," the woman said. "I only saw him once. Just enough to say handsome, handsome."

The woman poured more coffee into her cup and added the cream.

"Did you ever notice," she said, "how cream looks prettier in coffee than milk?"

She did not ask him about the boy once he was inside the door but only lay her head against his chest and whispered, "Did he show you the picture of his father?" and when he shook his head, took his hand and led him to her mattress. The floor of the room had been cleared of clothes and toys, as if she were trying to do what might please him. When he lay back, he could feel his shoulder blades on the floor, and when she unbuttoned her shirt in the light through the window, nothing inside him resisted. He did not like the smell of her body.

"Kiss me," she said.

The man's face was gray as the sky, his yellow hat pulled to the tips of his ears, his beard drawn sharply to his chin. "I have been ill," Reynolds said to him. He watched the grass sway over his knees.

"Inside me," she said. Her skin was damp to the touch. He could scarcely feel the burning of his own. She moved on top of him. "Inside me," she said. "There. There."

Reynolds sat beside him in the grass that even in the cold smelled sweet. He didn't move, didn't seem to notice the company. Over a hill, a flock of crows flew low over a harvested corn field; the wind, that occasionally fluttered the man's hat brim, brought their cries back irregularly over the grass.

"Listen," she said. "Listen. It can be good, but you have to move." He lifted his back up off the mattress.

"I know," Reynolds said to the man, "I know that if you sat here in the grass, and she was asleep on your lap, you would have let those crows take the whole field before picking up your gun and waking her." For a moment the man lowered his eyes towards the grass, and Reynolds could see a burst of feathers in the sky.

"There now," she said. "I can feel your breath. And you like that, don't you? Don't you?"

Reynolds turned to face him on his knees and took up his hands. Behind his shoulder, the pale disc of the sun shone through the clouds. "But there are those things you did with her, right? I mean, you watched her mother weave clover flowers in her hair, or, or, you could see the paths she'd trampled in the grass before she went to bed when you got up in the morning. And that was something, wasn't it? You'd remember that."

"You're close," she said. "Aren't you?" Her movement on top of him was hardly rhythmic, her belly looked loose and gray in the dim light.

Reynolds vision had blurred in the cold. "I would like to know that she'd take care of me. That if, twenty years from now, I were dying, she'd bring me a cup of tea, hold my wrist, and say, 'Well. Drink.'"

"Come into me," she said. Her shoulders were heaving. He felt the man's hands, smoother than they should have been, squeeze his once, and then his voice, distant, like a child's.

"Come into me," she said.

"I'm sorry," the man said.

"Now. Now."

"But if you had been my son, the boy could still hold my hands better than you would have known them."

In the sudden light of the room, he saw the boy standing in the door frame and saw the breathing of his mother; for the first time he felt the wetness of his thighs.

"You see," the woman said, her voice not triumphant, but tired. "He is no different. No different, Tommy. Do you understand now? Now do you understand?"

Reynolds's table was near the window, where Raphael had stood for five minutes listening, his face red with embarrassment.

"So you see, Raphael, I've been ill, I admit that. And I don't blame her, you realize."

Raphael smiled faintly.

"I don't believe for a minute we could have gotten along. But I still don't understand how he got back, how the boy got back all that way."

"Don't worry, Mr. Reynolds. Children heal quickly," Raphael said and tapped his fingers twice on the table. "A drink now. We'll talk, but, other customers, you know?"

"Yes," Reynolds said.

Through the window he saw him then, sitting on that same curb, huddled over something he was working with his hands. Reynolds was out the door and nearly across the street before he began to recognize the ridiculousness, again, of his tie and short sleeves.

"Tommy," he said. He felt the shame of saying his name for the first time. The boy's knife slid over the wood, and the long, even slivers fell from the block.

"Go away," he said, without looking.

"Tommy."

"Go away, or I'll stab you with it."

But Reynolds couldn't move, not yet, as what struck him first, as he watched, was the memory of his body, and then it no longer mattered that he could see the shape of his own head in the boy's hands, but instead the movement of the boy's fingers, how he pressed them into the empty eye sockets, along the nose, and between the lips of the mouth.

"I love you," Reynolds whispered, knowing that was not what he meant even as he said it, knowing that the boy could not hear. "You are my love, my love, lover."

He shook his head.

"Not that now. No . . . no . . . not that. But loveliness . . . loveliness . . ."

He shook his head.

"The Harlequin": Autobiographical Sources

When writing about the autobiographical material that informs a story (or a poem, or a novel, or a sculpture), it seems to me one risks exposing the story to clinical examination, particularly when the characters and artifacts of the story are as much of psychological origin as they are of physical (or actual) origin. Such an examination inevitably reduces a story, and, unless he suffers from an inflated estimation of the literary value of his own life's experience, embarrasses its writer. Worse yet, any reader offered autobiographical sources is bound to make auto-biographical interpretations. If a writer describes his father, and this description is similar to one of his characters, that character mistakenly becomes the writer's father. The reader has found a comfortable slot into which he can insert a story so he no longer has to be moved or troubled by it. The writer has given the reader an excuse for the story.

I mention this not as a disclaimer, but as a sort of precaution. I like to believe that any story I write has more resonance, richness, and form than my personal history. So as I begin to examine "The Harlequin," remember that the sources I've actually lived have stewed so long in my imagination that even to me they're almost unrecognizable.

"The Harlequin" had its origins—if any story ever has a pointed origin—in a dream I had four years prior to the story's completion. This was a particularly troubling time for me: I was newly married, my wife was pregnant with my first son, and I was out of work with no prospect for long-term employment. Some of the circumstances of my marriage were similar to my mother's and father's, who married in their teens and were divorced fifteen years later when I was eleven years old. The dream was long and involved, but the single scene that gave form to "The Harlequin" (is it the curse of writers to refer to one's life experiences as scenes?) ended it. In the dream, my wife and I were sitting in an apartment that at the time we would have been unable to afford. She was unwrapping presents for our unborn son, and happy, when she drew in a sudden breath, and where the wall of our apartment had been was another room. Inside was a ten- to twelve-year-old child standing in a playpen, and the child was retarded, incapable of speech.

When I woke, I wept bitterly out of recognition: the child represented, I imag-ined, my own truncated childhood, as I perceived it after my mother and father's

separation. The dream informed "The Harlequin" in several ways: certainly with
the boy, standing "in the sudden light of the room," as well as his imposed
childishness, and his disinclination to speak. But far more important is the degree
to which the form and symmetry of the story were established by the dream.

In stages, and with each story I've completed, this exploration of symmetry has
displaced the exploration of the power and perversion of language in my writing,
though the two, of course, are interwoven. I do not see this fascination with
symmetry as different from a physicist's, though it is certainly less informed.
What fascinates me is the surprise of form, its inexplicability, its coyness, its
sleight of hand. I pretend at symmetry of form and the rhythm of symmetry,
though I pretend with all seriousness, then, rereading one of my stories years later,
laugh at my pretension and its mockery as form. This is what makes it so difficult
for me to write and is why I write so slowly.

I was interested that this self-revelation about my childhood occurred in a dream
that I could not or would not conjure up while I was awake, and I felt more acutely
than I ever had the demands of the subconscious and memory. The first draft of
"The Harlequin" opened with the character of Reynolds dreaming about the boy
and his wooden figures. But any dream that appears in a story is usually so
symbolically laden as to redden the face of any reader who is the least bit self-
conscious. In part, a dream is self-staging, and Reynolds, at the outset of the story,
is already something of a rooster in that regard. I knew that I wanted the story to
alternate between what, for the story, was "real" and "surreal," but I did not want
the story to be about dreaming, and I did not want to separate by anything more
than white space "real" and "surreal." I wasn't interested in their separation, but
rather their continuity and the artifice of their display as continuity, that display a
culmination, a production similar to my dream.

It was through drafting and redrafting the first page of the story that the title
"The Harlequin" occurred to me. I knew before I titled the story that Reynolds,
while certainly the main character, was not the central, or perhaps I should say
centering, character—that role belonged to the boy. As the story is played out,
Reynolds is no more important to the boy than the boy's other "fathers," his
presence largely sexual, and his sexuality, for both Reynolds and the boy, unspeakable. A harlequin most often appears in a pantomime—thus the suitability of the
title—wearing a mask, variegated tights, and carrying a wooden sword. Reynolds's
admiration of the boy's wooden soldiers—the bayonets of their wooden rifles like
real metal, the serenity of their faces that mask their violent deaths—coincided
with the title effectively, though I had used the soldiers long before I thought of the
title. The form of the story, too, is variegated; it's lent its internal symmetry
largely through the obsessive urgency of Reynolds's experience of the variegation.
The harlequin's garment for Reynolds, through most of the story, is no different
than his skin.

I can see already the degree to which I must intellectualize my autobiographical material before I can work with it. Without this distance, the sources are too warm, too moist.

I should speak briefly to the artifice of this story, which is deliberate, if not consistently structured. (The artifice, too, is variegated, though this seems more excuse than intent). The scenes alternate, as I've said, between what is real and surreal, or more accurately between what is experienced externally and internally by Reynolds. But while this alternation is consistent, the distinction between the realms of the story is not. Reynolds reads the first half of the Bobby Shafto nursery rhyme (both rhyme and picture extracted from a Mother Goose book I read to my children) in Caroline's apartment; the second he learns from the ballplayer, one of Caroline's other lovers, who is sitting next to Reynolds at a baseball game Reynolds played when he was a child. This, of course, is impossible, unless the rhyme is recorded somewhere in the recesses of Reynolds's memory. I did this in part because I didn't want Reynolds to have the excuse of reality and unreality, because revelation does not always occur in actual experience (which again points back to my dream) and because the experience of memory is convoluted. But I did it, too, for the sake of its artifice.

All writers, of course, work with artifice; most try desperately to hide it, others, such as John Barth and Donald Barthelme and other post-modernists, parade it, exalt it. None of this work can be ignored. I'm no longer comfortable with the presumption and pretension of veracity; but neither am I comfortable with the egoism and affectation of the self-consciousness of language and form. To do the first seems to me slightly archaic, to do the second is to establish a textual persona that is in love with its own reflection. In "The Harlequin," I wanted to batter and pervert the form of the story because I think this is fascinating and dangerous, but I did not want the texture of the characters' lives disturbed by my intrusions. It is too easy for a writer to pull off the arms and legs of his characters for the sake of intellectual cleverness. More difficult is to make the characters feel their existence in a story with all earnestness, despite the form or the artifice of form that provides a medium for their existence. This is what I attempted, though unsuccessfully at times, in "The Harlequin."

At this point, I've discussed the autobiography of writing the story more than the autobiographical sources that informed the story. The two seem intertwined. But let me move on to that which is more personal and, I confess, embarrassing.

The story is, in part, about fathers, their presences and absences. Reynolds's father leaves his home when he is quite young (roughly the boy's age); the first four memories that the boy invades, at least those that appear in the text, are associated with something Reynolds's father says or does. Reynolds spends much of the story trying to father the boy, which, of course, he is incapable of doing because he is unable to come to terms with his own past, let alone the boy's. The boy himself searches for a father that his mother won't allow him to have; he systematically displaces his need for a father with the wooden figures that approximate the faces of the men that have been his mother's lovers. The figures almost become icons for the boy. And even Reynolds, at times, looks for his father in Caroline's lovers. This is part of the incestuousness of the story.

My father left home when I was eleven. My memories of him to that point are largely physical: my hand red and sore after a game of catch where I would not admit he was throwing too hard, the power suggested by the immovability of his flexed biceps, the thick, menacing growths underneath his fingernails. He was absent often—pursuing his education, seeing other women (though to my knowledge there were only two), and of course working, working hard, because we had so little money. He did not love my mother. At the time, he loved his children principally because his blood obliged him. So I remember his absence more than I do his presence, and though we became much closer as I grew older, and at times he desperately tried to sketch his face into my memory of childhood, he could never quite fill it in. Memory is retrograde, but fatherhood is not.

The day he left, I grieved, but only for a short time, because I would not allow myself grief. I remember standing at the window as he backed out of the drive in his used Rambler, my older sister saying to us, "Don't wave to him, don't wave," then when *he did,* our hands flying up as if attached to strings. That night my mother took us to a restaurant and bought us hamburgers and French fries, usually a treat we received only twice a year. And I could not help but to feel that as a kind of compensation or distraction, even substitution. And yet a substitution for what? As I've said, my father was largely absent. At the time, and rather melodramatically, as a child will, I believe I saw his leaving as taking away even that sense of absence.

Obviously, there are connections between this material and the story. The way the boy invades Reynolds's childhood memory (unsuccessfully, of course: as the story progresses, Reynolds's memory is increasingly twisted towards his sexual attraction to Caroline, and in the penultimate scene the artifacts of his memory are more Caroline's than his own), the way Reynolds feels the boy's poverty as the boy does not, the way Reynolds watches his brother use a cheeseburger bun to wipe off the mist his breath makes on the window. More important is the connection between my personal sense of absence and that of Reynolds and the boy. I had to deal with what I call this loss of absence, through which I imagined I had to become an adult. Reynolds's situation is similar, though he never sees his father again after he leaves. The boy, Thomas, knows his father only through his mother's words and his grandmother's photograph. Each of us (so strange to speak of one's characters as persons) had to try to fill this absence with other material from our lives. (But Reynolds and the boy are confined to the material provided them in the story; I am not.) This is, in part, how the story is pressured: the urgency of these characters trying to fill in an emptiness that is unspeakable, ineffable, because one cannot fill in something that is not there. And this is a part of Reynolds's epiphany:

he watches the boy carve a figure, and it is not so immediately important that the figure is modeled after Reynolds, but rather that the boy's creation of the figure is the closest Reynolds will ever come to understanding what it is to father.

I use the word father only because of the sex of the characters and the auto-biographical sources of the story. Because the story is about mothers as well. I do not dislike Caroline, the boy's mother, for the simple reason that she is so passionate, even though her passion is often calculated. Her relationship with her son had its seed in a conversation I had with a woman soon after my first son was born. She told me that she had too often pushed her son towards the arts, that she had not given him the opportunity to grow up as other children do. This is a temptation, I believe, of anyone who imagines herself as an artist. I have pushed my son toward drawing when he would have preferred to do something else. I have read him books to soothe him when he would have liked a lullaby. And, in my own restless search for material for my writing, I have taken some of the simple horrors of my son's childhood and tried to transform them into something pretty.

One image in the story that is repeated three times is the boy's slipping under the bathwater. This happened to my son once when I had left the bathroom to get a towel, gone only for an instant, and when I came back he was entirely submerged. Like most parents, I didn't hesitate to pull him out, but it was as if my mind stuttered, stopped for a moment, and locked that image into my memory. He lay on his back, motionless, his face entirely under water but his eyes open, and his expression was not one of fear, but rather confusion, uncertainty, and perhaps recognition: in it was the merest suggestion of something primeval, a simple depth of understanding of which I was no longer capable, fearing water as I do. In the story, I used the image to suggest the same, and I did not want Caroline completely to recognize its meaning. But I was interested in creating a character who would not only mentally hesitate—a thing over which I am still horrified and occasionally ashamed—but, because of her immersion in herself and her son's life, hesitate physically as well. Caroline is like no mother I've known, and it is not my purpose or intention to present her as a poor one; she is, I think, more aware of the darker side of motherhood than most.

The image of the boy under the water is also woven into the sexuality of the story, which I cannot neglect to mention here. But I would be unable to supply the autobiographical origins of it. I can say only that I do not intend it to be sociological. I do intend it to be pervasive. And for the story to work at all, it must be unspeakable, for the characters, for me as its writer, and, if I've done my job, for a reader.

I can see that I've spoken of the characters in this story alternately as persons. I do not think one takes credit for one's characters as much as responsibility for them. The same can be said, finally, for the story as well. I can easily list the autobiographical sources for many of the images of "The Harlequin": the woman singing in the bar, who is also the fat lady at the circus and the loud fan at the ballgame, I met in an Irish pub in Pittsburgh; the grandmother in the story was inspired by a woman who sells apples near my mother's home; the amusement park and the circus are any number that I've been to, always fascinated by their display but disturbed by their seduction and deformity. Caroline's mattress was like the one I bought at a garage sale and slept on for seven years; the tricycle and tire swing I saw at a farmhouse my mother and father once considered buying.

I can just as easily list the sources that were appropriated from non-autobiographical material: Caroline's father I plucked from a Van Gogh print that hung on the wall above my typewriter while I wrote the story; the two lines of the Irish ballad were sung by a woman on Garrison Keillor's *Prairie Home Companion*. Reynolds's host in the bar came in part through my love of the sound of language but also from a character in a Thomas Mann story; the restaurant, Reynolds's drunkenness, and the use of the name Raphael for a character opened the story principally because I was reading Malcolm Lowry's *Under the Volcano* when I began writing.

I could go on like this and attempt to pursue every image to its origin. But such a pursuit would be finally meaningless. The artifacts and characters of any story seem less interesting than their juxtaposition and orientation with each other. When I've completed a story, regardless of how many drafts it has gone through—and this one has gone through more than I'd like to admit—I always have the sense that the final form has been predetermined; it seems distant, peculiar to me; I feel as if I've managed the material rather than controlled it, much as one can only manage, but not control, one's memory. I don't believe any writer can articulate the blueprint of his soul or the blueprint of language that urges him towards expression. Finally, I believe a writer is more of a conduit than a creator; the question that is left for each to struggle with is nothing less than for what or for whom.

WRITING THE NOVEL I'D LIKE TO READ

by Emily Ellison

On any given weekday morning, I hand my daughter to her sitter, walk to the far side of the house, and close the door to my study. On most days that door is heavy enough and thick enough to muffle the sounds of the baby's walker wheels rolling over wooden floors and the sound of her spoon banging against the highchair tray and, sometimes, her squeals and cries. Most days the door—literally and figuratively—separates me from the rest of the world. On many other days it does not.

As a novel writer, this is my greatest obstacle, the toughest part of my job: my daily entry into one world and the closing off of all others. On most days, like the door, I am fairly efficient. On other days I am not. Since the time I began writing this essay, the baby has had two ear infections and three colds, and the sitter has been out sick four times, once with what we thought was a light stroke, the other times with the colds she probably caught from and then passed back to the baby. Both my husband and I have had food poisoning. We've flown to Miami and to New York on business. And the living room ceiling caved in from a leak in the roof; the roofers couldn't find the problem until it rained, and since we have been in the middle of a four-year drought, we waited two months before a hole the size of a grand piano could be patched and the plaster stopped falling. A new crew of workmen is due any day; because of the water damage, the floors have to be refinished. Many other things have happened since *The Picture Maker,* the novel I am finishing now, was first started: our daughter was born, my husband had a major job change, and for a few weeks a relative came to stay with us while she received chemotherapy treatment from a nearby hospital. In the past, I might have been defeated by these interruptions. Presently, because of the good folks who live in my head during the writing of this novel, I keep coming back to this room, keep listening to them, keep writing.

Toni Cade Bambara has written: "The short story is a piece of work. The novel is a way of life." This explains, in part, why I am a novel writer. It is the life that I have been living since I was in my twenties, a life that, fortunately or not, seems to suit my personality. It is a lonely, private occupation; but I have never minded being alone, and I'm always hungry for privacy.

There is also a structure to the life of novel writing that I need, that, I believe, I would not find if I wrote short stories. The late Raymond Carver once said that when he was working on a story, he worked day and night. "Sometimes I don't even know what day of the week it is. And when I'm not working, I fall into bad habits: stay up late, watch TV, sleep-in too late in the morning; I suppose I work in fits and starts.''

I no longer have the luxury of fits and starts, or of writing day and night as I did when I was younger and had fewer responsibilities. And because of my fought-against but persistent nine-to-five work ethic mentality, sleeping-in and daytime TV depress me and make me feel worthless. If I wrote short stories, I'd have too much time on my hands between the numerous endings and beginnings. With a novel, I know I'm in for the long haul. I know reasonably well what's in front of me for the next year or two of my life.

Because of the work I do and because of my other responsibilities, this life is divided into four-hour intervals. There is a part of me that would often prefer the less regimented schedule Raymond Carver described. But my daughter wakes at six and the sitter doesn't arrive until ten, so for these four hours the baby needs to be fed and dressed, listened to, and played with. During this time she rarely has to share me with my other self; it is a mistake, I have learned, to begin plotting the next scene or mentally writing dialogue on the baby's time. If I do, I miss her demand for more banana, or a particularly endearing way she crosses her legs while in the highchair, or I miss a step or a word or a fall. I miss her life, which seems to be passing at a far faster pace than anything I put on paper. And when I begin to feel I am robbing myself of time with her, I am seized with guilt and a sense of failure, two of the greatest deterrents for a writer. So. Those four hours from six to ten are hers, and mine. And after the sitter arrives, the next four are mine alone. Behind the door.

When the sitter leaves at two P.M., the next four hours are mine and my daughter's again; the four after that we share with her father. It is only after ten o'clock each night, after meals and baths and conversations and other obligations and pleasures, that I am able to return to my room if I want and edit what I wrote that morning or think about what I'll work on the next day. The next eight hours are mine again, if I have the energy. Usually I don't. Usually it is only when I'm finishing a novel that the pace and my energy increase so that I may write all night, or that my loved ones give me up for a period of days or weeks.

Simple arithmetic shows that twelve hours of each day are mine to spend in my life as a writer, the other twelve in my life as mother, wife, daughter, friend, and citizen. Half and half. It seems a fair deal, but in truth it is imperfect. Half of me is always on one side of the door, trying to keep out the other for a small stretch of time; half of me always wants to be where I am not.

The room where I go each day is like no other in the house. It has a stretch of wavy windows on two long walls. My favorite books are here, my most cherished piece of furniture (a hundred-year-old roll-top desk my husband salvaged, refinished, and put back together), and a fabric-worn, comfortable old chair, perfect for curling up and thinking, for which I compete with the dog. Newspaper articles, essays, short stories, files clutter the floor. Notes written to myself are stuck here and there on little yellow squares of paper. I close the wide, heavy door to this room, with the baby and the sitter in another part of our home, with the bills and the telephone and baskets of laundry, dust motes and pet fur and grocery lists and unanswered letters left behind me. For a while I look out at the comings and goings on the street below in this busy part of town, and I work at forgetting all that I care about on the other side of that door.

I love this room. It is the place I feel most at ease, most my self, safest. It is also the only place in my home I consider dangerous, the only room that is scary.

It is scary because the pages I wrote yesterday are not necessarily followed by ones of equal quality today, or tomorrow. The fact that I finish one novel (or a dozen) does not guarantee that I will know how to write the next. As yet I have found no formula that will at last show me how to do what I do. I keep relearning every day, relearning with every book, every chapter.

It is scary because this is the room where I hold the greatest chance of failing. For every novel I complete here, one or two, or three, will probably get scrapped. Here I know that even the novels I finish may not get published, and if they do, publication does not necessarily mean they hold any literary value.

It is a scary place because it's where old bones are exhumed, forgotten emotions are remembered, and mean moments are relived. It is a place foremost where questions get asked and not so many get answered.

Toni Morrison has been credited with saying she writes the kind of books she writes because they are the kinds of books she'd like to read. I underlined that quote when I first read it and later typed up a version of it, meant as a reminder to myself, and hung it near my desk: *Write the kind of books you would like to read.* Of course. It seems so obvious. So basic. But had I done that in the past?

My first novel was written when I was in my mid-twenties, written about as fast as I could type it, and completed in less than a year in an apartment in Fairhope, Alabama. I was the youngest person in my apartment complex by a good forty years, and about the only noise I heard during the day was a neighbor dead-heading her marigolds in the common ground behind the residents' back steps. I spoke to almost no one during those months, sometimes didn't even answer the doorbell when I was working. I ate at my desk, when I remembered to eat, and often wrote until late at night or on into the next morning. That novel was written in a steady rush not because I was in a panic to be published but because I had the notion I would not have what it takes to be a writer if I couldn't get it done in the amount of time (twelve months) I had allotted myself. The result was not a bad book (it was accepted by a publisher quickly and received its share of good reviews). But, I knew immediately, it was not the kind of book I liked to read. I knew that, but I wasn't sure why.

With one novel under my belt at a fairly early age, I should have been encouraged. Instead, my spirit was flattened, I was full of self-doubt, and I was fearful

I'd never be able to write anything that would please me. Again, I had strong notions of what writers must be, and my lack of oomph made me pretty sure I wasn't one of them. It was simply a fluke, I decided, that I had been published at all.

Despite all the negative information I kept feeding myself, I started my second novel quickly after finishing the first and as soon as I'd moved from the apartment to a tiny house a couple of blocks from Mobile Bay. The idea for the new novel had come to me months before, while I was still midway through the first book. I was anxious to get to this story, anxious to write, but I couldn't. I sat in that damp little house, surrounded by unpacked boxes, and all I could do was make endless notes in a spiral-bound artist's sketch pad about my characters and where they lived, what they wrote, who they talked with, what they believed. But I couldn't begin page one. Well, I decided, if it wasn't clear before, it certainly was now: real writers didn't stall; when they sat down to work, beautiful prose flowed, one good page followed another. Simply, I didn't have what it takes.

I closed my spiral notebook, repacked boxes, and moved to Atlanta, where I began working as a newspaper reporter. Almost three years passed before I opened my notes from Alabama, quit my job, and began writing *First Light*. This time I was ready and I took my time, wrote more slowly, more carefully. And when the book was finished and published, I was proud of it for the most part, glad my name was on it.

But when it came time to start the third novel, I was as uncertain as I had ever been about how to start; sometimes audiences at readings would ask questions about the process of writing a novel, how it was done, and I'd find myself making up answers because the truth was, I didn't know. I could remember *where* I had written *First Light*. I knew by heart every corner of every room where it had been difficult, or where the writing had gone easily. I remembered some of the problems I had had in making a scene come together. But as far as actually writing the novel—making the pieces fit—I felt as if I were suffering from sort of author's amnesia because I couldn't remember how it was done.

Two more novels were started and stopped before I began *The Picture Maker,* the novel I am completing now. The idea for it came, as the idea for *First Light* had, midway through the book before it. But it was centered on an incident similar to one that had happened to my family when I was a child, and as much as the story kept surfacing while I was trying to write something else, the idea of it seemed too autobiographical. I prided myself on the fact that the first two novels were not autobiographical, since this was something I had read authors should stay clear of and I knew was often a criticism of the work of beginning writers.

So I pushed down this story, and its characters who had begun to speak, and tried to write something else. I outlined what seemed like a good book and for several months worked steadily trying to make something happen. But the characters from that novel wanted nothing to do with me, and I couldn't get them to talk no matter how hard I tried. The notes and sketches and bits of imagined dialogue for that book were put on a shelf, and efforts for another novel were begun. This time I took as my protagonist a sixty-year-old Italian sculptor. Months more went by before I realized *he* didn't like me either. You could almost hear the sigh of relief in my editor's letter when I told him this book, too, had been put aside.

All the old insecurities returned. The fact that the first two books had been accepted and published was indeed an accident, I realized, a true fluke since it had happened twice. What I had guessed all along was now painfully obvious: I wasn't a writer after all. I wondered if they'd give me my old job back at the newspaper. Or maybe I could become a freelancer and do author profiles on some of the people I had met who *were* real writers.

Two things happened that set me to writing again. First, I reread an essay, from the *New York Times Book Review* by the Pulitzer Prize-winning novelist Alison Lurie, something I had filed away years earlier. She described how she had gone for years without having a manuscript accepted and how her first and second novels had been rejected by a long list of publishers. She described the even more heartbreaking details of how those closest to her didn't understand how important it was for her to write and gave her little or no encouragement. And then she said it wasn't until after the death of a friend, when she began trying to write about this demanding, exceptional woman, that her work changed. "While I worked," she wrote, "not worrying for once about whether my sentences would please some editor, I experienced a series of flashes of light."

Had I been worrying about what an editor wanted, I wondered, or at least worrying about the kind of book I thought I should write? I still certainly had some strange and distorted notions about how a writer was *supposed* to write (I tried following the daily routines of other writers I read about, for example, to see if their magic would work for me). But no matter what I did, it was rare when I experienced any "flashes of light."

A few days later I found the quote attributed to Toni Morrison. Was I writing the kind of books I would like to read? Not the first time, no; but even with *First Light* I found that the section I kept going to when I gave public readings was the last fourth of the book, written in less than a month in a burst of energy and inspiration, when the rest of the novel had taken more than two years. It was the character Samuel's thoughts that interested me the most and most touched my heart. And it was his section of the book that I enjoyed reading.

I remembered hearing that Eudora Welty, when accused by an interviewer of loving all her characters, had replied that she guessed she did love them all. Did I love mine? I loved Samuel, but the others I wasn't so sure about. I understood them, was sympathetic to the ways they acted, but I wasn't certain I loved them. And if I, their creator, didn't have a warm spot in my heart for them, what could I expect of a reader? Maybe this was the reason I had such difficulty reading from the earlier sections of *First Light* and why I couldn't read from my first novel at all.

I noticed that writers occasionally bring back a character or two to live in a later novel years after their first appearance on the page. There were Reynolds Price's Rosacoke Mustian and John Updike's Harry Angstrom. These writers had to love such characters, I knew, to bring them back *again* to share their homes and their lives and their minds for still another year or more. Well, the only character I had missed seeing, the only one I'd think of asking back was Samuel.

All right, then. There was something wrong here, I realized. I'd wasted valuable time, strayed some from the real reasons I had wanted to write in the first place. It was time for me to zoom in quickly on what my real goals were and to think about the designs of fiction that were important to me. I began listing the novels I most admired and enjoyed and the characters who remained, even after many years and many readings, my favorites. In the fiction I liked best, generally not all that much happened. The stories were, for the most part, about normal people living average, sometimes even mundane, lives. Fiction by John Cheever and John Updike, Anne Tyler, Flannery O'Connor, Alison Lurie, J. D. Salinger, Eudora Welty, James Joyce. And the characters these writers created were not necessarily "good" individuals, not always even particularly sympathetic or smart; but their author had made me feel as close to them as I would to a family member, someone who might anger me from time to time, someone with whom I might not have much in common, but someone I cared about immensely nonetheless. There was honesty in the writing, a rendering of emotions that rang absolutely true.

In my opinion, I had succeeded at this only once. Surprisingly, I was filled with hope instead of depression. At least there was one fellow of mine out there I could say I loved; and at least I had written one section of one novel that was the kind of fiction I liked to read.

I tried calling up those characters who had been tapping at my door more than a year earlier. Thankfully, they returned in good humor, eager to speak; they even brought a few others with them, folks I had not expected. As they began talking, I knew that what I was taking down wasn't autobiographical as I had feared. A certain event, a turning point in most of these people's lives, had happened similarly to my family. But I wasn't writing my family's story at all; most of what I was putting down were made-up incidents, imagined conversations. It was only the *emotion* that I drew from my memory. And yet, these characters seemed as real to me as any people I had ever known. In my writing before, I had cared greatly about characterization. But I had been the one *creating* the characters; this time it felt as if I were merely listening, listening carefully, and what I wrote was as honest as I could make it, as true as I knew how. That was it, then. That was the difference: for the first time I felt I was telling the truth. Not *fact,* but truth—a big difference.

The reason I had wanted to write this particular novel was very clear to me: walking home from a doctor's office one afternoon, it suddenly occurred to me that I was now the same age my parents were when I was in high school. How had that happened, I wondered. I still felt the same as I always had, but here I was a grown-up person, the same age my parents and their friends had been when they had seemed so knowledgeable and daily had to make such large decisions. If this were true for me, was it also true for them and others? Had they at this age felt as they did when *they* were younger? Had they been full of doubts and questions too back then (and even now), when I assumed certainty and answers were always there for them? I wanted to know more about the passing of time, and how people stayed the same, or changed, to cope with the daily things that happened to them.

I started *The Picture Maker* in what is now its center, and I started it in the present. I also began writing in third-person. Soon, though, I realized, I was going to have to drop back in time, back twenty or thirty years, to learn certain things about these people. And it became obvious that a third-person narration was not going to work. I had always wanted to write in the first person, but I was scared of it, afraid it wouldn't give me the distance I needed. For this book though, and these particular people, first-person was what was required, with each of my seven main characters taking their turns to speak. Since it was their voices I was hearing, I had the distance I wanted, much more it seemed than if these people were being observed by an omniscient narrator.

Strange things started happening. What was going into my word processor and coming out my printer was things I didn't know that I knew. Words were being spoken in ways that I would never talk. Half of my characters had lived twice as long as I had and lived through events I knew little about. They spoke not as if they were talking to someone, not even to me, but more as if they were looking in a mirror and telling the events of their lives to themselves. In my mind at least, they were ordinary people. But, as Anne Tyler has said, "Even the most ordinary person, in real life, will turn out to have something unusual at his center."

A writer friend of mine not long ago said he was having trouble beginning a new novel. He said it was because he didn't have anything to say. I thought about that and about the kind of writing I had done in the past, where it seemed *I* had been saying a lot. With this book it seems the characters are the ones who have something to say, and I'm just the one asking questions. But this is the reason I wanted to write novels in the first place: not so much to say something, but to *ask* a thing or two.

I have wasted time along my way to becoming a novel writer. A great deal of it was spent comparing myself to others, believing that writers were supposed to fit a particular mold. We, like everyone else, come in all kinds of packages with all kinds of peculiarities and needs and work habits. For the most part I have stopped comparing, and I have stopped expecting beautiful prose to flow every day, or even most days; I know good fiction comes from me (and from most people) with an awful lot of work and revision. At last I have learned there is only one real secret to getting a novel written, and that is to stick with it.

At last, I have worked out a pattern to my life, a schedule that suits *me* for now. Later, as my life and my obligations change, it may no longer work. I may find that I can carve out six hours from each day that is mine to spend as a writer; or I may find only two.

It is an imperfect way to write. Work takes longer to complete this way, and no matter which world I am in, part of me is always wishing I were in the other. It is no different, nor more difficult, than for anyone else who divides his or her time between work and family; it is just that a writer spends his or her time in isolation with no one else determining the office hours. There is no boss expecting a writer to show for work if the baby is sick or the plumbing clogs or the ceiling drops or a relative comes visiting, when sometimes it would be so nice if there were one.

Soon I will be finished with my novel. This time when my characters who have lived with me so long are packed up and sent to my publisher, I will not just miss them. I will grieve. No doubt I'll spend days expecting to bump into them in the hallway or wishing they were there to talk with me on my way to the grocery store or as I stand waiting to catch a bus.

This time I wish I could say I've gotten it right, that I've written a book that will totally please me. Maybe I have, but probably I have not. At the very least, this time I've written the kind of book I'd like to read.

I think. I hope. Maybe.

• Ben: 1963 •

(from The Picture Maker)

Packing up, leaving. I ain't staying here. Already stayed way too long.

That's what happened, stayed past the time I ought to. Should have left at the end of last summer, got on out of here. Walked out to the highway and stuck out my thumb. Rode down to Atlanta, or somewheres. I can get a job.

What did he mean anyway, saying I was his best hand? And what was she doing, bringing me my own little skillet of cornbread out here? Saying you ought to come to church with us sometimes, Mr. Bolt. They're nothing to me. Those children don't even know my full name, just call me Ben. Well, you look at them all dressed up like that—her so straight and pretty, both little girls each with a ribbon tied to their hair, the boy up in his arms dressed in yellow britches—and you think, now that's the picture of the American family. Well, this ain't no ball game, buddy. I'm gone!

This was the first place I come to after Raleigh. Got off the bus at Greer. I was eating me some supper, wondering should I find a place to spend the night, and I heard these boys talking about how there was work down the road. They said this man named Glass that owned a peach orchard was hiring.

I guess I had figured I'd go on further than here, some place on down the highway so Maxene wouldn't find me. But I don't know, this didn't look like a bad place, and I thought I'd stay a week or two, earn enough to get me back on the bus, heading south again.

But I stayed right on through the whole summer. I was picking at first, but Henry Glass, he comes over to me and says he's never seen such a worker, how would I like to be his foreman. I say I don't know, I guess I could do it temporary. I tell him right there that I don't plan on staying. And he says sure, he understands. So I'm foreman for a while out in the orchards. I drive the truck up and down, checking on how fast the coloreds and Indians are working. He says I'm doing good. And then he moves me up to the canning house, and I work there. I see that everything's running smooth, that the boys are backing the trucks up proper to the soaking vats, that the big wheel is turning in the water and the peaches are moving down that conveyor belt. But all the time I'm thinking, Got to get on going, can't let Maxene find me here. I'm thinking where I'll go next. I listen to what people say. What kind of jobs are where. But then this Henry Glass, he says they've got this old trailer out behind the canning house, don't I want to move in there. Nothing fancy, he says, but it's a free place to live, comes with the job, and I'll be right there if anything goes wrong.

And I think, well no, she won't find me here, not in my own trailer. So I stay for a while. He keeps me on through the fall and winter, and now the spring too.

I'm the only worker, all the summer help is gone (migrant workers mostly), and I take care of the equipment, help him put out the smoke pots here in the spring in case it gets down too cold. We spray the trees together and he says, Watch the wind!

Sometimes I ride into town with him, and I'll buy me a *Life* magazine. Sometimes I pick up a newspaper, thinking maybe I'll see my name and picture there, like I'm wanted or something. He tells me about when he used to play ball. I guess you could say they start treating me like family, sometimes asking me up for supper, him talking to me like he's known me forever. Every once in while he says to me, Bolt, you ought to settle down, did you ever think about that? I don't say nothing. I just listen and maybe nod. He don't even guess.

And all this time I'm thinking about what's happened to Maxene and the girl. Maybe nothing. Maybe they're still right there, right where I left them in that green house in Raleigh, with Budd buried in the back yard and my *Life* magazines stacked out on the back porch between that old freezer and wringer washer where she had me keep them. Rubber bands on every doorknob. Her hair curlers rolling around in every drawer. Tubes of lipstick lined up on her dresser like a row of round metal soldiers.

Maybe they don't even know I'm gone. Or maybe she talks to the neighbors and says, "Good riddance. I always hoped he'd take off."

I didn't leave 'em helpless. I did it right. Maybe I even always had it in the back of my mind, the whole plan, every detail—like somebody drew it out for me with a pencil. Like somebody said to me, All right Ben this is what you do: You go to the toolshed and take out that money you been saving that she don't know about. Then you go over to the landlady and you pay the next three months' rent, tell her you came into some extra and don't like it around the house, that you'd just as soon get some things paid ahead. You get a receipt for it, and you put it in this yellow folder. And you put nearly all the rest of that money in there too (keep out enough to get you somewhere, pay for some food) and then you close it up and put her name on the front in big letters so she can't miss it. And you write this note to Maxene and you tell her that this should keep them going for quite a while and then they can go on back home to her folks like she always wanted. Whatever she wants to do. And then you write on there: Good luck, Benjamin Bolt. You fold it, and you put that out on the kitchen table after she's gone to bed. And then you walk out of that house without a sound and you walk straight to the Greyhound station and you wait there for the next bus, and then you head out.

So that's what I done. And halfway down to here on the bus I think, I don't even have a picture of the girl. I was always talking about buying a camera, and Maxene always said, Yeah, I guess you think you're going to send some pictures off to *Life* magazine and they'll send you a million dollars. Just let her talk, I'd think, don't say a thing. But I always thought I'd buy one some time, try to keep it a secret, just every once in a while snap a picture or two of Evelyn when she and her mama wasn't looking. Not even let them know. But I didn't ever do it, and the only picture we had was when she was just a baby. Some cousin of Maxene's came to visit, and she took a snapshot of Evelyn getting a bath at the kitchen sink in a turkey roaster. Holding her up, drying her off in one of those big slick towels.

I don't know much about babies, but I always thought she was a pretty little girl. I liked holding her, giving her the bottle. But Maxene always said No, that's not right, you don't hold it like that, you're letting her drink air. I'd hand it over, go out on the back porch and throw a stick to the dog. I'm sitting there throwing, the dog coming back every time just like clock work, letting me take it from his mouth so easy. And she comes to the door, Hey I could use some help in here, Mister. I throw the stick one more time and the dog comes back, standing at the bottom on the steps, his tail just wagging, waiting, the stick dropped at his feet. And I'm back inside and, Wash your hands, I'm told.

All along I keep thinking, sooner or later she'll get to know her daddy. But it just seems like everything goes so fast, one long slow day right after another. I come home and Evelyn's in her playpen, just in her diaper, and I go to her and pick her up, and Maxene snatches her so fast and Evelyn starts to cry, and Maxene says, See what you've done? And I go out to the kitchen, that baby smell still in my lungs.

Pretty soon she cries every time she sees me, and I'm thinking, She's that scared of me? Or is it the snatching she's scared of, what happens every time I pick her up? So I keep my distance, and little eyes watch me when I move around the room.

And she's getting bigger every day, older. And I'm thinking, She looks just like Maxene. Even sounds like her. And I begin to think too that maybe there's nothing left of me in her, every thing that was ever there Maxene's got rid of like she had this big eraser and just rubbed me out.

Maybe it wasn't her fault. Maybe I misled her.

When I met her I told her I had this good job with the railroad. I thought it was. No Rockefeller or nothing, I knew that, but it paid something and I liked it. But I guess she thought it was going to be more. Right away she says, This is all? Her girlfriends had things she said, stockings, hats, they rode around in automobiles, went to picture shows all the time, why wasn't there any of that? So I start saving, thinking: One day I'll get her something. I planned to spring it on her in one big lump instead of a little trickle here and there. But I think maybe it was the trickles that she wanted. Maybe every day a little surprise. Candy, stockings, tubes of lipstick.

So she gets them herself with the grocery money, and she shows them to me like she got them from another man. And all the time Evelyn's growing closer and closer to being her mother, and she stops looking at me like she don't know who I am and turns to looking at me like I'm this bum, like one of them guys who crawl up in the boxcars and freeze to death while they're sleeping it off. And every day I come home and her mama says, Goody, goody, the breadwinner's home, while Evelyn keeps her head down playing with paper dolls, not even looking up. And I go outside and free the dog from where she keeps him chained up and I toss to him, and he brings it back to me so faithful, slobber all over the stick, his jumps so light and easy.

She's watching me out the window all the time, I feel it, and every once in a while she'll call out, You better keep that dog out of my flowers, Mister. I just throw, watching that poplar stick turn and glide in the air. Later she'll come to the door, hold it open a crack and say, If you're hungry come get it, and I'll put the dog back on his chain and after supper I'll bring him out any scraps, give him a fresh pan of water.

Right before I left I was up for a promotion. Nothing much, just the next level and a little extra money. Every day she's waiting out on the porch on the glider and she says as I'm coming up the walk, Did you get it? They hadn't said yet, I tell her, but I have this bad feeling. I was working hard, it wasn't that, but there was this new guy in charge and he wasn't much for me, I could tell. I don't know why, just one of those things some people have, something against another and there's no real reason that you can put your finger on. So the day they announce it, I don't tell her. I keep it to myself for almost a week. But somehow it's almost like she knows. She's pacing, something strange on her face. She's there every day, getting farther off the porch, closer to me when I'm coming down that walk. Every day it's Did you get it? Did you get it? Every day. And every day it's like that poor old dog's chain's getting shorter, and when I ask her about it, she says, He's digging and if he don't stop he's going down to one last notch, Mister.

He's just a yard dog, just a howling old brown yard dog, but none of this ain't his fault.

Finally I've got to tell her, I know that. But I think, I'll tell her about the savings too, tell her that promotion don't matter, that I've got money put away. We can buy some things, what is it she wants? So I move up that walk and she's there on the bottom step, her mouth stretched tight and crooked and she says, "So did you get it?" And I say, "No, but wait, it doesn't matter."

But she's back in the house, the front door banging and I go in after her, and she's in my closet and she's pulling down the gun, and I say, "Whoa here. Hey now, what's going on?"

"I told you he was digging," she says. "Told you he was in my flowers." And she goes to the back porch and pumps the cock. And I say, "Hey now wait a minute here." But she takes aim, and she shoots that yard dog right through the throat.

That's when the plan come to me, just like I'm looking at this picture somebody has drawn up. But I go out there and I bury Budd first. I dig a hole right in the spot where he's been digging, right where he's got it started for me. I dig it deep, following the lines of my plan as I'm shoveling. And when the hole's done, I put him down in there, the chain, the water pan, even the old pile of rags he slept on. All of it. And I cover it up. I stay out there past dark, and then I go on out to the toolshed and get that wad of money where I've had it hid, wrapped up in newspapers and string. When I see her light go out, that's when I go in. And I follow all the rest of the plan like I told you about.

I didn't take nothing, not even the *Life* magazines I had piled up on the back porch, the ones she kept saying needed burning. And that's when I come here.

Temporary, like I said, that's what I thought this place would be. I didn't mean to get stuck anywhere.

Right-hand man, that's what he told me. Yesterday I helped her carry in her bags of groceries. I brought 'em in and she unloaded 'em. After the last one, she says, "Oh, Mr. Bolt, there's some things from the drugstore in the floorboard of the backseat." Some bottles of liquid vitamins for the children that she said she got at a Rexall one-cent sale, could I get them for her? But then she says, "How about a cup of coffee first?" And I say I don't reckon that would hurt.

One of the girls was at the table drawing, and every once in a while she'd turn it up for her mother to see and her mother would say, That is lovely, simply lovely. I wondered if Evelyn knew how to draw like that.

He came in too and we all had some coffee. I ended up staying for supper. We watched some singing on the television, and the oldest girl she sang along, pretended she was holding a microphone in her hand, her eyes closed tight and throwing out the words to "Blueberry Hill." When the song was over she opened her eyes and looked over at us and her mother said, "Silly," and all of us clapped. All three of the children fell asleep on the floor, and she dozed off too, stretched out on the sofa, her stocking feet crossed one over the other in his lap.

It was too warm in there. They still had the furnace going this late in the year, and you could smell the pork chops from supper all the way in the living room. I forgot all about those vitamin bottles.

It was about an hour ago somebody come to tell me. I was here in the trailer frying bologna, listening at the radio. Somebody knocked and I went over and cracked the door. It was this woman, dressed up like she'd been to church. "Mr. Bolt?" she says, and I say, "Yes?" I'm thinking, *I'm found.*

She says, "Mr. Bolt, there's been this bad accident," and I think, *Evelyn.* But she says, "It's Henry and CoraRuth, Mr. Bolt. It's a car accident and they're hurt real bad, critical, one of the little girls is already dead."

Stop, I want to tell her. Don't tell me anymore. Don't tell me which one.

"Someone said you'd be the one that would know what to do here," she says, "that you could take care of things for Henry." I don't know what I say, *OK* or *Thank you* maybe. I close the trailer door, and for a time I think I can still hear her out there talking to a rusty wall. I smell the bologna burning, and then something spells out: GO.

I've cleaned this place up, leaving it just the way I found it. Every dish washed, everything swept out. I've got my jacket and my shirts, the new *Life* magazines down in a paper bag. There are all these cars parked over at the house, people coming in and out. Every light burning. I'm waiting until it's completely dark and then I'll head out to the road. Hitch or hike, wait for a bus, it doesn't matter.

No pictures, I think, not of anybody I ever knew. Just these ones in the magazines. But I look over at the lit house and I know that isn't true. I think about all those children asleep last night on the floor, her with her feet in his lap, me and him sitting there with our shirts open watching until the television goes off.

We all got pictures, I think, up here in our heads, and everywhere we go we have to take them with us.

A Selected Reading List: Novels

Isabel Allende. *The House of the Spirits.*
Mariano Azuela. *The Underdogs.*
Beryl Bainbridge. *Watson's Apology.*
John Barth. *The Floating Opera.*
Saul Bellow. *Herzog.*
Thomas Bernhard. *Concrete.*
Doris Betts. *Heading West.*
Elizabeth Bowen. *A World of Love.*
Paul Bowles. *The Sheltering Sky.*
Andre Brink. *The Wall of the Plague.*
Hermann Broch. *The Death of Virgil.*
Bo Carpelan. *Voices at the Late Hour.*
Fred Chappell. *Dagon, the Inkling.*
Albert Cossery. *Proud Beggars.*
J. M. Coetzee. *Life and Times of Michael K.*
Jose Donoso. *Curfew.*
William Duggan. *Lovers of the African Night.*
Ralph Ellison. *Invisible Man.*
Monroe Engel. *Fish.*
William Faulkner. *Light in August.*
F. Scott Fitzgerald. *This Side of Paradise.*
Paula Fox. *A Servant's Tale.*
E. M. Forster. *The Longest Journey.*
Lynn Freed. *Home Ground.*
George Garrett. *Death of the Fox.*
Jean Genet. *Miracle of the Rose.*
Nadine Gordimer. *The Conservationist.*
Graham Greene. *Brighton Rock.*
Ricardo Guiraldes. *Don Segundo Sombra.*
Thomas Hardy. *A Pair of Blue Eyes.*
John Hawkes. *The Cannibal.*
Henry James. *The Golden Bowl.*
Ruth Prawer Jhabvala. *How I Became a Holy Mother.*
Josephine Johnson. *Now in November.*
Elsa Joubert. *Poppie Nongena.*
Franz Kafka. *The Trial.*
Janet Kaufmann. *Collaborators.*
Par Lagerkvist. *Barabbas.*
Rhoda Lerman. *The Book of the Night.*
Malcolm Lowry. *Under the Volcano.*

Bernard Malamud. *The Assistant.*
Andre Malraux. *Man's Fate.*
Wright Morris. *Fire Sermon.*
Carson McCullers. *Reflections in a Golden Eye.*
Vladimir Nabokov. *Bend Sinister.*
V. S. Naipaul. *A House for Mr. Biswas.*
Anais Nin. *Seduction of the Minotaur.*
Flannery O'Connor. *Wise Blood.*
Alan Paton. *Too Late the Phalarope.*
Georges Pernanos. *Diary of a Country Priest.*
J. F. Powers. *Morte d'Urban.*
Reynolds Price. *A Long and Happy Life.*
James Purdy. *Mourners Below.*
Nahid Rachlin. *Foreigner.*
Mewa Ramgobin. *Waiting to Live.*
Erich Maria Remarque. *All Quiet on the Western Front.*
Conrad Richter. *The Town.*
Philip Roth. *The Ghost Writer.*
Nayantara Sahgal. *Rich Like Us.*
Paul Scott. *The Raj Quartet.*
Christina Stead. *Miss Herbert: The Suburban Wife.*
Robert Taylor. *Fiddle and Bow.*
Aleksandar Tisma. *The Use of Man.*
Sigrid Undset. *Images in a Mirror.*
Douglas Unger. *Leaving the Land.*
Robert Penn Warren. *World Enough and Time: A Romantic Novel.*
Virginia Woolf. *To the Lighthouse.*

WRITING POETRY

KEYS TO THE WRITING OF POETRY

by Herbert Scott

Sit awhile wayfarer,
Here are biscuits to eat and here is milk to drink . . .
—*Walt Whitman*

In the eighteenth century Alexander Pope wrote that poetry is "What oft was thought, but ne'er so well expressed." Perhaps since he wrote during what we now call the Age of Reason, he neglected to add "What oft was *felt*." Today, although we might say that poetry is generated by thought *and* feeling, the poet's problem remains the same: how does one express in a new way what has been thought and felt since the advent of humankind? Ezra Pound, in his advice to poets, writes "Go in fear of abstractions." Thought and feeling are, of course, abstractions. If the stuff of poetry is, then, abstract, how do we avoid abstraction? The answer is simple. We must objectify idea and emotion. We must make them concrete. We must create scenarios for them, give them body, voice, place, movement.

When I was fourteen, I worked for several months as an apprentice gravedigger at the Summit View Cemetery near Guthrie, Oklahoma. Digging the graves of children haunted me. It seemed obscene and totally unacceptable that children should die. I hated how small the graves were. When we dug the graves we used a shovel for the first three feet (dirt) and a pickax for the final three feet (clay and slate). I thought it reprehensible that gravediggers received a bonus, beyond their hourly wage, of fifty dollars for digging an adult's grave and twenty-five dollars for a child's grave. These strong feelings stayed with me. Years later I wrote "The Apprentice Gravedigger." I knew, as a writer, that I must objectify my feelings, give them physical presence. The apprentice gravedigger is speaking:

I don't like to dig
the children's graves.
They cramp you in,
not room enough
to swing your axe
or work a sweat.

I'd like to climb in,
brace my back,
and push them longer.
If I was stronger.

I needed an *image* that embodied the energy of the emotion. What I wanted the reader to understand from this was the apprentice's refusal to accept the horror of the death of children, and his desire to believe that if he could somehow push the graves longer children wouldn't have to die.

We experience our existence through the *senses*. We store in our memories images of love, hate, fear, and so on, not the abstractions themselves. Jesus taught by parable because we *remember* stories, and the paraphernalia of stories: the characters, objects, scenery, all the strongly drawn and well-observed detail. And *then* we experience the ideas, emotions, and symbols these images evoke.

Students of writing must get weary of hearing that one must learn to write images, even *think* in images. Pound writes that "It is better to present one image in a lifetime than to produce voluminous works." One of my favorite definitions of poetry is itself an image. From Wallace Stevens: "Poetry is a pheasant disappearing in the brush." For me, this calls to mind how beautiful, mysterious, and elusive a good poem can be. It is much easier to be general and abstract in one's writing than it is to pay close attention to detail, to present images. One Monday morning a student came to my office to tell me that he had written ninety poems over the weekend. Of course he had written none. His ninety poems were similar to the poem I will attribute to a not-so-mythical beginning writer who, asked to write a poem about his relationship to his mother and, overwhelmed by the enormity of this task, writes "My mother loves me./I love my mother./The end." Well, that seems to take care of it. No need to write any more poems on *that* subject. What this writer hasn't learned, among other things, is to chew one bite of his pie at a time. What he might remember is snowy winter afternoons when he was a small boy in Paw Paw, Michigan, how he would walk home from school, how he was a good boy remembering to wear his mittens, but how wringing wet they had become from his gathering of snow into missiles to hurl at trees and passing cars, and how stinging cold his fingers were. And how, when he opened the door into his warm living room, his mother hugged him, laughing, and told him how cold he was and tucked his hands under her arms to thaw, and how he could feel her heart beating against his cheek and her breath stirring the hair on the top of his head until he was warm again and laughing and could smell the ham and navy beans simmering on the stove in the kitchen.

Imagery

For our purposes, let's reduce the act of writing the first draft of a poem to a simple three-step process: (1) careful observation; (2) accurate recreation of that observation; (3) speculation about that observation, perhaps in the creation of metaphor, perhaps in questions we ask ourselves and/or the reader.

The poet must have supreme concentration, must *see* things clearly and accurately. The best hitters in baseball say that when they are concentrating well they can see the rotation of the seams on the baseball as it comes toward them from the pitcher's hand at ninety miles an hour and instantly know whether the pitch is a curve, a slider, a fastball, etc. A poet must concentrate that well and see that clearly. It is this intensity of vision that opens the world to us and allows us to experience it in new ways. And our focus must be as narrow. We must see the world an inch at a time. Stevens says, "Imagination applied to the whole world is vapid in comparison to imagination applied to a single detail.''

As the hitter sees the ball leave the pitcher's hand, he is already beginning his swing. Everything happens almost simultaneously. Everything comes together: the hitter's training, ability, experience, knowledge, conditioning, technique, and, hopefully, the bat and the ball. The hitter wants to make contact.

How do we bring everything to bear at once, how do we make contact? First, of course, we must observe, see. Fine, so far. Consider a poem as an act of communication, first with one's self, then with others. The hard part, of course, is the communication with others. How often we have stunning ideas, heart-plundering emotions, if we could only get them down on paper. What we do get down never lives up to those marvelous visions in our heads and hearts, those home runs that keep leaping out of the park. But if we learn the fundamentals and work hard, we will make contact. We know we're probably not going to be .400 hitters as Ted Williams and Elizabeth Bishop were, but the rewards are there for the .250 hitter as well.

We as aspiring poets must recreate or reimagine in words what we have seen. We must name things. We must be like Adam naming the animals. By naming something we acknowledge, identify, and experience its uniqueness.

In the following poem the poet, by naming, brings to us and our experience the speaker's sense of loss. The details, piled one on top of the other, create both the world of the speaker and the imagined world of the brother, and the distance between them, traversed only through the image of smashed pumpkins.

My Brother
by Gina Cole

Montez, I wish I knew you when you were a nappy-haired
Squirt playing stickball after dark,
Hanging out at Joe's Corner Store with your pals,
Benny and Nate, smoking Luckys, or
Smashing Halloween pumpkins on 64th Street.
But, big brother, you were a daddy before I was born.
Before I played kickball in the vacant lot where Mrs. Crumm
Burnt up with her woodstove on Thanksgiving; before I raced

*Up Delano Hill with my best friend, Evette, to buy Bazooka's
and candy cigarettes; before I hated Halloween after
Derek Cameron slammed my bright, warm jack-o-lantern
        against Lincoln Street.*

The use of names of persons, places, brands, can be effective, as they are here, in furnishing an interesting surface to the poem. Even Mrs. Crumm is named. Bazooka's and candy cigarettes add something that "to buy gum and candy" wouldn't provide. Delano Hill and Lincoln Street give the voice authenticity: we believe the speaker knows those environs.

Here is another example, from "The Apprentice Gravedigger," of naming.

One day, as I was digging a grave, I heard a rustling in a tree behind me. This is how I recounted, in the poem, what happened next:

*I killed a king snake sunning
in the branches of a cedar,
cut him with a spade
until he spilled
his breakfast on the grass.*

*Five sparrow babies,
slick and sweet,
poured out like heavy jam,
the fruit still warm.*

*I nudged them in the grave.
The snake, the birds, the man,
together in the ground.*

This section if it is successful is so because it includes images that allow the reader to experience in some measure what the speaker has experienced. In large part it accomplishes this by *naming*. If this section read, "One day I saw a snake in a tree and I killed it and it had a lot of birds inside and I pushed the whole thing into a grave," the reader would have the necessary information but not the experience itself. What kind of snake was it? A king snake. The reader sees a black snake three to four feet long. What kind of tree? A cedar. The reader sees the snake draped across the flat cedar branches "sunning" itself. How was it killed? Cut by a spade. The reader sees the severed snake. What was inside? Five sparrow babies. What did they look like? Heavy jam.

I tried to be as specific and concrete as possible, to reimagine the experience in such a way that the reader could also see it. When I came to the image of the birds, I remembered the half-digested sparrow babies pouring out like a thick, strawberry jam—the one simile or "speculation" in the passage.

The importance of that close attention to detail cannot be stressed too strongly. The best poets see things the rest of us overlook. Elizabeth Bishop, one of our very best, has often been described as having a "painterly eye" because of the richly textured surfaces of her poems. William Carlos Williams would never go without his glasses because he could not bear to miss any small detail in the surrounding environment. Charles Simic looks closely at simple implements such as knives, forks, spoons, and brooms and makes us see them in amazing new ways. As Stevens tells us, "The real is only the base. But it is the base."

A Poem Is Somewhere Waiting for You

Proust wrote that we who have survived childhood have more material to write out of than we can ever use. In the unconscious mind resides every experience of our lives, even experiences from the womb. Part of the process of writing is to free the Unconscious, bringing to the surface that which heretofore seemed unavailable to us, that which we thought we had forgotten, and that which we have never remembered before now, for whatever reason. Writing is often a way of thinking about one's life. Reimagining or recreating the past allows us access to our lives.

Childhood is everyone's subject matter; therefore, it is a good place to begin looking for poems. It is also a good place to continue to look for poems. Many fine poets write about their childhoods throughout their careers. For instance, Philip Levine's book *1933* appeared when he was fifty.

Here are some ideas for beginning a poem suggested by a memory of childhood.

Most of us have a special place from our past—perhaps we were born there or spent years of our childhood there—which will always be with us. Write a poem that takes place in the town, city, neighborhood, or rural area where you grew up. The poem should focus primarily (or completely) on *one* time and *one* event (incident, happening). Call to mind various neighbors, family friends, relations, members of your immediate family, your best friend, your worst enemy. Who was the strangest, or most original, or craziest, or most lovable person you knew? Capture that person in action, on locale.

Approach the poem as participant and/or observer. Recreate that time, place, and event for the reader. Here is a childhood poem in which the poet is an observer:

Katherine's Hair
by Dave Marlatt

I once saw my Grandma with her hair undone.
Long, white, wild.
Wind blew it about as she leaned on a dying elm.
I'd seen her first communion picture.
Dark brown pipe curls
Overflowing her shoulders
Onto the white gathered dress
Aunt Kate made.

Her eyes are the same.
"Oh don't look at me."
The wind blew from the East
Shooting maple seeds.
Pulling long strands
Across her face.
With both hands
She gathered her hair
From the wind.
Caught it up
With Ceylonese combs
Carved from ivory.

The poet calls to mind a time he saw his grandmother in the yard with her hair undone, an image that shone for him through time and space. Note how effective Marlatt's use of the grandmother's voice is. I can think of dozens of poems where the use of the subject's voice makes the poem. See, for instance, William Carlos Williams's "The Last Words of My English Grandmother" and Gary Snyder's "Hay for the Horses."

Ways to get started:

What are the images from your childhood that shine brightly through time and distance? Write them down as they occur to you.

Begin the poem "I remember . . ." and list what you remember.

If you fear you are going to have trouble being concrete and specific, make a list of things that must appear in the first draft. Here is a list you may use: (1) the name of at least one person; (2) a road or street; (3) something growing from the earth; (4) an animal; (5) an implement; (6) a part of the body.

Leaf through an anthology of poems; note the ones about childhood and the ones that focus on a single event or occurrence.

Our emotional ties with the past and with place make them valid and important material for writing. As you write, be receptive to whatever images come to mind, allow what was heretofore closed to open. Afterwards, consider your emotional and intellectual responses to that time, place, and event. Consider its significance.

Here is another poem examining childhood experience:

Catching Suckers
by Joseph Freye

In the spring
on the island
when the creeks are full
the suckers run up them
to spawn.
And each spring we meet them there.
We pile into the old truck

and bounce to Sucker Creek.
And they are lying there thick like slimy cordwood does
in the morning after a storm.
We splash about
and they bounce off our boots.
Carefully we slide our fingers
under the fish
and stroke their bellies
to trick and confuse them.
And then we grab them up quick
and hoist them high,
still swimming in our hands,
and gulping air through
the O rings of their lips.
I catch one in each
hand
and hold them for a picture.
My father laughs
as they spray spawn
into my hair and onto my blue jeans.
I toss them back.
My little sister catches one
by the tail
a beautiful smallish
grey-pink sucker
and we laugh with her until we cry
when she
kisses it on its mouth.
It squirms loose
and is lost in the mass
of writhing backs.
Mom even wades with us
tottering and giggling on slick rocks.
My brother
as he grabs for an enormous fish
comes close to slipping in.
He fills his boots in a deep spot
and grins as his prize
wiggles sperm about
his arms.

First Drafts

In a first draft, write everything down. I write on yellow legal pads. The large expanse of paper makes me feel comfortable, gives me plenty of room. In a first draft let yourself go. Don't censor yourself. If you get off on a tangent, the tangent may very well be the real poem. The idea is to free the Unconscious, to let it inform and structure the poem. The poet's task is *not* to know what the poem is about. It is the poem's task to know. If you are able to see your material clearly and to free yourself of preconceived notions and other such encumbrances, the poem will have a chance to surface, to become.

When you are writing a first draft, keep it going as long as you can. Keep it alive in your head while you are not able to work on it outright. You might keep at a first draft for several days. During this time, don't make final decisions. If three metaphors come to you that are all doing the same thing, write them all down. You may know you can use only one, but at this point you are not the best judge of which one, and you may be able to use a second one elsewhere. Don't worry about line breaks at this time. Don't stop when you don't immediately find the right word. Keep going. These are matters to be considered later.

After the draft is finished, let it cool awhile, if you can. Begin something new. Distance yourself. Return to it with a fresh eye. You probably loved it when you first finished it. Now you may hate it, think there is nothing there. Trust neither response. You, at this point, are your own worst critic. When you are feeling more objective, go through the draft and underline the lines you like best. Write them out on a separate sheet of paper. That may be the poem.

Revision

The process of revision is usually one of paring down, tightening, condensing. I have suggested that a first draft should include more material than the poet will finally use. It is much easier to cut an original version than it is to add to it. In a way, the poet has to enter the wilderness of that first draft and discover the poem hiding there.

I have suggested one approach to revision would be to underline the lines or images that seem to work best, then to write them down on a separate sheet of paper. Some first drafts will not be as ungainly as I have described. Some may be close to the length and shape the poem will take when finished. In either case, here are some ways to consider your poem as you work to complete it.

1. Often the beginning of a poem is an introduction to the poem itself, or is the poet thinking about the poem, getting into it. See what your poem might gain by removing the first line or first several lines. Perhaps the opening lines "give away" the poem, undercut its effect. Is your first line too flat? Which line in the poem would make the most stunning opening? Which line would get the reader into the poem more quickly?

2. The concluding line or lines of an early draft often tend to sum up the poem, as if the poet were afraid the reader won't get the point. If your poem says too much, cut back to the final strong image. It is usually better to conclude with an image than with a statement, especially if the statement explains the poem. Trust the reader and the reader's intelligence. None of us like to have mystery explained away. Our pleasure comes through thinking about and puzzling over various matters—such as poems.

3. Rearrange the poem. Move lines around. Move stanzas around. Perhaps the last section would work better as the opening of the poem.

4. Make each line of the poem justify its existence. How would the poem read without a certain line? Consider each word in the poem. What articles, prepositions, conjunctions, modifiers might be removed?

5. Much of the strength of a poem rests in its strong verbs and particular nouns. Which verbs are weaker than they should be? (Should *moves* be *jogs, wobbles, canters, weaves,* etc.?) Which nouns could be more specific? (Should *tree* be *eucalyptus, willow, blackjack oak, elm?*)

6. Often a passage will gain energy and movement if you change forms of *to be* to an active verb. Check your use of passive verbs and see which ones can be changed. How many lame constructions such as "there was" can you remove from your poem?

7. Which words in your poem don't seem quite right? Now is the time to look for the exact word you need.

8. While you are working on a poem say it out loud over and over again. Listen to it. What doesn't sound right? What does your voice tell you about where lines should break, where stanzas should break? Is the poem's music working? What are the rough spots? Where does the movement become static, awkward, unsurprising? Perhaps you should vary sentence structure, try different line lengths, and so on.

9. Extreme measures. Perhaps, finally, there are only three or four lines in the poem that you really like. Do these lines work by themselves? (The right title might help.) Or you might start over, with these few lines as your beginning. Or you might look at these lines in conjunction with other good lines from other failed poems. Does anything good happen? If nothing else, save these lines. They may be just what you need somewhere down the line.

10. See what you might gain by rephrasing different figures of speech. For instance, try changing similes to metaphors. "I climb like a fever to the forest" might become "I climb a fever to the forest."

11. Try changing the point of view in your poem. "It is difficult to love this woman in your arms, her face familiar as your own." Or, "It is difficult to love this woman in my arms, her face familiar as my own." What is gained or lost in each version?

12. Questions. Poets often ask questions in poems. Two who do so very successfully and for different reasons are W. B. Yeats and Elizabeth Bishop. Look at Bishop's "Filling Station." Try adding questions to your poem, playing off them or leading up to them.

13. When you feel you have a polished, finished poem, or at least feel that you have taken it as far as you can, go back and look at earlier drafts to see if there is something that you took out that you really liked. There is the possibility that you have taken out too much, revised the poem right out of the poem. Try to get that particular image back into the poem. At the very least, save it.

14. Never throw away a previous draft. If you revise on a computer, be sure to print versions as you go along.

Point of View: The Position of the Poet in the Poem

There are innumerable ways to present a poem.

In Stafford's "Traveling Through the Dark," the speaker is *inside* the poem as *observer* and *chief actor*. We follow his actions as he comes upon the dead deer on the mountain road, stops his car, discovers the presence of a still-alive fawn in her belly, and, finally, pushes her over a precipice into the river below.

In Gary Snyder's "Hay for the Horses," the speaker is *inside* the poem, but chiefly as *observer,* our authority on the scene. The chief actor in the poem is the old man who has driven a truckload of hay from the San Joaquin valley to the fire camp in the mountains.

In James Wright's "A Blessing," the speaker is inside the poem as *observer, actor,* and *interpreter.*

In Wallace Stevens's "Disillusionment of Ten O' Clock" and in Elizabeth Bishop's "Filling Station," the speakers are *outside* the poem as unnamed and unidentified *observers* and *interpreters.*

I say "speaker" rather than "poet" because the speaker *may* be the poet, but may as easily be a *persona* of the poet, a voice the poet has created to speak his or her poems that may or may not approximate the poet's private voice.

A somewhat different persona, more easily discerned, occurs when the poet assumes the identity of a specific person. Thus, in Bishop's "Crusoe in England," the speaker is not Bishop, or a persona of Bishop, but Robinson Crusoe living out his last years in England after his rescue and the subsequent death of his beloved Friday.

In another poem the speaker may address directly the reader, or a friend, or a historical personage, as if in a letter or in conversation. Philip Levine addresses a poem "To a Child Trapped in a Barber Shop."

It is helpful to examine these poems and others in order to gain an understanding of the latitude one has in approaching a poem. If your initial draft of a poem isn't working, perhaps repositioning the speaker in relation to the poem will produce better results. The different effects achieved can be quite startling.

Your own *voice* will develop naturally as you continue to write and to pursue your own way of seeing things, your own subject matter, imagery, and motifs. Theodore Roethke's voice is distinctive for a number of reasons, not the least of which is his use of the lush imagery of the natural world, which he gleaned from a childhood spent among his family's greenhouses in Saginaw, Michigan.

Metaphor and Simile

A *metaphor* makes a direct comparison of two things essentially unlike one another by saying one *is* the other: "The wind is an old friend who enters without knocking." A *simile* is a comparison of two essentially unlike things, using such connectives as *like* and *as:* "Here and there houses rise up out of the flatness like forgotten promises."

Metaphors may also be implied: "The white sheets fold their wings in the cupboard." This line implies that the sheets, probably while drying and flapping on the clothesline, are large birds, which now are sleeping or nesting.

How does one make metaphor? I believe it all goes back to *seeing* things more clearly than ever before. We must observe with such intensity and concentration that the imagination is set free. And the mind must always be questioning, seeing relationships, possibilities, reverberations. An eighth-grade girl considers her heart: "The heart is inside your body and lonely. Beating or pushing all the time to get out. But you can't let it go. It's your prisoner locked up in the darkness of yourself."

Read Elizabeth Bishop's poem "The Fish." In this and many other of her poems, one can see the creative process happening, see the metaphors rise up from the details she so closely observes. Charles Simic is also miraculous in his use of metaphor, as is Conrad Hilberry in his book *The Moon Seen as a Slice of Pineapple*.

I include here a few examples of metaphor from first-year writing students, chosen from a week's batch of poems.

> *The fog is pulling apart,*
> *a sheet of wet tissue.*
> —Joel Bodine

> *The creek flowed by, ankle deep,*
> *reeking of dead fish,*
> *yet he'd stand there gazing*
> *as though the rings of oil spills*
> *were rings from the dead fish jumping.*
> —Fawn Butler

> *I was a Forenza girl, queen of the suburbs,*
> *risen from condominiums and dogs named Tiff.*
> *I walked as if the air rested upon my shoulders*
> *like a fallen halo.*
> —Marie Ashley

> *After supper, when all the dishes*
> *were washed, dried, and put away,*
> *Grandma would fill the kettle*
> *and Lydia would begin her walk down,*
> *cats drifting behind her like a kitchen aroma.*
> —Julie Paavola

> ### Drought
>
> *The wind wakes dust devils*
> *in whirling black cloaks.*
>
> *Parched corn leaves click their claws.*

Stalks crack and scatter the ground
with piles of bones. The earth,

dry and crossed as a plowman's hands,
peels like thin wood shavings.

Famine, in loose overalls, jigs
as the wind pulls him from his nails.
                    —Tyler Kundel

It might be instructive to look at an early draft of Tyler Kundel's poem:

The wind rushes through the field,
and wakes dust devils in whirling black cloaks.
Parched corn leaves
flutter and click like claws;
their stalks sway, as if to moan,
then crack and scatter to the ground
in piles of bones.
The leathered earth,
dry and crossed as a plowman's hands,
peels like thin wood shavings.
A scarecrow,
Famine in loose overalls,
jigs as the wind
pries him from his nails
to dance across the land.

The revision is considerably leaner, and the simile of the parched corn leaves becomes a metaphor. In the final image the poet trusts the reader to see the scarecrow without its being named. The poem is rich in simile and metaphor which rise out of the poet's accurate observation.

The Use of Line in Free Verse

The poet should be aware of the possibilities inherent in the free verse line, how the line can and should work for the poem, how line and subject go hand in hand, how the line shows the reader how to read the poem.

By rule of thumb:

1. The most emphatic position in the line is the last word since the eye rests there momentarily before it moves to the next line.
2. The short line is delicate and slows the movement of the poem. (See William Carlos Williams's "The Red Wheel Barrow" especially.)
3. The long line is powerful, rhetorical, keeps the poem moving. (See Walt Whitman's "Song of Myself" especially.)
4. The line may be based on patterns of speech (where one, when talking, pauses naturally for emphasis, or rhythm, or breath, or meaning, or because of grammatical patterns such as prepositional phrases and clauses.)

5. A line may be based on a complete image or thought. (See James Wright's "A Blessing.")

6. A line may be end-stopped; that is, end with a semi-colon, colon, dash, or period. A preponderance of end-stopped lines slows the poem, keeps it stopping and starting. This works well in a poem such as William Stafford's "Traveling Through the Dark," in which the action of the poem stops and starts and pauses.

7. A line may be enjambed, or run-on. In such a line the thought, image, and action continues without significant pause from one line into the next. This keeps the poem moving. Gary Snyder uses enjambment well in "Hay for the Horses." The action of men unloading hay is reinforced by the lines that move the poem along at a steady pace.

In the following poems, notice how the lines work for different effects. "Mother at the Mirror" has short, enjambed lines that move the action slowly but without pause. In "Crow Box" the first stanza stops and starts. Five lines end with periods. The second stanza is two sentences, the second of which is six lines long, which builds momentum for the poem's conclusion. The lines are considerably longer, workman-like, with no surprising enjambments.

Mother at the Mirror, 1939

> She says
> her lean evening
> prayers
> for the flesh
> fingers dipped
> in Pond's
> cold cream
> blessing
> her face
> before the birdseye
> maple dresser
> children tucked
> asleep
> beneath the rim
> of wind-whipped
> sheets.

Crow Box

> "Come with me," my grandfather said,
> "we are going to check the crow box."
> He took my hand and we walked
> down the lane to the ravine.
> There on a post sat a crude little box
> and I had to climb three rungs up the fence
> to see the yellow chick enclosed.

"But won't it die?" I asked.
"Bait, my son, one life for ten," he said.

Three mornings I carried oats in my pocket,
water in my hand, to check the crow box,
till the black bird was trapped,
its neck wrung. An old red hen
hatched the next chicks, in safety,
beyond the catalpa, in the high weeds,
and I took four of her brood
behind the woodshed
and cut off their heads.

Here are some suggestions for discovering the best form for your own poem:

1. Read the poem aloud. Where does your voice tell you the line breaks should be? Are there any lines that should include only one word? You can make any choice that seems appropriate.
2. Look at the content of your poem. Should the movement stop and start, or should it flow?
3. Think about stanzas. Does the poem need to be broken into units? A stanza is something like a picture frame. It surrounds and isolates, allowing the eye to focus on the unit by itself.
4. Be willing to try any form until you discover what works best for that particular poem.

Some poets use the term "organic verse" rather than "free verse." This suggests that each poem's form grows naturally (organically) from the poem itself. Each has form, but each form is unique. Robert Frost said that writing free verse was like playing tennis without a net. This remark was not meant as a compliment, but the free verse poet can, at least, accept it as a challenge. He or she must invent the net too.

Formal Verse

The beginning writer often wants at once to write poems with rhyme and meter. This is a bad idea since one can rhyme forever and turn out page after page of metronomic, sleep-inducing lines that have no relationship to poetry.

It is far better to learn to present images first. Then one should study the work of masters such as Shakespeare, Yeats, and Bishop to gain some knowledge of the inherent complexities and possibilities of formal verse.

The process of describing or analyzing the meter of a poem is called *scansion*. The best way for me to show the subtle skills that must come into play to make a formal poem work is to *scan* one. In scanning a poem, one notes the poetic foot and the number of poetic feet in a line.

Poetic Feet

Iambic (iamb): unstress, stress—two syllables (˘ -)
Trochaic (trochee): stress, unstress—two syllables (- ˘)
Spondaic (spondee): stress, stress—two syllables (- -)
Anapestic (anapest): unstress, unstress, stress—three syllables (- - ˘)
Dactylic (dactyl): stress, unstress, unstress—three syllables (- ˘ ˘)

Common Poetic lines

Dimeter—two feet
Trimeter—three feet
Tetrameter—four feet
Pentameter—five feet
Hexameter—six feet
Heptameter—seven feet

The following poem is written in iambic pentameter. Each line has ten syllables (five two-syllable feet). For the most part the feet are iambic. (˘ ¯) There is one trochaic variation (- ˘) and three spondaic variations (˘ ˘). The important thing to notice is the *variation in stress in both the unstressed and stressed syllables*. It is this subtle variation *within the limits of the form* that makes the verse effective and keeps the rhythm from becoming predictable and monotonous. In this poem, for instance, it is remarkable that line *five* and line *ten* are both *iambic pentameter* yet are strikingly different rhythmically.

The Wood, The Weed, The Wag
by Sir Walter Raleigh (1552?-1618)
To His Son

(1) Three things there be that prosper all apace
(2) And flourish while they grow asunder far;
(3) But on a day, they meet all in a place,
(4) And when they meet, they one another mar.

(5) And they be these: the wood, the weed, the wag.
(6) The wood is that which makes the gallows tree;
(7) The weed is that which strings the hangman's bag;
(8) The wag, my pretty knave, betokens thee.

(9) Now mark, dear boy, while these assemble not,
(10) Green springs the tree, hemp grows, the wag is wild.
(11) But when they meet, it makes the timber rot,
(12) It frets the halter, and it chokes the child.

It is instructive to note the most obvious variations in Raleigh's poem and why they are there. For instance, the only trochee in the poem appears in fourth position in line three and gives tremendous emphasis to the key word "all" which foreshadows the poem's conclusion.

The second major variation occurs in line ten where seven of the syllables receive heavy stress, slowing the poem and suspending the reader in that moment of seemingly limitless joy and possibility.

The final, brutally effective variation comes in line twelve where three very quiet, weak syllables in a row set up the harsh and violent alliteration that closes the poem. It's almost as if we experience that instant of silence after the trap door opens, before the body drops and the slack rope tightens.

It is my purpose here merely to suggest some of the complexities involved in the writing of structured verse. Whether or not we intend to write in meter, it is important for us as writers to understand the accomplishment of our great poets, past and present. A good way to begin to gain such an understanding would be to read, and own, one of the many fine handbooks on poetry currently available. X. J. Kennedy's *An Introduction to Poetry* is particularly noteworthy.

Music in Poetry

In Wallace Stevens's poem "Thirteen Ways of Looking at a Blackbird," the speaker says he doesn't know which he prefers, the blackbird's song or just after. In contemporary poetry the preference seems to be for the latter, for a music so subtle that it is more remembered than heard, an almost subliminal experience. The feeling one has after *hearing* such a poem might be akin to waking up in the morning and feeling utterly happy but not knowing specifically why.

Language is less formal, more conversational in contemporary poetry than in previous periods. Williams, for instance, follows the rhythms and patterns of speech in his poems.

Speech, of course, does have its own rhythms and music. The poet must hear as well as *see*. When I was a student and first in the presence of practicing poets, I was amused to hear them talk about their "ears": "She has a good ear"; "I like his ear though it's very different from mine." As poets we must hear the music around us, in voices, in the sounds of nature and machinery, etc. We must listen carefully as well as see clearly.

Rhyme, when used now, is quieter, disguised, sometimes hidden within the line or muted by enjambment. Meter is often modulated to sound like speech. One doesn't notice at first, for instance, that Stafford's "Traveling Through the Dark" is written in iambic pentameter and employs some rhyme.

When one writes in free verse, by definition one gives up patterned rhyme and regular meter. How does one, then, keep music in the poem?

You can develop your ear by listening to voices, by reading poems aloud, by examining a poem that pleases your ear until you know what makes it work. Think consciously about the sounds of words. Use words that repeat sounds subtly.

Assonance is the repetition of vowel sounds.

Shadow, bowl, clothes, frozen, loaf, for instance, repeat an *o* sound. If these words were to appear in proximity to one another, say over a space of five lines, they would create a subtle music.

Consonance is the repetition of consonant sounds. (Repetition of consonants in the primary position is, of course, alliteration.) *Father, booth, wither, thistle* repeat the *th* sound.

Slant rhyme, also called half-rhyme or off-rhyme, usually repeats the final consonant but varies the vowel sounds. *Dead, hid, sawed, loud, sad* are slant rhymes.

In order to become aware of how such sounds work, you might write several lists of words that evoke a quiet music and practice using them as if you were writing a poem. For instance:

> My father found the dead *bird curled* like a leaf on the *hard* ground.
> Maggots, like beads or *pearls,* the yellow beak half open . . .

I have underlined one sequence of sounds. Also note *dead, beads, beak, leaf, half.* If you make yourself conscious of using music in your writing, its use will eventually become second nature, part of your own "ear."

Symbol and Meaning

Here is a writers' joke: Two would-be novelists meet by accident on a busy street corner in New York. After they exchange amenities, the first asks the second, "How's your novel coming?" The second replies, "Great! I'm almost finished. All I have to do is go back and put in the symbols."

The joke, of course, is that you don't *put in* symbols. Meaning must rise out of the poem or story. If you see clearly enough and write honestly and accurately enough, the meaning will take care of itself. It would, however, be naive to imply the poet throws the poem up for grabs.

The poet does, in large part, control the response of the reader through the *careful selection of detail* and by choosing *the right words* to convey image and meaning. When Louise Gluck, in her poem "The Racer's Widow," has the widow see, in her sleep, the crowd *coagulate* on asphalt, she also makes the reader see the spilled blood of the dead husband. Words are our tools. The professional chooses, carefully, the right tool for the right job.

Subject Matter

Poems come out of experience, *actual* or *imagined*. Dave Marlatt has seen blackbirds gather in the trees in southwest Michigan during late fall and writes this poem:

Before the Snow

We call it a convention
When the birds come in the fall.
Filling the bare burr oaks
With thousands of fluttering black leaves.
They all move at once
From the shagbark hickory
That once shaded the Bissell schoolhouse.
Turning to the North
And back to the South
They head for the rotten spruce trees.
Pulling carpenter ants
From split and cracked trunks.
Their chattering can be heard
Across the stock pond
Echoing off scarred sugar maples.
They've come to talk
About the nesting last spring
And whose blueberries they stole.
They stop.
Getting word of a swarm of gnats
Warming themselves over Roy Nickol's manure pile.

Elizabeth R. Barney is alive and well, but imagines how drowning would feel:

Drowning

Horribly I fill.
My eyes are open.
I am kicking.
I can hear the water rattling
as I breathe it
sinister, heavy,
thicker than I imagined.

Julie Galvin discovers poetry in a bowl of breakfast cereal:

Good Mornings: Cheeriness, Cheerios

Spoon in my cereal,
a silver fish in a white lake.
I am looking for the golden Cheerio.
I am fishing for answers in my milk.

My breakfast stares at me;
the sightless eyes,
oat O-O-O's.
Open mouths
floating in silent criticism.

I stir them up.
I swirl them into dizzy
OOOOOOOOO's.
They circle me; they
moan at me.

I catch them with the mouth
of a silver fish.
I eat them with the mouth
of my mouth.
I drink the lake.
I swallow everything whole.

I imagine them
in my stomach;
great round eyes and great
oval lips.
I hear them soundless
echoing O remonstrances
in my cavity
—off my canyon soul my cavern
brain—
great O-O-O's
inside me.

What is *your* subject matter? Nothing is much more depressing to a writer than to sit down to a blank piece of paper and wonder, "What am I going to write about today?" This, too often, generates poems about pencil sharpeners, blank walls, or how hard it is to write. It is much better to have some idea of what your particular subject matter is. What do you feel strongly about? What is your background? Family, children, friends, lovers, work, travel, places—your relationship to and feelings about some of these may be subjects for poems.

The poet Mark Van Doren was gracious enough to read an early manuscript of mine and note that my subjects appeared to be elderly persons, children, and death. I had never thought about subject matter until then, but his analysis made sense. I had grown up around my grandmother and her circle of friends. I had five children. And death—like childhood—is everyone's subject matter.

Write about what you care about, what stimulates you intellectually. Write out of experience, both real and imagined. What each of us has to offer that no one else does is a unique genetic make-up and, therefore, a way of experiencing the world that is different from anyone else's. What we have is our own individual lives and our apprehension of them.

When you begin to write in an area, don't be satisfied with one or two poems. Write a sequence of poems about trout fishing, or your father, or your job. I have written some fifty poems about growing up in rural and small-town Oklahoma, and an entire book using materials gained from twelve years in the grocery business. When you are writing within a specific context, one poem often generates the next. An added bonus to this approach is that when the time comes to put together a chapbook (usually twelve to twenty-five pages) you will have poems that work well in conjunction with one another.

A Checklist

1. Check out individual collections of poems from the library. Immerse yourself in one or two poets for a week or two at a time: The broader your reading experience, the more you will learn about writing and possible approaches to it. Anthologies are a good place to discover poets, as are periodicals, but reading an entire volume by one poet is more rewarding.

   Begin your own collection of poets. You could do worse than start with the selected poems of Williams and Stevens and the collected poems of Bishop, all available in paperback editions.

2. Be flexible and ambitious in your approach to poetry. Try various subject matters, techniques, kinds of imagery: prose poem, narrative poem, poem of place, social criticism, personal history, realistic imagery, surrealistic imagery, persona poem, letter poem, character sketch poem, family poem, love poem, hate poem, etc.

3. Where to write: somewhere that you feel comfortable and where you will not be interrupted. Isolation is often essential. Also try a public place where no one knows you (bus station, park, etc.). A constant flux of visual images will often start something.

4. How to get started on a poem: go for a brisk walk to get the juices working. Read some poems by someone else; they might trigger something. Start writing whatever comes into your head—nonsense, or whatever, until something begins to happen. Discover the routine that works best for you.

5. When to write: carry a notebook. Write down images and thoughts as they come to you. Always try to be open to your surroundings. If you wait to write something down that occurs to you, you often lose it. Attempt to write

something every day. If nothing new comes, go to your notebook or work on revisions. Try working on a new poem in the morning while you are fresh. Work on revisions after you have written yourself out.

6. Read your poem aloud while working on it.

7. Remember to create images. Use as many of the five senses as possible. Describe small, intimate, particular details. Be specific and accurate. Use *names* and *places*. Use *moving* images rather than *static* ones. Use strong verbs and metaphors. Avoid the overuse of adjectives and adverbs.

8. Nothing is more important than the hard work of revision.

9. Stimulate and challenge and open your mind: read books, go to poetry readings, concerts, ballet, the theatre, art museums and galleries, good movies. Think about them. Try to capture in words what you saw or heard.

A Glossary of Terms: Poetry

1. **Allegory:** An extended metaphor in which a literal "story" is told to evoke a "story" of an interior state which is difficult to verbalize except through a literal story. The story's characters and actions represent something else and must be read "through" in order to observe the elusive abstraction such as holiness or bravery.

2. **Alliteration:** Repetition of beginning consonant sounds in words, as in Frost's "the only other *s*ound's the *s*weep."

3. **Allusion:** In an allusion, something outside the poem is being referred to, usually something biblical, mythical, or historical, although many allusions in contemporary poetry are to shared cultural events, such as Woodstock or Marilyn Monroe, which may not survive in history as long as myth or biblical stories.

4. **Analogy:** Two like relationships are compared; for example, a mother and child may be compared to Christ and Mary or the Madonna and Child.

5. **Apostrophe:** An address in a poem is made to an absent person or thing.

6. **Association:** What a word causes one to recall, be it a person, object, emotion, or sensation.

7. **Assonance:** Vowel sounds which are similar, with the vowels surrounded by different consonant sounds: t*i*me, m*i*nd.

8. **Ballad:** A narrative poem, meant to be sung; usually presented in quatrains rhymed a-b-c-b, which constitute a ballad *stanza*.

9. **Blank verse:** Verse written in iambic pentameter that is not rhymed.

10. **Cacophony:** Discordant sounds usually used to accentuate meaning in a poem.

11. **Canon:** Widely used now to indicate a nation's shared body of literature but originally used to indicate the work of a single author authenticated as written by that author.

12. **Canto:** In a narrative poem a division similar to a chapter in a novel.

13. **Classical:** Referring to Greek and Roman literature. A *classic,* then, is usually meant to signify that which has endured or may endure.

14. **Cliché:** A figure of speech that has been used so often as to be tiresome to read again.

15. **Conceit:** When a comparison is made between two things that would not normally be compared. A conceit may also compare persons.

16. **Concrete:** The opposite of *abstract* and, therefore, language that is imagistic. In *concrete poetry* the poet seeks to arrange the words of the poem on the page in a manner which suggests that which the poem is about or means.

17. **Connotation:** Subjective understanding of what a word *de*notes—a word's implications.

18. **Consonance:** A repetition of consonance sounds, with the vowels preceding the consonant differing: rain, ruin.

19. **Convention:** The use of a style or subject matter that has become accepted practice through repeated use.
20. **Confessional poem:** A poem in which a poet reveals more about his or her personal life than has previously been conventional to reveal. When the confessional poem itself becomes a convention, confession by the poet becomes so standard a strategy that the term loses significance.
21. **Couplet:** A pair of rhymed lines.
22. **Diction:** Choice of words, vocabulary.
23. **Didactic poetry:** Poetry which offers lessons to the reader; in contemporary poetry, often used to humorous or ironic effect.
24. **Dramatic monologue:** A poem spoken by a fictional persona who reveals his or her idiosyncrasies or peculiar circumstance.
25. **Envoy:** A concluding stanza that dedicates the poem to an important person.
26. **Epic:** A long narrative poem written in an elevated style about a heroic person.
27. **Explication:** The explaining of a poem's meaning, line-by-line, word-by-word.
28. **Figurative language:** "Pressured" language; the words mean more than their literal meaning.
29. **Foot:** One stressed syllable and one or more unstressed syllables in a metric unit.
30. **Found poetry:** Like "found sculpture," words arranged in such a way as to invite or suggest a "poetic" reading—often lines of prose.
31. **Free verse:** Poetry written in organized cadences not based on strict meter.
32. **Gloss:** To explain an unusual word in a text, usually by a footnote.
33. **Hyperbole:** Exaggeration in order to make a point.
34. **Image:** A word or words used to stimulate a response of the senses.
35. **Inversion:** Inverting a normal word order.
36. **Irony:** In poetry, irony occurs when it is clear that the meaning is opposite of or different from what is said.
37. **Lyric:** A poem that expresses personal emotion.
38. **Metaphor:** Comparisons expressed without the use of *like* or *as*.
39. **Meter:** Patterns of stressed and unstressed lines.
40. **Narrative:** A poem that tells a story.
41. **New criticism:** Analysis of writing that focuses on the text apart from extra-textual considerations such as a writer's "intention" or history.
42. **Onomatopoeia:** Words used to imitate sounds, such as *hiss*.
43. **Paradox:** A true statement that seems to contradict itself.
44. **Pastoral:** A poem using a rural landscape or the persona of a "country" person.
45. **Prose poem:** Prose which is taken to be poetry.
46. **Quatrain:** Four lines of poetry in a group, often rhymed.

47. **Rhyme:** Words or syllables that are alike in their endings.
48. **Rhyme scheme:** Pattern of rhyme in poetry.
49. **Scansion:** Determining a poem's metrical pattern.
50. **Simile:** Comparisons using *like* or *as*.
51. **Symbol:** A word meant literally but which also stands for something else.
52. **Syntax:** The way words are arranged in sentences.
53. **Tone:** The speaker's attitude as evidenced in word choice.

A Selected Reading List: Poetry

Philip Appleman. *Open Doorways.*
John Ashbery. *Three Poems.*
John Berryman. *The Dream Songs.*
Elizabeth Bishop. *The Complete Poems, 1927-1979.*
Robert Bly. *Silence in the Snowy Fields.*
Rupert Brooke. *The Collected Poems.*
Fred Chappell. *River.*
Robert Creeley. *For Love: Poems 1950-1960.*
E. E. Cummings. *Collected Poems.*
Peter Davison. *A Voice in the Mountain.*
James Dickey. *Drowning with Others.*
Hilda Doolittle (H.D.) *Collected Poems 1912-1944.*
Alan Dugan. *Collected Poems.*
Stuart Dybek. *Brass Knuckles.*
Richard Eberhart. *Collected Poems: 1930-1976.*
T. S. Eliot. *Collected Poems: 1909-1962.*
Robert Frost. *The Complete Poems.*
Louise Gluck. *First Born.*
Robert Graves. *Collected Poems.*
Donald Hall. *Kicking the Leaves.*
———. *The Town of Hill.*
Robert Hayden. *Angle of Ascent: New and Selected Poems.*
Seamus Heaney. *Death of a Naturalist.*
John Hollander. *Blue Wine and Other Poems.*
A. D. Hope. *Selected Poems.*
Langston Hughes. *The Panther and the Lash.*
Ted Hughes. *Lupercal.*
Randall Jarrell. *The Complete Poems.*
Patrick Kavanagh. *The Complete Poems.*
Weldon Kees. *The Collected Poems.*
Ted Kooser. *Sure Signs: New and Selected Poems.*
Philip Larkin. *The Less Deceived.*
D. H. Lawrence. *The Complete Poems.*
Denise Levertov. *Jacob's Ladder.*
Robert Lowell. *Lord Weary's Castle.*
Hugh MacDiarmid. *MacDiarmid: Complete Poems.*
W. S. Merwin. *Carrier of Ladders.*
Marianne Moore. *Collected Poems.*
John Frederick Nims. *Selected Poems.*
Mary Oliver. *Twelve Moons.*

Michael Ondaatje. *There's a Trick with a Knife I'm Learning to Do: Poems 1962-1978*.

Katha Pollitt. *Antarctic Traveller*.

Ezra Pound. *The Cantos*.

Adrienne Rich. *Poems Selected and New: 1950-1974*.

Theodore Roethke. *The Collected Poems*.

Carl Sandburg. *Chicago Poems*.

May Sarton. *Collected Poems (1930-1973)*.

Phillip Schultz. *Deep Within the Ravine*.

Anne Sexton. *All My Pretty Ones*.

Karl Shapiro. *New and Selected Poems*.

John Silkin. *Poems, New and Selected*.

Charles Simic. *Dismantling the Silence*.

Louis Simpson. *Caviare at the Funeral*.

Gary Snyder. *Regarding Wave*.

——. *Turtle Island*.

William Stafford. *Stories That Could Be True*.

Wallace Stevens. *Collected Poems*.

Mark Strand. *Reasons for Moving*.

Dabney Stuart. *Common Ground*.

Dylan Thomas. *Poems*.

John Updike. *Midpoint, and Other Poems*.

Peter Viereck. *Terror and Decorum: Poems, 1940-1948*.

David Wagoner. *Sleeping in the Woods*.

Robert Wallace. *Views from a Ferris Wheel*.

Richard Wilbur. *Things of This World*.

Peter Wild. *New and Selected Poems*.

William Carlos Williams. *Collected Later Poems*.

John Woods. *The Salt Stone: Selected Poems*.

James Wright. *Collected Poems*.

William Butler Yeats. *Collected Poems*.

For the Living and the Dead: A Consideration of Three Poems

by Herbert Scott

Hearts

"I prefer the dark meat," Mother says,
"so much more flavorful."

"Moist, delicious," Grandmother says.

Father and Grandfather love breast and wishbone.

"Brother loves the heart,"
these women croon, my sisters, too.

Chicken heart, goose heart, duck heart, turkey heart.

"Come to the kitchen, Brother,
your heart is ready!"

Oh, steamy heart gleaming on a white plate.
Jewel, crown, mouthful of joy—
how they sing its praises!

And I, most favored of boys, come
to that warm, stirred room
and chew the heart down.

This is the final version of the poem, in many ways a bare bones version which includes only one-third of the original draft, one I am happy with because it is economical, somewhat elliptical, and, I believe, subtle in its suggestion of the family dynamics that inform the poem.

I began with a memory. I was the third of four children, the only boy, in a family that needed to be very careful in matters concerning money. My grandmother—my mother's mother—lived fifty miles away, on a farm. I was a naive child and could be convinced of almost anything, and often was. In the first draft of "Hearts" I tried to record everything I could remember concerning one particular indoctrination.

Hearts

"I prefer the dark meat," my mother said. And chicken was cheaper
than beef or pork, and my grandmother raised spring fryers, the yard
sprinkled with Rhode Island Reds and White Rocks. And turkeys, great
twenty-five-pound gobblers for Thanksgiving and Christmas. In the
summer my grandfather paid us a dime apiece to discover the turkey
nests, to count their eggs, hidden in bushes, ravines, wild plum thickets

about the farm. At night the black walnut tree by the garden fence hung heavy with turkeys. "The dark meat is juicy, more flavorful," my mother said, disseminating her propaganda, campaigning for the whole bird to disappear beneath the magic wands of our forks. My father and my grandfather loved the breast and wishbone, so we children must love the dark meat best. Yes, I loved the drumsticks, but buried them, half-eaten in my bureau drawer next to napkinfuls of moldering spinach and rhubarb. My mother loved the gizzard, my grandmother loved the back, my sisters loved the liver, but no one loved the heart. "Brother loves the heart," my mother said, and all agreed. Yes, brother loves the heart, the chicken heart, the goose heart, the duck heart, but most of all the turkey heart, that wonderful huge doorknob of a heart. "Oh Brud, come to the kitchen, your heart is ready." And I would go to that stirred, warm room, my grandmother, my mother, my sisters, in aprons, smiling from damp faces, the overhead lamp lifting its skirt of light along the wall, and on the table a gleaming plate, and on that plate a jewel. Oh how they sang its praises, this chorus of women, and I believed, and chewed it down.

The title of this poem, in a way, defines its subject: How the expression of love is generated and defined within a family by familial needs. Father and Grandfather, who provide the wherewithal that furnishes food for the family table, love breast and wishbone. Therefore, Mother and Grandmother must *prefer* the dark meat. Way down the family pecking order (or food chain) is Brother, who must love the heart, the one *part* not yet spoken for. The important thing here is the women and their ready acceptance of their roles as dispensers and maintainers of love and order within the family. Brother who "loves" the heart and the warmth that emanates from these women acknowledges his part in the family dynamics by chewing the heart down.

Each character is known by his or her position in the family, not by a given name. The sisters, while not identified individually as Brother is, are initiates in the female hierarchy and are part of the chorus that sings to Brother that he loves the heart, while Brother is uninitiated and remains distanced from the male hierarchy.

Understanding what the poem is about, though not articulating it consciously as I have here, I could go forward with the business of shaping it from an ungainly, a prosy first draft into the final version. I could see that much of the information— the kinds of chickens, the searching for turkey nests, the moldering food in my dresser drawer—was, at best, peripheral and could be pared away. I also felt that I needed my grandmother's voice in the poem. Grandmother and Mother by speaking become real presences. Father and Grandfather by not speaking remain distant.

Since there is a fairly large cast of characters for such a short poem, I framed each character in a one- or two-line stanza to give the reader time and space to move from one to the next. The last revision I made was to change the tense from past to present. This made the action seem more vivid and immediate.

The Woman Who Loves Old Men

She loves the brown moles
widening to pools of oil
on their faces, their eyes
turning to milk, the tiny
forests of their ears;

and the shoulders,
wearing thin as skulls,
the slow glaciers of flesh
sliding from bone;

and oh the white bellies,
the pure salt of their bellies,
she could bury her face forever
in such perfect snow.

Yes, she marries them,
and they roost in her arms
like tired birds as she listens
for the last drawn croak
before that certain stillness.

And they, thankful, never know
it is their deaths she loves,
their bodies she lays out
like polished wood, as she dreams
of the one who will marry her twice.

I'm not sure what generated this poem. When I was in high school, an attractive woman in her thirties lived across the street with her eighty-year-old husband and two small children. As I get older, perhaps I wonder who will love me. Neither of these things do I think about consciously, but perhaps they have some connection with the poem. An earlier draft of this poem is quite different:

The Woman Who Loves Dead Men

When he sees her across a room
smile at him like an old friend
he wonders if he has known her before.
He loves her fallen breasts
swelling at her waist like heads
of cheese. He knows she will take him
to her mouth like a feast.
And yes she marries him, and he roosts
in her arms like a tired bird,
and she listens for the last drawn croak
before that perfect stillness,
and yes she wears weeds and cries
long tears, and yes he is thankful,

and never knows it is his death
she loves, his body she will lay out
like polished wood, her image pressed
in his eyes like a flower. And she
will carry him in her chest like an extra heart
as she waits for the man who will marry her twice.

Much of the description of the woman has disappeared from this earlier version. "Her breasts swelling at her waist like heads of cheese" turns up in another poem, "As She Enters Her Seventieth Year She Dreams of Milk." One of my favorite lines, one I felt I couldn't give up, "She will carry him in her chest like an extra heart," had to find another home as well. In the final version the focus in the poem shifts from the woman to the old men she loves. Yet the main questions in the poem remain the same. Why does she love these old men? Why does she love their deaths? Who is it that she dreams will marry her twice? And what does that mean? These are questions I can't answer. My wife, Shirley Clay Scott, tells me this is a poem about poetry, that the woman is a muse and the old men are poets whom she loves and marries but who finally fail or betray her by not surviving their physical deaths. The one who will marry her twice is a Stevens or a Yeats who will lay *her* out like polished wood. It does please me to think of the poem in this way.

The Dead

It is the dead who are always with us,
handsome and winning, on their best behavior.

We carry them in our chests
like an extra heart.

Companions who never falter,
who live in us their second lives.

And how can we deny them?
We who held them in our laps too long,

their languorous arms about our necks,
the breath of their sweet skin swarming.

How can we say:
This is the last kiss goodnight?

We who do not yet know
forgiveness was never possible.

As one can see, the "extra heart" line found its home here. That pleases me more than anything else in the poem. I do know what generated this poem. I know a woman who divorced her first husband twenty years ago, remarried, and subsequently had a son by her second husband. But after the tragic death of her first husband, she became obsessed by her memory of him, and her second husband became obliterated in the shrine she made for the dead man of her life. As a result she lost both men.

Why can we not live in the present? Why can we not let go of what is already lost to us? What is there in us that keeps us betraying ourselves? These are some of the questions that sponsored "The Dead." Interestingly, the original title was "For the Living."

For the Living

We must not let the dead
sit in our laps too long
their arms folded about our necks
the sweet breath of their skin swarming.
Yes, I know it is impossible
to say: this is enough, or this
is beyond redemption. I must
lay you in your grave
brush the hair from your forehead
like miraculous water
smooth the dear flesh
along your bones one more time.
This is the last kiss goodnight.
We must walk about as if our lives
were still going on. We must pretend
our words are little breathing animals . . .
We must let the dead go.
They have been waiting for this.
We must understand forgiveness
was never possible.

One reason I have chosen this poem to discuss is that I no longer know which version I prefer. One problem inherent in the act of revision is the danger of compromising a poem's initial impetus and spontaneity. While one may gain clarity and cleanness of image, the loss may be equal to or greater than the gain. What occurs here, I will leave to the judgment of the reader. I *will* note that I rather prefer the relaxed yet ceremonial quality of the earlier version—the intimate gestures of brushing the miraculous hair from the forehead and smoothing the dear flesh along the bones—rather than the reduction to only the stark legislated kiss of the revised version. I also like the volition given the dead, who have been waiting for their release. In "For the Living," we see the ritual of the living making peace with the dead and with themselves. And we experience more of the selfless pain of loss that is, finally, a purer affliction than is the guilt we cannot yet accommodate.

Sitting Down in the Profession, or In Training for Olympus
by John Woods

In his *Collected Poems,* Auden tells us that the bulk of the poems he had chosen lacked significance, since, if had limited himself to those poems for which he was sincerely grateful, the volume would have been "depressingly slim."

I imagine we all hope for that time in our writing when we have the skill to express our strongest emotions or our deepest commitments: neither to bury with technique nor bore with sententiousness.

The desire to be interesting, even fascinating, and the desire to be sincere and committed seem irreconcilable. In the sixties (the time, not the magazine), it came to pass that skill in an art, professionalism, became associated with the Academy, actually the "entrenched academy," and the poetry of ivory towers was the expression of Fascists, racists, and, if there is worse, worse. "The sonnet is a Fascist form," someone is supposed to have said, though I've never found the source.

I see we have survived the Academy and the Mongols and can get on with it.

Since I am not to tell you your deepest emotions nor your strongest commitments, I will talk to you about craft. No poem was ever written that didn't get started first. It doesn't matter where a poem starts; it matters where it goes.

Unless you have a bad back or other playful habits, you sit down, you sit down in the profession.

Be comforted. Sappho sat this way, Shakespeare, a long procession of S-shapes back through time.

One way to start is by adopting a persona. Of course, we always show only one facet of ourselves in a poem, but I mean speaking as someone entirely different. One advantage of persona poems is that they get you out of your self or allow you to approach your self in a new manner.

Speak as a personage from history, real or imaginary. The poet owes nothing to the truth, neither the truth of cartographers or cost accountants, nor the truth of philosophers or cosmologists. Frost says, "The fact is the sweetest dream that labor knows." But I suggest that the poem makes the fact and the truth, in the way that the physicist creates the atom by looking for it.

Indeed you might go back to histories, eighteenth-century diaries, forgotten correspondence, etc., and make a poem that tries to be true to someone else's truth. But why not a poem spoken by Sigmund Freud's twin sister? Or a poem in which the persona is berated by the lies in his wallet?

Speak as the opposite sex. Speak as a spirit, an unborn child, a prehuman. Speak as an anatomist. John Logan has a poem to his liver; Kathleen Frazier to her legs; Dennis Saleh to his penis; Herb Scott to his elbow; Auden to his five senses.

Speak as an animal, a machine, a natural force, a number, a waterhole, an electric chair, as T. S. Eliot's truss. Invent dialogues between or among them.

Another way to start a poem is to accept an external obligation. In painting, we know the still life, the portrait, the landscape. In poetry, the sonnet, the sestina, the ode. The modernists among you are flinching and yearning for the exit. James Wright once said that to admit to having written a sonnet is like admitting you loved your own wife.

I suggest that our identification of form in poetry is misplaced, if we concentrate on sonics: rhyme, meter, and rhythm. The obligations accepted in the first line of a sonnet—the tone of voice, the persona, the metaphorical covenant, the pattern of imagery—are much more important determiners of form than the metrics.

Nevertheless, a poem moves through time, especially if read aloud, somewhat like music; and that movement creates responsibilities. Rhythm, meter, rhyme are like snags just under the surface: they make the poem swerve.

This is a "free verse" age, and for good historic, perhaps esthetic, reasons. The avant-garde is not only pushing bravely into the unknown, it is fleeing bad practice. With a combination of run-on and end-stop lines, with slant rhyme, with internal assonance and alliteration, it is possible to have a poetry of subtle music, not the "Anvil Chorus."

Deciding to write a sestina, say, is deciding to write a poem. After you have chosen (or have been chosen) by your six words, you ride (or are ridden by) them through six stanzas and the envoi, perhaps not thinking of your strongest emotions and deepest commitments. Sitting down in the profession.

But, unlike the school figures of Olympic ice skating, we can dump the sestina anytime a line or phrase suggests a new and better direction. Of course, we can always invent new metrical forms.

It is possible to write good poems or bad poems starting from anywhere, but it is not possible to write any poem without starting, unless you want to be a conceptual poet.

In Dylan Thomas's last unhappy year, he was invited by Igor Stravinsky to come to Hollywood, where a studio awaited the poet. They were going to collaborate on an oratorio, or something, called "The Creation." Where do you go after "In the beginning"?

The next suggestion for starting out is writing a poem in reaction to an occasion, the occasional poem. The problem with such an approach is that it usually leads to rather pedestrian results: poems on current events, newspaper articles, etc. Our poets laureate are expected to respond to holidays, the birthdays of our leaders, the dedication of nuclear plants, etc.; and only the most chauvinistic among us could resist satire or despair.

Poets have often written poems in reaction to the other arts: other poems, graphic arts, dance, music. Such an approach asks the reader to be educated or apologetic or irritated. Such poems ask, "This is my taste; what's yours?"

Poems tied strongly to external events have a power only partially earned by the poem. Fine, let there be poems that barely survive the year; next year, they may need footnotes, but not deserve them.

There have always been poems that depend on the reader's knowledge of other poetry. According to David Wagoner, Theodore Roethke would start his classes by saying: "This semester we will read the bulk of poetry written in English." I'm not speaking here of literary reference or allusion; the matter of whether or not we have an educated readership must be dealt with in another "venue," as we have learned to say.

One can write imitations, parodies, appropriations, translations, or "renderings." These are lesser arts, perhaps, except translation; but our mission is to start a poem any way we can, when the muse is out of town.

There are poems, or sustained poetry, written for performance. Anyone who reads in public comes to realize that some of his/her poems are more accessible than others, more acceptable, funnier, even; and he or she needs such platform poems for the situation, however irrelevant it may be on the way to Olympus. On the way to Olympus, we sometimes need some local stroking, some *right ons*!

The public poem also includes song lyrics, oratorios, opera, and film. Dylan Thomas said that he thought the camera should be the poet. Most experiences I have had with my poems set to music have led me to think that no one could hear the words, but they were strangely carried by the glamor of performance.

I'm not sure if there is any audience for narrative poetry, such as that by Edwin Arlington Robinson, John Masefield, or Stephen Vincent Benét. In one of my nightmares, a local dentist has hired me to edit his six-hundred-page manuscript about his first eighteen years, written in rhymed couplets.

I think there is still a possibility for the long poem. Considering the difficulties in printing any collection of poetry, such an undertaking would be heroic. No journal would print it, I imagine. The sequence poem is a different matter. Often one writes a poem or two that circle about a common concern, of place or time or mood. Each poem is strengthened by its companions: "Five Love/Hate Poems for Sally"; "Thirteen Ways of Looking at a Blackbird"; "Eight Gargoyles at the Laundromat." Sometimes only a Zen mystique can hold these poems together, a willingness of the reader to go, as my students say, "with the flow."

Sometimes a poem, or an idea for a poem, is too static; it needs to be opened up in some way; it needs some movement, through time or space. One way to try to open up a poem is to analyze it through time: once, now, soon. Often I ask my students to consider a family ceremony—Christmas, church, dinner, the visit of a certain uncle—in such a time order. The family ceremony places the poem, provides the imagery; *once, now, soon* acknowledges change in those images and their import.

One can plug into the energy of archetypal cycles: dawn, afternoon, evening; the seasons; birth, death, rebirth. We appear to have survived the excesses of

Freudian analysis in literary practice, where anything longer than it is wide is a phallic symbol. Overheard in the hall: "I know it's a phallic symbol, but what's it a phallic symbol of?"

We appear to be coming down off the big wave of interest in Jungian analysis: the Shadow, anima and animus. I insist in pedagogy and practice that these intellectual systems can indeed open up a poem but that the system is not the poem. The poem must be located in the senses first.

W. C. Williams has simplistically ordered: "No ideas but in things." All right, but, still, ideas. To this end, a poem may be opened up by analyzing it along the sensorium. We are accustomed to taking the term *imagery* too literally. We do believe that sight dominates our senses, but sight need not dominate the imagery of our poetry. One class exercise I occasionally use is to present a situation. It is an October afternoon. It has rained heavily, and the gutters are still rushing, etc. Place yourself in the scene and exercise all five or six of your senses. Remarkably for most, such an analysis by category opens up the poem.

I tend to sermonize about the need for placing the poem in the senses. So many poems shout out of a cloud or treble through a telephone that they seem lifeless, totally free of experience. I can't miss the dead father or cruel lover or happy spaniel because I'm not allowed to know them, to see their particularity.

There are two things I want to say about imagery. First, imagery is irresistible. One does not question a tree, especially one that has left bark scars on your breast. The poem that says: "You left me and my life is over" is not as seductive as "At night tears get in your ears." The second idea is that one cannot write a poem of hard, accurate imagery without moving into metaphor. Sharp images are like active elements: they have a high valence; they attract each other, forming new compounds.

The point is that the idea can be present in the thing: ordering the things orders the idea. One of Wallace Stevens's poems ends with a two-word sentence: "The the." Thinginess. Many poems express emotion in abstract language. Pain, love do not come over our thresholds carrying placards. They overwhelm us; our tears, our laughter are involuntary, not considered. I send the writer back to the scene of the event and ask him or her to reconstruct the poem from its original materials: was it raining? Did you hear a dog barking in the distance? Were the mums turning brown? Were the insides of your thighs damp?

Most of us want to look good. We don't want to seem ridiculous or out of control. We don't want to admit pimples or diarrhea on prom night. As a teacher, I have to strike a balance between what might be seen as a prurient interest in someone's private life and the strong feeling that the emotions expressed in a poem are earned by the context, the revealed experience, the gestalt of sensual memory.

I try to make the point that one uses one's life; one is not a victim of factuality. If your poem requires that your mother was chased into the synagogue by a motorcycle gang, then chase her in there! But make her a real mother in a real synagogue and let's smell the leather.

My last few ideas become steadily more giddy.

Collaborative poems, trading first lines or rhyme schemes. Acrostics, poems in which the first letter of each line reads downward: To My Mother. Curses, hollers, chants, hangovers, blessings, confrontations, harangues, spells, stomps, remedies, recipes, poems from the balcony, poems from the backseat, epitaphs, announcements, menus, operating instructions, warranties, warrants, bills of lading, Dear John letters, kiss-offs, sex manuals, confessions, prayers when you ain't got a prayer, what to tell your children about sex, explanations and excuses, Santa lists, dreams.

There's concrete poetry: poems shaped like swans, altars, wings, pyramids, bouquets. Found poetry. Accidental poetry, scat poetry, nonsense improvisation.

Another way to get started or restarted is by altering the writing environment. Robert Creeley tells us he carries a notebook to write in because he doesn't want to associate writing with a particular place. I'm just the opposite, though my recent acquisition of a word processor has spurred me considerably.

Try composing on a tape recorder as you drive, watching the road, of course. Keep a journal. Write something every day. Tape poems to the wall. Make a huge desk so you can spread things out.

Finally, if all else fails, write poetry that expresses your strongest emotions and deepest commitments.

Some poems come out of specific autobiographical instances, or so it seems. An innocent writing student will present three stanzas of impervium. The poet will tell his readers that he was writing about a cardinal he saw in his backyard. He will be puzzled when informed that there is no cardinal, no backyard, even, on the page.

I don't know how far or deeply the urgency of the autobiographical instance carries into the text. If the instance (a memory, after all) had a verifiable reality, it quickly joins the folk residue, the aside, the joke, the poem. As the instance moves into text, it is captured by the gravity of other poetic concerns, the stubbornness of the language, perhaps even the pleasant groin-stroking of one's Kareer.

I have been asked to speak about three of my poems. I understand that I am to say How They Grew. The specific autobiographical instances from which these poems grew are none of your business. They are also none of my business. We are all burdened with enough experience to provision a lifetime of poems.

The Girl Who Had Borne Too Much

That girl has borne too much,
there, in her locked bed.
We need to see the caul flaming,
the drooled lip, ancestral greed
stamping its old medallion
on the childish brow, something

dragging a swollen foot
at the edge of our shadows.

But whatever walks her night corridors,
its hair burning, does not lie
in her arms. Now her face is smoothed
back to childhood.
            Child, and whoever
wears your young body in the bad nights,
we know that the whore
may breathe sweet milk,
and a lean christ lie back at ease
in the fat-rinded murderer.

This poem is rather vaguely placed in a ward of a mental institution: the "locked bed," the "corridor." Usually I would take considerable time to establish the situation in the senses: a male nurse reading *People,* a volley of coughs, an ambulance's flasher crossing the window, perhaps a far shout. The devices we are fond of.

The poem is interested in the poignancy of illness in the young and guiltless, if our beliefs allow such an idea. But it's not the pity we feel that interests us; it's the plainness of the lives that are so tortured: their featurelessness. I am amazed that the mass murderer watched Captain Kangeroo or had dandruff.

The parents of mentally ill children are only partially comforted by the current theory that mental illness is a chemical imbalance, not much at all by the possibility of genetic predisposition, and not at all by the suspicion they have been lax parents. But their children are beautiful and loved and inexplicably ill.

This poem claims that some romantic or desperate vein in our consciousness needs some explanation more cosmic than chemical imbalance for the extreme behavior we are capable of and skilled at. Our vulgar, simplistic, and melodramatic needs are not satisfied, except in art. If it is not what we do or are capable of that determines what we are, perhaps it is how we are presented.

Is it more important that Jesus was crucified or that he died between two thieves? Perhaps we were saved by the thieves.

Friend of Distances

What is your living, friend
    of distances, in the room
you illumine, where my
yesterday's weather hums
    on your phone?
Woman with Child
and oleander, time
to say I remember
more than your red bush,
    Fox! August, and the

asters are stupid, but
their fuses are lit.
The word is out
among the crawlers that apples
forge the sugar chains.
This botany means that
love need not answer letters
for all is known to
the knowers, friend of distances,
redtailed hawk who
reads the grass tremor
at eye's end, tell
me your living.
You once told me your tremor
in bed, in the bed
below the bed, when
you sighed time's thunder
in my ear,
deeply ancient
so that street names
flew and the town
was lost in its state,
and the servers
of processes, the faces
that would frown
us home, flattened
into snapshots in purse
and wallet, when oleander
veined the room.
August, now, and the slow
fuse burns along my hands,
and the asters open
their dim flames, your gifts
as I remember you
in them, friend of distances,
what is your living?

Men, yes, mostly men, have been wandering off from lovers and domesticity to war, to work, claiming they loved honor more, or that they were doing it for the family. Donne, in "Valediction Forbidding Mourning," employs the draftsman's compass and the malleability of gold sheet as metaphors to justify his absence and prove his fidelity, and, with the back of that pat hand, that full house, to tell his woman that her complaints suggest she ain't got no soul. Donne's poem is more than my playful reading, though it is a playful poem.

In my poem, the speaker is a time zone away, at least, from a friend, a woman with child. Her vegetation is southern; her hair is red. The imagery and metaphor of the poem are extravagant, in the Cavalier tradition. The speaker spreads his indulgent concerns throughout the landscape; he enlists the Yankee asters and apples to cohabit with the Rebel oleanders. He is indecorous enough to refer to her "red bush." Sirrah!

I could say more about this studied poem, the punmetaphors; but there are two matters I would like to address, as the politicos say.

First, I have referred to the "speaker" of the poem. Poet-teachers have learned to refer to the "persona," a Jungian term employed to deflect criticism from the innocent who wrote the poem onto the the innocence of the poem itself. No one believes in the persona.

I also had sonic interests in the poem. Of late, many poets have cast out all concern with music, avoiding, with good reasons, the excesses of Dylan Thomas and even the modest musicality of Richard Wilbur. Instead, we are delivered voices that come more from a stone-filled craw than from a throat. All right, bad practice requires strong medicine. One can tire of the bad rock of craw music.

I had strong musical interests in this poem. I accepted (I don't remember ever courting a rhythm) the pleasant stumble of dactyl/anapest:

> "**What** is your living, **friend**
> of **distances?**"

I also wanted the pleasure of partial rhyme, and I must trust you hear where I use it.

Resolutions: Ice Storm
(Dec. 31, 1986)

> *By late afternoon, the mist had thickened,*
> *the maples sifting into dusk.*
> *In the amiable shambles of people together,*
> *we hungered around the lamps, the wine,*
> *the pleasant chirp of dishware*
> *on the last rollcall of the year.*
> *We vowed small disciplines on this night*
> *of sackcloth and ashes.*

> *All night the trees exploded,*
> *power lines dragged and sparked.*
> *Electricity closed its shops.*

> *All across town, in the glare light*
> *of the new year morning, trees bowed*
> *in terrible metal, like Hiroshima,*
> *a sunken ship, the wreckage of Eden.*
> *Townsmen toured the ice museum*
> *in the crystal discipline of cameras:*
> *the cold spectacles, the oxides of silver.*

> *Grandpa told us we have promises to keep,*
> *so the sun opened its busy stores.*

The rose bowl of the TV stuttered on.
Half our sugar maple, trebled in gravity, lay
in the stiff, gray grass of the front lawn.
I could see through the ice to its rude mottle.
It is difficult to look out
from such beauty.

The circumstances of this poem seem clear enough. On New Year's Eve of 1986, the temperature was around freezing all day, and a light mist was falling. When people came out of the parties, they had to scrape thick ice from their windscreens.

Many of the parkway trees in my part of southern Michigan are sugar maple, quick-growing but fragile. The growing ice carapaces sought out their flaws. Limbs, power wires and poles bent, exploded and fell. In some areas, there was no power for a week.

New Year's Day was sunny. Citizens toured the city like tourists at Pompeii, Nikons whirring. Finally, though gradually, the event became history.

Since it was the time that flaws were tested and resolutions made, one might expect the poet to subject such matter to momentousness. For poets who believe in closure, a bang or a whimper, I see three possibilities. One possibility is to use the occasion of the poem to illustrate a larger, more comprehensive, even an abstract utterance: something about Life, Time, Mortality, a large, turgid proclamation, delivered from a "sad height."

In "Dover Beach," Arnold places his speaker where he can hear the waters, the heartbeats of genesis; a beach that faces Europe, from where navies of threatening ideologies have risen over the horizon; a speaker who is perhaps suffering from *post-coitus triste*. From his momentary angst, he proclaims apocalypse.

Another strategy is to bring the poem down to a personal level. The problem here is not to domesticate the poem into triviality or to make extravagent confessional demands.

The third closure that occurs to me is to discover a personal relevance that bears world-weight. If your last lines are personal, they are likely to be derived from the materials of the poem: they will be both familiar, earned, and, hopefully, transformed. As a teacher of poetry writing, I have been reduced to telling students to go forth and find a marvelous last line that will be both unheard of and inevitable.

I might have ended "Resolutions":

It is difficult to see through
such beauty.

I chose enigma.

Weaving In and Out of Control: Poetry, Gender, and Rules in the Writing Workshop

by Linda Mizejewski

"Sisters Again" and "Private Rooms" are the poems in which I dream the deaths of my parents—fictional events, as I write this essay. My mother and father are lively, healthy people in their seventies; they are not even really the subjects of these poems, so much as subjects of the dreams about relationship and loss. Written about five years apart, these two poems are also dreams that come out of very different sets of constraints and ideas about what poetry should be. I wrote the first during my M.F.A. workshops, the second when I was a teacher myself years later. Looking at them now, I can clearly see the history of an apprenticeship: an old but useful story about loving, resisting, and then leaving our teachers— who, like parents perhaps, are only wholly successful when left behind.

I went into those workshops with a headful of mythology about family and fathering. A Jesuit-educated girl from a northern steel town, I was still trying to deal with ideas about "being a woman poet" and was nervous that the Poetry Business meant either being One of the Boys or gracefully female/suicidal. My concept of the contemporary poetry scene for women was both warped and telling: there were the inimitable goddesses like Elizabeth Bishop, who wrote perfect and perfectly impersonal poems—and then there were the dynamic harpies and/or psychotics who dared to write about *women's* experience—and then failed, eventually, going out of control in their metaphors and lives. The women in the workshop would talk about Maxine Kumin and Linda Pastan as rare, brave proof that it was possible to be female and sane, writing solid poems.

"Solid" poems: no one would say then "poems that men could like, too," for that would undermine the dogma of the Universal Reader, the Universal Standards of good literature on which we'd bet our lives and careers. The story is all too familiar, but what still puzzles me is how the elitist, conservative politics of the New Criticism—a maintenance of absolute dualism between artist and artifact, culture vs. the masses, Eliot's sense of the impersonal act of creation—had survived Vietnam, Woodstock, Watergate and the Beatles' *White Album* to be embraced by young, liberal, iconoclastic writing students in 1976. We may have doubted all else, from America to the afterlife, but we could never doubt that meaning was "in" the poem—absolutely traceable, able to be valorized, clearly understood by the Reader (the universal one, workshop readers being the best and brightest thereof). The best poetry was the kind we could best describe with our critical vocabulary. The very worst was "out of control."

We accepted the language and we accepted the map: the landscape blocked out by Eliot and Arnold, the subject matter and the tradition. The alternative spaces I imagined as ghettoes populated by a wild, emerging "women's poetry" and various minority poetries—junked with pieces that broke the rules. It was surely no accident that the poets who were most "out of control" on the page were the women writing about "women's experience." Little wonder that in my own writing I avoided subjects like mothers and mothering. Instead, I mythologized an impossible daddy and wrote him to death.

In all my ambitious-but-failed poems of those years, there was almost a perverse turning away from my own life. I wrote about strained marriages, models with artists, and, of course, dying fathers, even though I had never been married, never known any artists, hadn't lost a parent. Yet I wasn't able to track down my self-imposed limitations. For who could argue against the evidence of the Norton anthologies or Arnold's eloquent entrusting to us—the lucky educated ones—the inheritance and ideology therein? I remember reading Arnold's essays in those days and making no connection to the artificial exclusiveness of what I believed was the Literary Imagination—virtually emptied, in my case, except for the wish for the passing father. Arnold's contempt for persons with unpleasant-sounding, working-class names like Higginbottom struck me only as historical detail. Yet I thought about changing my own name during that time, making it prettier for publication: mythologizing the father but cleaning up the unfashionable Eastern European name.

I was finally able to write my dying-daddy poem because the subject matter got displaced and successfully subverted by experience: a real sister, a genuine experience of the childhood bed. When I visited with my family in Pittsburgh that summer, just before my sister's marriage, I realized how I would lose an important sense of "home" when she left: sleeping in the same the bed we'd shared for almost sixteen years and still shared when we came home for summer vacations. Thinking with a laugh that she was still my most familiar and comfortable bedmate and also the person with whom I could still fight most amiably, I realized right away the richness of the possibilities: our old positions, back to back, taking the same sides. Those were the phrases with which I started to build a narrative.

Sisters Again

Summoned back from separate states
for a half a night in Emergency,
we share smokes and matches while we wait.
She's come in denims; I'm in tweed.
And when the beckoning nurse appears,
we know already: this is a scene
rehearsed in separate dreams for years.

We make arrangements, go back late
to the place we're willed. We use old keys,
and in the dark remember where
the steps begin and lights go on.

We wait a while to go upstairs,
where we make the bed that's ours again.
Here—contenders, favorite girls—
we'd whispered the furious arguments,
and cried in silence, and overheard
what the other called for in nightmare:
rescue, presence, father, light.

Tonight we wind this room's stopped clock
and find the nightlight—that charm against
bad dreams, the dark—inside our old desk
with some years-old aspirin we take with Scotch.
Undressing, we glimpse each other's scars,
think curiously of each other's men,
and when the lamp goes off, we lie again

beneath the set of refracted bars
the shutters make with passing lights:
across our faces the same dark grid.
In our old positions, back to back,
we have taken the sides we always did,
not speaking of the beds we've left
to take our father through one last night.

So while the narrative is completely fictional, the energy of the poem is real: the sense of connection and relief, the hint of the sexual dynamic in the past—the childhood contention for the father—now displaced by other sexualities—the glimpsing of bodies, the other men. The father as wish becomes the father as child—but I was perhaps able to write the poem because the father isn't "really" there at all, and I was dealing instead with a much more defined relationship with another woman.

Because I began with lines that were so nicely iambic—"our old positions, back to back"—I originally tried to work this into a sonnet, and then, as the narrative got longer, into a double sonnet. It crashed. The five-beat line was tempting—"and when the lamp goes off we lie again"—but the lines I liked best were leaner: "rescue, presence, father, light." Two more syllables would weigh it down. Yet I wanted to keep a rhyme scheme, and wanted to play the tight rhymes against the half-rhymes—there's a grate to "clock/Scotch" that reminded me of swallowing old aspirin. And so I broke the rules. In spite of some workshop colleagues who regretted the loss of "real form," I decided this poem would have its own form: tightly connected with sound, rhymes to emphasize key words, but no traditional pattern.

What I learned best and most usefully in workshop is probably the insistence on real detail, and some of the poem's imagery comes directly from this kind of questioning. If the good poem is like a dream, it's a believable dream. How do we know this is a real sister, different from the speaker, not just a prop? Thus the detail of our clothes. What kind of room is this? The clock, the engineering of shutters.

As a result, the voice I developed was that of a reliable narrator, so to speak.
Look: here are the keys, the old aspirin, the nightlight in the desk. Verifiable. This
is real. A real sister who doesn't dress up to go to the hospital. There is a small
world alluded to here, the kind we know from nineteenth-century fiction, with its
boundaries and outlying regions: the other beds we've left, a childhood full of
arguments, histories of men. The voice narrating this history is calm; it speaks in
thoughtful sentences that never hesitate or go out of breath. It seems to be in
control.

When I finished my M.F.A. and became a teacher myself, I at first imitated my
own teachers and demanded the same kind of coherent, controlled microcosm in
each poem, the perfect surface, the same logical development of metaphor. But
those standards were under heavy attack by then, and I was realizing that the
superior Universal Reader for whom we'd all been taught to write was not universal at all: he came from a certain class and race, and he had no vocabulary to
explain poetry that came from other languages, cultures, traditions. I was learning
to love poetry I could only barely "understand" in the old terms—Marilyn Nelson
Waniek, the sassy bad mouth of Ai, the last poems of Sexton in which she truly
goes out of control. In short, I was becoming a different kind of reader, and this
was the beginning of becoming a different kind of writer.

By the time I started "Travellers' Advisory," three years after the workshops, I
was much more willing to begin with the "real" microcosm and then explode it, to
have patience with the speaker who is angry in something other than iambic
pentameter. And—not coincidentally—the dying-father subject didn't at all interest
me as much as the subject of mothers, as if the prize for dynamiting Eliot's
landscape were another map.

Travellers' Advisory

> The advice is don't go home.
> Your mother's white apron
> at the door ribbons out
> to an ice-pall seven interstates
> long; the county roads
> glaze like her cakes—temptation,
> slicked by her own floured hand.
>
> The advice is tell the lover
> no; listen to the frozen wires
> tingle in the connections but
> insist on the radio prophecies that
> death is pulled up like troopers tonight
> over every ridge,
> the guardrails are cracking,
> the exits vanishing
> all over tundra Ohio,
>
> and beg forgiveness:

Mother, lover,
I swerve always out of fatality
wearing your secrets and amulets.
I wear your cheekbones,
your kisses, rings, the safety
of you pinned like scapulars
next to my ribs to remember
how to steer toward the skid
and how to hard wheel back
to touch you,
all my chains jangling

in a bracelet one of you
buys me every year saying
luck *because*
I take advice so badly, buckling
up, winter soldier, even now
to drive this storm
to find one of you, or both.

My real maps had changed. I'd just moved north again after five years in Arkansas and Virginia, and as an inexperienced snow-driver, I took every travellers' advisory with terrified seriousness. Again, the worst possibility was going out of control: having the car skid in crazy circles on the ice. Self-imprisoned by one of those blizzards, I started this poem because I was trying to understand something about taking risks, disobeying the voices of the authorities—and I was also rethinking what I'd learned in my workshops.

The world in this poem is recognizable—it begins with the "real" details: radio announcements about snowstorms, plans to go home, plans to meet a lover. But these are not the carefully arranged spaces and events of "Sisters Again." What the radio announcement says, the first two stanzas, is both precise and crazy—highway exits do seem to vanish in snowstorms, but now Ohio is a tundra full of ghostly soldiers; a beautiful, deadly road rolls out from the apron of a waiting mother.

When I started this poem, I had no idea what answer I really wanted to give the radio warning, and so I began by doing what it commands: making an apology for not showing up. But my apology also had to characterize a certain kind of speaker who, after all, is listening to this warning and hearing, *believing* such a wild, spooky description. And facing this problem, I eventually saw the solution: the speaker's voice is prone to the same dreamy hysteria—she's the one reading so much into a simple travellers' advisory. So she begins by talking about how she imagines herself driving: kept safe by a kind of magic girdling held in place by people who love her. But if she believes so much in this magic, then she would have to disregard the warnings, wouldn't she? So what starts out as an excuse turns into an apology for taking chances, for refusing to take advice. That is, the "logic" of the poem came from the voice, this breathless nervousness that spins out long, convoluted sentences.

I don't think I would have risked that long last sentence in my workshop days.
The last sentence of "Sisters Again" is a convergence of several events: the
childhood, the death, the present moment in the bedroom, their beds elsewhere. It
is parsed carefully into four lines, four stresses per line, each line a reference to
one set of events. It looks like the bottom four tiers of a huge, delicate wedding
cake. But my last sentence in "Travellers' Advisory" looks like the path of a
skidding car. It jumps across a stanza break; it changes direction and intention; its
grammatical hooks are piled-up verb phrases that move the speaker here and there
and finally out the door, bundled up for action. The voice in this sentence is no
Reliable Narrator. Yet the sentence relies on a grammatical precision instilled and
drilled by my New Critical teachers—whose voices never entirely disappear, of
course; and the sentence would be impossible without the image of the scapulars—
that "real" 1950s detail which my workshop teachers would have coaxed onto the
page.

One snowy afternoon, I chanced the icy roads so as not to cancel the poetry
reading I was scheduled to give, and there I met the man I married. And so I
gained a mother-in-law, another mother I loved very much, whose death shortly
thereafter made me sharply confront the mother-body-self connection. We spent
long, terrible weeks in the hospital with her. And like much else, I knew I had to
write about it in order to deal with it.

Private Rooms

Born here before the annex,
I've found the seams
where the pocked, pre-war walls
have scissored open
into the new wings.
Fathers closed out
of the blood those days,
she must have been steered alone
to Delivery and the sutured sleep
from which we both
came out alive.

Now I slip my mother's feet
into terry scuffs, and take
her weight to cross the room's
twelve feet—much further
than she can go alone.
Lighter than she has ever been,
she leans, wavering,
as if newly opened,
or just come out of
the gauzy dream where,
white, breaking, hollowed,
she has left me behind.

She will step out of
this air, above
the awkward weldings
and laced bellies, past
all recovered lives.
Hold me, hold on,
But the strange new space
in which I wake without her
starts to be the world.

This was the same hospital in which she'd given birth to her children over thirty years before, and it was now in the process of renovation. Walls and corridors were being stripped and rebuilt; the 1940s bricks and seams showed through. The violence of the demolition and construction—the noise, the mess, the odd juxtapositions of new and old—seemed to match the violence of what was happening in our lives, the stress of the loss. It was impossible not to be struck by the impact of cycles, time, continuations and destructions. The babies born here after the war were now hefty men supporting their mother from the chair to the bed.

I wanted most of all to write a *physical* poem about death—not just death, but the death of a woman who had given birth to the speaker, the death of a body that had knit someone out of itself. I wanted to confront the messiness of both processes, getting in and out of life. And I wanted to deal with the sheer astonishment, the anger that the body of the mother, the life-giver, isn't immortal—that the world into which she brought children, the world she seems to have constructed for them, will continue without her. So the wrecking, stripping transition of the hospital building itself gave me something to hang this on.

As in "Sisters Again," I wanted to create a convergence of different times within the poem, but this was more complicated because the speaker cannot of course remember her birth; this is where the renovation imagery was useful. The remnants of the "pre-war walls" are actually visible, reminders of a different era so that particular details can come into focus: the days when fathers weren't allowed inside delivery rooms and when women were put to sleep at the crucial moment of delivery. And the latter fact could get expanded in another imagining of birth in the second stanza: women woke up from the operation and had let a child into the world—but also had parted from it, the cord broken—and for the speaker facing the mother's death, it's a child "left behind."

But I had to go further in time, from the present moment in the hospital room to the imagining of a world without this mother. For surely that was the location of the poem's anxiety and loneliness. Once I'd finished the second stanza, I was stuck for days. Up to that point, the poem was workable because it was physical—the verbs were strong, violent, active. There were "real" terry scuffs, a twelve-foot room. There was a 1940s delivery room with fathers waiting outside. But how graphic could I be about the impending death?

Again the voices of the workshop teachers: the poem has its own integrity, the answers to its own problems. And this was true—the "answer" was in the second stanza, in fact, in the very last place we've seen the speaker, helping the mother step across the room. Her next "step" so to speak, is into a very different kind of space we can't imagine, except that it's not this world we know, this air, the kind of space in the torn-up hospital among the patched-up lives. And once I realized I could hang onto my space/construction imagery, then I could handle the time problem, too, moving from the simple future tense—something we know will happen—into a trickier, in-process future that's already begun because "the world" has already become a certain kind of place marked by absence.

And what a precarious world it is, in this poem. In the earlier poem, "Sisters Again," I'd made certain the speaker was located firmly in time and space. I'd been careful to give her cigarettes, scars, a position in the bed. There is a real house, with keys, the staircase, light switches. As for the speaker who inhabits this physical world—there is a rhyme and metrical scheme so that her voice sounds even-handed, each line ending with a firm, stressed syllable.

The physical world of the later poem is much more unreliable—walls "scissor open," fathers are "locked out" of delivery rooms, the speaker's own birth had taken place in the mother's exhausting dream. This world isn't true to fact so much as true to a certain kind of vision and moment, to a sensibility seeing the hospital building give way as the world seems to give way. Describing this wobbly world, the speaker's rhythms are often broken, and lines end tentatively in prepositions or in the middle of phrases. This voice is on the edge of going-out-of-control.

When I look at the distance between the two worlds of the two poems, "Sisters Again" and "Private Rooms," I measure the distance of how far and how much I learned to risk after leaving my teachers and their "advisories." But surely we are all unreliable narrators in telling the stories of our writing workshops, how we survived and transcended them. I think my reaction to our old killer phrase—the dreaded "going out of control"—was mixed and biased by the particular female imagery I associated with that phrase; like the word "hysteria," it seemed to have a gender, a face, a story. The story was being female and failing at something men naturally do better—perhaps iambic pentameter. The misconceptions and limitations I brought to the workshop were my own as well as others; when a woman from the English Department there suggested I try to publish in some feminist journals, I thought quickly, with contempt, that I preferred the "real" ones.

What I understand now is that any writing workshop is really a reading workshop, and even as a student I must have suspected this because we used to talk about a specimen called a "workshop poem": a slickly produced piece that was entirely "right" and unassailable but lacking in the genuine stuff. The "stuff" was what fell out of the boundaries of our vocabulary and our criticism, what could not be parsed and scanned. Surely we need to give our writing students a language they can use to think through their problems. Yet they also need to know how each set of terms arrives with its own limitations and disadvantages; they need to see many different kinds of poetry so they can make their own choices about what they want poetry to do. Looking at the two poems in which I dream the deaths of parents, I would not want to make an argument that one is better than the other. But I can imagine now, as I couldn't before, such arguments for and against each of them.

When my mother looked at the poems in my M.F.A. manuscript ten years ago, she read them as straight—though strange—autobiography, and said, "This is good, but I'm not in here at all." I told her poets do nothing but lie.

Sources for "Albert Einstein, Plumber," "An Elderly Woman Resists Falling in Love," and "Self-consciousness"

by Daniel Lowe

Poetry is easier for me to write than short fiction, because, frankly, I know less about it and have had limited experience with the form. Ignorance and inexperience are hardly credentials I should laud in a first sentence, but I am making a point: because of my lack of experience reading and writing within a form, that form demands less of me as a writer. Had I never written a poem—and read relatively few—I could jot down most anything and call it fine. On the other hand, if I had written hundreds of poems and read thousands of others, all of that work would be brought to bear each time I sat down at my writer's desk. That is pressure, indeed.

Before I undercut my authority entirely, I should say I spent the first three years of undergraduate school calling myself a poet. But because I've written comparatively few poems since then (though I have read many), I do not call myself a poet now. (The label itself has almost no meaning anyway.) But I am still interested in writing poetry, principally because the form pressures language—and consequently my adult sensibilities of language—entirely differently than short fiction. And because of the differentiation between the forms, each informs the writing of the other. I want to believe that my fiction is stronger for my having written poetry, and that my poetry is stronger because I have written fiction.

"Albert Einstein: Plumber," is one of the poems I wrote as an undergraduate. That was over ten years ago, so I have some difficulty recalling its sources. But my memory of the seed of the poem is distinct: one of my professors, while discussing the horror with which Einstein regarded the bombing of Hiroshima and Nagasaki, quoted Einstein as saying, "If I had it to do all over again, I'd choose to be a tailor." I had loved Einstein since I was a child, when I wanted to be an astronomer because I did not know what a physicist was. (Now that I do, I still have some regrets about choosing to be a writer—if that was a choice.) I admired his intellect, his genius, his affection for Mozart, but above all I admired his humility: when I looked into his large, dark eyes in photographs, I thought I could see how his theories had humbled him.

Albert Einstein: Plumber

"If I were a young man again
I would choose to be a plumber . . ."
                    —Einstein

On the streets of Zurich,
in 1945,
the old plumber
wanders down the sidewalk
like a wind-tossed lunch sack,
a hard roll tucked
between the wrenches
in his tool box.

When he greets the street children
they tug at his pants leg
and beg for the peppermint sticks
that line his pockets each morning.
They tear at the wrappers,
and his face is lit with a half-smile,
as if he knew a joke
he didn't want to tell them.

At noon, he breaks
from a clogged drain pipe,
eats the hard roll
and watches the sun
pour like a liquid over the Alps.
Forty years earlier
he scribbled on a blackboard
and uncovered God's equations,
then quickly erased them
for fear he'd robbed
the vault of the universe.

At five P.M.
he loosens his monkey wrench
and shuffles along the streets
toward home. On the corners,
redfaced newsboys shout
the war is over,
the battles won
with tanks and guns,
and American army nurses
bend like licorice whips
in the arms of sailors.

The quotation from my professor stirred my imagination; I began to think about what sort of tailor Einstein would have become. When I considered the seams he'd found in time and the universe, I began to conceive of how he would alter garments, and I suppose my conceptions could have filled any number of science fiction books. But I knew that anything I would write about such clothing would be a betrayal of Einstein's statement. His wish was *not* to draw attention to his work. Finally, I found this more interesting: a man who had recognized the enormity of his theories and decided not to reveal them because of how they presaged the nuclear age and instead became a tailor. I had already written out several very good lines about Einstein's tailor shop when I decided I needed to go to the library to get more information on his life.

I spent several hours afterward cursing my professor for getting the quotation wrong. Not only had I wasted all the writing I had done, but the occupation of plumber seemed far less romantic than that of tailor. At the time, whether I knew it or not, I was seriously interested in the Romantic in writing, both in terms of the sound of language and its imagery. "Albert Einstein: Plumber" does not sound particularly pretty, but it is a Romantic poem and very likely sentimental at times.

Once I had traded in needle and thread for a monkey wrench, the poem was rather easy to write. I began with an image of morning, Einstein as "an old plumber" walking along the street "like a wind-tossed lunch sack," lines of sweetness and vulnerability that again I might argue are sentimental. Then I simply took Einstein through his work day. The poem is nothing without the children eating the peppermint sticks and the image of the nurses as licorice whips. These as much as the chronology of Einstein's day hold the poem together.

Those last three lines— "and American army nurses/bend like licorice whips/in the arms of sailors"—own any power the poem might have. They are probably closest to my writer's sensibility. I developed the images themselves from the classic *Life* magazine photograph where a woman is kissing a sailor as she's draped across his arm in celebration of the Allied forces victory in World War II. The kiss itself and the sweetness of the image of "licorice whips" is essentially a romantic longing for the innocence of a world without nuclear weaponry. But I used the word "whips" very deliberately. It has connotations of brutality that I intend to balance most of the poem's nostalgia. (After all, we cannot forget that World War II was also about the Holocaust, which had nothing to do with the advent of the A-bomb.) If the poem does not resonate on that image, it fails.

I will say one other thing about this poem: it is among the most political I have written. And while I agree with those who argue that all writing is political and ideologically charged, I would also argue that the best overtly political poems are those that don't use contemporary politics as their means and their ends. I admire poets who try to bring about social change through their poetry; this is among the most useful services poetry provides. But I am less interested in poetry strictly bound by a particular political time period because, *in* time, those poems may be regarded nostalgically or referentially. Regrettably, I believe "Albert Einstein: Plumber" is one of those poems.

"An Elderly Woman Resists Falling in Love" is a poem shaped by my response to a story, Gina Berriault's "The Diary of K. W." The story is affecting on many levels, but the one I was most interested in was how an elderly woman had fallen in love with a young man who lived in a room above hers. The story is told with an utter lack of sentimentality, narrated through the entries the woman makes in her diary. I suppose I was taken, as I am often taken, by desperate love: in this case, a woman's body and mind responding in ways that her sense of her own physicality must necessarily deny.

An Elderly Woman Resists Falling in Love

I.
I have just gone to the market
and in the sack of groceries
found, to my surprise,
rinds when I had purchased oranges.

II.
I am not screeching for dignity.
I've nothing to implore.
The world spins its own cocoon.
(My children wait to see it scorched.)

III.
When I was younger, I loved birds,
but I did not want to be needed by them.
Now, I refuse to feed pigeons.

IV.
My blood has soured;
my skin smells of garlic.
I would sprinkle vinegar on your chest
before kissing it.

V.
I have always loved the ocean, but despised sand.
My own brackish eyes
do not have a speck of grit in them.

VI.
Your body would slip like water into mine.
But even now, nights I wake sweating,
and your face looms,
your mouth whispers, "Learn, learn."

"K. W." retains her dignity in Berriault's story, principally because she is so self-aware. In the poem, I was interested in writing of a woman whose self-consciousness was honed even more sharply, so that, feeling the threat of love, feeling the threat of desperation, she would resist the seduction of each. Finally, I do not believe in this resistance, as it has been my experience that such love is the most compelling, or that love is most deeply felt at moments of desperation. (Again, the Romantic in me takes his voice.)

The poem was easy to write, probably because I didn't take it as seriously as the preceding two paragraphs may indicate. The only stanza that truly interests me is the last one; the others are written for impression and sound. The first stanza reads:

> *I have just gone to the market*
> *and in the sack of groceries*
> *found, to my surprise,*
> *rinds when I had purchased oranges.*

The intent of the imagery is fairly simple here. From what I understand through reading and through speaking to others (and now, alas, through some of my own experience) is that aging surprises, and that age is revealed to many of us only in moments of brutal self-honesty or vulnerability. And in those moments it is difficult to avoid bitterness. The first stanza of the poem establishes this and leads to the second one, where the woman turns to resignation as a more appropriate response to aging than bitterness.

The sound of the first stanza is fairly simple, too. I liked the hard g's of "gone" and "groceries," the hard k's of "market" and "sack" (rather than bag, which has connotations—"the old bag"—I wanted to avoid), the softer, similar sounds of "gone," "found," "rinds," and "oranges." I write this way because it pleases me to hear such language, even as I believe that writers can love sound too much and become slaves to it.

But there was no elaborate metaphor or plan that went into the writing of the first stanza. I wrote it because Berriault's story was on my mind, and because, one afternoon after I unloaded groceries, oranges were left at the bottom of the bag. The next four stanzas were written much the same way, though they approach love and the experience of age from different angles and are deliberately ordered.

The last stanza is most interesting for me because in it lies the heart of my response to "The Diary of K. W." The exertion of falling in love seems to me among the most difficult aspects of love, particularly the demands that one's lover makes on one's capacity to love. Love is, in part, a violent accommodation. So the woman in the poem must sweat her lover's body out because she no longer has a body where there is room for another. And the word "learn" is fearful enough to keep her from falling in love *because* she has lived so long, and knows its urgency and its summons when spoken by a lover.

"Self-consciousness" is probably the most difficult poem of the three for most readers to understand. Of the three, it is also the poem I'm closest to. I have found this true with most of my work in both fiction and poetry. The material that is closest to me takes on a form and language that is not often highly accessible. I am never deliberately obscure, as I think such writing is insidious and pretentious. But the difficulty of my best material—my difficulty in working with it, my sense of its ineffability—is often mirrored in the form of the story or poem. And I believe that finally, if my writing is to be distinguished at all, this is what will distinguish it. I suppose in part I'm discussing style and voice here, but only as they're tied into form and language. (The separation of them is probably artificial.)

Self-consciousness

It is that evening
in a weighted summer
between too much rain
and too much rain,
when the deformity of light
the color of our insides
suffused into the sky
loosens the loose children
who announce their inscrutable skins
and bicycle slick-wheeled past
porches where men and women
make presents of their hands.

We could not touch anything
through that night of stupid rain.
Not our own children
dreaming of colors,
the sanctimony of our bodies,
that mockery of our limbs
that lay in the yard.

And it is difficult to remember light
in the conspiracy of closed doors,
the windows of our fathers' cars,
the temporal oddity of our mothers
that made us hesitate,
then run run run
into transfiguration.

I wrote "Self-consciousness" at a time when I was having enormous difficulty writing anything. Each time I sat down at the typewriter, I felt as if I was also standing behind my chair, watching as I wrote. Everything I set down over a period of months seemed pretentious, narcissistic, self-indulgent, or repetitious. None of these feelings is uncommon for writers, but at some point they must be left behind in order for work to get done. I could not leave them behind. So one evening following a fitful day of writing, I walked outside after a rainstorm, and the air had the peculiar, pink tint of sunset, where the houses, the street, the children playing in the puddles, were all tinged with color. The children were joyful; I was mournful. And it occurred to me that the color of the light was a suffused red, the color of blood, the color of my insides if I flung them into the sky.

I was struck so heavily by the self-consciousness of such a thought that I was ashamed. I said to myself, "Gee, how self-absorbed shall we become?" the pronoun itself in reference to the writer sitting at the desk and the one looking over his shoulder. I wrote the poem in part to rid myself of both of them for a while and to articulate what I had felt for so many months.

The first stanza draws a sharp distinction between the self-consciousness of my perception of the color of the light and the comparative joy felt by children and others who are appreciating it. The children's skins are "inscrutable," as are the hands of the men and women, because the narrator of the poem cannot understand or can no longer understand their simple connection to the elements of light, rain, bicycle-riding, and so on.

(But this seems easy to say. The children's skins are also inscrutable because they are, for me, inscrutable. I don't want to give a reason for the image because I don't want the poem to be reasoned. But this is much different from saying I don't want it to be understood.)

In the second stanza, I use "we" as a point of view for several different reasons. The first is that I wanted the poem to be about self-consciousness, not about isolation. The second is that utter self-consciousness precludes, as I have felt it, the touching of another. I wanted this "other" in the poem for that perspective, and I wanted the man and woman in the poem to have children themselves, in part because I do and in part because this underscores the inscrutability already mentioned in the first stanza even as it leads toward the third. The last is that I don't believe a poem about self-consciousness needs to have the word "I" in it. This is a personal bias. Poetry that is deeply and intimately revelatory doesn't have to be confessional. I say this even while I do admire some confessional poets; still, while I admire the courage of such poets, I do not often admire their craft or their work with the form. In terms of writing, I would argue that it is easy to spill one's guts, easy, though immodest to say, "Look at the pain and celebration of my life." I do not so much admire poetry that documents personal suffering and joy, because there it is in the world. I do admire poetry that embraces such themes and presents them in language and form in ways they have never been.

Is it elitist to demand such intellectual rigor? I think not. I would never ask poets to stop writing confessionally. But I would stop reading these poets because I can respond emotionally only to so many poems from so many writers. I must be interested in the poems, in how the emotionality is presented, how it is encased, how its structures represent it. My emotional response is deepened by this effort. I cannot be interested in so many poets writing about the same things in the same ways.

The poem "Self-consciousness" must turn on the last stanza, particularly the last two lines, if it is to work at all. The narrator of the poem is trying at once to recollect the moments of childhood when he was less self-aware along with those that provided the first hints of the self-consciousness he now feels. Thus "the conspiracy of closed doors"—children turned away from rooms of adult conversation even as light comes from under the door. Thus "the windows of our father's cars"—an image I use because my own father returned home many times from a week's absence, his face obscured by sun on the windshield as I watched from the window, the mystery of his absence trailing him as he entered the house. And thus "the temporal oddity of our mothers"—those moments when children see their mothers as women, women separate from motherhood before those moments collapse into a need for mothering again. The hesitation the narrator recalls is, I suppose, the recognition that childhood ends. But the direction of the running itself—childish in its rhythm—I intend to leave ambiguous. I am unsure whether the sprint into transfiguration is a headlong retreat into childhood or a rush into adulthood, or both. I am playing, here, with the brilliant light of Christ's transfiguration, the comparatively unselfconscious light of childhood, and the incandescent light of maturity that can leave myth and innocence bare. I do not want nor do I intend to offer a simple resolution for the dilemma the narrator is facing.

This, finally, is the most deeply autobiographical source of the poem. My self-consciousness as a writer is now a thing with which I constantly battle. I haven't found a simple resolution for the problem, even as I'm capable of tracing its origins. Those origins collide in the last line of the poem; the form of the poem reflects, perhaps feebly, my own interior state. This is more than I would like to say about myself. But this is also what I admire in poems, in stories, in almost all work written by other writers: language that reveals a writer's most intimate material in a form that describes how it has been learned and felt. As I've said, this becomes more difficult as writers better know the form, and I believe many writers become overmastered by such knowledge. But that difficulty must be managed through effort, concentration, and interest if a writer is not to become a slave of self-repetition or literary fad.

Discovering the Voices of Biblical Women

by Anne Colwell

"Mary Tells Her Side" is a poem that I carried around inside, in fragments, for a long time before I came to write it. One of the fragments involved women in the Bible and my attempt to understand my own experience by reinterpreting theirs. Another thread came from a more specific consideration of Mary Magdalene—her love for Jesus and her conversion. An act of conversion is a manifestation of great love, and any conversion, any great love, has that double edge; it is both the only salvation and the worst destruction, the ruination of the "old things." I had thought about conversion first in terms of celibacy, because of a conversation I had with a friend about his decision to become a priest and his idea that celibacy was a passionate, sexual choice. I also thought about conversion in terms of active sexuality, of falling in love, and the problem of choosing a life. But I have found that I can never write from this kind of fragmented thought, a more or less intellectual consideration of theme. I need a concrete image. I need to imagine real people, feeling real things.

Mary Tells Her Side

We could only find one room
in that whole dusty city
though we knew every street.
So all of us lay,
stretched on the floor
or propped between chairs
in the darkness.
My back to the cool of the wall,
I lay on my cloak
with my hair wound soft
beneath my head.

Long after the others were sleeping
with their fitful cries and mumbles,
I lay still and quiet
and listened hard
for his breathing.

I can't remember
him coming to me
or hearing him cross
the sleeping room.
But I knew.
I knew his touch.

> And when his fingers
> brushed my breasts
> my nipples opened up like flowers,
> like purple spikes of hyacinth.
>
> And all night in that molasses dark
> thick and sweet, my hands burned
> and my feet flamed
> and my hair, loose between us, became
> a woven crown of fire.
>
> And all night in that dark he came
> with the deep light and burning
> that I had known,
> that I had seen him inspire.
>
> But after that night,
> after that night I was ruined.
> The old things were gone.
> And I never was again
> without the sound
> of wings in my head,
> without the ache
> in my small, dark womb.
> And after that I never could again,
> I never did,
> with any man.

When I imagined Mary Magdalene and Jesus and the group of men and women that followed him bedding down for the night in a rented room in the crowded city of Jerusalem, this image brought the fragments together. I pictured Mary Magdalene lying perfectly still on the floor of a dark, crowded room; I imagined her listening hard to distinguish the sound of Jesus's breathing from all the other night noises. I wanted the poem to be about her love for him and how that act of conversion had ruined her.

I wrote the beginning of the poem twice but could go no further than five or six lines. The problem, I now see, was that I tried to start at the end. I thought I knew where the poem was going. The poem was written in Mary's voice, but she was describing her life from the moment of her conversion on, instead of describing the love and passion of the moment of conversion. I had let the original intellectual side of the poem get in the way of the human scene as I had imagined it. I got frustrated. I felt inept. I put the poem aside for a few hours and turned to other, more comforting things.

When I came back to the poem that evening, I wrote:

> Long after the others were asleep
> I lay still and listened
> for his breathing.

Not good. But I had found my way back to the concrete image, to the real person, the Mary that I had imagined. I sat for a while, looking at what I had just written, unable to go on. Then I did what I often do when I'm stuck—I turned the page and wrote the title again on a fresh sheet of paper. (If I don't know the title yet, I rewrite the first line.) I also did something that I had never done before I wrote "Mary Tells Her Side"—I did not look at the drafts that I had written in the afternoon, but instead tried to reimagine the whole scene, without depending on words that I had written before that did not work.

I put myself in the place of Mary Magdalene, a woman probably around my age, following the man that she was in love with, following him with a large group of other men and women who followed him for their own reasons. She tells the story. Her story begins not with her alone, lying in the dark, but with the dailiness of her life, following this man, knowing the dusty city streets that they live in, being forced sometimes to sleep in one room, perhaps hungry, perhaps exhausted. After I understood and wrote that part, I could use the image of Mary in love with the very human sound of Jesus's breathing, lying quiet in the dark to listen to him.

I read what I am writing out loud throughout the writing process. I do this as a means to make myself conscious of the rhythm and music of the words. By music I mean the way the sounds of words echo or contrast with each other, and not necessarily traditional rhyme or meter. So, for example, the lines "Long after the others were sleeping/with their fitful cries and mumbles" in the first draft read "Long after the others were sleeping/with their fitful groans and mumbles"; I changed "groans" to "cries" because I liked the way it sounded with the word "quiet" in the following lines: "I lay still and quiet/and listened hard/for his breathing."

The words of this poem, unlike most of the poems I've written, came like a gift after I had found the right place to begin. Usually, I write a poem over and over before I'm satisfied with it, but this poem remains almost exactly as it was in the first draft. This ease might have come from living with the poem for a while before I wrote it. Or the words might have been there because I had imagined the scene vividly enough to live it with Mary; I could identify with her feelings because of things that I was feeling in my own life. As I was writing, I was aware of the importance of repetition in the poem, both for its sense of rhythm and its ability to invoke a ritual element. So lines like: "But I knew./I knew his touch," and "that I had known,/that I had seen . . . ," and "But after that night,/after that night I was ruined" imitate the rhythm of speech, have the reiterative quality of a ritual, and foreshadow and underscore the important repetition in the final lines of the poem, "I never could again,/I never did,/with any man."

I was also conscious of choosing images that seemed to me particularly vivid or sensuous. For example, the comparison "my nipples opened up like flowers,/like purple spikes of hyacinth" and the description of the night as "molasses" seem to capture the experience of the senses and, in doing so, to give some concreteness to

subject matter that is otherwise abstract. Concreteness becomes particularly important in the description of Mary's haunted emptiness, "without the sound/of wings
in my head,/without the ache/in my small, dark womb." An abstract description at
this point in the poem would have undercut the central idea. Mary's ruin must
seem as vivid, as passionate, and as complete as her conversion.

Not at the outset, but somewhere in the middle of writing the poem, I realized
the strong connection between the story Mary Magdalene was telling and the story
of the Virgin Mary. I am uncomfortable with how Catholic this sounds, yet the
revelation was not a theological one but a human one. Through writing the poem, I
became aware of things I had listened to and comprehended, but never imagined or
understood. I began really to believe that the experience of love was universal and
human and that even a love as unearthly as Mary's love, a love that the second-
grade catechisms had made distant, bodiless, and cold for me, could have been
real, immediate, and passionate. The fact that I discovered this while I was writing
the poem, discovered it through writing the poem, made "Mary Tells Her Side"
more honest, an authentic search for the expression of an idea I was working out
and not words chosen for a prefabricated end.

The experience of writing this poem changed the way I write and what I expect
from my writing. "Mary Tells Her Side" gave me confidence in what the words
can do if you let them go in the direction they want to and don't try to force them
in the direction you think you want to take. It is a scary way to write; it involves a
lot of risk, and it hasn't always worked for me. But when it does work, it
inevitably pays off, not only in the form of a better poem, but in the potential for
learning and for enlarging the circle of myself, my perspective, as a writer and a
person.

"Adulteress" was inspired by an image that I could never successfully incorpo-
rate into the poem. The image came from an impression I got while taking loaves
of bread from the huge ovens of the bakery I worked in one summer. The bread
was brown and smooth and heavy, and it reminded me of the kind of stones that
you sometimes see in the desert. I kept returning to the image of the bread and
stones, and, because this happened after I wrote "Mary Tells Her Side" and I was
practically obsessed with stories of women in the Bible, I connected the image to
the stoning of the woman taken in adultery. I thought I would write a poem about
an adulteress in which the stones that killed her were connected with and somehow
transformed into bread.

Adulteress

The first stone struck below my right breast.
I heard the pop and crack
like breaking small branches.
The next one bounced from my hand, outstretched,

and fell heavy to the dust,
uncaught, gray, and even.

They were two or three standing at my door
when I came out to bring them in—
But then the crowd blew up like a whirlwind,
twisting, like the wind through the desert,
rushing, gathering stones and sand.
And I stepped back to the sun warm wall
no shelter
to find that wind hard and hot
and full of hail.
Hard and hot with stones sent for
my face, my breasts, my arms, my belly,
sent like labor-sudden pains into my belly.

I looked down and saw them in the dust
lying beneath me, mute and gray,
and I fell to my knees and then lay still, still
gathering the stone children to me.

I began with two stanzas centered on images of a woman baking bread; I imagined her kneading dough and pushing her hair from her forehead with the back of her floury hand. These gestures, common to any woman who is baking, seemed ancient and beautiful. Then I tried to switch from that third-person characterization to a monologue in which the woman tells the story of her stoning. But before I even completed a draft, I cut the first two stanzas because the third-person voice felt forced and, when the image of bread reappeared in the woman's monologue, it sounded unnatural. Moreover, I thought starting the poem in the woman's voice, with the lines "The first stone struck/below my right breast" was more dramatic and cleaner than switching the voice in the middle of the poem.

I turned the page and wrote the poem again in the voice of the adulteress, imagining what she saw and felt, and working more carefully with the sounds of words and their music together. I found that when I concentrated on this, and stopped trying to turn the stones into bread (it was a temptation), the poem worked and even surprised me. Although I had not planned it, the stones, which I thought were bread, became children—"I looked down and saw them in the dust/lying beneath me, mute and gray,/and I dropped to my knees and then lay still, still/gathering the stone children to me." This image, an image that came from imagining what it felt like to be stoned, the crushing weight, the sound, the sudden pain, seemed more interesting and truer than the image of stones changed to bread. The "stone children" image connected the pains of stoning to the pains of labor and to the brutal sexuality of the crowd rising like a whirlwind, "hard and hot." I liked the way it sounded in the woman's voice and what it said about her character dramatically in those final lines.

I took this first draft of "Adulteress" to show to a group of writers who work at the University of Delaware and have been meeting on Saturday mornings for about a year now. I owe them much of the credit for the development of the poem. They criticized, encouraged, and made suggestions that forced me to examine the way I write—to revise and reimagine and learn. They noticed things working in "Adulteress" that I had not; for example, the way "full of hail" recalled the angel's address to Mary, "Hail, Mary, full of grace." Overall though, they felt that the first draft seemed skeletal, somewhat reserved and underwritten. The jump from the end of the second stanza to the beginning of the third was particularly problematic because I had not sufficiently prepared the reader for the transformation of stones to children. Simply ending the second stanza with a reference to the pain in "my belly" did not necessarily evoke childbirth as I had hoped it did. This was symptomatic of the sketchiness of the whole first draft.

So we discussed ways that I could flesh out the skeleton of the poem, suggestions like: give more specific details about the people who have come to stone her, if they live in her village she probably knows them, who are they and what they do; talk about "him," where is he, what was her relationship with him like; give some detail about her life before the last moment; and, the suggestion that proved most immediately helpful, lengthen the line to make room to expand the ideas.

In the drafts that followed, I tried all the suggestions that we discussed that morning. Lengthening the line proved immediately effective, improving the rhythm and providing room for description. I have a tendency to use short lines because I like the way they emphasize each word, but in the first draft of "Adulteress" the number of line breaks interfered with the music and limited the potential to develop detail.

Other suggestions, although they did not work ultimately, taught me about characterization, concreteness, and the emotions and ideas beneath the poem's situation. For example, whenever I tried to give details about the people who were stoning the woman, their relationship to her, their jobs, this characterization detracted from the horror and made me forgive, in some obscure way, that individual. By trying lines like "At first I saw them—the friend of my mother's,/the baker who whistled 'a mouthful of birds,'" I discovered that describing the actions of a rabble means that this individual perspective, whistling or friendship, is made impossible. Mob action destroys the individuality, the individual humanity, of the perpetrators. Whenever I tried to restore it, I lost something of the sense of the crowd. On the other hand, when I included details about the man and the relationship that would cause her death, I discovered that the adulteress had to be an individual, and her individuality was emphasized by the contrast with the nature of the mob. Whatever beauty or sadness she had came from being a human being, suffering alone, in a world turned suddenly inhuman.

Having learned from these drafts, these experiments, I wrote the poem again and tried this time to surround inanimate things, like the stones and the pain, with the detail and description that would not interfere with the individual characterization of the woman but would instead comment on her situation, and make the poem more vivid and concrete. For instance, the last line of the first stanza in drafts refers to the stone that hits her outstretched hand as "almost unheeded," a direct comment on the woman's experience (and a weak line). In the final draft, I changed the line to read "uncaught, gray and even," better because it describes on one level the stones and on another level those who are doing the stoning. Repeating the phrase "my belly" and describing the pains as "labor-sudden" at the end of the second stanza made the connection stronger between the pain and the woman's perception of the stones as children in the final lines. By coming into contact with the loving and human force of the woman, even the inanimate stones are transformed, and it is her love and forgiveness that bring about this transformation.

Even though the development of "Adulteress" seems circular, moving away from and then back toward the first draft, the intervening stages taught me important lessons about a poem I'd written and only partly understood. Experiments, even failed experiments, prove something if examined in the right spirit. The criticism and encouragement and support of the individuals in this group of writers gave me the gift of the "right spirit" about all my failed attempts at "Adulteress."

The Incurables' Curative Power and the Soul in the Basement

by Suzanne Underwood Clark

"Sunday Service at the Home for the Incurables" came to me in a flood one evening after I had sought to stir up a poem by asking myself the question, "What *really* matters to you?" I had been through a long dry spell and hoped there might be a trickle of inspiration down in the depths somewhere.

The answer was delivered at once: What mattered was a scene going back twelve years to some forty residents at the Home for the Incurables in Memphis, Tennessee; a gathering of clownsfolk singing off-key at the top of their lungs, "When the roll is called up yonder I'll be there." I wept every time I went (our church conducted monthly services at the home), moved by innumerable graces: the pure, childlike love for Christ demonstrated by these individuals, whose "incurable" palsies and paralyses had stripped them of all outward normality, leaving them as fools; the hope they expressed in their hymns and in conversations of having perfect bodies someday at the resurrection; the friendship and gratefulness they expressed to me for coming.

Sunday Service at the Home for the Incurables

> *Idiots*
> *jitterbugs*
> *drooling fools*
> *and spastics:*
>
> *Forgive my wretched poise*
> *and tidy clothes*
> *and manners acquired*
> *from much church and so little*
> *rubbing into your palsy*
> *and piss and men asleep*
> *from birth living*
> *in cribs.*
>
> *Undo me*
> *dear incurables*
> *singing*
> *"My Jesus" in slapstick,*
> *your hands with minds*
> *of their own*
> *shaking praise.*
>
> *Moving in your midst*
> *a tender light,*

> *a love unkempt*
> *and blind waits on you*
> *singly, touching each*
> *ragged grief, each buried*
> *rage and sings*
> *your circus hymns*
> *with reverence*
> *as one who well knows*
> *the pogroms of fools.*
>
> *Touch me, my gargoyle*
> *heart, and make me*
> *crow.*

"Idiots/jitterbugs/drooling fools/and spastics": these lines are given for shock value, to plunge the reader into the company of the incurables. The words are not intended as insults; on the contrary, they become, in the speaker's mind, words of praise.

The next stanza is a single sentence, written to convey the speaker's mounting sense of unworthiness and dissatisfaction with religiosity that fails to meet human needs. Again, I am aiming for shock: "Forgive my wretched poise/and tidy clothes/and manners acquired/from much church and so little/rubbing into your palsy/and piss. . . . " The iambic (more or less) rhythm is abruptly halted by the single syllables of "much church" (with "ch" acting as a brake). Varying syllabic patterns can be a useful way of signalling changes in the speaker's emotional disposition.

"Undo me" in the next section is another direct appeal to these saints and alludes also to Isaiah who saw the Lord and cried out, "Woe is me, for I am undone; because I am a man of unclean lips" (Isaiah 6:5). A description of their singing follows, providing a glimpse of an abandonment in worship that has a comic element more akin to the kingdom of God, it may be supposed, than the worship employed in most "normal" church services. The use of metonymy ("hands with minds of their own") underscores this abandonment; truly, the left hand that shakes uncontrollably has no idea what the right hand is doing.

At this point in the poem, I thought it necessary to shift focus from the incurables to the object of their worship, a presence unnamed who understands and cares for these people more than anyone. I depict him as "unkempt and blind," a servant who heals the injuries of spirit resulting from ridicule and rejection. The clown motif is reinforced by having the Christ in their midst sing their "circus hymns with reverence." He identifies completely with these misfits "as one who well knows/the pogroms of fools." "Pogroms" was intended to remind the reader of Jesus's Jewishness and his persecution and to bring to mind the sufferings of Jews and other "undesirables" throughout history, especially in Nazi Germany. The incurables live in their own kind of pogrom, cut off from society and their former lives.

The last three lines are intended as a prayer. "Gargoyle" was chosen to describe the speaker's sense of spiritual deformity and a desire to be like the incurables who experience joy, simple faith, and who are free, like children, to crow.

As the mother of three young children, I sometimes sneak down to the basement to find my soul. The perennial laundry there comforts, allowing me to think as I sort and fold, to disentangle myself from the madness upstairs. Such is the setting for "Hanging Wash."

Hanging Wash

> There is something good in the wash
> with its intimate steam:
> Clumps of years I sort to give the wind,
> the breath of shirts and socks,
> the braille of towels telling of flesh
> I know as well as my own hands:
> colonies of moles, cracks and rashes,
> fevers, leaks and hair
> that outlasts all other threads:
> those of sleeves we wrap around each other,
> gowns we stroke and shirts
> that clothe the heart, painted scar.
>
> Give your heat to me,
> body of wash, ragdoll.
> Time is pulling loose
> the very seams
> we hang by.

The poem was inspired by a simple impression: handling the wash one afternoon, I was struck by the human feel of the clothes. This would provide a metaphor I had been seeking for a long time as a means of expressing a growing heaviness. It was the revelation that my husband and children, so very dear and loved, were going to die someday. Like most mothers, I have secret fears of my children being badly injured or killed. But my dread had been intensified by the recent death of my sister, whom I loved deeply.

Over a period of time I had attempted several poems to convey the theme of love and loss, but they were not true and remained unfinished. But the poem in my basket was different. It held all I needed—textures, sounds, associations. I composed the first line: "There is something good in the wash with its intimate steam." The next line, "Clumps of years I sort to give the wind," suggested my theme.

The wash was a perfect metaphor. It was easy to think of shirts and socks as having breath, of towels that communicate. I was pleased with "braille" (line 5) as a useful and suggestive word. "Telling of flesh I knew as well as my own hands" made the necessary connection between speaker and subject. The writer, if he is to avoid being a mere "versifier," must allow the reader entrance into the speaker's true feelings.

Next, I knew I must provide details to demonstrate the intimacies of flesh. Words were chosen for sound relationships and connotative value. "Colonies of moles, cracks and rashes" served my purpose; likewise, "fevers" and "leaks," for these combinations offered alliterative effects as well as implying the range of acquaintance with flesh of my flesh. "Hair that outlasts all other threads," a phrase arising from the memory of my sister's hair at her funeral, echoed the central meaning of the poem, while permitting a bit of deep pain to surface.

The next section, three lines defining the brief threads of human life, was something of a challenge as I set out to convey without sentimentality concrete images of my relationships within the family. I could not afford to be careless on sacred ground. Images came to mind of rocking a feverish child in my arms at midnight, of sexual pleasures enjoyed with my husband, and of a thousand occasions for laughter and affection. "Sleeves we wrap around each other,/gowns we stroke and shirts/that clothe the heart, painted scar." "Painted scar" was inevitable, though it came only after hours of work. It was a pivotal expression, drawing together the theme of temporality with the notion of suffering as a companion to love, while anticipating the ragdoll of line fourteen. In earlier drafts I had played with "spool of time" and "skein," until discovering the ragdoll that belonged to the poem.

At the end, I felt a need for direct address: "Give your heat to me, body of wash." The idea was to communicate something of the speaker's desperateness as she comes to realize more fully her own mortality, folded in with the lives of those she loves. The final image, that of being hung up as time wears out one's seams, was well-suited (if the reader will pardon the pun), for conveying a sense of helplessness while hopefully suggesting the terminal nature of existence, to which we are all pinned.

Something About "Dinosaurs of the Hollywood Delta," "Snake," and "The Rise of the Sunday School Movement"

by Gerald Costanzo

If there is one thing which misleads me most often in the making of poems, it's a concern—too early in the process—with the relative "importance" of the subject. I've been publishing poems for nearly twenty years, and though I like to think I write them to myself as attempts to understand the present, I begin to think about the response of readers before the end of the first draft. I assume readers' expectations will be similar to the ones I have when reading a poem: that they will be *interested* in the development of a situation or of an image; that something may be *learned* from the poet's style or from the cumulation of statements; that they will be made to *feel* something from the encounter; that they might even be entertained a little.

Because my poems concern themselves initially with material which is accessible and, often, trivial, the writing becomes a means both for attempting to make the material significant and for discovering that the overt subject may not really be the subject at all. The impediment is in manipulating the work intellectually, in bringing "theories" to the writing table. I have to acknowledge over and over how much I am fascinated by the consequences of what seems minute. If I can convince myself to get "lost" in the material rather than to stand before it questioning, then the poem has a chance to be.

Whatever else I want for my poems, I want them to *communicate*. For me this means creating something far in excess of self-expression. It involves a period of conscious attention after that unknowable unconscious has had its chance. My poems usually get their start with a few words or an image. Something I've overheard or read perhaps. Before I get very far along, I begin to have a conscious intent for the material. When the progression stalls and the unconscious, over whatever period of time, treats the material and "gives" it to me again, no matter how much the intent has changed, it is my conscious discovery and acceptance or rejection of it that matters for the poem. If I accept a new intention by incorporating it into the poem, it is still my intention. I have always been uneasy about that which is "unknowable" in a poem: not that which is unknowable in the process, but in the artifact itself. As I write—given that the process is both a conscious and an unconscious one—I'm trying to learn what I'm trying to say, so that finally the poem is my explanation of the material—to myself and to a reader.

I once gave a reading in eastern Pennsylvania with Henry Braun. I remember someone from the audience, probably a friend of Henry's, asking him afterwards why he hadn't written about an ongoing experience which the questioner knew to be Braun's. A rather quizzical expression developed on Henry's face and he responded, "Well, you know, we write what poems we can." Often I have wanted to write about subjects which are not really mine or in a style which I could not make my own. Often I've failed to write good poems from a subject or style which is mine. We write what poems we can, and the safest thing I can say about the poems I want to discuss here is that they came close to achieving, in subject and effect, what I wanted them to be. For me this is not a common occurrence. Each has been printed in a magazine. Two received the Pushcart Prize, and the other was cited, having been nominated by a well-known writer who is not an acquaintance of mine and whose work I have always admired. Each has been included in an anthology in addition to the Pushcart collection. Still, wary of them as I may be, I imagine this is as secure as I'm able to feel about the quality of something I've written.

These poems are part of a "thematic" collection rather than of a collected miscellany. In the writing there were severe restraints involved with the conscious selection of theme. Each constituted a version of a singular motif; namely, a version of America in response to the present plight of the "American Dream." If that Dream is based upon the Puritan work ethic and the belief that there is room for everyone in an always-expanding economy; and further, that it is the fault of the individual if he or she does not "succeed," what are some of the consequences of the discrepancy between the Dream and these versions of "actual" American experience? Collectively the poems are my attempt to focus on some possible consequences of holding the belief that the "good things" in life are obtainable through a directed and diligent attack on the world around us and, concurrently, that any examination of one's inner life is both dangerous and un-American. Many of the poems in the sequence contain American cities or place names in their titles. Mostly they develop metaphorically (or through other tropes) to suggest what I hope is something poignant about the "turning" of life in contemporary America.

Dinosaurs of the Hollywood Delta

Joe DiMaggio, who was married for three years to
Marilyn Monroe, has ended a 20-year standing order
for thrice-weekly delivery of roses to her crypt.
The florist said Mr. DiMaggio gave no explanation.
　　　　　　　—The New York Times
　　　　　　　September 30, 1982

In times of plenty
they arrived from everywhere
to forage among the palmettos
of Beverly and Vine, to roam
the soda fountains and dime stores
of paradise. For every Miss Tupelo

who got a break, whose blonde
tresses made it to the silver screen,
whose studio sent her on a whirlwind
tour to Chicago, and to the Roxy
in Manhattan where she'd chat
with an audience, do a little tap

dance, and answer questions
about the morality of the jitterbug,
thousands became extinct.
Their beauty, it was said, drove
men to wallow in dark
booths in the Florentine

Lounge dreaming of voluptuous
vanilla, though the rumor persists
that they were dumb.
They were called Jean, Rita, Jayne,
Mae, *and* Betty. *The easy names.*
No one remembers now

how the waning of their kind
began. Theories have pointed
to our own growing sophistication—
as if that were a part of natural
selection. At first we missed
them little, and only in that detached

manner one laments the passing
of any passing thing. Then posters
began to appear. Whole boutiques
adoring their fashion: heavy rouge,
thick lipstick. The sensuous puckering
of lips. Surreptitious giggling.

We began to congregate on street corners
at night, Santa Monica and La Brea,
to erect searchlights
and marquees announcing premieres
for which there were no films.
We looked upward

as if what had been taken from us
were somehow etched in starlight above
their sacred city. We began
to chant, demanding their return—
to learn, for once, the meaning
of their desperate, flagrant love.

Nostalgia was upon me again. The poem didn't begin as a response to its epigraph, but rather as a recollection of that minor event. I don't read the *New York Times*: I despise the typeface. Probably I heard about it on the news. It has the appeal of an item from a slow-news day. At any rate, I recollected it just at the moment of joking with a friend about my sadness at "the extinction of dumb blondes in America." The thought stayed with me so that after several days I wrote it down. It still seemed humorous. The writing did not go well; I needed more information. As I have done many times, I telephoned the reference desk (either of the town library in Harwich, Massachusetts, where I live during the summer, or at Carnegie Mellon where I teach) and asked for a copy of the *Times* article. Librarians have always been my friends; so many (without their knowing it) have helped me with my poems that I could never thank them all. I recall one episode when, having described with serious tone and in great detail the events of a baseball game in Cleveland where beer had been sold for ten cents and a fan had caused a riot by racing onto the field and accosting a player, one librarian covered the phone with her hand and, greatly amused, said to another, "It's that guy again, ya know, who always wants us to look up those crazy things that don't matter." But by the next morning I had been provided with a photocopy of the story.

The florist said Mr. DiMaggio gave no explanation. I admire the dignity in his insisting that what is private remain private. Dave Righetti's turning down a million dollars worth of advertising endorsements after he had pitched a no-hitter—because he wanted to concentrate on the season at hand. Garry Trudeau's statement that ours is the only country on earth where, by refusing hyperbolic self-promotion, one is considered to be arrogant. I was born into an America where shame (for example) was as tangible as a hammer. People who committed offense went to prison or into seclusion and were seldom heard from again. Now they write up their heinous exploits for big bucks. How tiring this has become; how out of whack! How satisfying that Joe DiMaggio declines to be disrespectful or disrespectable.

From that altogether-too-passionate-and-(some would say)right-wing concern, the poem became an elegy: paradoxically, for lost values and for lost dumb blondes. This surprised me. The words came from . . . I don't know exactly where. But suddenly they were all there. As a reader of them, the one I didn't understand was the "Delta" of the title. I elected to retain it, I suppose, in the interests of alliteration and invention. Later, a student of mine, a science fiction buff, informed me that a delta is a term for a star which is the fourth brightest of its constellation. I hadn't known that and am uncertain of a connection in any case. The form, six-line stanzas, came from—as always—a desire for form. In this case, a certain tightness which would allow for some visual space. And lots of enjambment for a rapid pacing. And the attempt to place striking words and phrases at the ends of lines.

Concerning the subject: as with so many things I was of at least two minds about it. It had become serious in tone, and I had felt the rightness of that. If I haven't always been a feminist, raising a daughter in America has certainly made me sympathetic to them. Of course the sex-object image should be disdained. Yet what genuine pleasure many of their performances have given us. What sheer fun. If there were to be a congregation demanding their return, albeit with alterations, I'd be among the number. I'm still fascinated by the way those larger-than-life public and private stories mirror our hidden ones. Such flagrance! Such desperation!

Snake
for Susan Petrie

Because he lived
in one of those regions
where snake is the plural

of snake, when they told him
there were snake in his swamp
he understood. He did them in

with his shotgun. His daughter,
Magill, sometimes sobbed while
poling them out. The tears

in her eyes and the look in his:
a whole morning's religion—
and the corpse of snake

left be in the heat
not snake at all,
but several serpent.

I hadn't written much for a while, and what I had gotten done seemed lengthy, leggy, padded. "Snake" was an exercise, a poem more about the use of language than about a subject. Most of the poems in my first book had been short lyrics. It was a style I'd moved away from. The work had gotten longer and more narrative. Anecdotal, really. But much of it wasn't satisfying: I'd lost that punch that can come with conciseness. I gave one of my classes an assignment of the following order: *Write a narrative poem in which you use exactly seventy-five words (including the title). Be sure to tell the whole story.* It was an assignment I'd formulated for myself.

The narrative element of "Snake" was suggested by a friend who delivered it as fact: her father who lived in a rural area had killed some snakes on his property. He had asked his younger daughter to remove them. She had cried while accomplishing the task. I decided to call my exercise "Snakes." When I sat down to write it out, almost absent-mindedly I kept writing "Snake." Make that plural I told myself, and then I noticed that it was. Why? Because they live in one of those regions. From that point the outcome was inevitable: there would have to be one more singular plural. Most of the ones I happened upon were not printable. But "serpent" enabled a fitting resolution to this brief statement about the nature of power, fear, and good and evil.

I think there was a radio commercial which proclaimed the Sunday School Movement as if it were imminent, proclaimed it with a fervor I have always loved to mock, even in sober moments. I knew immediately that, whatever it was, I wanted to help "give it rise." As it happens, I'm not a religious person. This is a circumstance not without stress: how best to live a life, how to raise one's children, etc. My Catholic upbringing has, nonetheless, lent me (or burdened me with) many Catholic images for my earlier poems. And perhaps there is still a desire for religion. At least there is the realization that not to believe eliminates one of the few reassurances which life offers.

"The Rise of the Sunday School Movement" continued to develop out of my reading and from a dream. I manage to read eighty to ninety books each year, and sometimes it's just plain healthy to get away from reading literature for a while. I had purchased a second-hand copy of a biography of Aimee Semple McPherson, "the world's most pulchritudinous evangelist" (as she called herself), who in 1926 claimed to have been kidnapped and who in her subsequent reappearance was tried for fraud amidst allegations of having absconded with a married man who operated the radio station at her Angelus Temple in Echo Park, California. The state withdrew charges during the trial in 1927 after which Sister Aimee crossed the country on a Vindication Tour. But the tour failed: the crowds were sparse and fraught with hecklers. Later she was found dead in her bedroom, the apparent victim of an overdose of sleeping pills.

The story of Puritans being Puritans is a continuing one in this country, as evidenced by the recent difficulties of the Bakkers and Jimmy Swaggart. For reasons I can't explain, I have spent hours of Sunday mornings during the past fifteen years watching such evangelists on television. This has mystified the members of my family, who have taken to offering reasons why I do it. My daughter, now a college student who is a talented singer and actress, appeared in a dream. She was dressed in a white satin, flowing robe-like dress and she was preaching to a large audience. Later, in our home, she was still wearing the dress—which frightened me. The dress itself seemed to create a distance between us which had never previously existed. I asked her to change her clothes, and she refused, telling me that the dress was a part of her now and that she was helping many people. But because her fingers were festooned with diamond rings I doubted her motives. I awoke, and what I first thought of were the diamonds. My daughter has never worn much jewelry.

Powerful dreams often unsettle our waking lives so I spent a moody day. That evening I began to write—out of a need, maybe, to assuage the implications of the dream: a belief against the exploitation of others, yet an acknowledgment of human gullibility. The next morning, driving to breakfast, most of the poem came to me and I recited it and asked my wife to copy it down. Probably because it contained the name of her daughter, she punctuated her transcription with comments such as "you can't say that" and "that part will have to be changed."

We write what poems we can. And whatever the nature of the help we receive, the final choices regarding selection are ours. Without a continuing study of craft, it isn't possible to make even adequate choices. This doesn't necessarily mean red-pencilling textbooks on poetics. It does mean continual reading and filing away of methods of technique one encounters in poems.

Usually my poems are as complete as I can make them in about ten drafts. If I'm writing as well as I'm able to, it's usually because I'm on a regular writing schedule; that is, I'm spending time at it each day. In times when I have extreme difficulty beginning, I invoke the Raymond Chandler method: one must spend one hour each day in the writing room. I don't have to write; but I may not listen to music, read, or even gaze out the window.

Many poets have talked about their poems arriving as "gifts," almost as if they hadn't written them. I think it is the conscious periods of writing which prod that unknown part of the self into doing much of the work. I then rely on subsequent conscious effort as a guide for the poem toward communication. And I think it is possible to coerce the unconscious mind into "giving" us elements of craft as well as those of subject and image. One can just as readily say "I want to write a poem which contains a zeugma and is about an astrologer" as "I want to write about an astrologer." But we have to have learned the definition for zeugma before we can ask ourselves for an example of it.

The Rise of the Sunday School Movement

I am not a healer. Jesus is the healer.
I am only the little girl who opens the door
and says "Come in."
                    —Aimee Semple McPherson

I had wanted my daughter
to become an evangelist—
                    Sister Lizabeth Adrienne—

not to relive my life in hers,
nor for desire after the great abstraction

in lieu of the bits of carpentry
I've managed. No, like anyone
I just longed for a little pomp amid
all of the circumstance.
A progeny who could shout Sweet

Beautiful Jesus *and mean it.*
To have borne
a pillar in the rise
of the Sunday School Movement,
or one of the overdue

Northern Crusades. One who could
espy the dance halls of Venice,

California with the true conviction
of a Sunday afternoon; who could bathe
in the sea at Carmel and not

disappear for three weeks
in Mexico with her married lover;
who'd never be transported
back from the lost, paraded
in a throne of white

wicker from her private train car
to overdose on tablets
of the newest redemption.
The way I figured it
I'd be sitting at a corner table

in the Desdemona Club
nursing a brew. She'd be up
there on the large-screen TV next
to the bar, having taken over Billy
Graham's Asian Tour after his terrible

swift heart attack in China. The petite
brunette beauty from America!
She'd be singing Lord,
We Need Thee Every Hour *as*
the afflicted clutched at the hem

of her flowing dress. Maybe
I'd kneel among them, then
and there. Begin
to believe as we're able to believe
what reaches us by satellite—

bow down as she gave us
the beauteous word, all of us praising,
loving her, adoring the celestial
melody, possessed by our irrevocable
conversions.

Writing Toward the Center

by Fleda Brown Jackson

Most poems begin for me with a place, or scene, or dialogue that gives me a subtle ache, a longing that first strikes my consciousness in images rather than words. As I get several images on paper, I begin to hear them tuning up. They have things to say to each other that I often don't suspect at first. They are like orbiting moons, and what I have to do is find the mass, the center, the source of the ache that holds them to their rounds.

Sometimes the source is almost tangible. Two summers ago, I bought a map and drove north. My family has a cottage in northern Michigan that my grandfather bought seventy-two years ago. We spent most of every summer there when I was young, wonderful summers, better than any other time in my childhood. When I unlocked the cottage door year before last, I had not been there in fifteen years, long enough for Central Lake to have taken on mythological proportions. Nothing had changed. Our neighbors, who have been our neighbors for generations, had remodeled, but my family still pumps water and walks up the hill to the outhouse. Few people are lucky enough to have the bones of their childhood preserved, intact. I think I wrote the five-poem series "Central Lake" to put myself there and keep myself there, in my childhood, by giving it away, by opening it outward. I started the first poem, "Cottage," my first night at the lake. I was alone, the earliest to arrive for the summer. I said almost aloud, "This is like opening the door on my grandmother's bones." The chairs, lamps, rugs, pump organ, fireplace were all still in place like the furniture of a tomb, vulnerable, apt to shift and crumble before my adult eyes. This is the first draft, begun that night:

> walking into an apparition, dead still, ~~the jumble~~
> chairs and clothes lying, dishes,
> like opening the door on your grandmother's bones
> where you had left them, curled and vulnerable,
> now dusted with neglect and strangely smaller.
> Things look like what they are,
> what they were, their looming in your
> mind suddenly reduced, as if you had walked in
> This is why you came, to sift down the bones,
> to use the ones worth saving
> for some new articulation.
> ~~I am here deep in ash.~~ I have burnt
> bones in all my intermediate life,
> defied and corrupted and driven myself away
> to stand here knee-deep in ash.
> We work for two days, hanging screens,

> *scrubbing floors, making beds, laying out*
> *the dock. We live here, for a month,*
> *again, anachronisms, pumping water.*
> *No other cottagers on the lake have refused like us*
> *to change. This is as good a time as any,*
> *but we hang on like a dying breed, as if*
> *what we have is delicate, ~~and will soon~~*
> *~~break~~. Here was our beginning, from which*
> *death emerged like a doppelganger.*
> *Our shadow selves come dripping*
> *up the dock, track sand across the floor,*
> *play spin-the-bottle by the evening fire,*
> *and tremble to think whose mouth,*
> *and how, exactly, is best.*
> *Our solid selves watch,*
> *and try to believe.*

Except in my very best poems, which tend to shape themselves in me before they reach paper, my work lies mostly in finding the gravitational center of the poem. I usually reach it, if I find it at all, by elimination, by writing what is *not* the center and whittling away at it until the poem begins to feel free in its own body and muscle. If its body is a surprise to me, I then sometimes have to go back and add new material to flesh it out.

My first draft was a puzzle of conflicting centers. The issues: could I believe the past had existed at all—the final lines try to pull the poem together with this idea—or did my old self and new self exist simultaneously in the poem? I thought of death and life as so entangled that my dead grandmother was giving me intense life at the moment of the poem. But another subject was our family's hanging on, trying to hold back time. I thought at first my return to the lake was the center of the poem, my coming back to sift down and articulate what is left, to claim it. Certainly "burnt" and "ash" were the wrong images, implying an irredeemable loss, just when the speaker has begun to get the place in working order. For that matter, "curled" was an outrageous image to describe brittle bones, but I hung onto it through another draft.

The second draft broke into halves, what the "I" saw and who the "we" are, ending with a quickly eliminated exclamation that was a desperate attempt to unite the two. I thought I wanted the doppelganger to express the split between the individual past (that hints in the poem at needing healing) and the present that always needs healing, that the poem intends to heal:

> *It is like opening the door*
> *on my grandmother's bones*
> *where I had left them*
> *curled and vulnerable,*
> *now strangely smaller.*
> *This is why I came, to sift*

down the bones,
to articulate the ones worth saving.
~~*For twenty years*~~ *All these years*
I have ~~*defied and*~~ *corrupted*
my own heart, driven myself away.
Now I claim what's mine.
My grandmother's name is mine.
I have come to help hang screens,
scrub floors, lay out the dock,
pump water, throw the rowboat
into the lake. Nothing changes.
We are a delicate breed,
but deliberate.
Here is where we began, where
our deaths emerged like a doppelganger.
Our shadow selves come dripping
up the dock, track sand across the floor,
play spin-the-bottle by the bonfire
and tremble to think whose mouth the bottle says,
and how is best. Our solid selves
watch, and try to believe.
~~*Oh division, that makes me take these words!*~~

In reading this draft over and over, it came to me that it was the delicacy, the lightness, the vulnerability of the past that needed to be in the center. The form itself was growing lighter and thinner—from three or four stresses per line, I took it in the next draft to two or three. I cut the speaker's own past, her own regrets, from the poem. They seemed to present themselves, anyway, in the tone. The visual focus is on the bones, which the speaking voice has mythologized and which are now contrasted with the real dust of history, the real smells. "This cottage is nothing but split trees" becomes the hard core, the material reality of the poem. The split ("division") I took out of the second draft showed up here, but here it makes boards to build a house which can contain both past and present. The game of spin-the-bottle, leading to the kiss, the intensely trembling life in that image, led me back to my original image of the bones. The bottle points which way? Toward death, always toward the bones, no longer crusted but now melting, dissolving the way a dream dissolves in the daylight. The poem wavers between versions of what's real, and when the kiss meets the bones at the end of the poem, that's what's real—life, opening the door on death and becoming more alive in the intensity of that knowledge:

Cottage

It is like opening the door
on my grandmother's bones.
By this time,
they have grown vulnerable

> *as a crust of snow,*
> *almost a fiction, almost*
> *easier than the actual*
> *dust fallen from history*
> *along the rocker, the mantle,*
> *smelling like cedar.*
> *This cottage is nothing*
> *but split trees.*
> *I have come to help hang*
> *screens, scrub floors,*
> *lay out the dock,*
> *pump water, throw*
> *the rowboat into the lake.*
> *Old motions rise out of us*
> *like ghosts, light*
> *enough to go on forever.*
> *Our shadow selves come*
> *dripping up the dock,*
> *track sand across the floor,*
> *play spin-the-bottle*
> *by the fire, trembling*
> *to think whose mouth*
> *the bottle points to, and*
> *what way is best. No sooner*
> *than I lean against the kiss,*
> *the door cracks open*
> *on those melting bones.*

When I sent this draft to a friend, who has given me good advice on many occasions, he had several quibbles. Some I listened to, some I didn't. He objected to "crust," finding it "visually inappropriate for bones. That is, crust is almost two-dimensional, it is flat, it is the top of something." He suggested "as crusted snow," which would change the subject from crust to snow. I disagreed, justifying it as I explained above, as well as justifying it in the effect of the echo of the crust in the final sound of the door *cracking* open. He also objected to "history" as being "a little bit the Huge Palpable Abstraction, that seems inappropriate to the diction here." Again, I disagreed. "Actual" right above "history," each at the end of a line, seemed to provide a level of telling that the poem needed, but I'm less sure about my stubbornness on this issue. My friend did provide me with the most useful revision, the elimination of "not much protection" following "split trees." It was, as he pointed out, needless editorializing.

The two cut lines, "Now I claim what's mine./My grandmother's name is mine" became the kernel of the next poem in the series, "Out Back." The face-to-face loss and joy that end this first poem gave me the center around which the entire "Central Lake" group moves.

A poem that begins as even more explicit reportage still has to find its center of gravity. "Saving a Life" began for me as a half-page of notes following an evening walk with my husband, Dennis. He had been ill for some time, fighting over-whelming depression. We stood on the railroad bridge near our house in the damp and drizzle and watched a young man run down the tracks where the high-speed Amtrak metroliners shoot through about every twenty minutes. Shortly after, two police cars arrived and five or six policemen began fanning out across and down the tracks, talking steadily and professionally to the young man. I could hardly hear, but Dennis, meanwhile, had gone below and reported to me what he heard. When I got home, I recorded what actually happened and looked for a way into a poem. I wondered whether the poem was contained within the events we witnessed or in the interplay between the events and the watchers. I decided the poem was all in the interplay. Of course even in the telling of the events, there would be the speaker's voice, and that would be an interplay, but the inclusion of the background event of the illness seemed to give the poem much more resonance. But it also ran the danger of sentimentality. I hoped to avoid that by turning mostly outward toward the events, by letting the reader in on the interior resonance early, then leaving the illness to do its work silently through the rest of the poem. My first really completed draft looked like this:

> *For eight months Dennis kept company*
> *with vague and shifty illness, so*
> *we had to walk every night to make sure*
> *we were still alive.*
> *By Thanksgiving, clouds and drizzle*
> *set in like unintelligible voices*
> *from space, and someone*
> *wanted to die on the railroad tracks.*
> *Innocently, we circled the station*
> *into revolving lights that wheeled up*
> *one after the other like dance-hall strobes.*
> *Official vehicles, raising a static of news.*
> *The police were not going to let anybody die.*
> *They were fingers of a hand across*
> *all tracks, their voices surgically calm*
> *in the night. The man was either drunk or drunk*
> *with misery, throwing his reasons against them:*
> *his grandfather dead, his little cousin*
> *dead, his wife fucking some other man,*
> *hey man, he yelled down the dark,*
> *there's nobody left.*
> *Reasons enough, the cops should say,*
> *nodding their heads. What the train could do*
> *to him was hardly anything, we thought.*
> Go ahead, we don't blame you, *we wanted*
> *to yell. We thought then he might take*
> *his grief in his arms and roll away in time,*
> *like a man recovered from a heart attack,*
> *weak-kneed, but owning the trouble himself.*

Safer, they talked him to submission,
his wife arriving barefoot in the cold.
They led him to the cars like a prisoner,
dividing his suffering among them
until each piece seemed like nothing,
until he was too poor to argue.

That semester I was taking a sabbatical from teaching, and I was sitting in on W. D. Snodgrass's writing workshop. I gave him this first draft for comments. Here is what he wrote:

This is very strong, but I have trouble with the first seven lines. I'd rather have someone else's name in there; this makes it hard for me (at least) to think about it as a poem. "Kept company" is very interesting and I see how it relates to the real or imagined infidelity in the poem, but if it's going to be here, I think it has to be paid off, one way or another, at the end. Similarly, I have the feeling that walking "to make sure we were still alive" may belong at the end. I just don't like the "voices from outer space."

I left "kept company" for the time being, but changed "Dennis" to "you," which of course changed the focus and tone, and at this point, I took the poem to the small group of poets in Philadelphia who occasionally get together to help each other with our work. Here are the notes I left with, after our discussion of the poem:

3. *For ~~eight~~ months you had kept company*
   with vague and shifty illness, ~~so~~

   ~~we had to walk every night to make sure~~
   ~~we were still alive.~~

   By Thanksgiving, clouds and drizzle
   set in like unintelligible voices
   from space, and someone
   wanted to die on the railroad tracks.

   Doesn't get underway
   fast enough.
   Too much info. at
   beginning.

2. *Innocently, we circled the station*
   into revolving lights that wheeled up
   one after the other [like dance-hall strobes.]
   Official vehicles, raising a static of news.
   The police were not going to let anybody die.

   out of place?

   rhythm bad?

They were fingers of a hand across
all tracks, their voices surgically calm
in the night.

The man was either drunk or drunk
with misery, throwing his reasons against them:

1.   *his grandfather dead, his little cousin*
dead, his wife fucking some other man,
hey man, he yelled down the dark,
there's nobody left.

Reasons enough, the cops should say,
nodding their heads. What the train could do
to him was hardly anything, we thought.
Go ahead, we don't blame you, we wanted
to yell. We thought then he might take
his grief in his arms and roll away in time,
like a man recovered from a heart attack, (and still alive?)
weak-kneed, but owning the trouble himself. (alive to own the
         trouble?)
Who is safer? *Safer, they talked him to submission,*
they needed
to be safer . . . *his wife arriving barefoot in the cold.*
They led him to the cars like a prisoner,
dividing his suffering among them
until each piece seemed like nothing,
until he was too poor to argue.

I finally discarded the suggestion to begin with the part marked "1," even though that would have been an exciting opening. The suggested sequence just didn't seem to move logically or easily, and I would have lost the reverberations of the illness through the events following. I cut out the third and fourth lines because they seemed to lead away from the poem. The main trouble was now in the similes—"like unintelligible voices from space," "like dance-hall strobes," and "like a man recovered from a heart attack"—that also led away from the poem. I cut them out. One of the major changes in this revision was the change from past to present tense, which made the shift to "you" in line one more sensible, as if the speaker is reliving the events with the companion, to get them straight in her head. There was a question in our group discussion about the word "safer"—who is safer? Why safer? But it seemed clear enough to me that the safer route was not to leave the young man alone, but to rescue him from himself. So I left the word. The published poem was sleeker than previous versions:

Saving a Life

You keep your illness, examining
its vague and shifty facets
like a jeweler as we take our daily walk.
By Thanksgiving, clouds and drizzle set in
and someone wants to die
on the railroad tracks.
Innocently, we circle the station
into revolving lights that wheel up
one after the other, official vehicles,
raising a static of news.
The police are not going to let anybody die.
They are fingers of a hand across
all tracks, their voices surgically calm
in the night. The man is either drunk or drunk
with misery, throwing his reasons against them:
his grandfather dead, his little cousin
dead, his wife fucking some other man,
hey man, he yells down the dark,
there's nobody left.
Reasons enough, the cops should say,
nodding their heads. What the train can do
to him is hardly anything, we think.
Go ahead, we don't blame you, we want
to yell. We think he might take his grief
in his arms like a rock, then,
and roll away just in time, weak-kneed,
but owning the trouble himself.
Safer, they talk him to submission,
his wife arriving barefoot in the cold.
They lead him to the cars like a prisoner,
dividing his suffering among them
until each piece seems like nothing,
until he is too poor to argue.

As I cut, I ironed out some problems with sound and sense. For example, changing "then he might take all/ his grief in his arms" to "he might take his grief/ in his arms like a rock, then," puts heavy stresses on key words, rising on "rock" and dropping to "then," as if one's breath drops in the understanding that he can't do it or won't be allowed to do it. Also, the stress on "grief" instead of "all" seems much more to the point. Besides, "grief" is a harder sounding word than "all." It is a hard job, picking up one's griefs.

I finally cut out "kept company" and "eight months." All I needed was the suggestion of the illness, the effect of the illness on the observers of the central event. I added "like a jeweler" and "facets" to intensify the later image of the young man's trouble actually being his treasure, his to keep for himself "like a rock" before it's broken up among his rescuers. I hoped also that I had made some suggestion of the "prisoner" as one who was caught trying to steal a grief that we all want or need to share in, just as the "you" in the first line "keeps" the jewel of his illness for himself. I wanted the poem to end almost as a question—how can we rescue without robbing people of their own selves? I don't think the poem contains an answer or needs one.

"Breaking the Dark" may be the hardest poem I ever wrote. Several years ago, it was arranged that I and a few others would read at our local arts council. The group of us decided to pull together the evening of individual readings with one poem by each of us on the subject of hands. No particular reason for the subject, except that we each thought we could work with it in the few months we had to prepare a poem. The prescription just about guaranteed failure; however, I took it on as a moral imperative. I finally did arrive at a poem—not one of my best, but one that at last settled its bones around a legitimate center.

I began by writing a long prosy poem on the history and etymology of the word *hands*—what it means in hieroglyphics, in Latin, its magical qualities among the Fijian tribes, the Queen's hand curing scrofula, Christ at the right hand of God, the lost hands of the Venus de Milo. I tied this free association to the central image of a woman consoling a man, reciting all this history to him as she holds his hand. The result was a blank verse encyclopedia entry, and a failure.

My second try at least contained the seeds of my final poem:

Traveling Hands

These are not the hands
I started with.
In the movies, one frame
fades into the next
and the heroine blends
into twenty years later,
her hand cupped
over the Madeira,
her bones emerging,
veins shadowing
toward her fingertips.
She has turned
inside out, so you see
what you thought
all along.

These are the hands
I started with,
the same scars
of vanished warts,
the lifeline spanning
the palm. These hands

have been places,
like good leather luggage
grown subtle with what
it knows of depots
and lobbies of first-rate
hotels and the many hands
of bellhops.

These hands divide
and subdivide
into complicated lines,
but they crook
over the pencil,
driving words before them
like a grand old woman
in the Piazza San Pietro,
lashing her cane
at pigeons,
simplifying,
simplifying.

Each stanza tried to be a poem, each tenuously connected. I began again, carrying over the image of an old woman, and of truth emerging as the flesh wrinkles and draws back over the bone. This time I located the poem solidly in time and space:

[handwritten: Title?]

The Night Someone Pushed Me into the Fortuneteller's Tent

at the Washington County Fair in Fayetteville, Arkansas,
[handwritten: already had] *I went with a plastic fan, a mirror, and a stuffed rabbit.* [handwritten above: my]
to buy the day's last impious act against my books. [handwritten right: — to buy a thought as / tangible as all the res / — to buy parentheses / — the day's last evidence]

(Under cover of dark, one could pretend, at least,
there was a fair. The Tilt-a-Whirl whisked up
in lights, then disappeared at dawn by sober recollection.) [handwritten: come clean as picked bones in the ~~recollection of~~ memory]
One expected—what? A gypsy parody in skirts
and shirts, scarves, beads and tinsel, an armory
of rings. So: she was no disappointment, mummified
in color, but as if this nonsense only ~~trimmed~~ the theatre [handwritten above: draped]
for simpler ~~suppliants~~. She flicked her bangles back like flies, [handwritten below: a] [handwritten above: audience]
then took my hand. I had kept it from her

all my nineteen years, and now must pay.
She closed hers down, massaged my naked palm,

blind, exultant in the flesh. Her fingers traced

the lifeline, touched the scars of vanished warts,

the reddened cuticles. They taught themselves ~~with~~ arroganc̶e̶. fly

There was nothing in her rote cliches, her multipurpose prophecies,
grab-bag prophecies
but the fright of darkness took me in, the shapeless rumored

words, the white hands finding out my carbon self my bitter

~~my bitter~~ skin, ~~denying what I knew~~. Now, these are
I thought of it just now. But these are not. . .
not the hands I started with. The bones emerge,
(roll +)   the veins roll, shadow
the veins shadow toward my fingertips. I am turning

inside out; these hands divide and subdivide

into complicated lines. They grow garish, gypsy-like.

They crook over the ~~pencil~~, driving words before them,/chasing

~~off~~ the dark, making stories, simplifying, ~~simplifying~~.

The three-line stanzas may have been a carry-over from the original three-stanza poem. I don't know. I had planned to use the first line as the title, but when I cut the self-conscious third line, I dropped the title into line one. The entire parenthetical second stanza I at first dropped as extraneous, then later retrieved, at a different place in the poem. Other changes smoothed out the meter and switched more precise images for awkward ones.

The next revision, which I have not included here, continued to regularize meter and sharpen images. In the version that reached print, I took the advice of poet Jeanne Murray Walker, who told me she had hoped to hear the fortuneteller speak, that I'd led to that and left the reader disappointed. So I gave the gypsy a rote spiel and cut some of my "telling" about that spiel. That seemed much better. The Tilt-a-Whirl's daylight emergence as picked bones now provided the transition from past to present. This is where the image had belonged all along. I took out all overt references to writing in the last stanza. That seems to me the most significant change. Prophecy is now the focus, not the act of composing. The hands perform a stronger act: they "take," "make," and "break," rather than "crook," "sweep," and "chase" the dark. They do it in more confident iambics. The earlier version's last word, "simplifying," is absorbed into what actually happens in the printed version's final stanza. The hands make a code, or coda. They break down experience into its simpler parts, its picked bones.

Breaking the Dark

The night someone pushed me into the fortuneteller's tent
at the Washington County Fair in Fayetteville, Arkansas,

I already had a plastic fan, a mirror, and a stuffed rabbit.

One expected—what? A gypsy parody in skirts
and shirts, scarves, beads and tinsel, an armory
of rings. So: she was no disappointment, mummified

in color, but she flicked her bangles back like flies,
as if this nonsense only draped the theater to please
the literal fans. She took my hand. I had kept it from her

all my nineteen years, and now must pay.
She closed hers down, massaged my naked palm,
blind, exultant in the flesh. Her fingers traced

the lifeline, touched the scars of vanished warts,
the reddened cuticles: "You will marry young. Children
will come after a long wait. You will travel to the sea."

There was nothing in her grab-bag spiel, but
the fright of darkness took me in, the secret
rumored words, the white hands witching, finding out

my carbon self, gathering evidence. Then she was gone.
The dark physics of the Tilt-a-Whirl, so whisked up
in lights, came clean as picked bones to the shock of day.

—I can prove these are not the hands I started with.
Now they divide and subdivide by complicated lines;
bones rise up, veins shadow toward my fingertips.

These hands grow garish, gypsy-like. They take
the firefly hints that pulse the dark and make them
prophecy for strangers, a code to break the dark.

How "The Deadwood Dick Poems" Came Into Being

by Herbert Woodward Martin

The Deadwood Dick Poems
for: Judith Brown Yales

I
Between the spaces,
Deadwood Dick
I vision you, man
Image within the pupils
Struggling somewhere in mid-life against the stampede
Odds of Texas, Arizona, Nebraska,
Horses and other men.
You, with your love of the free and wind,
The best eye on the plain
I have found it necessary to walk through your blood,
Question tender and desert nerves that,
You might have preferred to deal with privately.

II
Early your father died.
He made you man at twelve
Through death, through the discipline
Of breaking colts for 10 cents apiece.
It was another horse
With which you earned your reputation and fee.
Too bad you lost your 25 cents by
Collecting it beforehand.
That animal-will which
First introduced you to stampede,
The rough paths and pasture;
that throttled you almost to the ground,
Taught your arteries tenacity.

III
You, Deadwood, master of rope and gun,
When the wind interrupts your sleep
The ground, I know in that instance is harder.
I sense, what your nights must have been,
Where even the sagebrush approaching by wind
Is ultimately feminine company,
Although, that wind continues to move
Between you and your dreams

In the heart of its burning.
Deadwood what loneliness must have been like in those days!
One learns, in time, to sleep quite well alone.
I have experiences, dust-storms of the heart
Where you dig in and cover your face
Until the disaster is over/or
You ride like hell through a hail-storm
Hoping the ice will not strike against your temples.
A man can shoot everything but nature.

When you were thirty,
Were you swift, learned and happy,
As young men are supposed to be?
How many men did you know, who
Were afforded death by the natural stampede of your life?
Was the open as free as history records?

A man could shoot everything but nature
And death which itself is a bullet,
And loneliness, that knife of grass
Which cuts the flesh silently,
Although, the pain is apparent hours afterwards.
A man will resist everything if you tell him his heart is no good.

IV
Nat Love, in your black leather from foot to white Stetson,
You, man, were rough.
No woman's hand could have held you.
No circumstantial embrace could have kept you for more than a night.
What I want to ask is how . . . no, why?
After so many years of riding
You never recorded a single soft encounter?
Were there no quiet, accidental moments in barns?
Or everlasting evenings in the plains of the flesh
Where, one lying next to another on the ground
Can hear the sound of everything approaching;
Feel the heat from gathered brush expire
See the moon disappear,
Hear the wind stop,
Or fall deeper into sleep like night into silence?

There are certain concerns a man must be discreet about.

VIII
Where are the dark wolves of your knowledge?
I question you, Deadwood.
You may answer with subtle implications.
I know we have moved sufficiently from understanding,
So that to touch is less likely to mean love,
And to speak means certain death.
How do you feel in the open

With the moon's coyote gaze upon you?
Or when you wake and find a rattlesnake curled between your heart
and stomach sleeping?
Where did you bury the knowledge of your
dark enemies?

X
You Deadwood who,
Woke one morning with Indians in your eyes,
Who suddenly turning from nightmare to tears
Bled real blood.
Exiting from that dream, do you realize the cause may have been,
That there was no woman to share the dawn with?
There is some excitement to be derived from riding a horse
But a horse is never companion enough,
Not, at least for a man named Nat Love.

Sunday night.
Deadwood,
The roads are deserted.
We discuss ourselves.

XII
Indians come in silence; buffaloes come with noise
Their sound comes first,
Like maddened cowhands paid-off and drunk;
Then they appear and nothing can turn them around.
A man and his horse lay dead from the stampede.
Indians come in silence, the buffalo comes with noise.
It is with such swiftness the most destruction occurs.

Since our memories do not always serve us well, it is good to have a draft or two to refer to, so that one can at least demonstrate how a process seemingly took place. I am lucky enough to have preserved the drafts of "The Deadwood Dick Poems." Thus, even if I do not remember every detail, there is still an indicative outline which I can perceive. So, when the question was asked: How did "The Deadwood Dick Poems" come into being? I was delighted because I now had a chance to go back to my worksheets and attempt to make sense of my initial notes and the subsequent drafts which followed.

As my memory serves me, this poem was written during the fall-winter semesters of 1969-1970. I was then Poet-in-Residence at Aquinas College, but I had also accepted a new position at the University of Dayton. To mark my going and coming, I thought it would be a fine gesture to give a farewell reading with a new long poem.

I started to look around for a subject, and I came upon a book titled: *The Adventures of the Negro Cowboys,* by Philip Durham and Everett L. Jones, quite by accident. I suspect that this book interested me because I was reading about a group of individuals which I was unfamiliar with. This was new territory for me. It was material which could take me out of myself. I could read, absorb, and then try to write. Although the cowboys were black, I was not involved with them in a personal way, and I thought that this fact alone would allow me to be objective. With this decision made, I settled in on reading the entire book and finally allowed my mind to concentrate on Chapter 14, titled: "Deadwood Dick."

Why did I choose this character? Mostly because he caught my imagination and because he had had an interesting life. I would like to have been like him, but that wish aside, he was an interesting figure because he had lived when the odds were heavily against him, and he had succeeded. Here was herosim I thought I might be able to write about.

The process began with reading, absorbing, and imagining other events that this character might have been involved in. Imagining was an essential building block to recreating this historical figure. Another step in the process was to allow myself to write without any controlling sense or any intent on revising; I wanted Deadwood Dick to talk until he was tired of telling me what he wanted me to know and tired of telling me what I was too inquisitive about. When he seemed exhausted, I would pose another question, and he would begin his monologue all over again.

I would often take dictation from about eleven P.M. until early morning. This seemed like the best time for the both of us, and for me it was a period when I was less likely to be interrupted by personal matters or professional duties. In effect, the lines came to me in an undiscriminating stream. What I wanted most was not to interrupt this figure with my own perceptions. I did not want to interfere. I wanted to act as a recording device for Nathaniel Love's story.

I had an affection for the name Nathaniel because it was one of my father's given names. Also, as I read, I thought that the name Nat Love had many more metaphorical possibilities. Nat Love soon meant natural love. His story doesn't record any romance, so far as I know, and for that reason I posed a good many questions, some of which go unanswered. The reason they go unanswered, I suspect, is that they were none of my business, and even when I was given the answer, I think this character expected me to exercise a certain amount of discretion. All writers edit; all writers should expect to edit. All writers are expected to exercise options over what gets included and what gets left out of a manuscript. Still, as Ezra Pound suggests, we need to know as much about our subject as possible, even when a piece of information does not advance the narrative or proves unnecessary.

So I read.

I imagined.

I listened to what my persona had to say.

I recorded what was dictated to me without censorship.

Some of the lines dictated make up Section II where I discuss the early activities of the persona. Here is what I used:

> *Early your father died/and/ made you man at twelve*
> *you had an early Bar Mitzvah. I would say breaking*
> *horses colts for 10 cents a piece. But it was the large*
> *horse for 25 cents that you earned and lost by collecting*
> *fee beforehand. That horse was the first to*
> *introduce you to the stampede, the rough paths, and*
> *pastures and throttled you almost to the ground. Yet,*
> *there was a tenacity in your veins which turned them*
> *to muscles.*

The ideas for the section are here, but there are too many words. There needs to be a strict ordering of the action and ideas. It is possible to see the numerous cuts, the shifted lines, and how I tried to connect the ideas into a cohesive whole. Try to observe and think why I made the choices I made. Try to think what different choices you might have made. The suggestion is that we all have varying responses, differing points of view, and ways of ordering information. Here is the final published version:

> *Early your father died.*
> *He made you man at twelve*
> *Through death, through the discipline*
> *Of breaking colts for 10 cents apiece.*
> *It was another horse*
> *With which you earned your reputation and fee.*
> *Too bad you lost your 25 cents by*
> *Collecting it before hand.*
> *That animal-will which*
> *First introduced you to stampede,*
> *The rough paths and pasture.*
> *that throttled you almost to the ground,*
> *Taught your arteries tenacity.*

This initial draft, also, has the first hint of humor in the poem. Besides that, it sports two musical references: William Warfield, the black American bass-baritone, and Gustav Mahler, the Austrian composer. Mahler remains in the poem, but Warfield doesn't. Perhaps the question here was staying power, and one has to wonder if Mr. Warfield will not require a footnote in two or more decades should my poem last that long. I say this despite the fact that this gentleman was a first-rate singer and actor. Still the idea was relief. Thus, the tone of the poem had to change. And it would not be quite correct to make fun of so imminent a musician, while on the other hand Mahler's career could absorb the spurious reference. The following lines are the impetus for seciton VI. I hope you are able to see the fun in those single critical quotes.

> *I have been listening to Mahler/he knew what it*
> *was to wander. Had he know/n/you personally or*

> *otherwise you might/(the loneliness of wandering*
> *concerned) have inspired him/No doubt someone*
> *would be singing your songs, preferably myself: I*
> *see it now Bronco Love singing Mahler's "Deadwood*
> *Dick Lieder" I am always thinking the critics*
> *would have hailed me as nothing less than*
> *"moving." Just as history tells me your friends*
> *revered you. History should say that about a man*
> *when it can.*

The anonymous singer-narrator is better than a specifically named individual. So I combined two traditional names: Uncle Tom and Jim Crow. I tried to dignify the name by calling the man James Thomas Crowe. Even the use of the final "e" adds dignity to the name. Notice too how Bronco Love almost got changed to the Nat Love Love Songs, which to my mind is a clear allusion to T. S. Eliot's first masterpiece. The allusion was too close, so I edited it out of the next version. Finally, the history line is almost there, and in the cleaned-up version of the second draft it is there. This combination of words I can't explain. I defer to luck.

> *VI*
> *I have been listening to* The Songs of the Wayfarer
> *Mahler knew, at least, what it was to wander.*
> *Had he known you personally or otherwise*
> *You might have inspired him*
> *To write you a song cycle.*
> *No doubt someone, preferably myself,*
> *Would be singing your songs now.*
> *I see it this way:*
> > *TONIGHT*
> > *In Philharmonic Hall*
> > *James Thomas Crowe*
> > *Will devote his American Debut to*
> > *The World Premier of Gustav Mahler's*
> > *DEADWOOD DICK LIEDER*
> *I am thinking the critics would have said nothing less than:*
> *"Moving"*
> *"A monumental performance"*
> *"A major song cycle"*
> *"A major singer"*
> *History, tells me your friends revered you like this, and*
> *As I think Mahler might have.*
> History should say the best it can about a man.

When I reread what is in the drafts now, I supect that I tried to understand the many lessons of poetry I had been taught. From the shape and form of the draft it looks as if I arranged bits and pieces, images and sounds, rhythms and thoughts into an orderly sequence. Ordering is no doubt where my work began. An author must try to make sense of his material. How would I arrange this man's life in a particular progression from beginning to end? This was no doubt a time to question the persona again. Did he sense a rightness in the progression of details? I do not wish to suggest here the mystery of writing poetry. There is a good deal of that and some of it has validity. What I do want to suggest is an involvement with and an understanding of the character I was writing about. Every writer must find a way of doing this, and it means simply that you leave nothing to doubt.

So I think I began the poem with the idea that the character was coming alive on the pages I was writing, but he was coming alive as a person who could occupy time and space. I think the following lines suggest, as well, seeing the character moving between the states he lived in as well as the men he associated with. Observe:

> *Between the spaces,*
> *Deadwood Dick*
> *I vision you, man*
> *Image within the pupils*
> *Struggling somewhere in mid-life against the stampede*
> *Odds of Texas, Arizona, Nebraska,*
> *Horses and other men.*

What I wanted to create was a sense of this character's being stopped for a photographer's session. My eyes were the lenses; I wanted to capture as near a likeness as possible. As this session begins, the questions also begin, so in effect the poem has its beginning. After the first stanza it seems as if I tried to sequence this poem in a chronological order. It also looks as if I tried to write the second draft in such a way that Nat Love's story would be *shown* and not *told*. Sections I and II are exactly as I composed them in the second draft. Section II became Section VIII while Section V was intended to be Deadwood's response to some of the questions I had asked. The reader can tell when Deadwood is responding because his thoughts are printed in Roman type. At any rate, this section gets expanded into three stanzas and becomes Section III. The new Section IV has eighteen lines, the last two were cut, no doubt because they contributed nothing to the poem. Section V was originally one stanza, but it gets revised several pages later and becomes two stanzas. Sections VI, IX, and X are the same in draft II and the published version. Section IX looks like the one I may have had the most difficulty with. James Thomas Crowe is there and six lines which appear at the end of that section. It seems that everything else in this long stanza was invented or inspired from some notes that seem to have nothing to do with the idea in this section. Maybe my attention was at its highest level. I do know if I had the time and space to discuss and reprint Draft II one could see exactly what gets eliminated and what gets retained.

Again, the question: How "The Deadwood Dick Poems" came into being is an interesting one for me. It is possible for two reasons: one, it helped me to understand the process I used to write this poem; two, it helped me in some way to define the word *poetry* and, in some way, the act of poetry as well. Definition is a way of understanding how one's craft might be executed. The act of defining is only one approach among many. This is to say that each definition is a way to write a poem. Some approaches are better than others. The perceptive writer will realize this truth early on. Also he or she will recognize which definition works best for him or her. This is important because it can save endless hours of vain experimentation. A writer should always want to be daring with language and ideas. This is, in the end, one of the ways in which range can be developed and expanded.

Because language operates on a number of levels at the same time, a writer must try to be precise, remembering that he or she may mean one thing while his or her particular combination of words may suggest another. Constant awareness of this possibility is necessary for every writer. We are, as poets, metaphorical jugglers. This activity alone requires concentration because we must juggle: sound, meaning, colors, rhythms, rhyme, high and low diction, and sequence our ideas in a persuasive fashion. This suggestion implies a sturdy diet of concentration, of recreating an event in quiet tranquility, to borrow from Wordsworth. We are makers on a small scale. Therefore, what we create must take place visually on the page first and in the imagination second. This picture must happen in terms of images and actions. Writing this poem I wanted to give the reader a photograph, an image. I wanted the reader to be able to imagine visually what I was depicting, as well as see the action. This is, in effect, the act of showing and not telling. You will hear for the rest of your writing lives *"Show! Do Not Tell!"* Using words is like performing a magician's trick. You are narrating a story, but your language must be so vivid that it begins to take place right before the reader's eyes. This is the magic of words. This is the poet's, indeed, all writers' special gift. Treasure it!

The Poet as Translator of Sight

by Sharon Klander

One of my early creative writing professors, when asked by our class how to break a writer's block, advised us simply to *Look out the window and write what you see.* This advice recalls the inclination of all romantic prospect poetry to move from description into reverie. I believe that inclination to be the most natural in my writing process, to allow my sight to see beyond my self—to "The field out back''—so that when my eye eventually turns back, it is informed by the *real,* the "wild yellow-green'' of a particular landscape within which I can order my musings, longings, even conclusions. The three poems discussed below each owe a large debt to the sight that surrounds them; they begin by looking out the window of a particular circumstance. However, while sight may begin with an act of the eye, it is by no means limited to that motor function. In each of these poems the moment of sight is merely a touchstone for reverie, for the raid into memory, where sight is formed by innumerable layers of not only all the bodily senses, but also the intellectual and emotional senses, the knowing, believing, fearing, guessing. The poet's job is first to see and then to translate that multilayered sight to the reader, to coax sight into lines of a compatible beat, stanzas of compatible length, into images powerful enough to *give* sight—both visual and aural—as the essential means of placing oneself in the world.

Letter Home

The field out back paints a wild yellow-green
to protest the passing summer. In a month
there'll be nothing to compare it to, no way
to keep the brilliancies we'd turn in our minds
like cinnamon candy's first burning, the sweet
aftertaste. Winter sleeps soon enough. Soon
enough the greeting cards sugared with false
ice, our breath those gray, uneven circles

we follow. If you were here, how the days
would deepen the blue cast of old belief.
I've felt you go through me like water, like
wind, then held on past morning. Tonight
moths wing their slight ticking at the window
by instinct, intent on one small light.

From the first line of "Letter Home,'' I place the speaker within sight of "the passing summer,'' and then draw the reader into a tone of loss as mimicked in nature's inevitable plunge from summer, through the "brilliancies'' of autumn, and finally to winter's sleep. I chose the Petrarchan sonnet format for this poem so that the turn from octet to sextet could coincide with the turn from description to reverie, from "our breath those gray, uneven circles/we follow" to "If you were here, how the days/would deepen the blue cast of old belief." However, I did not hold the sonnet to a formal Italian rhyme scheme and did not always adhere to strict iambic pentameter, because the "we" and the "you" of the poem are less specific than are usually found in the traditional love sonnet. In this way I hoped to allow the reader the same access to the poem's observation and reverie as that of the speaker; "no way/to keep the brilliancies we'd turn in our minds" could thus be a universal submission to the forces of natural change.

By the time I move the poem from "we" to "you," from octet to sextet, reader participation in "Letter Home" can be strong enough so that even the two lines that lend themselves most easily to a specific love narrative— "I've felt you go through me like water, like/wind, then held on past morning"—can be accessible. In order for this to happen, the "you" must be understood as idealization, as the longing for a kind or type of person, as much as it is taken for a particular name, face, memory from the past. This, in addition, establishes and maintains the original force of nature as the primary force of the poem, making "Letter Home" a message to all homes, a longing to be at home anywhere.

From this longing for a home within the world, I move to a preoccupation with the human being's original home—the womb—in "To Mother on My Birthday."

To Mother on My Birthday

You say it happens every year, 5:15 sharp, the same
dull ache in back, in front. You think this is it,
the baby, and then you remember. Maybe you get up
for some water, an aspirin, and there,
through the bathroom window, first light

against the bare oaks, the dawn-tipped, fallow garden.
Original sin is fatal recurrence, the alluring turn-
in-place of maples run out of color, then
promising color back, the stubborn silence we hold
between us until it builds like scales on our eyes

we'd need a conversion to remove. Here, miles from you,
I watch the day fill with frenzied snow
falling to stunned, quiet cold. Two children
out front, circling the man they've made.

In light of that more fundamental beginning, I inform the sight of the poem not only with the expected natural surroundings, the "first light/against the bare oaks, the dawn-tipped, fallow garden," but also with issues that are more specific to a rocky familial relationship. In this context the world of nature, while exhibiting the same recurring changes, "the alluring turn-/in-place of maples run out of color, then/promising color back," expands to include a belief system that attempts to explain why there are seasonal changes at all, that shows the seasons as a result of some aberration of the perfect first garden of Genesis by fatal "Original sin." Here the natural sense of loss shown in "Letter Home" is explicated on a more personal level, the initial event that touches the poem off pinpointed by date and time, the ensuing reverie one that, because of its contemporanity with the natural processes of birth and recurring seasons, spills over from the moment of the poem to a continual "stubborn silence" held by the "I" and "you" until it "builds like scales" that would take "a conversion to remove." Moreover, with this reference to the Biblical conversion of St. Paul, the Christian belief system that has already informed the natural surroundings of the poem continues to inform the ways in which the antagonist and protagonist placed within these surroundings respond to their world.

I wrote the first two stanzas of "To Mother on My Birthday" in five lines each so that the uneven number could provide a subtle tension that I could then try to resolve in the form of a balanced quatrain. However, because the content remains unresolved, with the speaker remaining "miles" from her mother, the only real resolution the poem can achieve is, once again, in nature, in the "frenzied snow/ falling to stunned, quiet cold," in the attempts all children make to bring life from nature, "circling the man they've made." What begins as recurring false labor, moving through landscape description, ends back out the window, observing another false labor of sorts.

What We Wished For

How can I separate this night from that one,
with the stars their usual set lumens, the moon
that full solace? I still look for you

in the loose leaves of worn address books,
in photos shot years ago, when watered gin
spilled from plastic, ebullient toasts.

What could we possibly have wished for
that would outlast this debilitating distance,
this penciled list of disconnected numbers?

That night we danced past the clear sky
into a late rain, when the only lights left
colored the courtyard in misplaced

Christmas. Later, you held me swimming sick
in wet clothes, held my head through hours
I begged you not to watch. It was just one night,

but nothing since could match that gentleness,
your low voice in the dark calling the dark away.
I've imagined your life on the coast,

the pungent salt air that couldn't heal

a lost marriage, or soothe desperate mornings
prismed in each new sun, when you'd welcome

the water's white foam at your doorstep, its warm,
continual arms bound to go out with the tide.
Oh, to look back without the old paralysis!

Tonight I can find only a friend of a friend
who says you moved west to the desert,
where a thing hits just once in the sand

with no water to reflect, where, on the hottest
days, rain never reaches the ground.
And all I hope is that memory covers

where our feeble loves can't, that this night,
collapsed into pale, steady showers miles
from your window, touches your face

in a single referent gust that cools like a hand
you kiss, then hold.

Of the three poems discussed here, "What We Wished For" gives the most details of the most specific circumstances. Nevertheless, it still begins, as do the less specific "Letter Home" and "To Mother on My Birthday," by looking out the window, by moving from physical sight into emotional reverie. I begin by claiming that "this night," the night outside my window, is the same as "that one," because of what looks the same, "the stars their usual set lumens, the moon/that full solace." This sends me back into reverie over the "you" and the "just one night" that initiated a relationship since lost. But while the losses and changes in nature run parallel to those of relationships in "Letter Home" and "To Mother on My Birthday," here the sight, the surrounding, the nature of one night is the only thing that can call up a changing or lost relationship. The night doesn't run parallel, it stands apart in order possibly to save. This is especially clear in the image of the rain: first, the "late rain" danced into; then, the "pale, steady showers miles/from your window" that the speaker hopes to somehow send to the "you" "in a single referent gust" "to the desert," where, "on the hottest/days, rain never reaches the ground."

I originally composed this poem with no stanza breaks, hoping to bolster the details with the piling-on effect such a form can give. However, I realized that the music of the lines was lost in that rush, without the breathing space that white space could provide. I then decided that, while white space would highlight the lines, the sheer volume of detail still needed the discipline of a standard stanza in the same way that some novels benefit from the organizing principle of chapters. Thus, I revised the poem into three-line stanzas at a fairly regular long line. Once again, the established stanza length is shortened at the end, this time to indicate some possibility for the content, the story, to continue despite all the indications to the contrary throughout the poem. Even the last line is halved, as if to leave room for the "you" to complete it—another way that I could fit the poem's form to the seat of the poem's longing.

Wallace Stevens once wrote that the real is only the base, but it is the base. And while my poems often begin with a real emotion, it is only after I look away from that emotion to its place in the real world that I can begin to translate to the reader both the natural world and its objects and my emotional response to that world. As a poet I observe; I see with all my senses; and then I translate that sight onto the page in whatever language I can find. Each of the three poems given here contains at least one requisite window, a window on which I am intent, as if by instinct, as if there were "one small light" to find beyond the glass. It is my goal as a poet to use that window so that any reader can see.

Poetry from Concealment

by Eve Shelnutt

We live in an age of confession, using in much of our poetry what Mallarmé termed "blunt speech," the descriptions we make with words of the mundane realities. As much as the lessons in privacy taught me by my family might lead me to ask is there nothing left about which we would not speak, I don't suggest that subjects for either speech or writing should be excluded; rather, that what we say in poetry can either suggest the silence behind our writing or fail to suggest it. And to preserve the essential fact of silence, its truth, seems to make all the difference. We might thereby avoid nausea over words. But we have few formalities left, those gestures of both speech and manners which once implied that something—and I think that something was silence—needed to be protected.

What now in poetry does not destroy the fact of our profound silence before which words parade so gaudily? The question constitutes my problem with poetry, and it is no accident that when writing I move back and forth between poetry and fiction, using the still-formal structures of the story form as relief from the ostensibly personal in poetry.

I say "ostensibly personal" because I am aware that we consider poetry the medium in which fiction is stripped away. Poetry is thought to eliminate the middle-man of story, even when poems contain stories, as most do on some level. The distinction is in the convention of the writer's pact with the reader—the *poem* is the *soul* of the writer. And fiction is not? As a writer of stories, this distinction seems to me a conceit, and my thinking about poetry has been shaped by a resistance to the supposed differences between revelations in poetry and fictional forms. Kafka: could a poem have revealed him more than "The Hunger Artist"?

I have no allegiance to personal revelations in poetry, no more, that is, than to personal revelations in fiction, within characters' stories. What could I possibly write that would not reveal myself? I have disavowed the idea that my poetry should, must, ought to be a transcription of the events of my life, in sum an autobiography merely made palpable through form. Indeed, a deep irony over the "realities" of my life has overtaken me, so much being a matter of accident, of timing good or ill, of the legitimate actions of others and the abrasions of them when our wishes conflict. And yet, of course, I remain vitally interested in the spectacle of my daily life since, against this backdrop, in this time and place, what I am and am becoming occurs.

Writing is for me an act of distillation, perhaps even a concoction *made* during a process I simply think of as distillation. I am not sure anything is being distilled except *as* it is created since so much of who I am seems to evolve within a relationship to language. And if for me the most interesting personal relationships are with those whose sensitivities to language are on a seeming parity with one's own, the awesome burden of relationships is that we are guardians of our refusals to speak as well as the readers of what is wrested from silence.

All of this is preface, for what I chose to do here began several weeks ago when I realized that it did not interest me to write about poems I had written in the past, poems published as if finished in the several books of poetry I've written. Abandoned into print, they are in a sense finished, but more significant to my consideration was the fact that, since writing them, I had been writing fiction and living. My poetry, my relationship, to the form, would be changed by both, and I wanted to ask what my relationship to poetry was now. I decided, then, to write quickly and not to consider what I might have to "say" in poetry, to consider little about the act of writing poetry except where a word or two might lead me. I could say, to begin, that I was in a particular mood during the time—it was mid-July and hot. It seemed that the heat was a dome keeping noise out.

Eight of the poems written during that two-week period are presented here only to provide examples of a process that interested me.

Letter from Camaguey, Cuba, 1948

Our daughter has decided:
tears are a substitute for blood.
Salt mounds her tiny eyes
each with a crow surveying
the impossible distance
and it is perfectly clear
nature has rational patterns,
she the phenomenon varied
only in time and scale.
Believe me, I am learning.

When her eyes are shuttered
but sweetly dreamless
the crows fly to Cayo Pedras
to open the fist of light
in your room where
according to Yolanda's tears
a woman unties your shoes,
licks dust from your swollen lips.
Such efficient courting pleases you
after all these years?

And your denghi fever comes in spurts
when melancholy rains the roof,
when, thinking of us, you glimpse
a unity of design, a pattern
ingrained in serpentine rock.
Sweat pastes the woman's fingers
to your chest and you think:
Is she so poor, so embittered

that she must *be beautiful?*
I am turning lovely once again.

Perhaps you should not have had a daughter
when vengeance is time and its savouring.
The crows, I should warn you,
will relate the homology of limbs:
arms of mammals, wings of birds,
and when you return, when her blood
is blood again, you will lean
innocently over her bassinet and lift
the woman Yolanda to your chest
lightly with one hand.

"Letter From Camaguey, Cuba, 1948" began only with the name of the place, which words I had seen when leafing through a book. It is a way I often begin, thinking that, while flipping through a book, quickly so that another's associations with the words won't influence me, if a word leaps out it has arrested me for some reason, a reason residing in the silence of myself. As seemingly arbitrarily, I wrote as a title "Letter From Camaguey, Cuba, 1948" because it is a title that limits my considerations, lest a word's invitation to break into silence causes a profligate response, a chaos of associations.

Who, in 1948, is writing the letter? If one does not write autobiographically, as we say, it seems not to matter whose world I enter. A woman's? Why would she write a letter? I decided quickly that a woman would write the letter, not because she interested me, having then no words by which to reveal herself, but because all I sought was a context for language. And needing a context herself, I decided that she would have an infant daughter. It was this time not so much a decision as an image—after writing the title, I had glanced up and "seen" a portion of a house, the screened porch containing a bassinet, the gauzy mosquito netting having been thrown back, and the baby revealed sleeping. The stillness on the porch was such that I knew the father, the husband, was absent, living in another town because his job, I decided, had taken him there.

What job? I got up then and wandered past bookshelves, seeing there a book on archeology, thinking, Why not? It was a choice of expediency. I know nothing about archeology, but no matter, neither does the man's wife. I began to feel a sympathy for her, for I was bemused by recognizing that I write *around* my lack of knowledge, always, since there can never be enough. And the woman lived in some recognition of *her* absence of knowledge: she had scraps, single words. And a daughter.

I imagined the woman's silence in the house, the baby sleeping *as* the husband's embodiment and also as a surrogate into his world, her *fiction,* which the letter would describe, since, as I imagined the husband, I was aware of imagining not the facts of his situation but him only as she conjured him. This image coincided with my musing about writing resolutely about a place to which I had not been;

what had begun as expediency had now gathered substance, the substance of sympathy for our hapless situations as humans. We know so little, must imagine so much.

As I wrote I revised only for line length and for sharpness of language, taking out excessive words in order to better capture what I now felt so strongly was the woman's state. What absorbed me was how, as "she" wrote, the baby became in my mind transformed into something awesome. And because of that, I felt by the poem's end that the husband had in some way betrayed his wife, although not, I suspected, with another woman. Yet I felt she was entirely right in her warning to him—a mother reminding a father of what between them had been created in the child. And he was away. I felt that archeology had been redefined or its definition broadened, so enclosed in her being was the daughter Yolanda—precious, sequestered by youth, and to be discovered.

As it developed, the poem was "about" my feelings of awe before a child, who both *is* and *is not* until discovery, the nature of which is an unearthing that must be delicate, and a bringing to light. More than I had known, I had been thinking of a particular child I had met who has astounded me, so much of his rareness so early discovered. On another day, I might well have blamed the woman for her vengeance, for the tools of her vengeance, which discount her husband's perspectives, the claims of his needs, and, in fact, I suspect that I will at some time assert his case since out of writing other writing grows.

The Visit

> Craving held immobile too long—
> it is the look in our sisters' faces,
> almost as correct as a scar, the wound:
> our thirst for victims touched by grace
> and sweetness though we are nearly blind
> and, moving to the dirge of circumstance,
> must say instead I love you,
> terrified and cruel.

"The Visit" exhibits another mood, another impulse in language. It began as I sat thinking about the title of a story I had written, "Craving," and it was the word *craving* that incited the poem. In the story a father is dying, living with a daughter who needs him to die gracefully, as she thinks of it, and it is her arrogance-in-health that the father resists, for the daughter would have him spend his remaining time performing the rituals of summing up. She wants a closed circle; he wants to go on living, so begins courting a young woman, taking her dancing. Of the past that the daughter wants to be enclosed, the father says, "It'll keep." The craving is the daughter's folly, for it seemed to me that the father was right; even the daughter knows in some recess that he is right, yet she is poised on the edge between two conflicting awarenesses, of her need for closure and the fact of impending death which stops everything while resolving nothing.

In the story, I allowed the daughter to learn to let the father spend his days creating more chaos while also giving the joy of himself to others. But on the day that I wrote "The Visit," I was thinking that the daughter could have gone mad had she not relinquished her state—"craving held immobile too long"—and in the story she had not done so alone but with the help of a man who loved her. What if he had not been there? The question led me to consider how much we are guardians of one another's fates; and why are we guardians so infrequently? As much as over anything, I am astounded by the isolation of humans and by what contortions, vital contortions, we save ourselves from interior chaos, creating, thereby, the world's images which confound in their variety, beautiful and ugly in seemingly equal proportions, that which is ugly a reflection of our fear of interior chaos—the fear and not the chaos itself, for it seems we don't know what lies there, having only available for assessment that which we bring forth from it. And what we bring forth is surely also a contortion "almost as correct."

I wrote "The Visit" very quickly, as it stands. What troubled me and absorbed my time was the title, for I had decided, *for* the sake of language, not to specify that the visit I imagined was to two women in a hospital's psychiatric ward, visits made years apart by two different people who now know one another and have in common the unspeakable experience of having seen another human's—a sister's—face become changed by experience in a place neither had been themselves.

I tried the titles "The Sane Confess," "Confessions of the Sane," "After Visiting the Psychiatric Ward," etc. And yet I found that I did not want to bring into the poem the immediacy of a hospital. And that refusal changed the poem or left it as it was, "The Visit." I had decided, apparently, that it did not matter where such faces are seen or by what terms we designate an occurrence we can only guess at from our own trepidation, our actions of turning away, of turning craving into action for whatever salvation action may bring.

I have no idea, then, what a reader might read into the poem, which, to me, seems to be "about" the cruelty of human necessity, the terrors attendant to action, which, so far as we can see, has historically involved victims—those who do not make it out from a place of chaos or silence because they would not fight, assume the compromises of the battle, in order to surface. My concern is that enough context for a reader's understanding has not been made, even as I sought to make every word carry weight. The conflict over the title involved what silence I can surround the poem with and over what would be lost were the noise of context, as in "psychiatric ward," to be provided. My penchant is for less explanation, less "noise."

The Plan of Deliberate Lovers

The light is changed by her waiting,
softer than the light preceding words
although she holds a book in her lap,

thinking, If I could say those words . . .
meaning: When *will he come speechless*
as light breathing its colorless breath?
Her arms ache as if all the world's
transcribed impediments had lain on them
blocking her heart, its light beating,
lightly so that when he came
she would hear him push as though through
jungle heat, vine, ravished beasts,
half-beasts happy to be themselves,
and therefore brilliant.
She whispers, I was wrong to read memory
aligned in rows so orderly they suggest a habit,
like cannibals salting a kill.
Her arms turn pale; pages, blank in the rarest book;
only then the hidden red of her blood retaining
the possible letting, now, now
so that light becomes a river, their passage
so swift the others' cries are as soundless
as a village burning in the distance.

In "The Plan of Deliberate Lovers," the lines issued both from the title and from the fact that I had been reading, was too restless to read. Earlier I had been writing, which had absorbed me into a sense of timelessness, and as I read the sense of time had returned. I put down the book and, walking to the typewriter, thought about a sense of timelessness, how in writing and in lovemaking, time, as felt, disappeared.

The title, which I will mention again later, came only late. As I began I remembered that, after I had become too restless to read, I had sat watching light come through a skylight above my chair. I often do this, yet this day my observation of light as it seemed to move had affected me more deeply than usual, possibly because my watching occurred in a state of restlessness, which for me signals my waiting for something. These facts of experience seemed enough to begin with, surely personal but abstracted from language by sensation. Here is the first draft of the poem:

The light is changed by her waiting,
older than the light before words on a page
like those in the book she holds in her lap
thinking If I could say those words . . .
when she means, When will he come wordless,
like light breathing its burnishing breath?
Her arms ache as if the world's books
altogether had lain there
blocking her heart, its light beating,
lightly so that when he came she would hear him
push through as though through jungle heat,

its fecund brush, ravished beasts happy
to be itself, themselves, and therefore solid.
She was wrong, she thinks, to turn the book's
pages of half-remembered love stuttered
in rows so neat they suggest compulsion,
the last throes of exhaustion when lovers
transgress on light's delicate lessons,
like cannibals of light salt the feast
with words. The arms she rests on the colorless
chair are colorless; pages blank in the book,
only the hidden red of her blood expectant
with hue, the possible letting, now, now
so that light can become a river, their passage
on it swift, so swift the cries of others
are as soundless as a deserted city, burning.

This draft displays a writer who, it seems to me, has been inattentive, and I recall reading the draft in disgust, which, on another day, would have caused me to abandon the poem. I reminded myself that it was a process I was pursuing, here were words to be worked with: had the jungle image been carried over from the Cuba poem somehow? What I was reminded of was Conrad, of his novel *Victory* in particular. I then wrote the title, "The Plan of Deliberate Lovers," thinking of Lena about whom Conrad writes that she had come to her relationship with Heyst "with her whole soul yearning." And, because of this, her fate and Heyst's are bound together as if they had planned it. But I wanted the woman I wrote about, and the man she loved, to escape *because* she had begun in the poem just having read a book. The fact of the book became important, to be used. I imagined that if her reading had prepared her for anything, it was to recognize when to stop reading, when to whisper—and I imagined that she whispered to him what to do, what they both would be required to do in order to save themselves *as* themselves, lovers. It seemed I had written about timing, about how its perfection can erase noise, cause a silent conflagration of noise.

Collaborators

Were *we naive to talk across a table?*
The ice broke, quickened, and I went under
as you watched me enter a region known for its beauty
though only we had gone there, each alone, alone
as a tenor singing an aria on the radio
or your father drumming on a pane of glass:
something hurts him and yet sometimes he is happy—
a remembered lime tree giving off the scent of a woman
or schoolgirls carrying prayer books in their hands.

The tenor? His breath has warmed the water.
This might well be Italy, its serious black,

and I want to live in a district so remote
that we put aside our taste for the perfect dwelling:
a boathouse, incautious scenery bewitching.
Remember: I did not once shudder or open my mouth
to the coarse expression of drowning
though sweet is the image of drowned and perished beauty.

I would love your father if I could.

In "Collaborators," I knew when I wrote the title, my first choice of the poem, that what interested me was speech between two people when nothing they say can be wrong because, knowing one another, they attend to everything about one another that accompanies their speech. I imagined that this fact of their relationship changed the manner in which the speaker of the poem attended to objects and places in the world—she has, by virtue of the effect of the man to whom the poem is addressed, become immersed and, surfacing to speak, sees the world differently, and not only the world, but language, that which names the world. These feelings, I thought, would cause her to allude to all that she might have said differently: "Remember: I did not once shudder or open my mouth/to the coarse expression of drowning/though sweet is the image of drowned and perished beauty." But she is past romanticism, so profoundly has he affected her. And thus released, she is free to say what she feels: "I would love your father if I could." But that line was many drafts in coming, as if it had been necessary for me to retype over and over the self-serving lines of romanticism in order to release her to plain speech, to the depth of feeling and silence from which her last statement comes. I felt the words as great relief.

September

Too much to do,
and now a dog comes
scratching at the door;
not mine, but sleek
from her wanderings.
Why not let her feed
from my open palm?
I can ask her
the terrible questions:
"Is he happy or, at least,
has he walked, recently,
past the effusive houses
to crouch beneath a tree,
calling to touch your neck?"
And: "How deep, then,
was his silence?"
Daily, what must be done
bores my heart.

I want to put on my fur and,
letting myself out quietly,
know what this mongrel knows
and, if not, why
when she is so peaceful.

I had been reading Elizabeth Bishop's poetry before I began writing "September," although I think no trace of Bishop clings to the poem, since it seems to me that such traces would be impossible, so unassailable is her work. What I envy in her poetry is her utter ease with language. I wanted to write as directly as possible, to embellish as little as I could, to suffuse the casual with what for the poem's persona is crucial. Because of this as my beginning proposition, the poem as it stands is the only draft. Stopping there allowed me to look at what at least one poem written in this manner might sound like. Writing it was a matter of choosing tonalities for each line, but the tonalities arose from the choice of images, from, for instance, the choice of a dog as the animal—most ordinary, the humble dog as carrier of the fact of love, here equated with knowledge. And it amused me to imagine her putting on a fur, implicitly a dog's fur, without glamour. She is aware that the affectations of glamour would be beside the point, so deep are the man's silences.

Matisse, 1919

The vase is attached to its background
since moving it forward would cause trembling
not of the hand but of the eye viewing the hand.
Just once I should like to enter Brueghel's eye
against which objects crowd so rashly,
but we must one day look on the blankness of heaven
and how startled should we be?
I will paint a modest empty space, as it is,
a supplication of light.

The poem "Matisse, 1919" was written, I believe, simply because I often consider his work, by both looking at reproductions and remembering the retrospective show I saw several years ago in Washington. In 1919 he painted in a manner he would later free himself from at least partially. I imagined his defense to himself and possibly to others of his arrangement of objects and people, which held so much color and density, almost as if he was obsessed with pushing light back *into* objects, to hold it *there*. But why? The poem became the answer as I imagined Matisse would construe it. But the poem also seemed to approach questions I had been having about freedom and isolation. What *is* a "modest, empty space, *as it is*," and what constitutes "a supplication of light"? The poem did not answer my own questions but rather provided a place for them to be asked, the poem a "sounding."

When Light Is Fading

Have I taken something from the air
as a kitchen girl after work
will gasp in the orchard
awaiting the end of waiting,
the world so full of apples
and the mutilation of apples?

Who can suffer bravely the lore
of women rolling crusts, men's deeds
flung like scraps against a wall
as the dogs snarl wordlessly
doomed to hunger? The women suppose
she knows nothing as she asks,

Have we not had enough of calamity,
that knife scarring our hands,
peels curled on the tiles,
the wailing children? Have you
cleaned a table after an old woman
has eaten? Trust me,

I who know the human howl over plates
would do nothing shocking.
Notice how the apples hang lightly
by their stems? Calmly I would touch
the knowledge of your body,
gathering the tumult in.

"When Light Is Fading" began as it does— "Have I taken something from the air"—because I had been thinking about the days of writing, how the drafts had accumulated, how a decision to write had culminated in work that interested me. Time had seemed to disappear, and I found it disturbing to have to stop to attend to mundane chores. It is sobering to love the process of writing so completely, when the demands of the world recede, those honored by everyone above writing, but by the writer, lost elsewhere. As I thought of the complexities involved in writing, I "saw" a woman, a girl, really, leaving a kitchen full of the world's common demands—food, children, gossip, tales, dogs. The girl, by necessity and proximity, is filled with it all and wants to be emptied in order to make room for love; and by implication—that she waits for the lover outside the kitchen—love is not to be found in the kitchen, not even the rumor of it, for the kitchen is too calamitous.

I could have deleted the first line—I considered it—and written only about the girl. But what had begun the poem was my interest in imagination, in taking something from the air, which I imagined as having been prepared *for* by its absence. Because of the first line, I feel able to have the girl speak. I doubt she would have otherwise, yet it is difficult to explain why. Without the first line, I doubt that I would have thought of the words "human howl" or "knowledge of your body,'' for it was the tension I felt between what had prompted me to write "have I taken something from the air" and the girl's world that caused the girl's language. She must use words to explain herself to the lover, yet what she wants is for the words to be replaced with a more profound receiving of knowledge. It seemed to me that anyone who writes or loves must feel that something has been taken "from the air," inventions or answers to calamity more crucial to the writer or lovers than fecund calamity, for all its sociability. What I liked was her saying "I would do nothing shocking" followed by the phrase "gathering the tumult in," for what could be more shocking than to absorb another's knowledge? It is also shocking to try to write in such a way as to seek a break in daily babble, to seek the preservation of silence and all it contains. It is a sensual undertaking.

The Heir

With his sister he stands at a window
glazed by morning light and, on the other side,
by their mother's tears luminous
as the eyes of foxes startled each time anew
as if what we fear is not brilliantly cold.

Between the light of the father's leaving
and the woman who will stay put, so stunned,
the boy waves because he cannot help it,
such is his freedom; I know it
from this distance when yesterday

he touched me for the first time,
the arms flying up
to say wait, wait, it will enter you.

"The Heir" is "about" at least some of the knowledge required between two people who are about to touch one another in deeper exploration of knowledge. It follows from the previous poems thematically and, in the image of light, imagistically. I imagined a man who had stood at a window observing his father's leave-taking of the family, for good, and, absorbing the image into himself, conveys it to the speaker of the poem in his touch. Writing "The Heir," I asked myself what the girl Yolanda might convey of her childhood when she is older and a man touches her for the first time. Not only, I see, does a poem suggest other poems, but one poem reverberating against another can suggest a poem.

Technically what interested me was a way to suggest the boy in the man's touch, hence the words "the arms flying up," as if his touch were inevitable partially because they had flown up upon his father's leaving, or, rather, he "waves because he cannot help it." That is the heavy line; it is the woman of the poem who receives the "flying up," a gift of the man's self-resolution of loss and its attendant power to bestow the vulnerability of love again. I felt felicity in those words, which I then wanted to weigh down in the last line because resolution is also history and carries the weight of history: *wait, wait.* And what I imagined would enter her was that weight, this time felt not as the gathering in of a tumult—the softer image—but as something sharp, more painful.

The time of writing the poems is too close for me to estimate them aesthetically, except to say that they absorbed me and that what absorbs us is in part our aesthetics. What I wanted was a *whisper* of language that leaves intact silence, that which must be spoken and heard *through* our whispering.

AFTERWORD

I was asked not long ago to judge a group of student poems, selecting the "best" among a number that were to be included in an undergraduate student literary magazine. What struck me about the poems I read was how fine they all were. Immediately the question "Who *taught* these students?" came to mind because the poems demonstrated that the young writers had been guided to consider carefully a range of formal devices that would help them lift ordinary experience out of banality and into whole, unique poems that spoke of their authors' particular respect and appreciation for daily occurrences that most of us would fail to linger over, much less transform into poems.

It was gratifying for me as a teacher of writing to observe so clearly that far across the country in another university professional writers and student writers were engaged in a process similar to that my own students and I pursue. Those of us who teach in writing programs believe that writing can be taught. That is, we believe in apprenticeship as a lifelong activity that writers engage in. But the way writers learn from one another need not be tied to the classroom. Everywhere that writers meet a mutual engendering occurs—especially when we read what other writers write as well as what they write *about* writing.

When we communicate, in whatever form, it seems to me that we reiterate both the excitement we feel about writing and the difficulties attendant to it. And in *The Writing Room* none of us has disguised the myriad problems we face as writers or how engaging the problems are for us. It could be said that we love the process, with all of its difficulties. As much as the stories, poems, and novels we manage to create reward us, we write, I think, because the struggle with language is endlessly stimulating.

All during the process of putting together *The Writing Room*, I was acutely aware of the fact that I was not making writing look easy. I've often wondered, in fact, if so many of us would even want to write if shaping language into forms that will represent our deepest feelings and ideas about the world were any easier. What compels us if not the fact that we work always with materials seemingly just outside our grasp?

The stories, poems, and novels we produce are documents of an exhilarating struggle. We work at becoming increasingly professional, it seems to me, so that we ourselves can dictate more of what constitutes both the pleasure and work of writing. Once we learn, for instance, how metaphor can work in poetry, we can begin to confront other more intricate questions such as how much we want our poetry to appear "decorative" as opposed to "plain," indicative of ordinary speech. In story form, as another instance, I realized that as soon as I had learned how to move a story toward resolution, I began to question what resolving a story meant to me.

Work with form is what allows us to enjoy the endless and fascinating questions raised by form as a shaper of material. Form is also what allows us to *discover* material. It is this discovery that most compels students I've taught: one piece of writing suggests another; one way of shaping material suggests another way of shaping material. Writer's block occurs, I've found, only to writers who work as if material *for* writing is not found *while* writing. The struggle with words produces material.

So *The Writing Room* is about work—rewarding work that puts its laborers in the company of other writers and readers who help the writer complete his or her work. The first reader is the solitary writer trying to figure out what he or she has written and what it may mean. The second reader is the imagined one who must be invited to participate in the writer's process. These are the two readers that the materials in *The Writing Room* focus on.

If writers are always apprentices, we remind ourselves of that fact when we share both our finished poems and stories and when we share what we can about the process that produced the finished work. For finally we know that our work is never finished. We live in the writing room, sending our work out as signals that we are there, engaged in a profession that is less lonely than others may imagine.

Contributors

Paul S. Allison received his BA in English and Writing from Indiana Wesleyan University. He is presently completing an MFA at the University of Pittsburgh. He has published articles in the *Pittsburgh Press, Scrivener,* and the *Prairie Journal of Canadian Literature.*

A native of Nyack, New York, now living in Bristol, Tennessee, **Suzanne Underwood Clark** received the BS in English from James Madison University and the MA from the Writing Seminars at Johns Hopkins University. Her poems have appeared in *Shenandoah, Copperhead,* the *New Salt Creek Reader, Wellspring,* and *Now and Then.* She is also the author of a nonfiction book, *Blackboard Blackmail.*

Originally from Berwyn, Pennsylvania, **Anne Colwell** now lives in Newark, Delaware, where she is working toward her PhD in English literature. Her work has appeared in *Caesura.* She is cofounder of the Last Day Writer's Workshop.

A graduate of Harvard and Johns Hopkins, **Gerald Costanzo** lives in Pittsburgh, Pennsylvania, and in Harwich, Massachusetts. He directs the creative writing program at Carnegie Mellon University, where he edits *Three Rivers Poetry Journal* and the Carnegie Mellon University Press Poetry Series. His books of poems include *In the Aviary* (winner of the Devins Award), *Wage the Improbable Happiness,* and *The Laps of the Bridesmaids.* He has twice been awarded a Creative Writing Fellowship from the National Endowment for the Arts, and his articles on poetry appear regularly in journals and magazines.

Emily Ellison has worked as a journalist and editor and is the author of two novels, *Alabaster Chambers* and *First Light.* She is also coeditor (with Jane B. Hill) of *Our Mutual Room: Modern Literary Portraits of the Opposite Sex.* In 1987 she was the recipient of the Atlanta Mayor's Fellowship in the Arts for literature. Her novel in progress is *The Picture Maker.*

Barbara Hudson is a graduate of the MFA program in fiction at the University of Pittsburgh. She lives in Pittsburgh, Pennsylvania.

Fleda Brown Jackson's poetry has appeared in *Kenyon Review, Iowa Review, Poetry Northwest, Ariel, Southern Humanities Review,* and other journals. Her first collection of poems, *Fishing with Blood,* was published in 1988. She teaches English at the University of Delaware, where she edits the literary magazine. She has published essays on William Dean Howells, as well as on D. H. Lawrence and other contemporary British writers. She is coeditor, with Dennis Jackson, of *Critical Essays on D. H. Lawrence* and past editor of *The Newsletter of the D. H. Lawrence Society of North America.* She was the recipient of the 1987 Delaware Arts Council Individual Artists Fellowship.

Sharon Klander, a native of Houston, Texas, holds a Bachelor of Journalism degree from the University of Texas at Austin and an MA in Creative Writing from the University of Houston. Her poems have appeared in the *New Republic, Denver Quarterly, Shenandoah, Nimrod,* and *St. Luke's Journal of Theology.* She is currently a PhD candidate and teaching fellow at Ohio University.

A graduate of the MFA program at the University of Pittsburgh, **Dan Lowe** currently teaches at Indiana University in Indiana, Pennsylvania. He has published fiction and poetry in the *Wisconsin Review, Rhode Island Review Quarterly, Montana Review, Long Pond Review,* and *Spitball.* He directs fiction and poetry workshops at the annual Ligonier Valley Writers Conference.

Herbert Woodward Martin is Professor of English and Poet-in-Residence at the University of Dayton. He has authored four books of poetry, the most recent of which is *The Forms of Silence*. He has also written a monograph, *Paul Laurence Dunbar: A Singer of Songs,* and served as editor of the *University of Dayton Review* special issue devoted to Emily Dickinson.

Born in Wilmington, Delaware, **Jane McCafferty** graduated from the University of Delaware and received the MFA from the University of Pittsburgh.

A computer science graduate of the University of Pittsburgh, **Don Minkler** has lived most of his life in Bethel Park, Pennsylvania, where he began writing at the age of seven. Each weekend during his childhood, he would begin the "ultimate" novel, usually becoming discouraged not more than twenty minutes later.

Linda Mizejewski's poetry and essays have appeared in *Harper's, Southern Review, Georgia Review, Calyx, Women's Studies,* and other journals. Her chapbook, *The Other Woman,* was the 1982 winner of the Signpost Press competition. She lives in Pittsburgh, Pennsylvania.

Herbert Scott is the author of three collections of poetry: *Disguises, Groceries,* and *Durations.* He teaches in the English Department at Western Michigan University.

Shirley Clay Scott, chairman of the English Department at Western Michigan University, is the author of *Myths of Consciousness in the Novels of Charles Maturin* and essays on Katherine Anne Porter, James Wright, Eve Shelnutt, and Judith Minty, among others.

Eve Shelnutt, a graduate of the University of Cincinnati and the University of North Carolina at Greensboro, is a native of Spartanburg, South Carolina. She has taught at the University of Pittsburgh and is now Professor of English at Ohio University. A much sought-after consultant for teachers of writing and founder of the Ligonier Valley Writers Conference, she has won numerous awards, including the *Mademoiselle* Fiction Award and an O. Henry Prize. The author of three collections of short stories, including *The Musician,* and two books of poetry, most recently *Recital in a Private Home,* she is currently at work on a novel. Her book *The Magic Pencil* is a highly praised resource for teaching children to write.

A former high-school English teacher, **Mary Anne Tumilty** is a graduate of Indiana University of Pennsylvania and has studied fiction writing at the University of Pittsburgh. "Light on the Retina" is her fourth story.

Jessie Vanamee is a native of New York City and a graduate of the University of Chicago. She has also studied at the University of Florence in Italy. After working in publishing, she entered the MFA program at the University of North Carolina at Greensboro. She is a recipient of the Randall Jarrell Fellowship.

A native of Iowa, **Beth Watzke** left home at eighteen to study acting and literature. She worked as a waitress, receiving room clerk, lab assistant, addressograph operator, librarian, and secretary, in addition to appearing in repertory theater and playing bass in various rock bands. She received her BA in Literature from the University of Pittsburgh, where she is currently working on her doctorate in Writing and Australian Women's Literature.

John Woods was born and reared in southern Indiana and educated at Indiana University. He served in the Air Force in World War II. Since 1955, he has taught at Western Michigan University, where he was appointed Distinguished Faculty Scholar and Distinguished Michigan Artist in 1978. He was an NEA Fellow in 1982 and is the author of eight books of poetry, the most recent being *The Salt Stone: Selected Poems.*